INSTRUCTIONAL MODELS

FOR PHYSICAL EDUCATION

THIRD
EDITION

Michael W. Metzler
GEORGIA STATE UNIVERSITY

Holcomb Hathaway, Publishers

Scottsdale, Arizona

Library of Congress Cataloging-in-Publication Data

Metzler, Michael W.
    Instructional models for physical education / Michael W. Metzler. — 3rd
ed.
        p. cm.
    ISBN 978-1-934432-13-6
    1. Physical education and training—Study and teaching—United States.   2.
Physical education teachers—Training of—United States.   I. Title.
    GV363.M425 2011
    613.7'071—dc22

                                                                2011006924

Holcomb Hathaway, Publishers, Inc.
8700 E. Via de Ventura Blvd., Suite 265
Scottsdale, Arizona 85258
480-991-7881
www.hh-pub.com

10 9 8 7 6 5 4 3 2 1

ISBN 978-1-934432-13-6

PRINTED IN THE UNITED STATES OF AMERICA.

contents

ALIGNING STANDARDS, CURRICULUM, AND INSTRUCTION WITH MODEL-BASED INSTRUCTION   3

DESCRIBING INSTRUCTIONAL MODELS FOR PHYSICAL EDUCATION   17

iii

3   AREAS OF KNOWLEDGE FOR MODEL-BASED INSTRUCTION IN PHYSICAL EDUCATION   45

4   TEACHING STRATEGIES FOR MODEL-BASED INSTRUCTION   77

7 ASSESSING STUDENT LEARNING IN MODEL-BASED INSTRUCTION   151

part two

EIGHT INSTRUCTIONAL MODELS FOR PHYSICAL EDUCATION   171

10 COOPERATIVE LEARNING
Students Learning With, By, and For Each Other   227

11 SPORT EDUCATION
Learning to Become Competent, Literate, and Enthusiastic Sportspersons   263

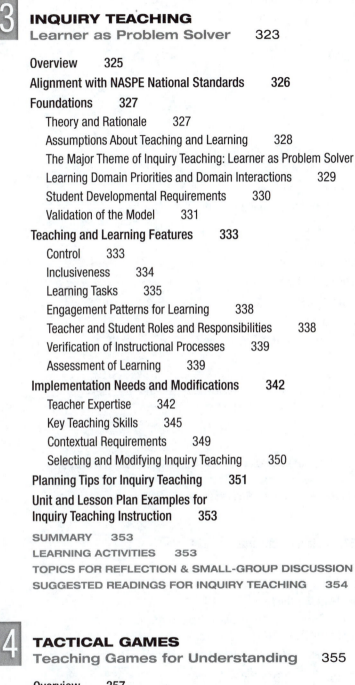

15 TEACHING PERSONAL AND SOCIAL RESPONSIBILITY
Integration, Transfer, Empowerment, and Teacher–Student Relationships   391

Dedication

To my wife, Terry,

without whom this edition

and much more in my life

would not have been possible.

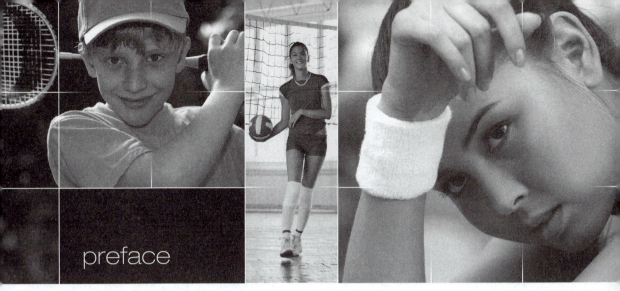

P hysical education has long been a teaching profession. Our earliest roots were established by people who were trained in medicine but used therapeutic and instructive techniques to help people learn and participate regularly in physical activity. And, while it is true that many contemporary professionals have interests quite removed from the teaching of physical activity, it still remains that most physical educators today carry out activity instruction as their primary function. Most of these educators teach physical education in P–12 schools, and a number of them teach in college level Basic Instruction Programs. This book is written for those and future teachers of physical activity so that they can approach their instruction from a new model-based perspective, increasing their students' knowledge, skills, appreciation, and participation in the many forms of movement available today.

The earliest teachers of physical activity defined "how they taught" as *the physical education method,* a direct and formal approach that called for teachers to follow accepted procedures closely and which gave students a limited role in the operation of classes. Essentially, the teacher gave directions and the students followed them. Most activities, regardless of context and grade level, were instructed with this approach. In the 1960s physical educators expanded the concept of method to include some innovative *teaching strategies* and *teaching styles,* the latter set forth in Musska Mosston's (1966) *Spectrum of Teaching Styles.* Both of these developments served to open up the possibilities for how teachers could plan and implement instruction in our field. A third movement began in the 1980s that viewed *effective teaching* as a constellation of decisions and actions that led students to increased levels of learning. Teachers developed a repertoire of effective teaching skills that they applied within strategies and styles. So, after the use of the physical education method for more than a half century, suddenly there were many innovative ways to instruct students in the growing content in P–12 programs.

The notions of method, strategies, styles, and skills are very helpful in promoting limited, short-term outcomes in physical education. In that sense they are "recyclable," as each one might be used for just a few moments in a class, and then give way to another—perhaps as many as three or four in a lesson. Because of that, these concepts lack a larger, more unified perspective from which to view the process of planning, implementing, and assessing instruction in physical education.

Over the past 40 years a fourth movement has arisen in the search for ways to teach physical education and other subjects. Although that movement has taken longer to grow, I would argue that its time has come as the best way to conceptualize how we teach physical activity to all students. Bruce Joyce and Marsha Weil published their first edition of *Models of Teaching* in 1972. In it, they made a case that instruction should comprise "structured, logically consistent, cohesive, and lucidly described *patterns* of teaching" (p. 1). Each distinctive set of those patterns is called a *teaching model,* which ties together theory, planning, classroom management, learning activities, and assessment. The scope of each model's perspective on instruction is much larger, and more holistic than our current notions of method, strategies, styles, and skill. A models approach is meant to address long-term learning outcomes—those intended for entire units and even programs.

We now have many well-articulated and effective instructional models. Most of them have been developed in other subject areas and adapted for physical education, such as Cooperative Learning, Personalized Systems of Instruction (PSI), and Direct Instruction. A few of them have been developed exclusively for teaching students physical activity and related concepts. Sport Education, Tactical Games, and the Teaching Personal and Social Responsibility models presented in this book were developed by physical educators for use in elementary, secondary, and college/adult instruction. What we now have is a group of models that have been developed separately, and which appear in isolated books and journals. What we need is a model-based *perspective* for instructing physical education that will help teachers to learn about, select, and practice these comprehensive patterns of teaching. It is my hope that this book will help to develop such a perspective.

Instructional Models for Physical Education, Third Edition, has two primary goals for its readers. The first is to familiarize readers with the notion of model-based instruction for physical education, including what it is, what they need to know to use it, the components and dimensions that determine a model's *pattern* of teaching, and how to select the "right model for the right job." The second goal is to describe each of eight instructional models from which teachers can choose. Those descriptions will provide the information needed to get up and running with any model selected, ensuring the model can be used with confidence and good results.

I also have a third goal for this book—one that is more ambitious than familiarizing readers with a model-based approach. For preservice teachers, that goal is for them to learn their craft from a model-based perspective, so that it becomes "how they teach." For practicing teachers, I want to change how they teach physical education! I don't want to simply adjust a bit here and there; I want teachers to gain a totally new perspective on the important educational mission carried out every school day. In short, I want readers of this book to go from **method to models** in their approach to teaching physical activity to students of all ages. I made that shift myself several years ago, and now teach physical activity courses with the PSI, Cooperative Learning, Direct Instruction, and Sport Education models. I work with many practicing teachers who have also made that shift. All of the example unit and lesson plans you'll encounter on the book's website (discussed below) were developed by these teachers and represent field-tested models that really work in physical education at the grade levels for which they were designed. It is my hope that readers of this book will become curious and innovative enough to take a model-based perspective, so that as a profession we can more often achieve the varied and diverse goals of contemporary physical education programs.

Since the second edition of *Instructional Models for Physical Education* was published in 2005, I have seen much progress in the use of model-based instruction in our field, and I have continued to see a growing number of excellent examples of units taught with that approach. With each new unit I see in print, or being taught by a teacher, I become more confident that this approach has a real opportunity to effectively align instruction with state and national standards for physical education—allowing more and more students to achieve the major learning outcomes in P–12 and college physical activity instruction programs.

I have provided in Chapter 1 information upon which readers can build that shows the importance and relevance of connecting planning and teaching practices to standards, and the NASPE standards in particular. Further, I have included tables in each of the models chapters (Chapters 8–15) that show the alignment of each model to the NASPE standards to help readers understand, conceptualize, and develop effective lessons that increase students' learning and performance.

Another important new feature of the third edition is the inclusion of a number of physical activity instruction units taught with the eight models; these are presented on the book's website, www.hhpcommunities. com/metzler. These unit plans also include lesson plans and assessments that have been field tested by students at Georgia State University and by inservice teachers who have adopted model-based instruction. These unit plans are available for readers to review and use in their own teaching. I also invite those physical education teachers who develop units for model-based instruction to submit their units to the website for other teachers to use. Guidelines for making those submissions are given on the site.

It is my continued hope that readers of this book will become curious and innovative enough to take a model-based approach in their teaching, just like those who contributed the excellent unit plans that accompany this edition. I believe that more teachers can lead students to the achievement of the varied and diverse goals of contemporary physical education programs through the selection and use of the instructional models presented in this book.

M. W. M.

ACKNOWLEDGMENTS

In the Preface I mentioned that I have become more confident that the model-based approach has a real opportunity to effectively align instruction with state and national standards for physical education. Much of that confidence comes from seeing the next generation of teachers—undergraduates in the GSU Health and Physical Education program—using model-based instruction, and often sharing that knowledge with their mentor teachers in schools! For that, I extend my appreciation to my GSU HPE colleagues Barbara Greene, Rachel Gurvitch, Jackie Lund, and Deborah Shapiro for promoting model-based instruction as "best practice" for our preservice teachers. I would also like to thank the many GSU HPE students who have not just "bought into" model-based instruction *because they were told to* but have seen the value for learners in that approach.

I would especially like to thank the GSU students, our former students, and the many teachers across the country who permitted me to include their excellent samples of model-based units on the website that accompanies this edition.

I would like to thank Colette Kelly of Holcomb Hathaway, Publishers for her patience and understanding through the events that caused the long delay in getting this third edition completed. I am also appreciative of her willingness to accept ideas that make *Instructional Models for Physical Education* more than "just" a textbook, such as the creation of the book's website. This site will serve as a "virtual community center" for preservice and inservice teachers who want to learn more about model-based instruction and to share their experiences and sample units for others to see and use.

Many individuals reviewed the third edition at various stages and offered ideas about how to improve the book. My thanks to all of the following people for their constructive comments: Bonnie T. Blankenship, Purdue University; Pam K. Brown, University of North Carolina at Greensboro; Russell Carson, Louisiana State University; Gary E. Clark, The Pennsylvania State University; David Cluphf, Southern Illinois University-Edwardsville; Kathy Davis, East Carolina University; Rachel Gurvitch, Georgia State University; Ken Hansen, California State Polytechnic University, Pomona; Mary L. Henninger, Illinois State University; Jennifer Faison Hodge, Capital University; Rhonda Hovatter, Ohio University; David Lorenzi, Indiana University of Pennsylvania; Kristi Mally, University of Wisconsin, La Crosse; Bryan McCullick, The University of Georgia; Heidi Henschel Pellett, Central Washington University; Lisa A. Pleban, Castleton State College; Brian Storey, Douglas College; Steve Stork, Georgia College & State University; Mary Lou Veal, Middle Tennessee State University; and Alexander Vigo, Towson University.

FOUNDATIONS FOR MODEL-BASED INSTRUCTION IN PHYSICAL EDUCATION

T his book is based on two primary assumptions about teaching physical education. First, instruction is most effective when it occurs within a coherent framework known to the teacher and communicated to students. Such frameworks will be called instructional models in this book, with eight models for physical education presented in Part Two. That part of the book will provide you with detailed plans for designing, implementing, and assessing each model. The second assumption is that teachers must understand the foundations for model-based instruction in order to select the best model to meet stated learning goals, match student developmental readiness, and manage the learning environment. Helping teachers gain that understanding is the purpose of Part One of this book.

It would be tempting for some readers to bypass Part One and search through Part Two for one or two "favorite" models selected from personal experience as a student or from one's teaching background. Although the descriptions of each model would give a teacher enough information to begin to use a model, eventually the teacher will be left with important questions: "Why am I teaching this way?" "How do I know my students are really learning according to the model's design?" and "How do I make modifications for my students and teaching situation?" Part One is intended to help teach-

1

ers answer those questions and many others, so they can make informed decisions about using model-based instruction in their school programs.

Instructional models are planning "blueprints" for physical education teachers to use as they help students achieve stated learning goals. Part One will help you understand where those blueprints came from, how they can help you build an instructional plan, how to select the right plan for your purpose, and how to know when that plan has given you the results you wanted. Equipped with that knowledge, you will be much better informed and ready to implement model-based instruction as a physical education teacher.

ALIGNING STANDARDS, CURRICULUM, AND INSTRUCTION WITH MODEL-BASED INSTRUCTION

Physical education programs can be viewed as a combination of personnel, learning goals, facilities, content and activities, and the ways in which the teachers instruct. Throughout the history of school physical education programs in the United States, these programs have tended to reflect larger patterns in American culture, people's needs and choices regarding physical activity, and trends in our educational system. Even today, the goals, content, and instruction in physical education continue to evolve in ways that call for new approaches in school program design and in how the teaching–learning process is carried out.

STANDARDS FOR PHYSICAL EDUCATION

In 1992, the National Association for Sport and Physical Education (NASPE) released *Outcomes of Quality Physical Education Programs* (NASPE, 1992). The work of the Blue-Ribbon committee that developed this report was based on the position that P–12 physical activity instructional programs must strive to meet a variety of needs in order for students to become "physically educated persons."

According to the NASPE *Outcomes* document (1992), a physically educated person is one who:

1. *Has* learned skills necessary to perform a variety of physical skills.
2. *Does* participate regularly in physical activity.
3. *Is* physically fit.
4. *Knows* the implications of and the benefits from involvement in physical activity.
5. *Values* physical activity and its contributions to a healthful lifestyle.

The 1992 NASPE Outcomes document clearly advocates for a balance among diverse goals and multiple purposes. As a guide for physical education programs today, the NASPE Outcomes document makes it clear that we can't promote one goal at the expense of the others. We must agree that a "physically educated person" is someone who demonstrates well-rounded knowledge and skill for regular participation in health-optimizing physical activity *and* who values physical activity enough to make it an integral part of his life, now and across the life span.

NASPE STANDARDS (1995, 2004)

The planning stage of the NASPE outcomes project led to the publication of *Moving into the Future: National Standards for Physical Education* (NASPE, 1995), which outlined goals and standards of programs for all grades and described some general instructional strategies for achieving them. Those standards were later revised (NASPE, 2004) and are shown in Exhibit 1.1. It is significant that the NASPE Standards document encompasses all three of the major domains of learning: psychomotor, cognitive, and affective. The

EXHIBIT 1.1   NASPE (2004) National Standards for Physical Education.

A physically educated person:

1. Demonstrates competency in motor skills and movement patterns needed to perform a variety of physical activities.
2. Demonstrates understanding of movement concepts, principles, strategies, and tactics as they apply to the learning and performance of physical activities.
3. Participates regularly in physical activity.
4. Achieves and maintains a health-enhancing level of physical fitness.
5. Exhibits responsible personal and social behavior that respects self and others in physical activity settings.
6. Values physical activity for health, enjoyment, challenge, self-expression, and/or social interaction. (p. 11)

psychomotor domain refers to the ability to move part or all of the body in skillful ways. The *cognitive domain* refers to one's intellectual ability to think, recall, conceptualize, and solve problems. The *affective domain* refers to inner feelings, attitudes, and socially acceptable behavior in a given setting. Learning domains will be discussed more in Chapter 3. For now, it is important to know that they represent different types of knowledge that students acquire from instruction. Unlike teachers of most other school subjects that emphasize learning in just one or two domains, physical educators have long recognized the need to help students learn in all three domains, further supporting the need for teachers to know how to instruct in a variety of ways.

PROGRAM ALIGNMENT TO ACHIEVE THE NATIONAL STANDARDS

The presence of widely accepted national standards for physical education is not enough to ensure that students actually achieve those broad learning outcomes. There are many other parts of a physical education program that must be properly aligned with these standards. Such factors occur at three major levels:

1. Program goals and design
2. Curriculum models
3. Instructional models

Having a proper alignment means that all these factors are working together in a way that allows the intended learning outcomes to be achieved by students in a physical education program. When one or more of these factors are not in the proper alignment, student learning is reduced or does not occur at all.

Program Goals and Design

All physical education programs have learning goals—what the teacher or teachers in that school would like students to learn from their physical education instruction. In some schools, those goals are stated clearly for all to see and understand. In other schools, those goals may be stated less clearly or are not formally communicated by the teachers. In order for those goals to be aligned with the national standards, the teachers in that program must formally state those goals and show how each goal relates to one or more of the national standards. Each program's design includes a unique combination of teacher experience and expertise, scheduling plan, instructional space, student characteristics, class size, and available equipment. It is the design of the program—how it is put together—that allows students to learn what is intended by the teachers. Some designs facilitate student learning of all the national standards, while other designs promote only one or a few of the standards. For example, students in programs with a strong emphasis on skill themes (Graham, Holt/Hale, & Parker, 2009) are more likely to achieve NASPE Standards 1 and 2 than standards related to physical fitness.

Curriculum Models

Presently there is no national curriculum plan for physical education—only the widely accepted NASPE standards. That means programs are trying to achieve the same standards even while there is no common structure or content for these programs. Teachers in the same district or even in the same school will identify one or more of the national or state standards for their students to learn, selecting what they consider to be an appropriate curriculum plan to provide an overall organizational structure for the content units offered in their own program. Sometimes this curriculum plan is simply a list of content units required for students during the school year, having little or no direct relationship to each other or the national standards. Those will be referred to as *activity-based* curriculum plans, in which the program is little more than a collection of content units with no central theme to bind them together.

The best curriculum plans will clearly specify which of the NASPE standards they are attempting to promote, show an intentional process for deciding which content units should be offered in the program, determine which resources are needed to help students achieve the major learning outcomes, and regularly assess the major outcomes as well as the curriculum plan itself. Those will be referred to as *standards-based* curriculum plans. The best of those plans will follow a distinct *curriculum model*—one that is implemented by all teachers in a school and clearly communicated to students, administrators, and parents. Each curriculum model for physical education is designed to allow students to achieve a recognized set of major learning outcomes, and it includes a carefully selected set of content units that can promote those outcomes. There are several widely recognized curriculum models used in physical education today. Each of these models has a *main theme* (Lund & Tannehill, 2010) that indicates the content emphasis and major learning outcomes designed for that model. As you'll see in Exhibit 1.2, the main theme of each model is usually captured in the model's label, so you can tell right away what the model is about. Although every model has the ability to address all six of the NASPE standards, in reality only a few models can address all of the standards equally well. It is important for teachers to understand which standards receive a *primary emphasis* and which standards receive a *secondary emphasis* in each model's design. It is also important to note that these primary and secondary emphases can be changed in each program, depending on how the program is implemented by a particular teacher.

INSTRUCTIONAL MODELS: ALIGNING INSTRUCTION WITH STANDARDS AND CURRICULUM

After a program's goals, design, and curriculum have been aligned to promote the NASPE standards, the next step is to bring the instructional plan into a similar alignment. It is not enough for a program to identify which standards are to be achieved by students or even to develop the right kind of curriculum plan for that purpose. Real achievement occurs from the way teachers instruct and how students are engaged in learning activities

Main theme curriculum models for physical education today.			EXHIBIT	1.2
CURRICULUM MODEL	MAJOR OUTCOME(S)	TYPICAL CONTENT UNITS	PRIMARY EMPHASIS ON NASPE* STANDARDS	SECONDARY EMPHASIS ON NASPE* STANDARDS
Fitness	Learning physical activities that lead directly to improvement of health-related fitness	Running/walking, weight training, aerobics, Pilates	1. Motor skill competency 3. Regular physical activity 4. Health-enhancing fitness 6. Value of physical activity	2. Concepts, principles, strategies, and tactics 5. Responsible personal and social behavior
Fitness Concepts	Learning facts and concepts that contribute to health-related fitness	Major components of health-related fitness, dieting and nutrition, wellness	2. Concepts, principles, strategies and tactics 3. Regular physical activity 4. Health-enhancing fitness 6. Value of physical activity	1. Motor skill competency 5. Responsible personal and social behavior
Games	Learning a variety of individual and team games	Basketball, softball, floor hockey, ultimate frisbee	1. Motor skill competency 2. Concepts, principles, strategies, and tactics	3. Regular physical activity 4. Health-enhancing fitness 5. Responsible personal and social behavior 6. Value of physical activity
Health Optimizing	Learning knowledge and skills for lifelong participation in physical activity for optimal health benefits	High-activity sports, dance and games, nutrition, personal fitness planning, lifetime sports	2. Concepts, principles, strategies, and tactics 3. Regular physical activity 4. Health-enhancing fitness 5. Responsible personal and social behavior 6. Value of physical activity	1. Motor skill competency
Lifetime Games and Sports	Learning a variety of games and sports that can be pursued throughout one's life	Golf, tennis, recreational sports	1. Motor skill competency 2. Concepts, principles, strategies, and tactics 3. Regular physical activity 6. Value of physical activity	4. Health-enhancing fitness 5. Responsible personal and social behavior
Multi-activity	Introduction to a variety of physical activities and sports	Content units can include a wide variety of physical activity, usually selected by the teachers	Depends on which content units are offered	Depends on which content units are offered

(continued)

EXHIBIT 1.2 Continued.				
CURRICULUM MODEL	MAJOR OUTCOME(S)	TYPICAL CONTENT UNITS	PRIMARY EMPHASIS ON NASPE* STANDARDS	SECONDARY EMPHASIS ON NASPE* STANDARDS
Outdoor and Adventure Education	Learning skills and knowledge for use in common forms of outdoor activity	Hiking, rock climbing, SCUBA diving, ropes courses	1. Motor skill competency 2. Concepts, principles, strategies and tactics 3. Regular physical activity 5. Responsible personal and social behavior 6. Value of physical activity	4. Health-enhancing fitness
Skill Themes	Learning basic movement patterns used in a variety of games and other activities	Balancing, changing direction, throwing, catching, object manipulation	1. Motor skill competency 2. Concepts, principles, strategies, and tactics 5. Responsible personal and social behavior 6. Value of physical activity	3. Regular physical activity 4. Health-enhancing fitness
Sport Education	Learning a sport from a variety of perspectives (e.g., player, coach, trainer, referee)	Any team sport and many individual sports	1. Motor skill competency 2. Concepts, principles, strategies and tactics 3. Regular physical activity 5. Responsible personal and social behavior 6. Value of physical activity	4. Health-enhancing fitness *(Note: Could be primary, depending on content unit)*

*Note that these primary and secondary emphases change depending on how the teacher implements the program.

that are also aligned with the NASPE standards. These are the day-to-day things teachers and students do that lead to the kinds of learning outlined in the NASPE Standards document. As with curriculum, the best instruction in physical education starts with a well-defined plan that can guide teachers and students throughout each content unit. That plan will be called an *instructional model* in this book.

Instructional models are based on an alignment of learning theory, long-term learning goals, context, content, classroom management, related teaching strategies, verification of process, and the assessment of student learning. Joyce and Weil (1980) define an *instructional model* as "a plan or pattern that can be used to shape curriculums (long-term courses of studies), to design instructional materials, and to guide instruction in the classroom and other settings" (p. 1). An instructional model should be used for an entire unit of instruction and includes all of the planning, design, implementation, and assessment functions for that unit.

Instructional models have strong theoretical foundations, and most have undergone much research in their development and implementation. They are usually field-tested in schools and other settings to ensure that they are capable of being used efficiently and effectively for their intended purposes. Most teaching models have been initially developed for use in classrooms, for outcomes primarily in the cognitive and affective domains. Several of these models, like some of those presented in this book, also showed great promise for achieving the instructional goals of physical education programs and have thus been adapted for use in our subject area. Some other models presented in this book were developed specifically for physical education instruction.

The remaining chapters in Part One will explain instructional models in much more detail. The key point here is that these comprehensive and unified plans for instructing physical education now represent "best practice" in teaching our subject matter to students of all ages. I would argue that models for planning, implementing, and assessing instruction will provide us with the most effective ways to achieve the NASPE standards within the great diversity of content and characteristics of our school physical education programs.

No "One Best Way" to Teach

If physical education programs and the teachers in them strive to meet NASPE's standards to help students become truly physically educated persons, teachers cannot instruct the same way all the time, and students cannot be engaged in only a few kinds of learning activities. Since programs should promote multiple learning outcomes encompassing all three learning domains, teach students with diverse characteristics and differing abilities, and include a wide variety of program content in the curriculum, there can be no "one best way" to teach physical education. Each time a teacher instructs a different content unit for different learning outcomes to a different group of students, that teacher must change her way of instructing in order to help those students learn more effectively and enjoyably. Sometimes those differences will call for only minor changes or small variations in a few teaching and learning behaviors. At other times those differences will require major changes in how a teacher instructs, calling for the use of a completely different approach, or what we call in this book an *instructional model*.

Instructional Models as Coherent Plans for Teaching and Learning

To achieve a variety of outcomes in all three domains and to address the range of students' abilities, physical education teachers will need to know and use a number of different instructional models. An effective instructional model will have a comprehensive and coherent plan for teaching that includes a theoretical foundation, statements of intended learning outcomes, teacher's needed content knowledge expertise, developmentally appropriate and sequenced learning activities, expectations for teacher and student behaviors, unique task structures, measures of learning outcomes, and mechanisms for assessing the faithful implementation of the model itself. The best instructional models link theories of teaching and learning to specific decisions and actions that teachers should incorporate into their practice. Each model describes a unique way, or a "blueprint," for a teacher to follow to help physical education students in the learning process. Each model also calls for its own set of decisions, plans, and actions by the teacher and students. The most effective teachers will know how to use a number of instructional models and understand which model to use for each unit of instruction, depending on learning outcomes, domains, student readiness, and content.

Each instructional model is a plan a teacher can select and use for a particular content and at an appropriate time to help students learn in the most effective way. The best teachers are not necessarily the ones with the largest number of plans (models) at their command; the best teachers are the ones who can select the "right plan for the job" in every unit to promote learning outcomes identified for their school's physical education program. It is more likely that a teacher's instructional plan will be determined mostly by the range of students' developmental stages at that school and by the specific content units to be offered. As you can now see, there must be a strong alignment between content, student ability/stage, stated learning outcomes, and the instructional model selected by the teacher in a course unit.

One of the major purposes of this book is to provide you with an introduction to instructional models for teaching physical education. When you are familiar with the idea of instructional models and know how to use them, you will be able to implement each one at the most appropriate time and then be ready to learn more models, making your personal set of plans even larger and more diverse. If you are using this book as part of a teaching-methods course, you will probably have a limited amount of time to learn and practice each model; so you will be a beginner, of sorts, on each one. That's OK. You will get more opportunities to improve during field experiences, during student teaching, and then as a full-time teacher when that time comes. Just like anything else you have learned well in your life, it will take time, planning, practice, hard work, and patience to improve your effectiveness with each instructional model you use.

If you are an experienced teacher, you can focus on those models that are aligned with the NASPE standards, your program goals and design, and your selected curriculum model. After you are familiar with a number of models, you can select the best model for each content unit and begin to understand how to plan for it, implement it, and assess its effectiveness in your program. Through that process you will also learn how to modify each model for maximum success in your setting.

MODEL-BASED INSTRUCTION IN PHYSICAL EDUCATION

I t is argued here that physical education instruction is typically based on content—the activity being taught to students. That is, the organizing center for instruction is most often determined by the content (e.g., softball, floor hockey, tennis, urban dance)—not goals or instructional models. If you mention a certain kind of content, a teacher will probably tell you how she teaches it to her students. "I teach badminton this way ...," "I teach invasion games this way ...," "I teach golf this way ...," and so on. And, as a profession, we tend to teach the same content in the same way to all students, regardless of grade level. Using volleyball as an example, the content, task structure, and sequencing of learning activities remain quite similar, whether the game is being taught to sixth graders or twelfth graders. The bump is learned first, then the set, then the spike, then the serve, followed by some rules and full game play. The drills and other learning activities used to teach each component are remarkably similar as well: the "triangle" bump drill, the wall set drill, and other easily recognizable tasks and organizational structures. All of this sameness stems from the assumption that there is "one best way" to teach volleyball and that this tried-and-true way will be equally effective for all types of students at all grade levels. Again, the content becomes the most influential factor (the organizing center) in determining how to teach a physical education unit. When this happens, the manner of teaching will be referred to as *activity-based instruction,* the most common way for teachers to design instruction in physical education today.

The unit content is important, to be sure, but it should be only one of many things to consider in how to teach a unit. It is likely that instruction will be more effective, safe, and enjoyable if content is considered along with other factors, such as:

- Intended learning outcomes
- Context and teaching environment
- Student developmental stage and readiness
- Student learning preferences
- Domain priorities
- Task structure and organizational patterns
- Sequencing of learning tasks
- Assessment of learning outcomes
- Assessment of instructional practices

A teacher must consider all of those factors *along with content* before making the key decision of how to instruct students in a unit. When a teacher analyzes all of these factors, which in turn leads to a unified, coherent, and comprehensive teaching plan for that unit, we will refer to the resulting manner of teaching as *model-based instruction.* The organizing center for the unit becomes the selected instructional model, chosen after considering all of the factors above.

In a model-based approach, when one or more of those major factors changes, this is likely to result in the selection of a different instructional model. This can be true even when the content remains the same. For instance, if two middle-school teachers are about to begin their own units of soccer and they have different learning outcomes for each class, it would stand to reason that the teachers would instruct in different ways—with two different instructional models. If Mr. Rupp wishes to promote higher levels of skill development with independent student progressions, he could design his unit with a Personalized System for Instruction (Chapter 9). If Mrs. Morales wishes to develop students' strategic knowledge, she could design her unit to be instructed with the Tactical Games model (Chapter 14). Both are soccer units in the same middle-school physical education context, but the decision about "how to teach" is not based on the unit content; rather, it is based on the preferred learning outcomes and the other factors listed above, which should lead each of these teachers to select a different instructional model for their respective units.

There are several good reasons for using a model-based approach in physical education:

1. It allows a teacher to consider and weigh several key factors before deciding which model to use in a unit. This consideration recognizes the relationship between all of those factors and helps the teacher make a *deductive* decision about instruction.

2. When the model is selected deductively, it is much more likely to match the context, content, and goals for each unit. Therefore, the effectiveness of instruction will be consistently high.

3. Most instructional models have research to support the theory behind them and their effectiveness in promoting certain kinds of learning outcomes. This research also provides teachers with field-tested ways to use each model most effectively in many physical education settings.

4. Each instructional model can be viewed as a blueprint for a teacher to follow in designing and implementing instruction. This blueprint helps the teacher make well informed decisions at all stages in a content unit.

5. A good instructional model will include ways for teachers to know if they are using the model correctly and to know if the model is working to help students achieve the stated learning outcomes. It provides teachers with essential feedback about their instruction.

6. Each instructional model provides teachers and students with descriptions of expected behaviors, roles, decisions, and responsibilities, all of which leads to increased clarity for everyone in the class.

7. The best instructional models are flexible and allow each teacher to adapt the model to the unique needs of learners and the context. These models recognize teachers' ability to make professional judgments and decisions based on their expertise, experience, and teaching situation.

OVERVIEW OF THIS BOOK

As I mentioned before, the purpose of this book is to provide you with knowledge about instructional models—plans that can be used to achieve a variety of learning outcomes in your physical education classes. When you know how to use each plan, you will be able to choose and implement the most effective way to instruct every content unit, providing your students with the best opportunity to learn what you intend for them to learn. In order to help you select, plan for, implement, and assess your use of instructional models, this book will follow a series of steps as you progress through the chapters.

Part One

In this chapter you learned that there is no "one best way to teach" physical education. In order for students to achieve the broad range of learning outcomes in the NASPE standards, they will need to learn within a variety of different and effective instructional approaches, called *models* in this book.

Chapter 2 will introduce you to the foundations, features, and implementation conditions necessary for using instructional models in physical education. You will then be able to apply that knowledge as you read the other chapters in Part One to understand fully what instructional models are and how they work in physical education.

Chapter 3 outlines the most essential types of knowledge needed by teachers for effective instruction in a model-based approach. As you will see, a physical education teacher has to draw from several knowledge bases in order to effectively arrange and carry out model-based instruction.

Chapter 4 identifies instructional strategies used to teach physical education using a model-based approach. Strategies are preplanned procedures for events that take place in physical education lessons to promote short-term learning outcomes. Strategies can be designed for grouping students in class, organizing learning tasks, getting and maintaining student attention, increasing safety, presenting information, assessing student learning, and other key operations.

Chapter 5 describes effective teaching skills for physical education that serve as the next level of building blocks necessary for model-based instruction. These are things that effective teachers do—and encourage students to do—before, during, and after class to maximize the potential for student learning. The teaching skills in this chapter were derived from research involving teaching in classrooms and in physical education over the past three decades.

Chapter 6 provides a comprehensive description of unit and lesson planning for physical education. It explains the difference between *just planning* and *being prepared* for teaching physical education. In this book, the planning process is viewed as a series of questions that a teacher should ask before the unit and each lesson in it begin. After the questions have been asked and answered, the teacher will have a better chance to implement smooth, coherent, and effective teaching episodes for all instructional models. A generic planning template is presented so that you will have a place to start in this important function of teaching.

Chapter 7 presents a variety of assessment strategies as they apply to model-based instruction in physical education. It begins with some key terms for that process and then explains several traditional, alternative, and authentic ways to determine how much students have learned in physical education content units.

Part Two

Each of the chapters in Part Two provides a complete description of one instructional model for physical education, based on the foundations, features, and implementation needs presented in Chapter 2. Each chapter will also show you how that particular model is aligned with the NASPE standards. The models (and their chapters in this book) are:

Chapter 8, Direct Instruction

Chapter 9, Personalized System for Instruction

Chapter 10, Cooperative Learning

Chapter 11, Sport Education

Chapter 12, Peer Teaching

Chapter 13, Inquiry Teaching

Chapter 14, Tactical Games

Chapter 15, Teaching Personal and Social Responsibility

These chapters will provide ideas for adapting each model to various teaching contexts. Examples of actual content units instructed with each model will be available at the Instructional Models for Physical Education website, discussed next.

Instructional Models for Physical Education (IMPE) Website

This edition of *Instructional Models for Physical Education* is designed to be more than "just" a book. It has been developed as part of an expandable set of resources that will provide you with many and different ways to learn model-based instruction for physical education. This book now has a website (www.hhpcommunities.com/metzler) that includes a lesson-plan template, sample lessons, and benchmark sheets for each of the eight models presented here together with more general information about using the models. The website is also interactive, with a Forum for sharing your ideas and questions about—and lesson plans for—model-based instruction with other students, student teachers, and physical education teachers.

As a reminder for you to incorporate the website into your learning experience for this book, you'll see the site's URL on the top of each left-hand page of this book. In addition, the following icons will alert you to

 Places to post and receive feedback on instructional–model based units you create as well as to find new units to use in your teaching.

 Opportunities to network and share teaching ideas and experiences with other future and practicing teachers.

 Printer-friendly resources for use your classes.

LEARNING ACTIVITIES

1. Make a list of your participation in physical activities at each stage of your life: preschool, elementary school, secondary school, college, and the present. For each stage describe: (a) your motivation for participating, (b) your goals, and (c) who taught you each of the activities.

2. For each teacher you just listed in the first activity, describe in your own words the methods he or she used to teach you.

3. If you presently teach physical education, coach, or instruct learners in physical activity of any kind, describe your own teaching methods.

4. In your own words, write a definition for "a physically educated person" in the form of a list. For each item on the list, explain how you would go about instructing to help students achieve that part of your definition. (By the way, use of the NASPE definition given in this chapter is not admissible!)

5. P–12 physical education programs have shown a clear evolution in the United States over the past century. What do you think those programs will look like in the year 2020?

6. From your answer in #5, what will learners need to know to qualify as "physically educated" persons? What will teachers need to know and be able to do to help students achieve that goal?

TOPICS FOR REFLECTION & SMALL GROUP DISCUSSION

1. Think for a moment about your personal philosophy of teaching physical education. What do you think students should learn and why? How would you instruct in a way to promote that kind of learning? After a few minutes, ask each member of the group to share his or her personal philosophy. After discussing your thoughts with your classmates, take a few moments to write them down, then post your opinion in the Forum section of the IMPE website for others to read. Be sure to check back for replies, and feel free to respond to those replies in the thread for each topic.

2. Try to identify the people, experiences, and other factors that influenced the development of your personal teaching philosophy. Share your recollections with the other members of your group.

3. Go back to the NASPE content standards for physical education (p. 4). Why do you think those particular standards are in place today? Would you like to see any of those standards deleted? Would you like to see other standards (learning outcomes) added? Justify your answers.

SUGGESTED READINGS

Lund, J., & Tannehill, D. (2010). *Standards-based physical education curriculum development* (2nd ed.). Boston: Jones and Bartlett.

National Association for Sport and Physical Education (2004). *Moving into the future: National standards for physical education* (2nd ed.). Reston, VA: Author.

National Association for Sport and Physical Education (1992). *Outcomes of quality physical education programs*. Reston, VA: Author.

2

DESCRIBING INSTRUCTIONAL MODELS FOR PHYSICAL EDUCATION

The word *model* has many different meanings, with several that apply to how a teacher might choose to instruct physical education. That word is often used to describe a good example of personal characteristics, such as a *model citizen* or a *model student.* It can have that same meaning for teachers when used to identify professional and pedagogical behavior that others view as highly effective and desirable. The word might also be used when someone demonstrates the way others should act or think—to *be a model* by example. That meaning can apply to teachers who display clear patterns of planning and instructional interaction that others can observe and emulate in their own teaching. *Model* can also be used to describe a scaled-down replica of a large object, like an automobile, airplane, or building. A scaled-down model allows the observer to see more easily, in miniature, what a larger object looks like from many perspectives, without having the real object to view. Instructional models also serve this same purpose for teachers by allowing the teacher to better understand a model's components and features before implementing the full version with students.

INSTRUCTIONAL MODELS AS BLUEPRINTS FOR TEACHING PHYSICAL EDUCATION

For this book, the most important meaning of the word *model* relates to the way a blueprint works as a plan for something to be built or procedures to be followed. The blueprint provides a detailed set of written and drawn plans, including instructions, measurements, locations, and materials that help both the architect and the builder understand what the structure will look like when completed, and it allows for efficient and correct decisions to be made during the building process. The "architect" in this metaphor is the person who has designed a model as a coherent plan to bring about certain types of learning and to achieve one or more program standards (such as the NASPE standards). That person develops the original blueprint that gives a model its defining characteristics and unique ways for teachers to instruct and students to learn. The "builder" in this metaphor is the teacher, who takes the blueprint (a model) and follows it to promote certain standards and other learning outcomes in physical education.

Context plays an important role in the design and implementation of all models, whether they are models for teaching or blueprints for building. Before an architect can begin to draw a blueprint, she must ask some important preliminary questions, such as: What will the building be used for? Who will be its primary users or occupants? Where will it be located? What is the construction budget? All those and other questions help to describe the context for the building's design and ultimately determine how functional the building is for those who will use it. Context is just as important for teaching, and must be considered in the selection and implementation of an instructional model for physical education. A teacher must be familiar with an instructional model and know how to change the model to fit a particular school setting, grade level, content, and class. It will be rare that a model can be used exactly as described in this book, so teachers will have to consider their context in selecting and implementing any of the models presented here.

ADVANTAGES OF USING MODEL-BASED INSTRUCTION IN PHYSICAL EDUCATION

There are many benefits pertaining to model-based instruction for physical education. Selecting and using the "right model for the right purpose(s), in the right way" can lead to effective teaching at all times, regardless of content and class contexts. Model-based instruction can offer physical education teachers several important advantages:

1. A model provides an overall plan and coherent approach to teaching and learning. All instructional models describe certain patterns of teacher and student instructional behaviors that effectively promote learning outcomes. Each model is a kind of "master plan" that helps a teacher make and carry out decisions that lead to student learning in a given unit. After a teacher has decided on the major learning outcomes for a unit and has taken the context into consideration, he must then select one or more teaching models that can help students best achieve those outcomes. If you will recall from Chapter 1, today's physical education programs can promote several different standards and types of student learning. Each standard and learning outcome will require a different set of plans and strategies for working toward those goals. Instructional models serve to provide alignment among national standards, learning goals, teaching, and student engagement.

2. A model clarifies learning domain priorities and domain interactions. Physical education programs today can strive for student achievement in any one or a combination of the major learning domains. A *domain* is a large category of related types of learning outcomes. Educators generally recognize three domains. The *cognitive domain* includes the recall of facts, the learning of concepts, and the ability to make decisions. It is usually demonstrated by verbal answers, written answers on tests, and problem-solving exercises. The *psychomotor domain* includes the learning of fine and gross movement patterns. It is usually demonstrated through skilled movement or the solving of generic movement problems. The *affective domain* includes one's feelings, attitudes, social interactions, and perceptions of self. For physical education, the affective domain usually refers to what one learns about self, others, and various forms of physical activity. It can be demonstrated on attitude questionnaires, in personal interviews/conversations, in verbal comments, and through observable personal behaviors and interactions with others in a physical activity setting.

Teachers usually attempt to lead students to learn in one or more of the major domains at all times, but one domain is likely to have a stronger emphasis at a particular moment. If a teacher says, "I want my students to get better at tennis skills," she is prioritizing the psychomotor domain over the others. If another teacher says, "I am not terribly concerned about skills—I want students to explore each new activity and feel good about it," he is emphasizing the affective domain. And finally, if a teacher says, "I really want my students to learn the rules and history of soccer," she is giving the cognitive domain the highest priority. It is also possible, and likely, that a teacher will strive for a balance encompassing all three domains within the same unit. Regardless of whether the domains are prioritized or balanced, the teacher must instruct in the most effective way for learning to take place. Each instructional model presented in this book will clearly state which domain it is primarily designed for or if it is designed for a balance among learning outcomes. Knowing the primary domains for each model, a physical education teacher can more easily select the most effective model(s) for achieving stated outcome(s).

In reality, no activity promotes learning exclusively in a single domain, even when one domain is prioritized over the others. Students will always learn something in the other two domains that are not emphasized at the moment. This is called domain interaction. Just as each model has a domain priority, it will also have domain interactions that further help the teacher decide which model is best for the intended learning goals in a unit. This interaction gives each model another aspect of its identity.

3. A model provides an instructional theme. Each instructional model represents a "big idea" for teaching and learning in a content unit. This idea is the unique way the teacher and students will operate. For instance, the big idea about Cooperative Learning (Chapter 10) is that students are responsible for learning as a team. The theme "Students learning with, by, and for each other" represents the major plan for learning and can be used to help students better understand the way classes will be instructed in that model.

If teachers and students understand that each model will call for different patterns of planning, decision making, responsibility, and learning activities, they will be more receptive to the new ways of teaching and learning described in some of the models. By simplifying these patterns with an instructional theme for each unit, teachers can regularly remind themselves and students that physical education class will be a bit different, and more interesting, than usual.

4. A model allows the teacher and students to understand current and upcoming events. The master plan in each model will be apparent to the teacher and students, providing a good basis for understanding the purpose and sequence of events in the unit. All instructional models allow the teacher to plan ahead and students to know where the learning plan is taking them. This understanding promotes increased student interest, cooperation, and managerial efficiency—all of which can enhance learning.

5. A model furnishes a unified theoretical framework. All teaching models are designed from a unified theoretical framework that begins with assumptions about how learning occurs, the developmental needs of students, the best ways to manage the teaching setting, and the learning activities that will lead to stated learning outcomes. If a teacher remains aware of those assumptions and implements instruction within the model's theoretical framework, the desired learning is much more likely to occur.

6. A model has research support. All the instructional models in this book have some level of research support for their effectiveness. After a model has been developed from a unified theoretical framework, it is common to conduct research on how best to implement the model by using classes of students to test the model's ability to promote the kinds of learning for which it is designed. Before selecting a model, it is important for a teacher to become acquainted with the research that shows how best to use it and, more important, when it should not be used. That background information will help a teacher learn the best ways to apply the model, implement it most effectively, and know its limitations.

7. A model promotes a technical language for teachers. Every instructional model contains unique terminology to describe its theoretical framework, design, and operations. We refer to that terminology as a *technical language,* through which all teachers have a shared meaning for words and terms applied in a model. That shared meaning allows designers, teachers, and students to communicate clearly and efficiently, increasing the potential for stated learning outcomes to occur. Teachers should be aware that some words and terms can have different meanings in different models, so it is important to know the terminology used in each model.

8. A model allows the relationship between instruction and learning to be verified. An instructional model will include a coherent pattern of decision making, managerial plans, instructional strategies, discrete teaching skills, in-class operations, learning activities, and assessment—all of which are designed for the primary purpose of increasing student learning of the stated outcomes. The model's designer, in effect, is saying that if a teacher makes decisions and carries out instruction in a way that is congruent with the model's theoretical framework and design, students are likely to learn what is intended. Since many teacher and student instructional behaviors can be observed and measured, as can many stated learning outcomes, it is then possible to examine this relationship within each model. This examination can become a useful way to test the effectiveness of a model in any given application, and it can become the basis for making systematic revisions for the model's next use.

Those teacher and student operations and *ways to teach and learn* will be called *benchmarks* in this book. Each benchmark indicates a certain operation or in-class process that the teacher and/or students will try to follow in each model so that the model is implemented according to its design, leading to a greater likelihood of increased student achievement.

9. A model allows for more valid assessments of learning. Assessment of student learning in physical education has received increased attention in recent years, and many good new ideas have been developed (Wood, 2003). However, assessment techniques are often developed with no clear directions for when and how a teacher might use it; the technique is simply a "nice idea" that each teacher must figure out how to use in his or her own classes. This decreases the chances that the assessment actually measures the intended learning outcomes in a correct, or valid, way. Every instructional model in this book includes assessment techniques that are designed specifically for that model and serve as valid indicators of how well students learned in that content unit. Instructional models promote improved formative and summative assessments of learning by monitoring student achievement throughout a unit and at its completion. Many models will promote the use of authentic and alternative assessments, reflecting the unique domain interactions within them.

10. A model encourages teacher decision making within a unified framework. Instructional models can help teachers make decisions within the scope of each model. Rather than decide how to teach from a long list of discrete skills, managerial schemes, and learning strategies, the teacher will have a reduced range of choices based on the unit content and the model's framework, design, and context. This reduced range of options can improve the congruence between decisions and actions within the unit, promoting more effective student learning.

None of this implies that a teacher cannot use her own personal and creative options within a model-based instructional unit. In fact, how the teacher makes and carries out decisions within a model's framework will depend greatly on her pedagogical content knowledge and other professional expertise. As you will see in Part Two, each model will specify that certain instructional operations need to be completed within its framework. Yet rarely will the model's design indicate that an operation must be done in just one way. In nearly all cases, it will be the teacher who provides the innovation to implement each operation in the model for maximum effectiveness.

11. A model directly promotes specific standards and learning outcomes. As a set of blueprints for teaching physical education, the instructional models in this book can lead students to high levels of achievement in all six NASPE standards and other learning outcomes stated for today's physical education programs. As discussed in Chapter 1, contemporary programs must strive to promote a wide variety of learning outcomes for students, and no "one best way" to teach will work by itself. Teachers must use a variety of models over a period of time to cover all the kinds of learning outcomes that currently define an effective program of physical education instruction.

FRAMEWORK FOR DESCRIBING THE MODELS

E ach instructional model in this book represents a unique way for teachers to make and carry out decisions that lead to student learning in physical education. Although models can differ in many ways, it is possible to describe attributes to show how each model is designed, how it works, how learning occurs in it, and when it might be used most effectively.

In Chapter 1, an instructional model was defined as a comprehensive and coherent plan for teaching that includes descriptions of students' needs and abilities, statements of intended learning outcomes, teacher's content knowledge expertise, developmentally appropriate and sequenced learning activities, expectations for teacher and student behaviors, unique task structures, measures of learning outcomes, and mechanisms for assessing the faithful implementation of the model itself. That definition separates it from smaller, discrete teaching skills and less-complex teaching strategies—both of which are included in every instructional model. Before you learn each of the models in this book, it is important that you understand how each model is designed and how it operates to promote student learning.

Each instructional model described in this book is designed with a combination of foundations, teaching and learning features, and implementation needs that make it a unique way to teach physical education. In order to understand how each model works, it is best to use a common framework to describe each model so that you can see how they all differ. Exhibit 2.1 outlines this framework; each item you see in columns 1–3 will be discussed in presenting each of the eight models in Part Two and will thus help you understand the similarities and differences among the models.

Framework used in this book to describe instructional models by foundations, teaching and learning features, and implementation needs.			**EXHIBIT** **2.1**
FOUNDATIONS +	**TEACHING AND LEARNING FEATURES** +	**IMPLEMENTATION NEEDS AND MODIFICATIONS** ➤	**DETERMINE WHICH MODEL TO USE**
Theory and rationale	Control	Teacher expertise	Direct Instruction
Assumptions about teaching and learning	Inclusiveness	Key teaching skills	Personalized System for Instruction
A theme	Learning tasks	Contextual requirements	
	Engagement patterns	Contextual modifications	Cooperative Learning
Learning domain priorities and interactions	Teacher and student roles and responsibilities		Sport Education
			Peer Teaching
Student developmental requirements	Verification of instructional processes		Inquiry Teaching
			Tactical Games
Validation	Assessment of learning		Teaching Personal and Social Responsibility

Foundations

An instructional model is much more than the set of operations and learning activities in it. Each model is based on a design that forms the foundation for all aspects of the model. That design is not always apparent to those who observe a model in action, but it should be fully known to any teacher who selects a particular model for physical education.

Theory and rationale

Each model is based on an articulated learning theory that leads its designer to a rationale for why and when a model should be used and under what conditions it will be the most effective. In effect, it describes a relationship between one or more theories of learning and operations in the model that "make it work" for its intended purpose.

The theory and rationale explain the central design concepts behind the model, often indicated by the model's label (e.g., Cooperative Learning, Peer Teaching, Sport Education). Physical education teachers should clearly understand the "big idea" behind each model they read about and consider using in their classes.

What does the model include? Each model contains a different set of managerial plans, decisions, operations, learning activities, and assessments. A model also describes a set of roles and responsibilities for the teacher and students within it. Teachers need to be certain they know what is expected of them and their students within each model, and they must make sure they can meet those expectations with pedagogical skills, content expertise, student management, and their own personal values for teaching.

What does the model not include? Each model is designed to meet specific types of student learning needs. Therefore, it is important for a teacher not to have unrealistic expectations and not to misuse a model by mismatching the theory, the stated learning outcomes, and the model's capabilities. For instance, a model like Direct Instruction (Chapter 8) is designed to give the teacher a high degree of control over task structure, task progression, and learning activity. It offers limited opportunities for students to make decisions in class. If a teacher wishes for students to participate regularly in interactive decision making in physical education, then Direct Instruction is not an effective model for that learning outcome.

Assumptions about teaching and learning

Little is known conclusively about the relationship between teaching and learning in gymnasiums and classrooms. An instructional model is often based on assumptions made by the model's designer: that is, if a teacher plans and implements instruction in certain ways, it should lead to some-what predictable learning outcomes for students. Some of those assumptions may be supported by research, but it is the job of the designer to set out those assumptions for teachers—in a sense, putting "the cards on the table" for potential users to make their own decisions about the validity of those assumptions. If a teacher understands most or all of the assumptions behind a particular model, that teacher is more likely to agree with and use the model in her teaching. As you can tell by now, there must be strong agreement between a designer's assumptions and the values held by a teacher who would use that model.

Theory extends one step past assumptions, in that it is based on some preliminary evidence an assumption is valid. Referring to instructional models, this means having some research to indicate that the model has a good theoretical foundation. Typically, that evidence is gathered through research and then applied in the design of a given model. This theory represents an "educated guess" that the model *should* work, but it is far short of demonstrating that it can and does work. Personalized System for Instruction, or PSI (Chapter 9), was developed on a theory based in operant conditioning and behavior modification. Fred Keller (1968) and his students used that theory to design an individualized learning model at the college level, basing the theory on their educated guess that it would be an effective way to promote increased levels of student knowledge in college introductory psychology courses. Their educated guess was correct, and the PSI model developed from that theory.

It is important that teachers understand the assumptions and theories behind each instructional model. This does not mean a theory must be abstract and removed from the realities of teaching physical education to children and youth. Quite the opposite is true, since a good theory must prove itself relevant and practical in a model that can be used in many contexts, in many grade levels, and for many types of movement content. Contrary to the popular view that theory has little to offer teachers in schools, when used as the basis of an instructional model *there is nothing more practical than a good theory*. Think about it!

The model's theme

All instructional models are based on one major premise or theme that defines the model and makes it unique. That theme summarizes the most basic idea on which the model is designed. A model's theme comes directly from its rationale and might also describe the major learning processes used in the model. The major theme of Peer Teaching (Chapter 12) is "I teach you; then you teach me." In that model, students assume many key instructional operations to teach their peers. While Peer Teaching does include other ideas and processes, that brief theme captures much of what the model is about.

Learning domain priorities and interactions

Each instructional model places a different emphasis on outcomes in the cognitive, psychomotor, and affective learning domains. That means learning in one domain is more likely to occur than in other domains because of the way the model is designed and the way students interact with the content. It is important not to view a model's domain priorities negatively when you disagree with them—it is simply a fact that each model is designed to emphasize different kinds of learning outcomes and should be selected only when those outcomes match the teacher's instructional goals. If not, then a different model should be selected.

What are the model's domain priorities? It should be mentioned that all the models in this book are designed to promote learning in all three major domains. In physical education it is not possible to exclude any of the domains, but most models are based on a hierarchy of learning domain goals. The Inquiry Teaching model (Chapter 13) places the strongest emphasis on learning in the cognitive domain, followed by the psychomotor and affective domains. That model places primary importance on students learning to "think first; then move." Students should acquire the underlying cognitive knowledge before they attempt to become highly skilled in their movement. Affective learning and psychomotor skills are not ignored, but those outcomes receive much less emphasis than those in the cognitive domain.

A few of the models promote balance among the three domains. As you will see in Chapter 11, the Sport Education model strives for student learning of motor skills, game rules, strategy, traditions, and personal interactions within team affiliation. Students can be in a learning activity that emphasizes one domain at any moment, but over the course of the whole unit, all three domains receive balanced attention.

What are the most likely domain interactions? A domain interaction happens when emphasis is placed directly on one domain but learning still occurs in one or more of the other domains at the same time. Since it is not possible in physical education to exclude any of the domains in the learning process, teachers must recognize which domain interactions are most likely to occur in each model. In the Inquiry Teaching model (Chapter 13), students learn to develop thinking and problem-solving skills. Therefore, the model works best when the cognitive domain has the highest priority in the unit. However, while students learn in that domain, they are likely to improve their movement skills as they use their bodies to explore possible answers—a result of the interaction between the cognitive and psychomotor domains. At the next level, this interaction will lead to increased personal efficacy and self-esteem—outcomes in the affective domain. The domain interaction for that model will look like this:

Cognitive Learning ⟶ Psychomotor Learning ⟶ Affective Learning

Domain interactions can serve to reduce some of the differences among models used in physical education and allow teachers to pursue several standards and many kinds of student learning in every model. So, while most models will have definite domain priorities, every model will have some interaction that promotes student learning in all three domains.

Student developmental requirements

Students are not passive participants in learning. They play a key role in the selection, implementation, and success of an instructional model. Each model assumes that students have certain physical, cognitive, and affective levels of development that can be increased through the corresponding kind of instruction—prerequisites, in other words. And each model gives students specific roles and responsibilities, so students must be able to meet their responsibilities for the model to succeed. Together, these factors determine student *readiness* for learning within that model. Since each instructional model represents a certain way that teaching and learning will occur in physical education, teachers must realize that each model will appeal to some students more than others. Individual students simply like to learn in some ways more than others, which determines their *receptivity* to a given model.

Student readiness for learning. For instruction to be most effective, it must correspond to students' levels of developmental readiness. Developmental readiness refers to a student's ability to understand and follow directions, behave safely and responsibly, and have a reasonable chance to succeed at learning tasks. Instruction that matches student ability in these areas is called *developmentally appropriate* instruction. If it matches just a little or not at all, it is considered to be *developmentally inappropriate* instruction.

In order for instruction to be developmentally appropriate, it must match student readiness in four areas: (1) comprehension of verbal, written, and modeled information; (2) decision making and responsibility; (3) social/emotional maturity; and (4) prerequisite knowledge and physical ability. Exhibit 2.2 shows some examples of developmentally appropriate and inappropriate practices for physical education.

	EXHIBIT 2.2
Developmentally inappropriate and appropriate practices for physical education.	

READINESS AREA	DEVELOPMENTALLY INAPPROPRIATE	DEVELOPMENTALLY APPROPRIATE
Comprehension of information	■ Teacher uses words and terms that students do not know ■ Teacher gives extensive written task structure to slow readers ■ Teacher shows students an "adult" version of the task in the task presentation	■ Teacher uses only familiar words and terms when talking to students ■ Task cards are brief, with pictures and drawings on them ■ Teacher asks a peer to demonstrate how the task should be performed by students of their age and ability
Decision making and responsibility	■ Students are expected to pick "fair" teams for games, but cannot do so ■ Students are told to work alone, without teacher supervision, but cannot stay on task ■ Teacher gives incomplete managerial directions and expects students to follow them correctly	■ Teacher selects fair teams before class ■ Teacher regularly monitors for proper engagement ■ Teacher gives simple, complete directions and checks for understanding
Social/emotional maturity	■ Immature students are placed in tasks that provide an opportunity to cheat ■ Unmotivated students work on individual projects with no supervision ■ Students are asked to do peer teaching but are rude to less skilled students	■ Teacher gives students rules to follow and monitors students' progress ■ Teacher provides students with a check sheet to remind them how to complete the project ■ Teacher shows peer teachers how to give constructive and supportive feedback
Prerequisite knowledge and physical ability	■ Teacher goes to advanced tasks before students have mastered basic skills ■ Teacher assumes all students have experience with the content ■ All students do the same task, with the same task difficulty	■ Teacher checks for student mastery before progressing ■ Teacher conducts a needs assessment before the unit begins ■ Teacher uses intra-task variation and "teaching by invitation"

Student receptivity to the model. There has been much discussion in the educational literature about *learning styles,* which describe how each person best receives, assimilates, and acts upon perceptual stimuli in the environment (Dunn, 1996). The concept of learning styles, however, does not attempt to describe the conditions under which an individual student prefers to be engaged in learning, or the student's receptivity. Since each instructional model essentially determines a unique learning environment, the notion of *learning preferences* set forth by Reichmann and Grasha (1974) works well within a model-based approach to instruction. Reichmann and Grasha identified three bipolar dimensions that determine a student's preferred learning environment: avoidant/participant (student attitudes toward learning); competitive/collaborative (views of teachers and/or peers); and dependent/independent (reactions to classroom procedures). Each dimension includes several pairs of descriptors that lead to a profile of each student's preferred conditions for learning. The design, operations, and types of learning activities within each model will generate a unique environmental profile for that model. The model will be most effective when its environmental profile matches the profile of the majority of students in a class. Exhibit 2.3 shows the dimensions and descriptors in the Reichmann and Grasha profiling scheme.

The attributes on the right side of the continuum should not be interpreted in a negative light—they simply reflect some students' preferences concerning how the learning environment is set up. Jonassen and Grabowski (1993) analyzed the bipolar ends of all three characteristics in the Reichmann and Grasha model to determine the kinds of teaching strategies and settings that would best suit each preference:

1. The *collaborative* student prefers working in small groups and having student-designed activities, group projects, peer assessments, and interaction with the teacher.

2. The *competitive* student prefers direct teaching strategies, opportunities to ask questions in class, and teacher recognition.

3. The *participant* student prefers class discussions, alternative assessments, individual learning activities, teachers who provide opportunities for analysis and synthesis, and enthusiastic task presentations.

4. The *avoidant* student prefers no required tasks in class, little interaction with the teacher and other students, self-assessment, and no tests.

5. The *independent* student prefers self-paced learning, independent study opportunities, student-designed activities, and indirect teaching strategies.

6. The *dependent* student prefers direct teaching strategies, teacher-directed assessments, and clear timelines for class activities and outside assignments.

Validation of the model

A *valid* model is one that has been shown to be effective in promoting certain standards and types of learning in physical education. In other words, the model works to help students learn what it is designed for, in the contexts for which it is an appropriate way to teach. For teachers who have not used a model, the most important question is, "How do I know it can work to help my students learn what I want them to learn?" Validation can come from any or all of three primary sources: research, craft knowledge, and intuitive knowledge.

Research. A large body of research on instructional models exists. Most of it has come from other subject areas, but we also have research evidence for many models as they have been used in physical education. This research describes

Student learning preference dichotomies (adapted from Reichmann & Grasha, 1974).	EXHIBIT 2.3

PARTICIPANT	AVOIDANT
has strong motivation to learn course content	has weak motivation to learn course content
likes to assume responsibility for learning	likes to assume little responsibility
participates with others	prefers not to participate with others
does what is required	does what he/she wants
COLLABORATIVE	**COMPETITIVE**
shares	is competitive
is cooperative	is motivated to do better than others
enjoys working with others	enjoys competing
sees PE as a place for learning and interacting with others	sees PE as a competitive situation in which he/she must win
INDEPENDENT	**DEPENDENT**
thinks for him- or herself	relies on teacher as source of information and structure
works on his or her own	needs others to provide direction
will learn what is needed	learns what is required
will listen to others	shows little intellectual curiosity
has strong self-confidence	has less self-confidence

optimal ways to plan and implement a model, or it can demonstrate a model's effectiveness in promoting student achievement. Both kinds of research are important for teachers who will decide which model to use for certain outcomes and in certain contexts. Teachers can become familiar with a model's research base by reading research journals, searching online, taking courses in instructional design, and reading textbooks—like this one—that contain descriptions of models. Some models have entire books that provide written research evidence in support of them.

Each of the chapters in Part Two will report research findings from the eight models presented in this book. Along with research on individual models, some research is now emerging about model-based instruction in general. Gurvitch, Metzler, and Lund (2008) conducted a series of studies to examine the use and perceptions of model-based instruction in physical education with student teachers, cooperating teachers, and P–12 students. Student teachers and cooperating teachers overall supported the use and effectiveness of model-based instruction, while noting some factors that inhibited those attempts. However, the majority of these teachers found the extra effort to learn and use instructional models to be well worth it. In one of those studies, Metzler and McCullick (2008) surveyed and interviewed a large number of P–12 students who had just taken units of instruction with varying instructional models. The results indicated that students: (1) knew the difference (and liked it!) between being taught with an instructional model and their typical physical education instruction; (2) could clearly identify the major components and learning objectives in each model they experienced; (3) liked the new and different ways of interacting with their teacher and fellow students; and (4) overall thought that they learned more from model-based instruction.

Craft knowledge. Craft knowledge is derived from many teachers' experiences of using an instructional model. It is based on verbal and/or written communication among teachers about "what works" and "what doesn't work" when implementing a model. Although research knowledge is more formal, and sometimes more valid, most teachers actually rely on craft knowledge (their own and others') when deciding if and how to use a particular model. Craft knowledge of teaching decisions and actions that work well for many teachers and in many settings can rise to the level of *best practice* and become the accepted way of doing things within a particular model.

Craft knowledge is valuable because it is based on many teachers' actual experiences with a particular model, content, and context. Through craft knowledge, an individual teacher can benefit from the experience of others and eliminate much of the trial and error that occurs the first few times they use a model. Craft knowledge can come from many sources: one's own experiences, interactions at professional conferences, conversations with teaching colleagues, practitioner journals like the *Journal of Physical Education, Recreation & Dance* and *Strategies,* and physical education–related websites like PE Central (www.pecentral.org) and PELINKS4U (www.pelinks4u.org). The many excellent examples of model-based instruction on the IMPE website represent the very best craft knowledge developed by physical education teachers who have used this approach.

Intuitive knowledge. While research and craft knowledge are much more tangible ways to validate the use of an instructional model, sometimes a teacher selects a model because it appears to be a good way to instruct certain content in certain contexts. It just "makes sense" to instruct that way at a given time, based on the teacher's general knowledge of the model and the learning goals for the content unit. Eventually, this will be replaced either by craft knowledge as the teacher gains experience with the model over time or by research knowledge as the teacher reads more about the model. Basing an initial decision on one's professional intuition is an acceptable way to select a model for the first time, but eventually that intuition should be supported by craft or research knowledge.

Teaching and Learning Features

Each instructional model will include several features that give it an identity. These features in large part define what the model looks like for the teacher and students, and they make each model different from the others. These features come directly from the learning theory and assumptions on which each model is based.

Control

Physical education instruction involves two major participants—the teacher and the students. Those participants will have a large number of verbal, nonverbal, and combined interactions in every lesson. The pattern of those interactions is determined largely by the design of the instructional model being used in the unit. One way to describe the pattern used in a particular model is by *control*. The concept of control has two parts. It can describe the origin and type of interactions between a teacher and students during instruction—who says what to whom and who makes what kinds of gestures to whom. It can also describe the nature of decision making and teacher/student control during class. Because all models are based on different assumptions and views of how learning can be most effective, each model will, by design, lead to different degrees of teacher/student control. Models that are strong on the *teacher-control* end of the spectrum (see Exhibit 2.4) give the teacher most or all of the responsibility for making decisions and initiating instructional interactions. Students are given few opportunities to make decisions, and they receive information and directions mostly from the teacher. Models that are strong on the *student-control* end of the spectrum allow students to make many decisions in class, to explore and be creative, and to initiate a lot of questions and other interactions with the teacher. Models that promote high levels of teacher and student *interaction* fall in the middle, with shared decision making, communication, control, and responsibility in physical education classes.

Teacher control: "The sage on the stage." Instruction that is strongly controlled by the teacher gives her the authority to make most or all decisions about content and class management. As the managerial authority, the teacher makes and oversees nearly all decisions about how students are organized, when practice

Control continuum.   **EXHIBIT 2.4**

Teacher control	Interactive	Student control
"Sage on the Stage"		"Guide on the Side"

segments start and stop, when learning tasks change, and what class rules apply. As the content authority, the teacher is viewed as the one who has the knowledge that needs to be transmitted to students according to decisions made solely by the teacher. Thus the teacher becomes "the sage on the stage" (King, 1992).

Teacher-controlled instruction is also characterized by communication mostly in one direction—from teacher to student. The teacher makes decisions and then informs the students what they will do or learn next, while controlling the selection and pacing of class events. The students *receive* more than they *initiate* when the teacher is strongly in control. Within some models, teacher control is used effectively to increase the level of student participation and increase the number of repetitions during skill practice.

Student control: "The guide on the side." Student-controlled instruction lies at the opposite end of the continuum. It is characterized by much less teacher control of decisions and class events and more open-ended, student-initiated learning activities. Teachers at this end of the spectrum view themselves not as authorities but as *facilitators* of student learning, placing students, not themselves, at the center of the learning process. For these teachers, the major functions involve arranging the kind of learning environment that gives students some direction and a task to accomplish, then standing aside to monitor while students go about the learning process—thus the "guide on the side" label (King, 1992).

With this kind of instruction the teacher still keeps a degree of decision making and control, the object of those decisions is to find ways to allow students to interact more freely with the content and each other—not necessarily with the teacher. For classroom management, it means that students have input in making class rules and that they take more responsibility for their own behavior. Students get to make more of their own choices about how they will be engaged in learning tasks (e.g., selecting objects to throw or to catch with, choosing the level of challenge they wish to pursue, and deciding when to go on to a new task). This will promote more student thinking and creative movement exploration by posing questions and problems to students, rather than telling (or showing) students how to move in certain ways. This kind of teaching also features in-class or outside assignments in which students have flexibility in managing their own learning processes. The teacher then serves as the main resource person to help students when they "get stuck" or need other assistance.

Interactive teaching. In the middle of the control continuum is interactive teaching, characterized by a balance between teacher- and student-controlled instruction. The teacher and students have approximately equal responsibility for decisions and share many classroom operations. Interactive teaching also involves frequent two-way communication between the teacher and students. Students are encouraged to ask questions, offer suggestions, and have regular input into the functioning of lessons. The teacher will ask for, and act upon, students' suggestions and ideas in class.

Key operations for determining a model's control profile.   A model's designation as teacher controlled, student controlled, or interactive is not determined by a single factor. *Key operations* within the model must be analyzed for their place on the control continuum. Seven key operations will be used in this book to determine the control profile of each model (see Exhibit 2.5).

1. Content selection   Who determines what is taught in the unit?
2. Managerial control   Who is mostly responsible for classroom management?
3. Task presentation   How do students receive task information?
4. Engagement patterns   How are student engagement patterns (involving space, groups, structure) determined?
5. Instructional interactions   Who initiates the communications during learning tasks?
6. Pacing   Who controls the starting and stopping of practice?
7. Task progression   Who decides when to change learning tasks?

Each model will have varying degrees of control in these seven operations, but most of the operations will fall in or near the same general area on the continuum. Therefore, the overall profile for each model will typically be described as teacher controlled, interactive, or student controlled to reflect its *predominant* place on the continuum.

It is tempting to prefer student-controlled and interactive teaching over teacher-controlled teaching. But it is not correct to pit these three ways of

Control profile for key instructional operations.   EXHIBIT 2.5

teaching against each other. Each way can be successful in developing certain types of learning outcomes, and the wise teacher will choose the model that most effectively promotes his stated outcomes. A teacher may choose to teach one unit with a strongly teacher-controlled model, the next unit with an interactive model, and a third unit with a strongly student-controlled model.

Inclusiveness

Physical education classes reflect the growing student diversity now found in almost every public school in our country. That diversity combines nearly every conceivable gender, race, religion, language, ethnicity, learning ability, and physical ability represented by students in our society. With those differences in student demographics and abilities come differences in the needs, experiences, and preferences students bring with them to physical education class. Today's philosophy of inclusion challenges teachers to select content and instruct in ways that meet the educational needs of all students. Inclusion is legally mandated for girls by Title IX legislation and for many physically disabled or handicapped students by the Individuals with Disabilities Education Act of 1997. But it is not just legislation that should compel physical educators to design inclusive content and instruction; we should strive to meet the educational needs of all children as part of our professional ethic.

The term *inclusive* describes any class that contains students with greatly differing characteristics, needs, and abilities, all trying to learn at the same time. The dilemma for physical education teachers is that by addressing the needs of one or more groups of students in the class, they may reduce the opportunity for other groups of students to learn the content. If a teacher progresses quickly through a unit, it is more likely that only the more skilled students will keep up, while the less skilled students fall further behind. If a teacher must take class time to communicate with a non-English-speaking student through a translator, attention is diverted from perhaps 35 or 40 other children who also need the teacher's time and attention. If a teacher decides to use written task cards at learning stations, how will that affect students who can't read at that level or who have a reading disability?

Each instructional model is based on some prerequisite abilities and experiences that students must be able to apply within the model. Those prerequisites play a large role in determining if the model can meet the educational needs of all students in an inclusive class group. Students' learning preferences also determine how inclusive a model will be with any given group of students. Students whose preferences match the kind of learning environment designed in the model will have a greater chance for success and will like the learning process being used. Students whose preferences do not match those in the model will probably not have that same degree of success and enjoyment. As a potential user of any instructional model, the teacher must be aware of which students can be served well by teaching that way and which students might be overly challenged by that model. Even more importantly, the teacher must ask himself if and how the model can be adapted to meet all students' needs.

Learning tasks

In many models, a teacher's most essential functions are to show students what will be learned, explain how the learning task will be set up, and determine when it is time to change learning tasks. These key operations are called task presentation, task structure, and content progression.

Task presentation. *Task presentation* refers to those processes used to demonstrate skills and learning tasks to students. Through this presentation, students come to see and/or hear how to perform skills to be practiced in upcoming learning activities. This is an important part of every lesson, accomplished in many different ways from model to model. Some models will use just one or two task presentation strategies, while other models will use a large number of them. Chapter 4 describes these strategies for presenting tasks in physical education.

Task structure. Most task presentations will include a description of *task structure* to inform students how the learning task is organized, how they will be grouped, how long it will last, what the performance criteria are, and what the expectations are for student conduct during the task. Refer to Chapter 4 for a more complete explanation of task structure. As with task presentations, each model will use certain kinds of task structures more than others, so a teacher would not necessarily need to be prepared to use a large number of them in a content unit within one model.

Content progression. Every instructional unit in physical education will contain a range of content to be learned and a planned order for learning it. For example, in a soccer unit, the students might learn the basic skills of ball handling, passing, trapping, shooting, marking, goal keeping, offensive patterns, and defensive patterns. Within each of those content areas of soccer, the teacher will use one or more learning tasks to help students acquire that skill and/or knowledge. The order in which those tasks are given to students, along with the ways the teacher decides to change from one task to the next and one content area to the next, are all included in what is called *content progression*. This progression describes how students move through the unit toward the learning outcomes intended by the teacher. Each of the models in this book has a different plan for content progression, as you will see in Part Two.

Engagement patterns for learning

The engagement pattern characterizes the manner in which students interact with the learning content—the way in which they are involved in the learning process. At any given time, the engagement pattern is strongly related to the learning activity and its task structure as planned by the teacher. Engagement patterns can be defined by the degree of student interaction with the content and by the grouping strategy used in the task structure.

Active engagement. The learning process is active when it involves direct personal participation by students. It is characterized by student movement, thinking, questioning, and decision making.

Passive engagement. The learning process is passive when students merely receive the content from other sources (usually the teacher) in the form of information given to them. It is characterized by student listening, watching, and reading. Exhibit 2.6 shows how students can be actively or passively engaged with some examples of content.

Active learning is not necessarily the kind preferred at all times. Sometimes a teacher can use passive learning strategies to get large amounts of information to students quickly and effectively. The key question for the teacher here is, "How do I want students to know this content?" If cognitive knowledge is sufficient, then passive engagement will do fine. However, if the teacher wants students to learn how to think *and* move, then active engagement should be planned.

Individual, small-group, or whole-class engagement. The engagement pattern is partly determined by how students are grouped, if at all, for learning tasks. Some models rely almost entirely on individual participation in learning tasks. Some models are designed for participation in small groups or teams of students—all of whom share the responsibility for team achievement. Still other models are based on the whole class participating in the same activities at all times. Most models will have one or two predominant grouping strategies for student engagement.

Teacher and student roles and responsibilities

Each instructional model will call for teachers and students to take on a unique set of roles and responsibilities within it. It is important that everyone knows

EXHIBIT 2.6 Passive and active engagement in physical education.

LEARNING OUTCOME OR CONTENT	PASSIVE ENGAGEMENT	ACTIVE ENGAGEMENT
Learning game rules	▪ Reading rules in a book ▪ Hearing rules from teacher	▪ Officiating a game ▪ Explaining rules to others
Pitching a softball	▪ Watching a teacher demonstration ▪ Viewing a DVD	▪ Practicing pitching drills ▪ Pitching in a game
Learning dance steps	▪ Listening to the teacher describe step sequences	▪ Following the teacher's lead at "half speed"
Learning self-esteem	▪ Listening to a definition of self-esteem ▪ Defining self-esteem on a test	▪ Achieving success in a game or activity, followed by reflection to develop a sense of self-esteem

those roles and accepts responsibility for carrying them out in the unit. This is often related to the model's control profile, defining who largely controls decision making and instructional operations in class. Sport Education (Chapter 11) and Cooperative Learning (Chapter 10) call for the teacher to assume the role of resource person and facilitator, while students assume a large role in decision making and shared responsibility for their team's learning. In Direct Instruction (Chapter 8) the teacher takes on the roles of instructional leader, the major source of task presentation, and the primary provider of instructional information (e.g., cues and feedback). Students take on a more receptive role, with their major responsibilities being to pay attention, follow directions, and stay engaged as directed by the teacher.

Managerial responsibilities can shift from model to model. In some models the teacher assumes nearly all control over class management decisions and interactions. Those teachers will expend considerable time and energy in "running the class." In other models, students take responsibility for a large portion of class management, allowing the teacher more time to interact with students for learning.

Verification of instructional processes

It is important for a teacher to verify that she is implementing a model in the way it was designed. Each model is a plan of action that should lead to intended learning outcomes for students, so from time to time the teacher must ask herself, "Am I teaching according to the way the model was intended to be used?"

As indicated earlier, each model is designed for unique patterns of teacher and student behavior in class. In essence, those patterns distinguish each model from the others, so a teacher should implement a model with an acceptable degree of adherence to its design plans. A teacher will always have to make some modifications, most often due to context, but those changes should not go against the basic assumptions in the model or cause major operations and features of the model to become unfamiliar.

Each model will have a series of *benchmarks*—patterns of teacher and student operations that should happen while they use that model. Those benchmarks help to remind the teacher of "how to teach" and "how students will go about learning" in that model, and they can be used to verify proper planning and instructional operations. Consider the following ways to monitor teaching and learning benchmarks in model-based instruction.

Systematic analysis of teaching and learning behaviors in class. Once a teacher knows what kinds of instructional patterns a model should foster (i.e., the benchmarks), those patterns can be analyzed by collecting data in live settings or by studying video or audio samples of classes. The behaviors to be analyzed should be those that reflect the model's benchmarks. For instance, the PSI model (Chapter 9) allocates very little class management time to the teacher and much opportunity for the teacher to provide feedback to students. It is quite easy to measure the amount of management time and teacher feedback in PSI classes, thereby establishing whether a teacher is implementing the model according to its design in those areas. Duration recording, event recording, and momentary time sampling can all help monitor certain kinds of teacher and student behaviors in physical education classes. Exhibit 2.7 shows how each technique can be used to verify different aspects of instruction.

Checklists of benchmarks. A list can be made of teacher and student benchmarks and patterns that are indicative of each model, "checking off" each time one of them is observed in class. The checklist can verify that a benchmark occurred, but it cannot distinguish between correct and incorrect instances of the benchmark. Chapters 8–15 provide teacher and student benchmarks for each model, and the IMPE website presents printer-friendly checklists using these benchmarks.

Rating scales for benchmarks. A rating scale resembles a checklist, with the added ability to render an evaluation of observed benchmarks. Each benchmark is followed by a series of evaluative criteria, such as "poor," "fair," "good," and "excellent," or a numeric scale of 1 to 10, with 1 being the lowest rating and 10 being the highest. The observer notes which benchmarks occur in the class and circles the word or number that represents his judgment of the quality with which the benchmark was carried out.

EXHIBIT 2.7	Systematic analysis of teaching and learning benchmarks.		
OBSERVATIONAL TECHNIQUE	**USED TO MEASURE**	**TEACHER BEHAVIORS**	**STUDENT BEHAVIORS**
Duration recording	The amount of time a defined behavior occurs in class	■ Management time ■ Task presentation length ■ Circulating in class	■ Management time ■ Practice time ■ Academic learning time ■ On/off task time ■ Waiting time
Event recording	The frequency of defined events	■ Use of students' first names ■ Feedback to students ■ Cues given to students ■ Questions ■ Checks for understanding	■ Practice trials ■ Success rate ■ Feedback received ■ Questions asked
Momentary time sampling	Occurrence/non-occurrence of behaviors at predetermined times in the lesson	■ Pedagogical moves ■ Location in class	■ Percent of students on task at any moment ■ Percent of students practicing at any moment ■ Student success rate ■ Appropriate task structure

Open-ended questions for written assessments.	EXHIBIT	2.8

- How did you feel in your role of team coach? (Sport Education model, Ch. 11)
- What were the two things you learned to do best in this unit? (Any model)
- What motivated you the most to stay on schedule during this unit? (PSI model, Ch. 9)
- Did you often get to figure things out on your own in your field hockey unit? (Inquiry Teaching model, Ch. 13)

Rubrics. A rubric uses a combination of features from checklists and rating scales. Each rubric contains a list of teacher and student behaviors that might be observed in a lesson. But rather than simply rate each item with a numeric scale, a rubric will include several descriptors that indicate what each level of performance should look like. During and after watching the lesson, the teacher and/or other observer considers each descriptor and identifies which one best represents what occurred in the lesson. One of the many benefits of a rubric is that the teacher (and the students, if the teacher shares it with them before the lesson) knows ahead of time what is expected for each level of performance and can plan to meet the highest level possible. A rubric can contain a list of benchmarks for instructional models, along with descriptors that indicate how well each item on the benchmark was carried out by the teacher or students. These descriptors are easier to understand than the numbers on a rating scale because they provide more in-depth information. A rubric to analyze student and teacher benchmarks in each model is available on the IMPE website.

Written student assessments. Teachers can also use the model's unique benchmarks to develop a short list of questions for students. Students' answers can be a good way for teachers to verify they are engaging in preferred instructional patterns. The questions can be open-ended (see Exhibit 2.8), or they can prompt students to circle or check one of a series of possible replies (see Exhibit 2.9).

Scaled questions/items for written assignments.		EXHIBIT	2.9
Please circle the response that best describes your opinion.			
The teacher was well organized in this unit. (Direct Instruction model, Ch. 8)	Disagree	Neutral	Agree
I improved my confidence in this unit. (Any model)	Disagree	Neutral	Agree
I really liked working with my team in this unit. (Cooperative Learning model, Ch. 10)	Disagree	Neutral	Agree
I was able to progress at my own pace all of the time. (PSI model, Ch. 9)	Disagree	Neutral	Agree

Assessment of learning

The most significant criterion for determining the value of any instructional model is its effectiveness in promoting student achievement of the intended learning outcomes. Determining the effectiveness of a model is not a simple task, since physical education has several ways to describe and measure learning outcomes. Getting informative and valid assessments of learning takes both time and the ability to ask and answer clear questions within that process.

The assessment of learning in model-based instruction involves asking five key questions that lead to the selection and use of proper assessment techniques in physical education:

1. What standards or learning outcomes will be assessed?
2. When will they be assessed?
3. What assessment techniques are valid for those outcomes?
4. Is the assessment procedure practical?
5. Can the outcomes be assessed with authentic techniques?

Each instructional model focuses on well-defined learning outcomes, so it is relatively easy to implement assessment procedures within model-based instruction. All of the models have clear plans for content progression, which can help a teacher identify the crucial times for assessments. And because each model defines a specific set of learning outcomes, many of the assessment procedures are "built in" to the model's design. Chapter 7 will provide much more detail on the assessment of student learning in model-based instruction, while Part Two will explain specific assessment procedures for each model.

Implementation Needs and Modifications

Each instructional model represents a plan of action that will require certain conditions and resources for effective implementation. Teachers need to be aware of what is required and to consider those requirements when selecting, planning, implementing, and assessing a model for physical education.

Teacher expertise

Both students and teachers must possess certain kinds of knowledge, skills, and abilities for a model to reach its full potential. Knowledge about content is always important, regardless of the model being used. Necessary pedagogical content knowledge—a combination of applied expertise in content, context, learners, and instruction (Shulman, 1987)—will change according to the model selected for each unit and class group.

Since each model will include a unique repertoire of learning strategies and effective teaching skills, a teacher should be proficient in the strategies and skills called for by a given model. The Tactical Games model (Chapter 14) depends on a teacher's knowledge of games as learning settings. In particular, it requires her to know how to sequence increasingly complex tasks from situated drills to modified games to full games. Those who choose the Inquiry Teaching model

(Chapter 13) will need to know students' cognitive development and have strong skills in the use of questions as the primary teaching strategy.

Key teaching skills

As you will learn in Chapter 5, many effective teaching skills can be used to instruct physical education. That skill list is long, but the good news is that each instructional model will not require a teacher to use all of the skills. Each model's unique set of operations, managerial functions, task presentation strategies, and task structures will determine which teaching skills are needed most for that model.

Contextual requirements

None of the instructional models in this book will work in all contexts. Student abilities and developmental readiness, teacher knowledge, content, length of the unit, equipment, facilities, and available learning resources must all be considered in selecting a model. At times, that analysis will lead a teacher to decide "I can't teach that way in this situation." Failing to consider contextual needs for a model will cause the instruction to be less effective and perhaps even counterproductive in helping students learn stated goals. In order for a model to succeed, contextual needs must be met in five important areas:

1. Student characteristics
2. Instructional time
3. Facilities
4. Equipment
5. Learning materials

Contextual modifications

Many times a teacher will not be able to implement a model exactly the way it is designed "on paper" or presented in this book. Contextual limitations, experience with using a model, and at times just plain common sense will lead a teacher to make modifications to a model before and during a unit of instruction. However, changes should not be made thoughtlessly. Modifications should be planned systematically with the aid of process and achievement assessment information whenever possible.

Special precautions must be taken not to significantly alter the basic operations that make each model unique or to violate the learning domain priorities of the model. Those two mistakes can lead to ineffective use of the model and to incorrectly thinking that "it doesn't work" when, in fact, the teacher changed too much of the model to allow it to work the way it was designed.

Potential modifications will be suggested for each of the models presented in Part Two. Those modifications will be made from the following list of planning and decision areas a teacher could change before and during a content unit.

1. Managerial plan

2. Content coverage

3. Content progression

4. Instructional materials

5. Time allocation

6. Assessment techniques

7. Task presentation

8. Specific roles and responsibilities for teacher and students

9. Students' developmental stages

Notice that certain parts of a model cannot be modified: underlying theories, assumptions about teaching and learning, domain priorities, and domain interactions. They pertain to the basic foundation of a model, so changing them will cause the model to be something other than what it's designed to be.

To help you understand what some of these modifications might be, each model in Part Two will include suggestions for making that model inclusive for all types of students. As you will see, each model calls for certain ways to get students engaged fully within the model's design. Therefore, most of the modifications will be simple adjustments made by the teacher to ensure that all physical education students have the opportunity to learn according to any chosen model.

Each chapter in Part Two also will include planning tips that show how to apply general planning principles to each model in this book. Just as there is no "one best way to teach" in physical education, there is no "one best way to plan." Although all models share similar planning strategies, they are all different enough to require variations in how teachers should prepare units and lessons for each model.

SELECTING AN INSTRUCTIONAL MODEL

The attributes of instructional models discussed in this chapter will serve only to generally describe how models are designed and how they operate. This is *necessary but not sufficient information* for a teacher who must select a model for an upcoming content unit in physical education. Perhaps the best way to select an appropriate model is to ask a series of questions that will lead to the best choice. Exhibit 2.10 presents a step-by-step process for selecting an instructional model for physical education. As that exhibit notes, sometimes the answers to a teacher's questions will identify more than one effective model for his or her situation. In that case, the teacher should use professional experience, judgment, and personal preferences to make a choice.

Note that the first two questions ask about the match between what the teacher wants students to learn and a potential model's designed learning domain priorities. This match must be carefully considered, so that you do not expect something from an instructional model that it is not designed to do.

Process for selecting an instructional model for physical education. 🖶 **EXHIBIT**	**2.10**

1. WHAT DO I WANT MY STUDENTS TO LEARN ABOUT _____ [CONTENT]?

Example: Team handball: basic skills, strategies, and rules

2. WHAT ARE MY DOMAIN PRIORITIES?

Example: First: Skills—psychomotor
           Second: Rules and strategy—cognitive
           Third: Confidence as a player—affective

3. WHICH MODELS HAVE THOSE SAME PRIORITIES?

Example: Direct Instruction
           PSI
           Tactical Games

4. WHAT ARE THE CONTEXTUAL REQUIREMENTS FOR THOSE MODELS?

Example: Direct Instruction: See Chapter 8
           PSI: See Chapter 9
           Tactical Games: See Chapter 14

5. HOW WELL DOES MY CONTEXT MEET THOSE REQUIREMENTS?

Example: Direct Instruction: Very well

           PSI: Very well

           Tactical Games: Not well; not enough space for several modified games at one time

                                           (Tactical Games model is therefore not a good choice.)

6. WHAT ARE THE TEACHER AND STUDENT PREREQUISITES FOR THE REMAINING MODELS?

Example: Direct Instruction: See Chapter 8
           PSI: See Chapter 9

7. DO I AND MY STUDENTS HAVE ENOUGH OF THOSE PREREQUISITES?

Example: Direct Instruction: Yes
           PSI: Yes

8. WHAT MODIFICATIONS WILL I NEED TO MAKE FOR EACH MODEL?

Example: Direct Instruction:

           1. Need a lot more handballs (to reduce waiting time)

           2. Need a large outdoor space and several goals for stations

           3. Need to teach students with a wide range of skill abilities

           PSI:

           1. None. I have everything I need to use PSI for this unit.

               (Select PSI because it needs no modifications.)

SUMMARY

This chapter presented a framework for describing instructional models for physical education. A teacher who wishes to use model-based instruction can examine any of the models in Part Two within that framework and use that information to select one or more models that will give students the best opportunity to learn the stated outcomes in an upcoming content unit. Instructional models are essentially planning and decision-making tools that teachers can use to provide students with the most effective instruction possible in a given context.

LEARNING ACTIVITIES

1. Analyze your own learning preferences according to the Reichmann and Grasha model presented in this chapter. What kind of learning environment suits you best? What kind of learning environment would most challenge you?

2. Individually interview five students from one class group to analyze each one's learning preferences according to the Reichmann and Grasha model. How many students are similar? How many are different, and what are those differences?

3. Reflect for a moment on how you currently teach physical education. Then analyze your teaching according to each of the attributes of model-based instruction presented in this chapter. From that analysis, write a profile of how you teach now.

4. Compare your findings about students' learning preferences in Activity 2 with your description of your own teaching in Activity 3 as it relates to learning preferences. How well do they match? What are the implications for student learning in your classes?

TOPICS FOR REFLECTION & SMALL GROUP DISCUSSION

Take a few moments to write down your thoughts, then post your opinion in the Forum section of the IMPE website for others to read. Be sure to check back for replies, and feel free to respond to those replies in the thread for each topic.

1. What are your "early thoughts" about instructional models for physical education? Does the model-based approach look as if it will support or contradict the personal philosophy of teaching that you described at the end of Chapter 1?

2. Why do you think physical education teachers need to know so many things to be effective instructors?

SUGGESTED READING

Gurvitch, R., Metzler, M., & Lund, J. (Eds.) (2008). Model-based instruction in physical education: The adoption of innovation. *Journal of Teaching in Physical Education, 27,* 447–589.

AREAS OF KNOWLEDGE FOR MODEL-BASED INSTRUCTION IN PHYSICAL EDUCATION

Physical educators must have expertise in many areas that directly or indirectly determine how they instruct and how well students will learn in each content unit and lesson. It is an oversimplification to suggest that teachers need to know about their students, physical education content, and instructional models. Effective teachers do need to know these things—but in much more sophisticated and interactive ways. The sophistication comes from having extensive knowledge in many areas of teaching; superficial knowledge is not nearly adequate to attend to the complexities of most physical education teaching settings. The interactive part arises when a teacher must apply several types of knowledge at the same time, often with little opportunity to consider the options or to consult with others.

If you recall, instructional models in this book are described as blueprints for teaching. The breadth of knowledge that contributes to effective model-based instruction can be thought of as the foundation needed to support the structure of the model as it is being built and during its extended use. Teachers without good foundational knowledge might be able to get model-based instruction

chapter

3

started, but their lack of knowledge may eventually cause the plan to fall apart and lead to reduced student learning. It is easy to see why this *knowledge base* is so necessary for effective teaching.

A KNOWLEDGE BASE FOR TEACHING PHYSICAL EDUCATION

Over the years there have been many attempts to define a knowledge base for teaching—all the things a person needs to know in order to teach a subject effectively in P–12 schools. Since research has not determined a definitive knowledge base at this time, any list of the kinds of knowledge teachers need will depend greatly on the list's author. Although many such lists exist in educational literature and in the opinions of teacher educators, there has been some consensus in the past decade on the knowledge base proposed by Lee Shulman (1987), as shown in Exhibit 3.1.

Teachers need to have knowledge at three different levels within each category: declarative, procedural, and conditional. *Declarative knowledge* is that which a teacher can express verbally or in writing. It encompasses a teacher's awareness of the many things that make for effective instruction in physical education. *Procedural knowledge* is that which a teacher can actually apply before, during, and after instruction. It is the ability to carry out declarative knowledge in ways that facilitate class management and student learning. *Conditional knowledge* informs a teacher about when and why to make decisions that fit the specific context of the moment. See Exhibit 3.2 for examples of each knowledge level. All three types of knowledge are strongly related to each other: declarative knowledge is a prerequisite for procedural

EXHIBIT 3.1 The seven categories of Shulman's knowledge base for teaching (1987).

1. Content knowledge	Knowledge about the subject matter to be taught
2. General pedagogical knowledge	Knowledge about teaching methods that pertain to all subjects and situations
3. Pedagogical content knowledge	Knowledge about how to teach a subject or topic to specific groups of students in a specific context
4. Curriculum knowledge	Knowledge about developmentally appropriate content and programs at each grade level
5. Knowledge of educational contexts	Knowledge about the impact of context on instruction
6. Knowledge of learners and their characteristics	Knowledge about human learning as it applies to teaching
7. Knowledge of educational goals	Knowledge about the goals, purposes, and structure of our educational system

Examples of declarative, procedural, and conditional knowledge for physical education teachers.	EXHIBIT 3.2

Declarative:	Knowing the concept of developmentally appropriate curriculum and instruction
Procedural:	Knowing how to write lesson plans that use developmentally appropriate teaching strategies
Conditional:	Knowing how to modify activities in class when they are not developmentally appropriate for students
Declarative:	Knowing the rules of team and individual sports
Procedural:	Being able to illustrate correct rules as part of a task presentation
Conditional:	Using different words and terms for 4th graders and 10th graders
Declarative:	Knowing three interesting rhythmic activities for 5th graders
Procedural:	Being able to monitor and provide accurate feedback while students practice those activities
Conditional:	Knowing how to motivate reluctant students to participate
Declarative:	Knowing why a certain movement pattern improves performance
Procedural:	Being able to plan and implement lead-up games that provide students with increased repetitions of that movement pattern
Conditional:	Knowing when it's time for students to progress from lead-up games to full games

knowledge—one must first have basic knowledge about teaching and learning in order to make that knowledge operational. Once a teacher can make knowledge operational one time or in one setting, conditional knowledge allows the teacher to generalize those operations to many other times and settings and "know why" before acting to "make it happen."

At this level, much of the knowledge you gain will be declarative, as you become aware of the major concepts included in each area and how they relate to model-based instruction in physical education. Procedural and conditional knowledge will be developed later when you select, plan for, and implement each teaching model in specific contexts. In the next sections, I will discuss each area in detail.

Learning Contexts

All physical education programs occur in some context that facilitates or inhibits the planning and implementation of instruction. The context refers to the sum total of all factors that can influence what and how content is taught and learned in a program. One of the key things to keep in mind is that most contextual factors are relatively predetermined and not in the teacher's control. For example, students, teachers, principals, and curriculum are situated in a broader social fabric that dictates what kind of movement is acceptable and what kind is preferred. Dance may be the dominant movement form in some cultures, while team sports may be the dominant form in others; therefore, teachers' curriculum and model choice are affected by the larger-scale culture around them. Most teachers have limited ability to change their context. The best teachers can do is become familiar with a given context and maximize the potential for teaching and learning in that place. This does not automatically imply that all contexts are overly problematic for teachers; many physical education programs occur in contexts that allow teachers a wide variety of positive options for instruction.

Every school has unique characteristics that offer opportunities and challenges for physical education teachers. It is important that all teachers in a school know that context well and understand how each part of the context can affect the physical education program. Rink (1997) emphasizes this point: "The context of the teaching situation affects how teachers develop, what skills they acquire, how they think about those skills, and what they think the goals are for their [physical education] programs" (p. 18). There are many ways to categorize and describe a school's context. For our purposes, I am highlighting five major factors: school location, student demographics, administration, physical education faculty, and instructional resources (see Exhibit 3.3).

Teachers should conduct a complete contextual analysis of their school regularly to determine whether changes have occurred and, if so, how they will affect the content and conduct of the program. Teachers can use the factors and subfactors listed in Exhibit 3.3 as a starting point for their analysis. This analysis will influence every part of the physical education program, including the selection and implementation of instructional models.

Learners

Some of what teachers need to know about students refers to contextual characteristics that describe how many students are in each class, their background, and their previous experience and knowledge of the unit content. Other important areas of knowledge focus on the teacher's familiarity with the general growth and developmental stages of school-age learners, student motivation, and learning preferences.

Growth and developmental stages

Knowledge in this area is essential to the planning and implementation of developmentally appropriate instruction for children and youth, as it gives teachers good starting and reference points for identifying student needs and abilities. Young children and adolescents develop as whole persons, with the cognitive, psychomotor, and affective domains in constant interaction. A brief description of the domains is presented below, although they will be discussed in more detail later in this chapter. To simplify the discussion in both places, development in each domain will be presented separately. Yet teachers must be aware that a person's development does not occur in separate compartments—it is fully interactive across domains.

Major contextual factors for physical education programs.		🖶 EXHIBIT 3.3
MAJOR CONTEXTUAL FACTOR	**SUBFACTORS**	**POSSIBLE IMPACT ON PHYSICAL EDUCATION PROGRAM**
School location	1. Urban, rural, suburban	1. Class size Outdoor facilities School security Travel to off-campus activities
	2. School district	2. Policies Personnel hiring
	3. Regional climate	3. Weather for outdoor activity Local natural resources for activity (lakes, mountains, parks)
Student demographics	1. Size of school	1. Class size Scheduling options
	2. Student SES profile	2. Ability to afford PE uniforms Ability to take optional for-charge activities
	3. Cultural diversity	3. Student experience and preference for movement forms Preference for traditional or alternative movement forms
	4. Community values	4. Students' range of experience with movement forms
	5. Academic ability	5. Ability to comprehend instructional information Ability to read task cards, keep score, or work independently
	6. Absentee rate	6. High rates require more teacher reviews High rates can lead to starts/stops in student learning
	7. Transitory student rate	7. High rates can lead to loss of continuity High rates lead to constantly teaching class rules to new students
	8. Students who are non-English-speaking	8. Teacher inability to communicate Student inability to communicate Student waiting/isolation until teacher can "catch them up" Excessively slow class progress due to needs of English learners
	9. Physical ability/ disability	9. Need for modified equipment Need for teacher's aides Teacher inability to instruct all students

(continued)

EXHIBIT 3.3	Continued.	
MAJOR CONTEXTUAL FACTOR	**SUBFACTORS**	**POSSIBLE IMPACT ON PHYSICAL EDUCATION PROGRAM**
Administration	1. District level	1. Program policies for all subjects Program policies for PE General budget allocations Hiring of new staff Approval for major renovations/repairs Curriculum guidelines
	2. School level	2. Departmental budget allocations Hiring of new staff Evaluation of teachers Support for PE policies Scheduling Permission for off-campus classes Space allocations Approval of equipment requests Familiarity with PE program goals and content
Physical education staff	1. Number of teachers and support personnel	1. Teacher/aide: student ratio Number of concurrent classes offered Ability to team teach
	2. Gender, racial, ethnic composition	2. Ability to provide role models for students Ability to relate to diverse student population
	3. Age	3. Ability to relate to younger generations
	4. PE teaching experience	4. Need for mentoring (new) Ability to provide mentoring (veteran) Ability to assimilate new content and ideas
	5. Content expertise	5. Determines what can and cannot be taught Determines match/mismatch with students' preferences and needs
Instructional resources	1. Teaching spaces	1. Class size Number of classes sharing space Available teaching stations
	2. Equipment	2. Student safety Student participation rate Ability to vary task difficulty
	3. Time and scheduling	3. Instructional minutes for each lesson Frequency of PE lessons

Cognitive development. Jean Piaget (in Phillips & Soltis, 1991) describes four phases of cognitive development in humans: (1) sensorimotor, (2) pre-operational, (3) concrete operations, and (4) formal operations (see Exhibit 3.4).

Many contemporary physical education curriculums are based on Piaget's stages of learning, with carefully planned activities, modified equipment, teaching strategies, and assessment techniques that strongly adhere to the appropriate cognitive stage for each grade level. At times, cognitive development is the primary focus of instruction; at other times, the instruction facilitates development in the psychomotor domain.

Motor development. Motor development refers to the way each person acquires, or learns, patterns of movement throughout the life span. Some movement patterns are more generic, like ones used in everyday activities (e.g., walking, climbing steps, sitting, standing, reaching, grasping). Those and many other motor patterns can then be applied in sport, dance, and exercise situations. The development of those motor patterns is the purpose of most physical education instruction and is therefore what this discussion will focus on.

Gallahue and Cleland (2003) present a scheme for describing motor development in children and youth. It comprises:

1. phases, which delineate major progressions from birth to adulthood;
2. stages, which differentiate learned motor patterns within phases; and
3. levels, which describe learners' proficiency (advances) within each stage.

Piaget's four stages of cognitive development.		EXHIBIT 3.4
COGNITIVE STAGE AND APPROXIMATE AGE RANGE	**LEARNER CHARACTERISTICS**	**IMPLICATIONS FOR LEARNING MOVEMENT CONCEPTS**
Sensorimotor (birth–2 years)	Makes initial relationships (operations) between movement and cognition Develops instinctual patterns (grasping, lifting, handling) through personal exploration	Learners at this stage are not ready for learning movement from others
Pre-operational (2–7 years)	Still learns in the "concrete" Cannot yet form or learn from abstractions	Learners need tactile experiences: holding, feeling, moving the body in space, with simple, explicit verbal directions
Concrete operations (7–11 years)	Begins to be able to learn with abstract experiences, but still relies on "concrete"	Can begin to solve problems Can explore relationships between thought and movement Can learn with logic Needs fewer and less explicit directions
Formal operations (11–14 years)	Mastery of conceptual learning Able to transform previous knowledge and experience into new structures	Can solve complex problems Can develop new knowledge for self Can learn from few or implied directions

Skill levels describe a learner's proficiency within each stage. According to this model, as an individual enters each new stage, he or she is at the *beginner/novice level,* characterized by uncoordinated, hesitant, conscious, and inefficient movement. The learner typically pays attention to all stimuli in the environment, because he or she has not yet learned what is important and what can be ignored. At the *intermediate/practice level,* the learner is able to practice with more efficiency and begins to approach the final, desired pattern or skill. The person begins to formulate learning strategies or little "tips" that facilitate practice and performance. Task focus increases because necessary information has been sorted out. The *advanced/fine-tuning level* involves a complete understanding of both task and process. The learner acquires automaticity, which makes it appear that the person is "not even thinking" about how to perform but "just doing it."

This model has many implications for the design and conduct of instruction in physical education—at all grades and developmental phases. If a teacher can identify a student's current phase, stage, and level, this knowledge can be used as the foundation for planning developmentally appropriate learning tasks and for measuring progress (learning) over time. This scheme can also provide teachers with a general starting point for entire classes and grade levels in the school by matching the age of most students with each phase and stage. For instance, most second graders are six or seven years old, which places most of them at the Mature Stage in the Fundamental Movement Phase. Instructional planning and task progressions can start at that point and then be adjusted after the content unit begins.

Affective development. Although we do have a useful taxonomy for the affective domain, we are much less knowledgeable about how children and youth actually learn and develop in this area (Snow, Corno, & Jackson, 1996). Therefore, teachers have fewer starting points for designing and implementing learning experiences that can lead to somewhat predictable outcomes in affective development. At least two major factors play a role here. First, affective learning is very private and individual, and teachers have very few indicators they can rely on to know students' needs and when affective learning has actually occurred. Second, there is a complicated and often poorly understood interaction between affective learning and learning in the other two domains. Theorists are sure that the other domains contribute to affective learning, but beyond that, the relationship remains vague and strongly debated.

Student motivation

One of the most essential factors in the learning process is the motivation to be engaged in the learning activity of the moment—whether that activity is listening, watching, thinking, or doing. Students' ability to learn depends directly on their willingness to learn. Effective teachers not only plan for developmentally appropriate content and effective teaching strategies, they also always consider a critical question: why should students want to learn this content in the first place? Keller (1983) reviewed many of the theories about student motivation and reduced them to four nearly universal concepts: (1) interest, or the degree to which the learner's curiosity is aroused and maintained; (2) relevance, or the degree to which the content and instruction address the learner's personal goals and needs; (3) expectancy, or the learner's perceived success in the task; and (4) satisfaction, or the learner's intrinsic motivations and/or extrinsic rewards for engagement.

Building on Keller's (1983) principles, Brophy (1987) developed a framework for classifying motivational strategies that teachers can use to get and keep students motivated to learn. The framework is built upon four essential preconditions: (1) a supportive environment, (2) an appropriate level of challenge/difficulty, (3) meaningful learning objectives, and (4) moderation/optimal use of strategies. According to Brophy, no motivational strategy will be effective unless all these preconditions are met for students.

The second level of his framework includes three principles: (1) motivate by maintaining students' expectations of success, (2) motivate by supplying extrinsic incentives, and (3) motivate by capitalizing on students' existing intrinsic motivation. The third level of the framework mentions specific strategies for stimulating student motivation to learn. Refer to Exhibit 3.5 for a complete illustration of Brophy's framework.

It is essential that a teacher be able to motivate students to become engaged, stay engaged, and learn the intended content and goals of instruction. There are many ways to motivate, but in the long run the most effective strategies will be those that are inviting, positive, and rewarding for students, rather than alienating, negative, or punitive. Physical education teachers need to develop a large repertoire of motivational strategies that adhere to Keller's and Brophy's principles.

Learning styles and preferences

Much attention in education has been given to styles of learning. Jonassen and Grabowski (1993) define *learning style* as "learner preferences for different types of learning and instructional activities" (p. 5). According to learning-style theory, each of us has an individual way of learning, determined by a complex interaction between personal abilities, past learning experiences, and the instructional environment. Psychologists and learning theorists have developed many ways to describe, determine, and measure individuals' learning styles. Unfortunately, so many theories have caused much confusion for teachers trying to better understand learning styles and consider them in their instructional practices. The various conceptualizations can be divided into two large groups: (1) those based on descriptions of the learner's perceptual and information-processing abilities (e.g., Kolb, 1981; Gregorc, 1982); and (2) those based on the learner's preferred contextual factors while attempting to learn (e.g., Dunn, Dunn, & Price, 1989; Reichmann & Grasha, 1974). The main difference is that the first type either places learners in categories (styles) and tends to describe them with one descriptor, such as diverger, assimilator, converger, or accommodater, or attempts to identify each learner's preferred perceptual mode, such as visual, kinesthetic, thinking, or listening. The sec-

EXHIBIT 3.5 Brophy's framework for classifying motivational strategies.

A. Essential Preconditions

1. Supportive environment
2. Appropriate level of challenge/difficulty
3. Meaningful learning objectives
4. Moderation/optimal use of strategies

B. Motivating by Maintaining Success Expectations

5. Program for success
6. Teach goal setting, performance appraisal, and self-reinforcement
7. Provide remedial socialization for discouraged students
   a. Portray effort as investment rather than risk
   b. Portray skill development as incremental and domain specific
   c. Focus on mastery
   d. Provide attribution retraining
   e. Minimize test anxiety

C. Motivating by Supplying Extrinsic Incentives

8. Offer rewards as incentives for good (or improved) performance
9. Structure appropriate competition
10. Call attention to the instrumental value of academic activities

D. Motivating by Capitalizing on Students' Existing Intrinsic Motivation

11. Adapt tasks to students' interests
    a. Incorporate content that students find interesting or activities that they find enjoyable
    b. Offer choices of alternative tasks or opportunities to exercise autonomy in selecting among alternative ways to meet requirements
    c. Encourage student comments and questions
    d. Include divergent questions and opportunities for students to express opinions or make other responses to the content
12. Plan for novelty and variety
13. Provide opportunities to respond actively
14. Provide immediate feedback to student responses
15. Allow students to create finished products
16. Incorporate "fun features" into academic activities
    a. Fantasy or elements of imagination
    b. Simulation exercises
    c. Gamelike features
    d. Peer interaction opportunities

E. Strategies for Stimulating Student Motivation to Learn

17. Model interest in learning and motivation to learn
18. Communicate desirable expectations and attributions about students' motivation to learn
19. Minimize students' performance anxiety during learning activities
20. Project intensity
21. Project enthusiasm
22. Induce task interest or appreciation
23. Induce curiosity or suspense
24. Induce dissonance or cognitive conflict
25. Make abstract content more personal, concrete, or familiar
26. Induce students to generate their own motivation to learn
27. State learning objectives and provide advance organizers
28. Model task-related thinking and problem solving

From Brophy, J. E. (1987). Synthesis of research on strategies for motivating students to learn. *Educational Leadership 45* (2), pp. 40–48. Reprinted by permission.

ond type tends to describe multifaceted conditions (preferences) under which a learner is likely to learn most effectively, such as the learning environment, the social structure, the emotional climate, and the physical stimuli received by learners.

A relatively simple scheme developed by Reichmann and Grasha (1974) is quite useful in helping to match student learning preferences with a given instructional model. It is based on three dimensions that describe a student's (1) attitudes toward learning, (2) view of teachers and/or peers, and (3) reactions to classroom procedures. The scheme shows how these key features of the learning environment combine to establish various typical student profiles, informing teachers about the ways students tend to approach learning and how they may best be motivated. That perspective goes well with the notion of instructional models, since each model is essentially a unique and different way to structure the learning setting.

The Reichmann and Grasha model, presented in more detail in Chapter 2 (see especially Exhibit 2.3), is one way to describe differences between instructional models and to help teachers choose the best model for student learning preferences. So, while it is generally helpful for teachers to understand the concepts of learning styles and learning preferences, the latter framework will be more useful in model-based approaches to instruction.

Learning Theories

The most fundamental design component for all instructional models is the learning theory on which it is based. The best way to define *learning theory* is to consider each word separately and then combine them. Shuell (1986) defines *learning* as an enduring change in behavior or in the capacity to behave in a given fashion, which results from practice or other forms of experience. Schunk (1996) defines *theory* as "[a] scientifically acceptable set of principles offered to explain a phenomenon" (p. 3). So, then, a *learning theory* is a way to explain or describe how learning occurs. The next step in this logic is significant for instructional models. If psychologists and instructional designers hold different theories and assumptions about how people learn (and they do), each theory will lead to a somewhat different instructional model. Since we have many theories of learning, we also have many and often contrasting instructional models.

All teachers have their own personal theories explaining how people learn best and how to teach physical education to them. When personal theories differ from the theory at the heart of a particular model, there is a tendency to avoid using that model and even to criticize it. It is important that a teacher have a personal theory, but it is even more important that she be open to other theories about teaching and learning so that she can choose the right plan (model) to pursue her intended learning outcomes for students. Holding on to one theory exclusively means that a teacher will teach the same way all the time.

There are many learning theories, but not all of them apply to educational settings or ultimately contribute to the design of instructional models. Those that do have relevance for this book are shown in Exhibit 3.6, along with a brief description of how each theory views the learning process.

Each theory will be explained further in Part Two as it applies to the foundation of each instructional model. At this time it is important that you recognize how learning theories contribute to the design and development of instructional models.

EXHIBIT 3.6	Major learning theories and their assumptions (adapted from Schunk, 1996).
LEARNING THEORY	**BASIC ASSUMPTION(S) ABOUT HOW PEOPLE LEARN**
Operant conditioning	Learning occurs through the consequences of human behavior. Behavior that is reinforced will be more likely to recur; behavior that is punished will be less likely to occur in the future. The three-term contingency $$S^D \longrightarrow R \longrightarrow S^R$$ is the basic building block of learning. The discriminative stimulus (S^D) sets the occasion for a response (R) to be emitted, which is then followed by a reinforcing stimulus (S^R) that increases the probability that the behavior will occur again when the discriminative stimulus is present.
Social cognitive learning, including self-efficacy	Learning occurs as people observe others in their environment and imitate that behavior. Socially learned behavior is reinforced in much the same way as operant conditioning. It is strongly determined by reciprocal interactions between the learner, the environment, and behavior. Learning can occur either by actually doing or by observing others.
Information processing	The learning "act" is conducted through internal (mental) processes. Learners select and attend to certain features in the environment, transform and rehearse information, relate new information to previously acquired knowledge, and then organize knowledge to make it meaningful. The use of the memory function is essential to learning.
Cognitive learning and processes, including constructivist learning	Learning occurs as a process of cognitive growth and development, through the expansion of one's ability to make meaning of previously learned facts, symbols, concepts, and principles. In the constructivist approach, students learn by *self-building* on existing knowledge. People hold implicit beliefs about learning that play a key role in this process.
Problem solving	This cognitive theory refers to people's efforts to achieve a goal for which they do not have an automatic solution. It relies on three main operations: trial and error, insight, and heuristics (self-developed strategies).
Motivation	The learning process originates with an innate need held by the learner. That need fuels the drive (or motivation) to engage in a behavior that reduces or eliminates the need. A need can be physiological, psychological, or some combination of both.
Humanistic theory	This is related to motivational theory, in which a person attempts to fulfill five levels of needs: physiological, safety, belonging, esteem, and self-actualization (Maslow, 1970). Learning occurs as a result of meeting subordinate needs, freeing the person to begin the learning process at the next higher level.

Developmentally Appropriate Practice in Physical Education

In 1987 the National Association for the Education of Young Children (NAEYC) published an important monograph (Bredekamp, 1987) that outlined preferred teaching practices based on the concept of developmental appropriateness. Developmentally appropriate practice in all subjects, including physical education, recognizes that the content of learning, the learning environment, and the instruction must match students' current developmental stage and readiness for learning. The second edition of the NAEYC monograph (Bredekamp & Copple, 1996–97) states that developmentally appropriate practice is based on the following 12 principles of child development and learning. (Keep in mind that although the NAEYC is referring to young children, these principles apply to all learners, as the developmental process continues throughout a person's life span.)

1. Domains of development—physical, social, emotional, and cognitive— are closely related; development in one domain influences and is influenced by development in the other domains.

2. Development occurs in a relatively orderly sequence, with later abilities, skills, and knowledge building on those already acquired.

3. Development proceeds at varying rates from learner to learner as well as unevenly within different areas of each person's functioning.

4. Early experiences have both cumulative and delayed effects on an individual's development; optimal periods exist for certain types of development and learning.

5. Development proceeds in predictable directions toward greater complexity, organization, and internalization.

6. Development and learning occur in and are influenced by multiple social and cultural contexts.

7. Humans are active learners, drawing on direct physical and social experience as well as culturally transmitted knowledge to construct their own understandings of the world around them.

8. Development and learning result from interaction of biological maturation and the environment, which includes both the physical and social worlds we live in.

9. Play is an important vehicle for children's social, emotional, and cognitive development, as well as a reflection of their development.

10. Development advances when learners have opportunities to practice newly acquired skills as well as when they experience a challenge just beyond the level of their present mastery.

11. Individuals demonstrate different modes of knowing and learning and different ways of representing what they know.

12. People develop and learn best in the context of a community where they are safe and valued, their physical needs are met, and they feel psychologically secure. (Adapted from Bredekamp & Copple, 1996–97, pp. 9–15.)

These statements about developmentally appropriate instruction go hand in hand with Gallahue and Cleland's stages of development for motor skills, discussed earlier in this chapter. The model addresses only the content portion of this concept, while the NAEYC guidelines are concerned with the entire instructional environment.

The Council on Physical Education for Children (COPEC) and NASPE's Motor Development Task Force followed the NAEYC's guidelines with their own position statements, carrying this concept into the realm of physical education. These statements include descriptions of instruction, curriculum, program philosophy, and learning progressions that adhere to the principles of developmentally appropriate practice applied in physical education. The position statement from the Motor Development Task Force (NASPE, 1995) defines an overall developmental perspective for physical education programs:

1. Developmental change is qualitative: children mature in ways that can be easily observed by watching their actions.

2. Developmental change is sequential: maturation happens in mostly predictable patterns that can be taught and learned.

3. Developmental change is cumulative: children typically retain previous maturation gains as they make new gains.

4. Developmental change is directional: change usually happens from a less mature pattern to a more mature pattern.

5. Developmental change is multifactorial: change typically happens in more than one area at a time (e.g., intellectual and emotional).

6. Developmental change is individual: each child matures at a rate different from other children. (pp. 2–3)

The task force's statement highlights one of the most important concepts about developmentally focused instruction: development is age related but not age determined. Teachers must realize they cannot teach all 8-year-olds or all 12-year-olds or all 16-year-olds the same way. While students at each of those ages will share many developmental characteristics, there will be some important individual differences that should deter teachers from instructing all students the same way all the time.

The concept of developmental appropriateness eventually leads to some specific curriculum, planning, and instructional actions. Yet the concept also serves to define a broad set of values and practices that should guide physical education teaching so that students can pursue learning in environments that are physically, emotionally, and educationally beneficial for them. It is the teacher's responsibility to establish and maintain that appropriateness at all times.

Learning Domains and Objectives

As discussed earlier, learning theorists recognize three major types of human learning that can be used to categorize the primary outcomes of instruction.

Each one is referred to as a domain, or a "territory," and includes specific kinds of learning that students will acquire within it. The three traditional domains are cognitive, psychomotor, and affective.

Cognitive domain

The *cognitive* domain focuses on intellectual learning that includes logic, concepts, facts, and recall from memory. The book *Taxonomy of Educational Objectives* (Bloom et al., 1956) includes a hierarchy of cognitive processes, moving from simple to complex:

1. Knowledge: The ability to recall previously learned information
   Examples:
   Student can identify the parts of a tennis racquet.
   Student can recall five parts of the golf swing.

2. Comprehension: The ability to grasp the meaning of information
   Examples:
   Student can explain the importance of proper footwork.
   Student can explain how leverage is used in weight training.

3. Application: The ability to use information in new and concrete applications or to use information in some way
   Examples:
   Student can adapt game rules to make competition more fair.
   Student can create two dances from the same musical piece.

4. Analysis: The ability to break down material into its component parts and to understand the relationship between those parts
   Examples:
   Student can observe a peer's performance and identify errors made.
   Student can identify proper strategy for a game situation.

5. Synthesis: The ability to put elements into a whole, which can involve abstract relationships
   Examples:
   Student can recognize similarities and differences between the tennis swing and the swing used in racquetball.
   Student can plan offensive plays for flag football.

6. Evaluation: The ability to judge the value of material with defensible opinions

Examples:

Student can judge a gymnastics competition.

Student can compare two dance performances.

Psychomotor domain

The *psychomotor* domain focuses on the development of physical skills and abilities, learning that is primarily acquired and demonstrated through movement. Skills can be simple or complex, and they can involve fine (small) or gross (large) movements. This domain, too, has a taxonomy (hierarchy) to help us classify the type of learning that occurs within it (Harlow, 1972). Some examples from each level of learning in the psychomotor domain are:

1. Reflexive skills: Involuntary actions that occur in response to a stimulus

Examples:

Student can recognize and move to avoid a potentially dangerous situation.

Student can hold herself in the proper posture.

2. Fundamental abilities: Innate movement patterns formed by combining reflex movements

Examples:

Student can run, walk, jump, hop, skip, leap, and so forth.

3. Perceptual abilities: Actions that require the translation of stimuli through the senses into appropriate movements

Examples:

Student can track a thrown ball through the air.

Student can strike a ball with two different implements.

4. Physical abilities: Combine basic movement and perceptual abilities into simple skilled movements

Examples:

Student can perform calisthenics.

Student can hear and follow square-dance calls to the music.

5. Complex skills: Higher-order skills that require efficiency, stamina, and the combination of more than one physical ability at the same time

Examples:

Student can learn the skills needed to play sports.

Student can complete a fitness "obstacle course."

6. Nondiscursive abilities:

The ability to communicate through body movement; to express feelings, thoughts, and meaning through actions

Examples:

Student can "act like a flower in bloom on a sunny day."

Student can create a dance that expresses happiness to the audience.

Affective/social domain

The *affective* domain includes the learning of feelings, attitudes, and values as they relate to movement. This learning can be about one's self and about others. In a sense, it is learning about one's self as it pertains to physical activity. Learning in the affective domain is sometimes difficult to observe and measure, since the outcomes of such learning are internal states known only to the individual. These states can be expressed to others but can often be miscommunicated or misinterpreted. One way to monitor affective learning is to observe the behaviors associated with a certain affect, such as watching for instances of good sport behavior during and after a competition or watching students pursue an activity outside of class (as an indicator that they value the activity). Krathwohl, Bloom, and Masia (1964) developed a taxonomy that can help teachers plan learning progressions in the affective domain:

1. Receiving:

The ability to pay attention, to watch, and to listen so that information can be received

Examples:

Student reads a history of women in sport in the United States.

Student listens to another student's description of her favorite dance.

2. Responding:

The ability to discuss, debate, or agree/disagree with things that are heard or seen by the learner

Examples:

Student can list five reasons why he likes physical education.

Student can discuss the pros and cons of competition in sports.

3. Valuing:

The ability to determine the importance of an action or event

Examples:

Student understands why we should exercise regularly.

Student expresses the need to follow rules of fair play.

4. Organizing: The ability to place values in relationship to other values and to organize in order to make judgments and choices

Examples:

Student can state a preference among health-related fitness activities.

Student can set goals and work toward improvement of skills or performance.

5. Characterizing: The ability to internalize values and carry those values out in one's personal life

Examples:

Student can follow game rules and etiquette outside of class time.

Student makes proper choices for healthy eating when less healthy selections are available.

Domain priorities and domain interactions. Learning in physical education occurs through students' direct engagement in planned instructional activities. As we have already seen, all learning activities will emphasize outcomes in one domain over the others, determining an intended *domain priority*. That means each activity will place the highest emphasis on outcomes in one domain and less emphasis on outcomes in one or both of the other domains. It is important to remember that a domain priority is temporary, and the emphasis can change any time students begin a different activity or the teacher decides to change the main learning focus of the present activity.

Rarely in physical education will student engagement result in learning solely in one domain. Even when an activity focuses strongly in one domain, student learning will take place in the other domains, although not as directly. Therefore, a *domain interaction* typically occurs when one domain is given the direct intent of the activity, while learning still occurs indirectly in the other domains. Physical education teachers need to know how to determine domain priorities for all planned learning activities and to understand the potential for interactions as students pursue learning in the primary domain of the moment. With that knowledge, teachers can be more confident that students are learning what is actually intended in each lesson segment.

Exhibit 3.7 shows how domain priorities set by the teacher lead to domain interactions as students are engaged in some common physical education learning activities.

Learning objectives

Understanding learning domains, priorities, and interactions represents primarily declarative knowledge in this area of teaching. The procedural part of this area involves the ability to write clear learning objectives that students will pursue during instruction. Teachers who can write good objectives have an understanding of the domain priority, domain interaction, how student

		EXHIBIT 3.7
Domain priorities and potential domain interactions.		
LEARNING ACTIVITY	**TEACHER'S DOMAIN PRIORITIES**	**DOMAIN INTERACTIONS ("——▶" CAN BE INTERPRETED AS "WHILE AT OR NEAR THE SAME TIME")**
Learning basic dance steps	1. Cognitive 2. Psychomotor 3. Affective	(1) thinking about the order and timing ——▶ (2) rehearsing ——▶ (3) enjoying successful practice and liking dance
Tag games	1. Psychomotor 2. Cognitive 3. Affective	(1) running and dodging ——▶ (2) acquiring strategy and tactics to avoid being tagged ——▶ (3) learning what it feels like to be "it"
Cooperative games	1. Affective 2. Cognitive 3. Psychomotor	(1) being part of a group; meeting the objective ——▶ (2) learning trial and error for strategies ——▶ (3) performing the physical movements needed to carry out strategy
Skill themes	1. Cognitive 2. Psychomotor 3. Affective	(1) recognizing movement concepts and examples/non-examples ——▶ (2) moving to demonstrate the concept ——▶ (3) discovering new ways to move and be creative
Practicing sport skills	1. Psychomotor 2. Affective 3. Cognitive	(1) learning necessary motor performance patterns ——▶ (2) learning positive sport behaviors and attitudes ——▶ (3) understanding applications for skills in game situations

learning will be organized, and how long it will take that learning to happen. Instructional objectives should include three components: the conditions under which the learning will occur; the behavior/knowledge/affect to be learned; and the degree of mastery needed to demonstrate that learning has occurred (Mager, 1984). The specific form and content of the objective will depend on the domain and level of the intended learning outcome. Exhibit 3.8 presents some examples of learning objectives written for various taxonomic levels in the cognitive, psychomotor, and affective domains.

As you can see, objectives in the affective domain are not as straightforward and can be a bit more subjective than those in the other domains—which again creates difficulty in actually observing and monitoring the internal learning that occurs in this domain. That is not to say that teachers should stay away from objectives in this domain; but they will have to understand the unique qualities of this domain and the special phrasing needed to write and assess objectives within it.

Physical Education Content

Physical education teachers need strong knowledge of the content they will teach in their programs. Content refers to the sports, games, dances, skill themes, fitness, and concepts students will learn in physical education. It encompasses the subject matter—what will be taught and learned. There has been some debate

EXHIBIT 3.8	Learning objectives for the cognitive, psychomotor, and affective domains.
Cognitive domain (application level)	Given an explanation of a 2-3 zone defense in basketball and locating the ball at the top of the key (condition), the student will diagram (knowledge) all five players in their correct position (mastery).
Cognitive domain (evaluation level)	Being shown two performances of a 3-meter dive (condition), the student will determine a score for each dive (knowledge) and correctly identify (mastery) the better dive of the two.
Psychomotor domain (perceptual level)	Using a single jump rope and self turning it (condition), the student will be able to make 10 repetitions (performance) without stopping (mastery).
Psychomotor domain (complex skill level)	Playing quarterback in a flag football game situation (condition), the student will be able to complete a downfield forward pass (performance) on 40 percent of her attempts (mastery).
Affective domain (valuing)	In a multimedia collage (condition), the student will express his five favorite (affect and mastery) activities in physical education class this year.
Affective domain (characterizing)	After eating at a local restaurant (condition), the student will make a list of foods she chose (affect) and determine how healthy (mastery) her choices were at that meal.

over precisely what content knowledge means for teaching physical education. Is it the teacher's knowledge about a movement or skill—the ability to observe it and evaluate it against some expected standard? Or is it the teacher's own ability to perform the movement or skill with great proficiency? Or is it some combination of both? Regardless of how content knowledge is defined, all agree that a teacher can never have *too much* of it! This essential knowledge can be acquired in several ways: through one's own performance experiences, by observing others' performances, by reading books or viewing other resource materials, by attending clinics, through conversations with teachers and other experts, and by actually teaching the content to learners.

Good knowledge of content allows a teacher to be more organized for instruction, to better articulate learning objectives, to provide safer environments, to develop better learning progressions, and to show increased discrimination when observing and analyzing learners' movement patterns and skills in class. In short, it promotes more effective instruction and higher levels of teacher confidence when planning and implementing instruction for physical education. Content knowledge combined with knowledge of context and learners is called *pedagogical content knowledge* (Shulman, 1987), and indicates that the teacher "knows his stuff" *and* how to teach it to students in his own school program. According to Grossman (in Griffin, Dodds, & Rovegno, 1996), teachers develop pedagogical content knowledge by combining four related types of knowledge and abilities:

1. They keep both broad and narrow goals clearly in mind.

2. They understand readily what various students already know and can do.

3. They are highly knowledgeable about curriculum content.

4. They vary instructional strategies. (p. 58)

Two types of content knowledge are important to physical educators: knowing how to classify movement skills and knowing movement patterns and how to analyze them.

Movement skill classifications

Physical education teachers can plan for a variety of movement skills in their lessons. Each type of skill calls for different task presentations, learning cues, student engagement patterns, and observation during practice. The expert teacher will know how to classify movement skills in order to better prepare learning activities under each one.

■ *Non-locomotor skills* do not involve traveling through space or using an object or implement. They are executed in a standing, sitting, or other stationary position. Some examples include static balancing, bending, stretching, twisting, and turning.

■ *Locomotor skills* involve bodily movement through space, without using an object or implement. Walking, jogging, hopping, skipping, and dodging are common types of locomotor skills.

■ *Object manipulation skills* are used to control some piece of equipment that is not held in the hand or somehow fastened to the body. Common objects in physical education are balls, hula hoops, batons, Frisbees, and shuttlecocks. The object is typically controlled (thrown, tossed, kicked, caught, or dribbled) with the hands or feet.

■ *Implement manipulation skills* involve a piece of equipment usually held in one or both hands, most of the time for the purpose of controlling an object. The implement is used as a "tool" in this sense. Common implements in physical education are bats, racquets, gloves, and clubs. They can be used to control an object in many ways, such as striking, batting, bouncing, dribbling, and catching or stopping. Because many implement manipulation skills call for the ability to control both the implement and an object at the same time, they require well-developed hand–eye coordination and visual tracking abilities.

■ *Strategic movement and skills* can include any of the previous movement types as they are applied in dynamic situations—typically games. These skills combine movement skill and situational decision making to produce a certain outcome, such as playing defense in team handball, stealing a base in baseball, running pass patterns in football, or being creative to solve a group initiative.

■ *Skill themes* (Graham, Holt/Hale, & Parker, 2009) combine basic motor skills with movement concepts to develop progressively more complex patterns of movement. A basic motor skill could be any skill in the non-locomotor, locomotor, object manipulation, and implement manipulation categories. Movement concepts delineate requirements for space awareness (where the body moves), effort (how the body moves), and relationships (between body parts, other people, implements, and objects). This conceptualization of learning forms the basis of an entire curriculum and approach to teaching, typically intended for elementary physical education (Graham, Holt/Hale, & Parker, 2009).

■ *Expressive and interpretive movements* are not viewed as skills to be executed with proficiency or used to produce an outcome. Sometimes a movement is made to express feelings, concepts, ideas, or themes. Many styles of dance, such as ballet, modern, and jazz, are based on expressive movements. These types of movement are often done with musical accompaniment. The teaching of expressive movement requires specific expertise by the teacher, including a knowledge of the "language of the body" that translates movements into meaning for the mover and the audience.

Movement patterns and skills analysis

Regardless of which type of movement is being taught, it is essential that the teacher have the ability to critically observe and analyze the movement patterns and skills performed by students in class. This ability is based on knowledge of the movement (what it should look like), the teacher's own performance experience, knowledge of students' developmental level, and observational skills to recognize key elements in the performance. *Key elements* are those parts of the movement or skill needed for proficiency. Knowing the key elements for a movement skill allows the teacher to focus on specific parts of the performance, rather than the entire performance. The teacher can then use these key elements as the basis for providing congruent, specific feedback to the learner.

Coker (1998) suggests five strategies for improving a physical education teacher's skill analysis effectiveness:

1. Determine the focus of observation. (What is being watched for?)
2. Determine the best viewing perspective.
3. Watch several skill performances to determine a pattern.
4. Avoid being distracted.
5. Use a video camera if it is practical.

Part of the teacher's expertise in observation and analysis in physical education is based on the knowledge of students' developmental stages relative to the movement or skill being learned. Young learners should not be expected to execute movements and skills with the same level of maturity as older and adult learners. There are acceptable versions of performance at each stage of development, from which the teacher should base his analysis of the key elements. Gallahue and Cleland (2003) describe four phases of motor development that contain ten differentiated stages within them. Teachers need to know the key performance elements for any skill or movement at each stage so they can analyze the observed performance within this developmental scheme. This helps the teacher make better performance analyses and provide usable feedback to learners.

Task analysis and content progression

Physical education teachers conduct a task analysis to identify the components of a skill to be learned and to determine the order in which students will learn each component. The ability to do a good task analysis is largely based on one's content knowledge and organizational skills. The analysis is accomplished in several steps. Let's use tennis as an illustration of this process (see Exhibit 3.9). The first step is to identify the final outcome in the learning sequence. This is referred to as the Level 1 task or Terminal Objective (Mager, 1984). For tennis that might be stated generally as "the ability to play a singles match at a beginner's skill level."

The next step involves listing all of the skills and knowledge needed to perform the Level 1 task. In this case, the list will be serving, forehand drive, backhand drive, returning serves, and singles strategy and rules (including scoring). These are the Level 2 tasks and are placed on the flowchart under the Level 1 task. The order in which students learn Level 2 tasks usually has a hierarchy, because some tasks are prerequisite to others on that same level. In this chart, students will progress through the tasks in a sequence going from left to right in Level 2.

Level 3 consists of the component skills and knowledge needed to perform each of the Level 2 tasks, placed in ascending order of progression. Students begin by learning the tasks lowest on each list, progressing to higher tasks as those are mastered.

The task analysis begins the process of deciding what content will be included in the unit, because it reveals how much content can be learned with the amount of instructional time and other resources available to the teacher. It is very common for the task analysis to result in a teacher's decision to cover less content in the unit than originally thought.

Content progression. A task analysis will provide a clear plan for the learning that must occur in the unit and the order in which students will learn content. However, it does not explain which types of learning activities students will engage in and how students will progress from one activity to the next in each lesson. That process is called *content progression,* which includes the planned sequence of learning activities that allows students to acquire the content listed in the task analysis. Rink (2009) uses a scheme for content progression in physical education, with five types of learning tasks: informing, refining, extending, applying, and repeating. The following list includes an explanation of each category and a sample content progression for dribbling in a sixth-grade soccer lesson.

1. Informing   The initial task in a new skill progression

    Example:

    Students are presented with a demonstration, then they dribble a ball in general space for five minutes.

EXHIBIT   3.9   Three levels of task analysis for learning tennis singles.

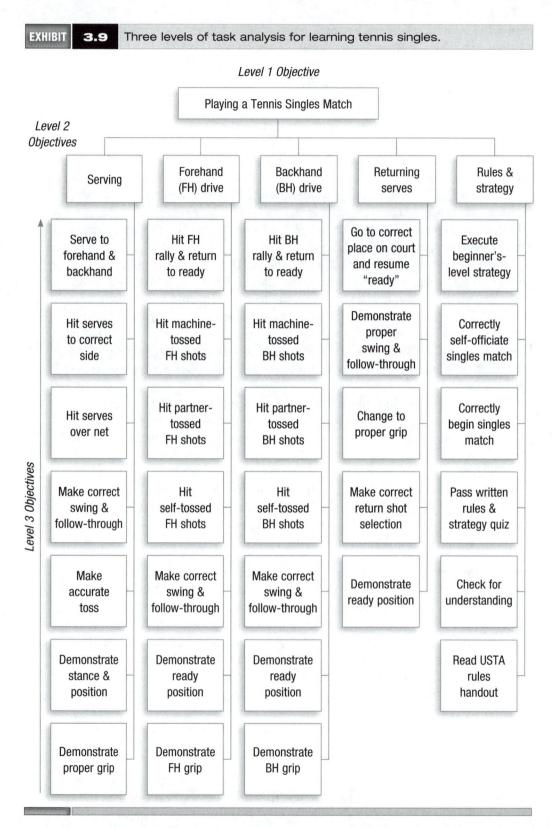

2. Refining

A task that promotes improved quality of performance

Example:

The teacher shows students three key elements for better control of the ball, and students practice in general space for 10 minutes to perform those elements.

3. Extending

A task that is slightly more complex or difficult than the preceding (similar) task

Example:

Students do a slalom dribbling drill for five minutes. The drill calls for them to dribble the ball through a course of eight cones placed on the floor.

4. Applying

A task to be performed to a stated performance criterion or performed against an opponent or standard

Example:

Students are timed as they dribble through the same slalom course. They are prompted to try to beat their "personal best" on each subsequent trial.

5. Repeating

Any previous task that is repeated for review or increased proficiency

Example:

Students' control has been reduced as they increase speed in the application task, so the teacher directs them to go back and practice the extension task for five more minutes.

Some of the models in this book will have specific content progression plans designed within them. When that is not the case, the teacher will need to prepare a content progression as part of the unit plan. Teacher knowledge in content development is critical for two important reasons. First, it helps the teacher plan good sequences of learning tasks that allow students to progress at a more even rate while building on previous performances. Second, it can help the teacher make well-timed decisions about when to move from one task to the next in class.

Time-based or mastery-based progression. Content progression decisions can be made in two ways. They can occur either according to a time allocation "budget" or when students have demonstrated mastery in the current learning task. In a *time-based progression,* the teacher estimates how much time it should take the majority of students to learn each task and then goes to the next task after that amount of practice time has elapsed. Task allocations can change when estimates are not accurate (when students need less or more time to practice), but the teacher's schedule generally guides the progression. In *mastery-based progressions,* the teacher determines a performance criterion for the current task and a group acceptance rate and then moves to the next task when both have been satisfied. For example:

> When 75 percent (acceptance rate) of my fifth graders can make 10 jumps in a row (performance criterion), we will move to the next task.

> When every student (acceptance rate) can pass (performance criterion) the written rules test, we can begin the tournament.

Time-based progressions allow the teacher to make long-range plans in a unit, but they entail the risk that some students will not be ready for a new task when it begins. And those same students are very likely to fall further behind as more progressions occur. Mastery-based progression ensures that most or all of the students can perform the current task before they move to the next one, but using even simple performance criteria and a relatively low acceptance rate can cause some learning tasks to take a long time to complete. The teacher needs to give careful thought to how students will progress through learning tasks, while keeping the advantages and disadvantages of each method in mind.

Assessment

More and more physical education programs are attempting to lead students to well-defined learning outcomes, such as those contained in the NASPE standards discussed in Chapter 1. In order to demonstrate that students are achieving those standards, there has been increased emphasis on assessment in physical education at all levels. Good programs not only need to have standards to strive for but they must also show that students have met those standards. Therefore, effective teachers must have a broad knowledge of assessment techniques that can answer the key question, "How do you know your students have learned what you intended them to learn?" The process of answering that question is called *assessment*.

Assessment in physical education is done for three important reasons:

1. To describe how much learning has taken place within a given amount of instructional time (a lesson, a unit, a year, or the entire program)
2. To judge or evaluate the quality of that learning (usually for grading)
3. To make decisions for improving instruction when not enough learning is occurring (i.e., one or more standards are not being met at a satisfactory level)

Until the adoption of standards for learning, assessment in physical education was often not conducted in any meaningful way. Students may have been given grades, but those grades were typically not based on observed or measured learning; most often they were based on nonperformance criteria such as dressing out, participation, behavior, and effort. When assessments were done, they traditionally included only fitness tests and skills tests, which address only a small part of today's comprehensive standards for physical education. In order to properly assess student learning in all the NASPE standards or other outcomes stated by a program, teachers today need to know and be able to use a wide variety of assessment techniques within model-based instruction. Assessment knowledge involves a number of different skills:

1. Linking assessment to standards or other stated outcomes
2. Understanding the timing of assessments
3. Knowing many assessment techniques
4. Selecting the best assessment technique for each situation
5. Implementing assessment techniques in practical ways
6. Organizing, analyzing, and interpreting assessment information
7. Using assessment information to describe student learning
8. Using assessment information to make program improvements (when needed)

There is much more to know about assessment in physical education than can fit in one section of this chapter. Therefore, Chapter 7 will provide a complete overview of assessment within model-based instruction for physical education, along with examples to help you understand the many and complex facets of this key part of a teacher's knowledge base.

The Social/Emotional Climate

Every physical education class is a small community with its own social and emotional climate that determines *what it feels like* to students when they are with the teacher and their classmates. A positive climate is one in which every student feels he or she is a valuable part of the larger group and can pursue learning in a comfortable, supportive, and nurturing environment. A negative climate is just the opposite. Students feel isolated and ignored, and their efforts to learn are hindered by unsafe and harmful conditions caused by the teacher and/or other students. Even when the climate in physical education is more negative than positive, teachers are quite able to change the climate so that it is positive for all students all the time. There can be many ways to promote a positive climate in physical education. Consider the following suggestions:

1. Establish firm and consistent expectations for student behaviors, and communicate those expectations often.
2. Do not pay attention only to inappropriate behavior; be sure to acknowledge and reward appropriate behavior when it occurs.
3. Include students in decisions about class management.
4. Acknowledge students' effort, not just performance.
5. Avoid being overly emotional.
6. Do not use derogatory, stereotyping language.
7. Avoid sarcasm.
8. Design learning tasks that are developmentally appropriate in all domains.

9. Make all learning tasks inclusive for all students.

10. Do not use physical activity as punishment (e.g., running laps for being tardy).

11. Interact with students often to let them know you are paying attention to their efforts to learn.

An overly negative climate can lead to student dislike and avoidance of physical education and eventually of physical activity itself. It can also lead to a dysfunctional cycle of events that makes the teacher's day stressful and emotionally draining. Students' reactions to a negative climate can cause misbehavior and confrontations with the teacher, who then feels inclined to respond with harsh words and strong actions, which only deepen the negative climate, stimulating even more misbehavior and confrontation. As you might expect, students leave class with negative feelings toward physical education and the teacher, while the teacher has a negative attitude toward students and little personal enjoyment to take from their day in school.

Teachers need to be aware of the concept of classroom climate and to know how to monitor it in their classes. They also need to be aware of when changes occur in the climate and whether those changes are positive or negative. They should know how to establish a positive climate with some of the previous suggestions and how to turn a negative climate into a positive one. The nice thing about classroom climate, unlike the climate outside, is that a teacher can establish the kind of atmosphere she wishes to have in her gymnasium and change it when it is not beneficial for student learning and enjoyment of physical education.

Equity in the Gym

In recent years much attention has been given to issues of student equity in education and in physical education. *Equity* refers to fair and equal access to social, developmental, and educational opportunities in schools and individual classes—regardless of a student's gender, race, ethnicity, abilities, socioeconomic status, and family/home background. That is not to say that all students will always get the same instruction or that they can all achieve to the same level; equity refers to the identification and elimination of factors that inhibit student access—for no other reason than being who they are—to opportunities to learn to their fullest potential. Inequity in the classroom can promote bias, prejudice, and stereotyping when educators make false assumptions about certain students and then base instructional practice on those assumptions.

Critical pedagogy is the study of fairness and justice in educational settings. It is based on the principle that schools and classrooms represent micropolitical contexts with definite and disproportionate distributions of power, status, and opportunity to learn. Sometimes that unfairness comes from a teacher's ignorance of inequitable practice, a lack of intent, submission to social norms and stereotyping, or a lack of experience. In the extreme, it comes from intentional bias and prejudice toward certain types of students. Whether intended or not, it leads to the establishment of curriculums, instruction, language, and interactions that favor some students while depriving other students of an equal opportunity to gain from the educational experience.

Our government and the educational system have tried, in part, to legislate equitable practice in schools and in physical education. Title IX of the Educational Amendments of 1972 specifically prohibits the segregation of boys and girls in sports and physical education. By implication, it also prohibits many covert practices that made for "separate but unequal" school physical education programs and instruction. The Education for All Handicapped Children Act of 1975 (Public Law 94-142) stipulated that students with disabilities receive a free and appropriate education in the *least restrictive environment*. In other words, a student with a disability should pursue learning in the regular classroom and gymnasium whenever it suits that student's educational needs. Many students who were previously scheduled into segregated special education classes now take physical education with nondisabled students, with the full expectation that their individual needs will be addressed in that setting. That practice was originally called mainstreaming: thus, P.L. 94-142 was often referred to as the "Mainstreaming Law." Today the term *inclusion* indicates that students with many different educational needs are now included in the same class on a regular basis. Students with severe disabilities are scheduled into adaptive physical education classes, but most students with special needs participate in physical education classes with their peers. The current legislation in this area is the 2004 Individuals with Disabilities Education Act (IDEA).

Title IX, P.L. 94-142, and IDEA have led to major strides in the establishment of equitable learning environments, but they have not come close to eliminating inequities in the gymnasium. Along with those stemming from students' disabilities and gender, other sources of inequity exist, such as students' race, ethnicity, religion, culture, sexual orientation, and motor ability. Napper-Owen (1994) mentions six types of inequities in physical education:

1. Organizational patterns that favor higher-skilled students (e.g., picking teams with "captains")

2. Gender-separated grouping for instruction (e.g., "The boys can play a game. The girls can stay on the side and practice, or whatever.")

3. Using teaching methods that don't address a variety of student learning preferences (e.g., always using direct instruction)

4. Using teacher–student interaction patterns that favor certain groups of students (e.g., always calling on high-skill students for demonstrations)

5. Using stereotyped (e.g., "girls' push-ups") or biased (e.g., "You throw like a girl") language

6. Inappropriate role modeling by teachers (e.g., "talking down" to girls)

Teachers can become aware of their own practices and patterns in class that may lead to student perceptions that "things are not fair here," thus resulting in imbalanced educational opportunities and reduced comfort levels for certain students. With an awareness of these patterns, a teacher can usually make immediate changes to promote equity in the gymnasium.

Curriculum Models for Physical Education

Contemporary physical education includes many options for program design and movement activities, and a growing number of programs are now based on well-articulated themes, following a particular curriculum model to promote student learning within those themes. Like the instructional models in this book, curriculum models are comprehensive and coherent plans for designing and implementing entire physical education programs in a school or district. They originate with program-level goals and objectives that lead to the selection of content units, instruction, and policies that allow students to achieve the goals of the program. Most models promote a limited number of student learning outcomes, all of which are strongly related to the model's stated purpose or theme. This reduced focus gives the program a better identity and makes planning decisions much easier.

Several good curriculum models have been developed for physical education programs at all grade levels. (Refer to Chapter 1.) These models have been implemented in many school settings, giving them strong support as effective ways to conceptualize, design, and implement entire programs.

Physical education teachers need to know the theoretical foundation and major learning goals of each model that is appropriate for the grade levels they teach. It is also important to understand what any given model *does not* attempt to do, so that teachers and students are not misled into false expectations. When the teacher has clearly identified the goals, it will be easier to select content units that are most effective in fostering those goals. It will also be easier to assess those outcomes at a later time.

DEVELOPING EXPERT PHYSICAL EDUCATION TEACHERS

There is much debate over exactly what a physical education teacher needs to know and do in order to be considered an expert professional. Even though Shulman's (1987) seven categories of the teacher knowledge base have been extremely helpful in recent discussions about what teachers need to know, they cannot be used to help us identify expert and non-expert teachers in schools. Some of the limitations come from the realization that good teaching (and expertise) is strongly based in context and involves a complex interaction between declarative knowledge, procedural knowledge, where the teacher instructs, and who the teacher instructs. So, a teacher not only needs to have all of the types of knowledge discussed in this chapter but he also needs to know how to adapt and apply that knowledge in his specific school, program, and classes. As you will recall, that is referred to as *conditional knowledge*.

An interesting area of research on teaching has focused on the expertise needed to instruct effectively in physical education and other subjects (Schempp, 1997). Manross and Templeton (1997) mention six characteristics of expert physical education teachers: (1) they plan thoroughly and completely; (2) they focus on individual student performance; (3) they develop automaticity of behavior; (4) they give creative feedback; (5) they attain command of their subject matter; and (6) they use reflective practices. All elements of the knowledge base outlined in this chapter are represented in one or more of these characteristics and require a precise, situationally specific combination of declarative and procedural knowledge.

SUMMARY

This chapter outlined a proposed knowledge base for teachers who will instruct physical education from a model-based approach. It represents categories of knowledge that provide the foundation for all the instructional models presented in this book. As you have surely noticed, this knowledge base is quite general, and most of it describes declarative knowledge for teaching. At this point, some of its components are rather abstract and lack specific examples to further your understanding. But that will soon change. The next level for building instructional models is comprised of instructional strategies and other teaching practices that originate from within this knowledge base and lead directly to the development of pedagogical knowledge (Shulman, 1987). Chapter 4 will be more specific, yet it too will remain somewhat general because the selection and use of each strategy will depend on which model the teacher is following in an instructional unit.

LEARNING ACTIVITIES

1. If you are a teacher now, reflect for a moment on *how you presently teach physical education.* Make a list of the ways you learned how to teach (e.g., from past teachers, from colleagues, at conferences, in your teacher education program). Cite how each source of knowledge influences the ways you now teach.

2. If you are not a teacher now, answer the last question describing *how you see yourself teaching in the future.*

3. Cite your personal knowledge in each of the 10 areas presented in this chapter. What do you know in each area? What do you still need to learn?

4. Get permission to interview a physical education teacher (or more than one at the same school) and have the teacher help you conduct a contextual analysis of their program using the blank copy of Exhibit 3.3 on the IMPE website as a guide. Once completed, compile your contextual analysis into a report and share it on the site and with other students in your class.

TOPICS FOR REFLECTION & SMALL-GROUP DISCUSSION

1. Many people think that good teaching is "obvious"—that there's not much to it and most people could do it well. Discuss this in your group. After you have discussed your thoughts with your classmates, take a few moments to write them down, then post your opinion in the Forum section of the IMPE website for others to read. Be sure to check back for replies and feel free to respond to those replies in the thread for each topic.

2. Discuss this statement: "Teaching physical education poorly is the easiest teaching job in any school; teaching physical education well is the hardest teaching job in any school."

SUGGESTED READINGS

Lambert, L. T. (2007). *Standards-based assessment of student learning* (2nd ed.). Reston, VA: National Association for Sport and Physical Education. (This is the lead book in the NASPE Assessment Series, which includes numerous resources for P–12 assessment.)

National Association for Sport and Physical Education. *Looking at physical education from a developmental perspective: A guide to teaching.* Reston, VA: NASPE Motor Development Task Force.

National Association for Sport and Physical Education. (2004). *Moving into the future: National standards for physical education* (2nd ed.). Boston: McGraw-Hill.

Strand, B. N., & Wilson, R. (1993). *Assessing sport skills.* Champaign, IL: Human Kinetics.

TEACHING STRATEGIES FOR MODEL-BASED INSTRUCTION

I f the types of knowledge presented in Chapter 3 form the foundation of instructional models, then teaching strategies can be thought of as the bricks and mortar that hold each model together, give it a unique look, and allow it to work toward its designed purposes. A *teaching strategy* is a set of preplanned actions intended to bring about a specific short-term goal within the lesson or content unit. Unlike most effective teaching skills that happen quickly and interactively during a lesson, a strategy is always determined ahead of time as part of the explicit lesson plan. Essentially, it is the way the teacher intends for each segment of the lesson to be operationalized—how it will get carried out by the teacher and/or students.

A predetermined set of teaching strategies makes each model look and operate according to the designer's plan, leading students to preferred types of engagement and learning outcomes. Some models will rely on many teaching strategies; others will use relatively few. However, as you will see in Part Two, each model will use only those strategies that are congruent with its foundational learning theory, its purpose, and its plan for implementation. Teaching strategies can be divided into two main groups of operations: managerial and instructional. *Managerial strategies* improve the organization of a lesson or unit, enabling the teacher to maximize the potential for student learning to occur. They are put into practice at any time in the lesson or unit. *Instructional strategies* directly facilitate student engagement before and during planned learning activities. They are used at specified times, according to the teacher's lesson plans. Both types contain specific actions, according to the design of a particular model, that teachers and students complete to promote learning outcomes within it. As you can see in Exhibit 4.1, teaching strategies *build upon* the teacher's knowledge base and rely strongly on procedural and conditional expertise in physical education.

EXHIBIT 4.1 Strategies and areas of knowledge for teaching physical education.

STRATEGIES FOR TEACHING PHYSICAL EDUCATION

MANAGERIAL	INSTRUCTIONAL	
1. Preventive	1. Task presentation	5. Task progression
2. Interactive	2. Task structure	6. Student safety
3. Grouping	3. Task engagement	7. Review and closure
	4. Learning activities	

AREAS OF KNOWLEDGE FOR MODEL-BASED INSTRUCTION

1. Learning contexts	6. Physical education content
2. Learners	7. Assessment
3. Learning theories	8. Social/emotional climate
4. Developmental appropriateness	9. Equity in the gym
5. Learning domains and objectives	10. Curriculum models for PE

MANAGERIAL STRATEGIES

All of the instructional models in this book depend on an effective plan for class management. This plan allows available resources to be used to their fullest potential to foster each model's unique set of domain priorities and student learning outcomes. Each managerial plan should be consistent with the model for which it is used. The most essential managerial plan is the one devised for *preventive management*, which maintains and maximizes appropriate student behavior and engagement in class. All physical education lessons and units require some amount of management time, planned for in identified lesson segments: the start of class, transitions, and the end of class. Many effective strategies can prevent or reduce managerial problems in complex physical education instructional settings.

Preventive Management Plans

It is not possible to completely eliminate student misbehavior or lost time in class, problems that divert class time from the opportunity to learn, contribute to teacher stress, and build a negative climate in the gymnasium. Yet a teacher can prepare a preventive management plan to greatly reduce the likelihood of behavior problems in class and thus increase time on task and student learning.

Management strategies at the start of class

It is important that a physical education lesson get off to a quick and stimulating start that can carry through the entire lesson. Siedentop and Tannehill (2000) call this *getting momentum*. When a teacher uses a good strategy for starting the class, she also sets the tone and expectations for the lesson, sending a clear message to students that "this is learning time."

Post the lesson plan for students. Too often students come to physical education class with no idea what their lesson will entail. They arrive at the gym and must wait for the teacher to give a vague or incomplete preview: "Today we are going to work on tennis serves . . ." And too often the students reply with, "When do we get to play?" In secondary schools, it would be simple to post an overview of the lesson plan in the locker room or entrance to the gym so that students know what to expect in the lesson. For elementary classes, teachers might provide a more complete preview of the lesson as it begins.

Post or announce special instructions for the day. Physical education classes can take place in many areas in and around the school, and they can be subject to the weather outside. When this requires changes in the regular class plans, students need special information for getting dressed or finding the location of class. Typically, the teacher must "pass the word around" through a few students or wait until all students have arrived in class to move to the new location. For secondary schools, a more time-efficient plan would involve the use of a written notice to students as they enter the locker room, before they begin to change out. In elementary schools, the physical education teacher could ask that classroom teachers make a brief statement about such changes as part of the daily announcements. Therefore, classes can come to physical education ready to make the needed changes in location, scheduling, or procedures.

Establish an instant activity. Some managerial problems occur because students find themselves with little to do at the start of class other than wait for the teacher to begin the lesson. As the number of students in the gymnasium increases before class begins, this waiting period can be the opportunity for misbehavior, because the students are less directly supervised by the teacher. A teacher can post an "instant activity" that students can engage in as soon as they enter the gym, reducing the chance for misbehavior to occur while the rest of the students arrive for class. See Chapter 5 for more information.

Contingency management

Contingency management for classrooms involves behavior modification techniques that have been shown to be highly effective (Alberto & Troutman, 2008). Such a plan contains an explicit statement of the relationship between student behavior and the consequences for it. If a student is observed or heard to engage in a predefined appropriate behavior in class, that student is rewarded, or reinforced, as a consequence. This increases the likelihood that the student will repeat or maintain that behavior. If a student is observed or heard to engage in a predefined inappropriate behavior, that student receives no reward, or can be punished—thereby reducing the likelihood that the inappropriate behavior will occur again. There are many contingency-based strategies for preventive management in physical education.

Good behavior game. In this strategy, students are assigned to a team, with individual members receiving a one-point deduction for inappropriate behavior observed by the teacher. Each team competes against the other team(s) to win the good behavior game for that class period. The teacher or an assistant keeps a tally sheet for each team during class, with the winning team earning a small reward at the end of the period.

Time-out. One of the most-often used behavior management techniques is "time-out," in which a student who has been observed or heard practicing an inappropriate behavior is removed from the class activity for a set amount of time. The designated time-out area is usually on the periphery of the gymnasium but within sight of the teacher. The student may observe the class activities but is not allowed to do anything else. The posted class rules specify the length of the time-out for each infraction, so students are aware of the contingency in effect and in some way "make their own choice" to be in time-out. When the time-out period has elapsed, the student can join the class activity in progress.

Assertive discipline. Established in the 1970s, this philosophy explains how teachers can arrange a preventive discipline plan in their classrooms (Canter & Canter, 2001). The teacher expresses clearly to students the classroom conditions necessary for learning to take place and then gets students to accommodate those conditions through appropriate behavior. For instance, the teacher might say to the class, "We need to make absolutely sure that the equipment is returned where you found it, so that the next person can use it without having to search for it." Once that need has been stated and all students understand it, the teacher then expects this to happen and becomes assertive with students to ensure that it does happen, settling for nothing less. If an expectation is not being met, it becomes the immediate focus of the lesson, and the rest of the lesson does not proceed until the teacher is satisfied with student behavior.

Student choice plans. Most preventive management plans are designed by teachers and imposed on students who have no choice or ownership in the plan. As students mature and develop, they possess an increasing capacity to make choices and hold themselves responsible for those choices. They can therefore assume a more active part in the process of making a discipline plan in physical education. Such a plan can be negotiated between the teacher and students by allowing students to suggest a list of class rules and consequences for infractions. Although there may be some student-choice rules that the teacher cannot accept for reasons of safety and liability, it is possible for the teacher to state the boundaries of student choice and let students decide within those boundaries.

For instance, a high school physical education teacher might ask a 10th-grade class, "What is a fair amount of time needed to change out for class and be in the gym, ready to start?" Through some negotiation, the class decides that 5 minutes allows students sufficient time without hurrying them or cutting into class time too much. That agreed upon, the teacher then asks, "What should happen to students who do not get dressed and to the gym in 5 minutes from the previous bell?" Some suggestions from students might be, "run 10 laps," "get 5 minutes of time-out once we start to play," or "stay at the end of class to help take up equipment." The teacher explains that because he is against using exercise as punishment, the class should vote on the second or third choice. The majority vote becomes the new class rule.

Interactive Management Strategies

Most class management episodes occur after the opening routine of the class and during the planned lesson segments. Some management strategies can be planned ahead of time, but most of the decisions must be made as the teacher directs students to end a current lesson segment and transition into the next one. This is called *interactive management* because it involves consideration of the many things going on at the moment, leading to some immediate verbal interaction with students. The success of many lessons will hinge on the teacher's effectiveness during these interactive managerial moments, since the interactions are often unexpected. They can cause major disruptions and loss of momentum if not resolved quickly. An effective physical education teacher may use some of the interactive management strategies described next.

Ask students to assist with equipment dispersal and return. When it is not possible to set up equipment before students arrive at class, the teacher can ask students to assist in getting it out for use and then returning it when they are finished. This reduces management time considerably and keeps students involved in the flow of the lesson. The teacher needs to give students clear directions to make this kind of transition quick and orderly.

Prepare for the next activity while the current one is taking place. Once the teacher decides that the class will change to another activity that needs different equipment or a new space configuration, he can get the upcoming activity ready while the first one winds down. When possible, the teacher can make a "change of scenery" quickly and safely, so that he may simply stop the current activity and immediately redirect students to the new one. For example, a teacher could direct students to perform stretching in a perimeter area while he sets up the tennis courts with cones for practicing serves. As soon as students complete their stretching, they can move to the courts to begin practice right away.

Establish a backup plan. What happens if it rains while the class is outdoors and you must finish the lesson indoors? What will the teacher do if a key piece of equipment breaks or fails during class? How will the class be restarted after a fire drill? What will you do if the principal needs the gym with little notice, forcing you to relocate your classes? These situations can be less disruptive if the teacher gives some prior thought to their occurrence and prepares a backup plan.

Prepare for some class emergencies ahead of time. Emergencies can include injuries or sudden illnesses, intruders, or unexpected environmental hazards (e.g., bees in the area, water leaks). In these emergencies, the teacher must stay with the class but arrange for help to be called for. If students must be sent to get assistance, consider who should be sent, if they know where to go, and exactly what they should say to the person being notified. A teacher can train a few potential messengers as part of an overall plan to cover emergencies. The idea is to be prepared ahead of time for any emergency situation.

Have a specific plan for student injury situations. Certain emergencies, such as a student getting injured or becoming ill during class, will require action and unanticipated decisions. Plans for these situations are similar to your emergency plan but require more on-the-spot decisions and actions: What will the rest of the class do while you are attending to that student? Who will be sent to get more assistance, if needed? How do you explain the injury to other students to reduce their fear of the same thing happening to them?

Use behavioral extinction for students who just want attention. Some students simply want to be noticed by the teacher and may initiate minor disruptions to get attention. When the teacher suspects that this is the case, a good strategy is to extinguish the behavior by simply ignoring it. Many times the student will stop because she fails to get the attention that reinforces the behavior to begin with. This strategy is far more effective than attending to every instance of attention-seeking or constantly punishing small misbehaviors. Both of those responses give the student just what she wants—some of the teacher's attention, be it positive or negative.

Learn to overlap classroom events. *Overlapping* refers to a teacher's ability to attend to more than one thing at a time during class. This ability is especially important in physical education, which often involves big classes, large spaces, and a lot of activity. For instance, the teacher should be capable of providing individual attention to a child who needs it while also keeping track of time so as not to miss the next class transition. Other examples include the ability to get class going while tardy students arrive one at a time or the ability to listen to a song on the CD player that cues a learning station rotation while also interacting with students as they practice.

Strategies for Getting Students into Groups

Many of the models in this book require that the teacher group students during class to promote effective use of time and to implement developmentally appropriate learning tasks. When the plan doesn't involve teaching the whole class at once, teachers can try several grouping strategies that show sensitivity to students' feelings, save time, and facilitate the immediate goals of the lesson.

Selecting groups randomly

Random group selection saves time by placing the grouping process under the teacher's control. It can save minutes and reduce the tendency for some students to want to be grouped for social reasons. Almost invariably, asking students to make their own groups results in increased transition time, elevated noise levels, some hurt feelings, and uneven or unfair groups. Physical education teachers can use any number of quick, random-based strategies for forming groups when student abilities or characteristics are not a factor.

Cut-and-go groups. Suppose the teacher wishes to form five groups and have each group stand in a different location in the gym. The teacher first points to five separate locations and assigns each one a number from one to five. Then she points to individual students while counting aloud from one to five, designating each with a number and telling them to go to their respective areas of the gym. The teacher repeats the process until all five groups are formed and in place.

Birth-month groups. The teacher says, "Everyone born from January 1 to the end of April is in Group 1. Everyone born from May 1 to the end of August is in Group 2. Everyone born from September 1 to the end of the year is in Group 3." The students get into their respective groups, and the teacher then balances the group sizes as needed.

Clothes-color groups (if students are not in uniforms). The teacher says, "Everyone who has on something that's red, get in a group. Everyone who has on something that's green, get in a group. Everyone who has on something that's yellow, get in a group. If you don't have on one of those colors, you can make up your own group." The students get into their respective groups, and the teacher balances the group sizes as needed.

Selecting practice groups by ability levels

Sometimes it is appropriate to form groups according to actual or student-selected ability levels. Yet it is discriminatory to make such groups based on assumed, totally subjective, stereotyped, or arbitrary determinations of student abilities. When the instructional situation calls for placing students into ability groups for practice or competition, the teacher needs to make it clear that the groups are determined by ability alone and not based on discriminatory decisions. Exhibit 4.2 contrasts discriminatory and nondiscriminatory group placement practices.

EXHIBIT	4.2	Discriminatory vs. nondiscriminatory group placement practices.

NONDISCRIMINATORY:

Students who scored 65 percent or higher on the unit skills test participate in the game on field 3.
Students who scored less than 65 percent on the unit skills test participate in the game on field 1.

Those who feel as if they know the rules of table tennis can go to the far end and start playing.
Those who are not sure of the rules can come with me for a review before playing.

DISCRIMINATORY:

The boys are on court 1.
The girls are on court 2.

The boys can practice at the "tall" basket.
The girls can practice at the lower basket.

The varsity players in class can practice here.
Everyone else can practice at the other end.

Choosing teams for games

We are all familiar with stories about hurt feelings and lopsided teams that result from "captains" (usually higher-skilled boys) being selected to pick teams for class games in physical education. Not only can this strategy be miseducative but it may also be the source of many students' avoidance tendencies toward competition and physical education. In addition, it usually takes many minutes to accomplish—minutes that could be spent playing the game. Teachers can use a few simple strategies to eliminate all the negative issues related to this process, thereby ensuring that class competition is fair and educational:

1. Determine balanced teams before class according to students' skill abilities and class demographics.
2. Form teams randomly by telling students to count off or by using one of the other random grouping strategies described above.
3. Modify game rules and scoring to foster more equitable participation patterns.
4. Do not punish or denigrate losing teams and players after the game; this will reduce students' concerns about unfair teams or playing with less-skilled teammates.

INSTRUCTIONAL STRATEGIES

 nstructional strategies refer to a wide range of operations intended to directly promote the intended learning outcomes in a lesson. While managerial strategies set the stage for learning to occur, instructional strategies serve to give students active engagement with the content of the lesson, which then leads to learning. Instructional strategies consist of seven operations: task presentation, task structure, task engagement, learning activities, student safety, task progression, and review and closure.

Strategies for Task Presentation

Students must get information about an upcoming learning task before they can begin the task. Rink (2009) calls the collected strategies for providing students with necessary learning task information *task presentation,* which includes five operations: (1) getting the attention of the learner, (2) sequencing the content and organizational aspects of tasks, (3) improving the clarity of communication, (4) choosing a way to communicate, and (5) selecting and organizing learning cues (p. 88). Chapter 5 will outline the specific teaching skills needed for effective task presentation. Below you will find some general task presentation strategies.

Communication strategies

Physical education teachers can use many types of communication to provide task information to students. The best type for any given situation is the one that provides the clearest task information in the briefest amount of time.

- *Teacher verbal lecture.* The teacher verbally communicates while students listen.
- *Teacher-modeled demonstration.* The teacher provides his own model of the information.
- *Combined lecture/demo.* The teacher models each piece of information as she tells it to students.
- *Active demonstration.* The students follow along as the teacher talks and demonstrates.
- *Slow-motion demonstration.* The students follow along as in the active demonstration—but in slow motion.
- *Peer-directed, verbal communication.* A student communicates verbally to another student, a group of students, or the whole class.
- *Peer-directed, modeled communication.* A student provides a model for another student, a group of students, or the whole class.
- *Task sheets.* Learning-task information is provided on sheets given to each student, and students read them individually.
- *Station signs/sheets.* Each learning station has its own information sign or sheet that students read when they first arrive at the station.

Physical education teachers do not have to rely only on themselves or other students to communicate task information. Several types of media can be used for that purpose:

1. Videos (commercial or produced by the teacher)
2. Wii sports and games

3. Photographs and drawings

4. CDs, DVDs

5. Podcasts

Set induction

The first task presentation of each class should include a brief *set induction* that serves four purposes: (1) previews the lesson content for students, (2) states the learning goals, (3) relates the content to other areas of learning, and (4) increases student interest and motivation. For instance, a teacher who has planned a fourth-grade lesson on balance could use the following set induction:

> "In today's lesson we are going to work on our dynamic balance—that's the ability to stay balanced while you are moving around. Can anyone tell me some sports that use a lot of dynamic balance?" Students mention soccer, football, tennis, and ice skating. The teacher picks up on the ice skating example and asks the class if they have been watching the Winter Olympics figure skating on TV the past week. Several students nod their heads, and the teacher continues. "If you want to be like those Olympic skaters, you need to have good dynamic balance so you can go fast, turn quickly, and land safely when you jump. Even though you will not be skating here, those same skills are important as you move around in general space. First, we are going to work on static balance in self-space, then move to some more difficult tasks using dynamic balance in three or four ways. While you are practicing, imagine that you are on ice skates and getting ready for the next Winter Olympic Games. OK, let's have some fun, you future Olympians!"

Checking for understanding

A good strategy to use after each task presentation is *checking for understanding*. This process involves asking a brief series of questions to determine how much of the presentation students retained or understood. Questions should not be rhetorical, such as "Did everyone understand?" or "Any questions?" The teacher should use purposeful questions that ask students to recall the most important information that was given to them, such as "Who can tell me the three main things to keep in mind when you try to strike a ball?" or "Why do we not want to 'high-stick' when we are practicing around others?" or "If you are not having success from a long distance, what should you do?" It is sometimes a good idea to spot-check certain less-attentive students, which will prompt them to pay more attention during future task presentations.

Strategies for Task Structure and Engagement

Task structure refers to the way a learning task or activity is designed for student engagement. Task structure as used in this book includes three components of what Jones (1992) called a *task system* (task presentation and task structure combined): (1) a set of operations or procedures used to pursue the learning task, (2) resources and conditions that are available to accomplish the task, and (3) a means of accountability that indicates the importance or significance of the task (p. 412). Operations include the location and organization of the learning environment and directions for safe participation. Resources and conditions include equipment and the number of minutes allocated for the task. Accountability includes expectations for student behavior, a proficiency goal, or an explanation of how the task relates to subsequent learning activities in the lesson or unit. Teachers can use several strategies to ensure that the task structure facilitates the learning goals of the moment and encourages the maximum and most successful student engagement.

Variations in task difficulty

Effective teachers will design learning tasks to accommodate several levels of student abilities at the same time, allowing all students to be appropriately challenged and to experience a high rate of success. This can be accomplished by planning varying levels of difficulty for each learning task and requiring students to demonstrate proficiency at a lower level before moving to the next one. This structure results in practice groups based on actual ability and allows students to work with others at the same ability level. The level of difficulty can be varied by progressively altering one or more aspects of a practice task, such as:

1. Distance to the target
2. Time required to complete (speed)
3. Size and weight of implement
4. Size, weight, and texture of object
5. Number of needed repetitions
6. Size or height of the target

Teaching by invitation

In this strategy, students are encouraged, or invited, to pick their own level of difficulty and challenge, choosing from pre-arranged setups (Graham, 2001). A teacher could set up three tossing stations for a first-grade class, each with a different type of ball (e.g., larger, smaller, bouncier) and target size (small, medium, large), and "invite" students to choose their own practice station. The teacher could add another variation of difficulty at each station by having three tossing distances, marked by cones. Again, students would be invited to practice at the distance they think provides the best challenge for their ability.

Developmental appropriateness

Are the students able to meet the managerial and performance requirements of the task? Managerial requirements refer to students' ability to comprehend and follow directions, assume responsibility, abide by safety rules, and stay engaged without the teacher's direct supervision. Performance requirements represent the match between the difficulty of the task and students' cognitive and psychomotor abilities. Tasks should be designed so that students can comprehend the purpose and form of the task and have at least a moderate level of success when they attempt it. Tasks that are too simple or easy can cause students to become bored; tasks that are too complex or difficult can make students frustrated. In either circumstance, it is likely that students will quickly choose to disengage from the task, alter it, or turn to off-task behavior.

Sequencing task segments for practice

Some skills are best learned when they are broken down into subskills that can be practiced one at a time, in a planned sequence. For *partial-skill* practice tasks, the teacher should provide a task structure that isolates the desired subskill for mastery through numerous repetitions. Exhibit 4.3 shows some examples of the partial-skill task practice structure.

At some point, it will be necessary to sequence all of the partial tasks into the *whole skill* performance. Sometimes whole skill practice will occur as the result of several partial skills sequenced together. Other skills, such as bowling delivery, basketball dribbling, golf swing, and swimming, can be practiced only in their entirety. When the whole skill is to be practiced, the teacher can use several kinds of *lead-up* task structures to maximize quality learning trials and to assist students as they attempt skills that have many performance components. A lead-up task emphasizes certain performance aspects when the learner does not engage in complete or full-speed practice trials. These tasks reduce the possibility of error and, at the same time, give the learner many

EXHIBIT 4.3	Examples of the partial-skill task practice structure.
MOVEMENT/SKILL	**PARTS TO BE PRACTICED IN ISOLATION**
Tennis serve	1. Toss
	2. Swing
	3. Follow through (starting at contact point)
Punting	1. Grip
	2. Step with kicking foot
	3. Step with other foot
	4. Drop ball
	5. Kick
	6. Follow through (starting at contact point)
Tumbling routine	1. Tripod
	2. Handstand
	3. Backward roll
	4. Finish

	EXHIBIT 4.4
Examples of lead-up task structures.	

TASK STRUCTURE	EXAMPLES
Slow motion	1. Tennis forehand and backhand drives 2. Dance steps 3. Football plays
Reverse chaining	Golf putting (start at hole and progress to longer putts)
Follow the leader	1. Aerobic dance routines 2. Basketball defensive "slide" drill 3. Obstacle course
Verbal guides	Calling out steps in a dance along with the music
No object	1. Golf swing with no ball 2. Tennis swing with no ball
Modified object or implement	1. Choking up on a tennis racquet 2. Using a "light" volleyball

correct repetitions through controlled practice. Exhibit 4.4 lists some examples of lead-up task structures for physical education.

Each of these task structures will provide students with increasingly successful practice trials as they learn the movement or skill. These lead-up task structures help students acquire the desired pattern quickly and safely, until they are ready to practice unaided in any way. Eventually, the task structure can progress to where students practice the complete task at full speed, with no assistance from the teacher.

Task structure for closed and open skills

A *closed skill* has few or no changing variables while being performed. The performer controls the pacing of the attempt, no one is playing defense, the playing area is constant, and the target does not move or change as the skill is being attempted. Indoor archery and bowling are classic examples of closed skills. The distance to the target is always the same, the target does not move, the performer can control when a shot is made, and the climatic conditions do not change. Task structure for these skills should be designed to create and maintain those unchanging conditions and to give learners many opportunities to repeat the precise movements needed for these tasks. Closed-skill proficiency requires good concentration and strong performance routines, so the task structure should allow students time to develop both under familiar conditions.

Few motor skills are completely closed. Many skills have some stable environmental characteristics, like the closed examples just discussed, but they have a few changing variables as well. In golf putting, the target (hole) is always the same size and does not move, and the player controls when and how the putt is attempted. However, the distance of a putt, the undulations in the putting surface, and weather conditions can make every putt different, causing the player to make small changes in how the skill is executed each time. For lack of a better term, we will call these *relatively closed skills* because they have more variables that are constant than changing. Performers must recognize when conditions have changed and learn how to adjust accordingly. The task structure must allow for a combination of consistency (to acquire the basic movement patterns and routines) and changing conditions (to learn how to apply those skills situationally).

For an *open skill,* many or all of the variables that impact performance can, and do, change as the skill is being executed. Many open skills also involve teammates and/or opponents that increase both the number and complexity of variables that must be considered as the skill is performed. Exhibit 4.5 shows examples of all three kinds of skills: closed, relatively closed, and open.

The task structure for open skills requires several stages of development. Similar to closed skills, the first stage requires the learner to practice the skill in isolation from interfering variables, often with partial-task trials and at a slower speed. The number of task components is gradually increased, along with the speed of the performance. The second stage introduces a limited number of open-task variables, typically through drills that involve opponents, obstacles, or specific performance criteria. The third stage features lead-up games that begin to approach the full number and complexity of performance variables. These might be scrimmages, half-court games, or reduced-numbers games (e.g., six vs. six in soccer). The final stage of the task structure would be practicing and learning these skills as they are performed in the unpredictable situations of a full game or competitive play. These last two stages would feature tasks that help students continue their development through "teaching moments." These are moments recognized by the teacher as opportune times to highlight the kind of decisions and skill execution that characterize open-skill proficiency.

EXHIBIT 4.5 Examples of closed, relatively closed, and open skills in physical education.

CLOSED SKILLS	RELATIVELY CLOSED SKILLS	OPEN SKILLS
Bowling	Golf	Tag games
Archery (fixed target)	Badminton serves	Field hockey
Darts	T-ball striking	Ultimate games
Line dancing	Juggling	Catching ground balls
Basketball free throws		Football pass defense
Gymnastics routines		

Grouping for task practice

Part of the task structure will be defined by how students are grouped to practice the activity. A grouping strategy should be based on the following considerations:

1. Safety
2. Maximum engagement opportunity
3. Objectives for the task
4. Student level of responsibility
5. Instructional model being used
6. Need for students to assist each other
7. Available space and equipment

After considering all those factors, the teacher has many options for grouping students in learning tasks:

- *Individual practice:* Every student has a personal practice space and needed equipment and is allowed to decide when to begin each trial. Students may or may not all be doing the same task.
- *Partner practice:* Students are grouped in pairs for practice. Both students can be practicing the same task together, or one student can be practicing while the other student assists.
- *Small-group practice:* Students are placed in groups of three to six for practice. This is a common grouping strategy for many learning tasks in physical education.
- *Large-group practice:* Students are placed in groups of 7 to 15, with all of them practicing the same task or playing the same game.
- *Whole-class practice:* A few learning tasks in physical education call for a whole-class practice structure, in which all students practice the same task together. This is typically a game structure, but it can also involve whole-class problem solving or initiatives.

As with all other parts of the lesson plan, student grouping should be carefully considered because changing grouping plans in class can decrease a lesson's momentum and cost excessive management time. However, it is possible to make a *progressive* grouping plan by starting students out in individual practice, then moving them into pairs, then small groups, then large groups, and so on, with each new task.

Strategies for Selecting Learning Activities

There are many ways to organize learning activities in physical education, determining how students will be engaged as they attempt to learn the skills, knowledge, and attitudes intended by the teacher. The kinds of student engagement correlate directly with the kinds of learning that can occur from the activity, so teachers must carefully consider all the following: the learning goals of the moment, domain priorities, domain interactions, student readiness, and the specific task structure to be used.

Learning activities when the psychomotor domain is primary

Learning centers. In this type of organization (also called learning stations), students work in small groups and rotate through several designated "centers" arranged around the gym or practice area. Centers can each be designed to focus on a particular skill (e.g., one for kicking, one for throwing, one for batting), or to represent a specific level of difficulty for the same skill (e.g., beginning, intermediate, or advanced basketball ball handling). Intra-task variation (Graham, 2001) allows students several ways to practice several forms of the same skill, all with about the same level of difficulty. To practice the overhand throw, for example, centers could be set up so that students do the following: (1) throw for accuracy, (2) throw for distance, (3) throw to a low target, (4) throw to a high target, (5) throw to a slowly moving target, and (6) throw to a partner.

Drills. It is often helpful to practice skills in a simple, controlled setting that provides the opportunity for numerous repetitions of one or two performance components. This can be accomplished with the use of drills in which students practice individually, in pairs, or in small groups. There are dozens of drills for each kind of activity in physical education. Students typically practice drills for short periods of time, due to their simplicity and the number of repetitions they offer. Teachers may set up several drills as learning centers that students rotate through in class.

Situated drills. It is possible to design drills that go beyond repeating isolated skill trials and take on some aspects of skill and tactical applications in game situations. For example, rather than have two students simply practice catching and throwing a Frisbee between themselves, a third student could enter the drill and try to prevent the thrower from getting off an accurate pass. This will make the thrower think about and react to the defender's position, select among two or three different kinds of passes, and prompt the receiver to move around to get into a spot where the thrower can more easily complete her pass to him. This task structure still allows for many repetitions, as does a regular drill, but the situated drill becomes more *authentic*—closer to the way skills must be applied in actual games.

Lead-up games. A lead-up game contains some of the features of drills and some of the features of a full game. A lead-up game is a simpler version of the full game that focuses on a few performance aspects, with many repetitions. Lead-up games are "bridges" between drills and full, complex versions of games; they allow students to acquire some relevant skills in a simpler version of the game that can later be transferred to the more complex version. Some common lead-up games are Newcomb (for volleyball), pickleball (for tennis and racquetball), Frisbee golf (for ultimate Frisbee), and floor hockey (for field hockey).

Modified games. Games can be modified in many ways that provide students with increased action, more opportunities to use strategy and tactics, and better competition. Instructors can modify the size of the field/court (cross-field soccer), the size/level of the goal or target (basketball with 8-foot goals), the number of players on a side (three vs. three volleyball), or playing rules (no strikeouts in softball).

Scrimmage. A scrimmage is a full version of a game with many anticipated stops in play at "teaching moments" that occur within the game's flow. A scrimmage does not entail keeping score or enforcing certain rules (e.g., eliminations due to fouls, proper player substitutions). It also allows students to replay certain events, so they can have a second look at some situations.

Games. Full games are common task organizations for many sport content units in physical education. To make games positive learning experiences, teachers need to keep the competition as fair as possible and eliminate any negative consequences for the losing player or team.

Role-playing. Many sport activities involve participants other than the players, such as officials, referees, judges, scorekeepers, coaches, and trainers. Students can learn much about a sport by assuming any of these roles. The Sport Education model (Chapter 11) is largely based on student role-playing in organized sport "seasons," during which students learn the knowledge, skills, and responsibilities associated with playing and nonplaying positions, such as coach, referee/official, or statistician.

Videos for self-analysis of key elements. Students can make short videos of themselves performing learning tasks in class and then use a checklist of key performance elements to analyze their skills. This allows them visual feedback on their skills for subsequent attempts.

Cooperative tasks. A growing trend in task organization for physical education involves the use of small student groups in cooperative learning activities. Typically the teacher gives each group a problem to solve or a task to complete and then directs the group to work together toward that goal, with little direction or intervention. For example, the teacher places students into "learning teams" and then directs the teams to come up with as many ways as possible to demonstrate the difference between counter-balance and counter-tension after reading a short definition of each concept. The teacher gives them 10 minutes for this activity; each correct demonstration earns their team one point. The teams must work at two levels: using each member's abilities to the fullest and achieving their given objective. As the name indicates, the Cooperative Learning model (Chapter 10) is based entirely on these kinds of learning tasks.

"Play-teach-play" (Graham, 2001). Sometimes teachers can engage students right away, even before giving them any key elements or a formal task structure. Once the students are engaged, it will become apparent to them and the teacher what information students need to do the task well. In "play-teach-play," students receive little or no task information before practice. As they practice, the teacher notes common mistakes and then stops the class with an attention signal. The teacher comments on those common mistakes and provides a short task presentation to help students improve. A second "play" segment follows, with more monitoring and then another "teach" segment. This task structure has two important benefits: (1) students become active right away, and (2) the task information is highly relevant, since it is directed to already observed mistakes.

Learning activities when the affective domain is primary

Reflection tasks. At times a teacher will want students to be introspective about their participation in physical education—to explore the personal meaning of their experiences. Teachers can foster this type of learning through tasks that direct students to reflect ("think back") on recent events in class. Reflection can occur through both written and oral activities in physical education. Some good reflection tasks include journal writing and "show and tells" to share something of personal meaning with the class.

Values clarification tasks. Similar to some reflection tasks, values clarification tasks focus on helping students determine their personal values in relation to physical activity, classmates, and themselves. Clarifying values does not mean that students learn the teacher's or some other person's values; it means that the teacher uses probing and clarifying questions to allow students to articulate and examine values in a public way. Some examples of learning tasks associated with this process are shown in Exhibit 4.6.

EXHIBIT 4.6   Values clarification tasks and questions.

VALUE TO BE EXAMINED	ASSOCIATED LEARNING TASK OR ACTIVITY	TEACHING STRATEGIES
Sharing	Floor hockey (after game)	1. How did it feel not to have the puck passed to you?
		2. Boys, why did you not pass the puck to the girls?
		3. What happened when your team did pass the puck to everyone?
Trust	Trust games (questions during and after games)	1. Why won't you volunteer for the "trust fall"?
		2. Why won't you let Sharon belay you on the climbing wall?
		3. How does it feel to rely on your classmates for your safety?
Persistence	Individual games	1. What did you do to make that great comeback to beat Mickey?
		2. Have you been practicing outside of class? Why?

Learning activities when the cognitive domain is primary

Critical thinking tasks. *Critical thinking* for physical education has been defined by McBride (1992) as "reflective thinking used to make reasonable and defensible decisions about movement tasks or challenges" (p. 115). Tishman and Perkins (1995) include four areas in the critical thinking process: (1) broad and adventurous thinking, (2) causal and evaluative reasoning, (3) planning and strategic thinking, and (4) a combination of several types of thinking (e.g., facts, opinions, and evaluations). Each of those areas calls for different kinds of learning strategies. Because one's critical thinking ability is related to developmental stages, learning strategies that promote critical thinking must be appropriately considered. Exhibit 4.7 shows some examples of learning strategies to develop critical thinking in physical education.

Checking for understanding. When a teacher has provided a task presentation or a learning cue, she must ascertain if students have understood what was just said or shown. Checking for understanding can be accomplished by asking students key questions based on the information they just saw or heard. The

Critical thinking strategies for physical education.		EXHIBIT 4.7
GRADES	**MOVEMENT SKILL OR CONCEPT**	**LEARNING STRATEGIES FOR CRITICAL THINKING**
Elementary*	1. Throwing	1. Students experiment with different components of the skill and describe how each one impacts performance.
	2. Spatial awareness and locomotor movement	2. Students make a "movement map" on paper with several locomotor movements, explain why each movement is on the map, then travel along the map with those movements.
Middle school**	1. Creative dance	1. Students choreograph a dance using the music and lyrics from a popular dance of their choice. Their dance must include four distinct "phases."
	2. Gymnastics	2. With partners, students link together two or more discrete movements into one graceful sequence.
High school [†]	1. Volleyball	1. Students use a study sheet to learn positioning and strategy.
	2. Fitness/wellness [††]	2a. Students interview each other about current fitness activity patterns.
		2b. Students complete a family health history, personal health history, and physical activity inventory.

* from Cleland & Pearse, 1995

** from Woods & Book, 1995

[†] from Blitzer, 1995

[††] from Greenockle & Purvis, 1995

best way to check for understanding is to ask questions that do not lead students to simple "yes" or "no" answers. Some good checking-for-understanding questions might be:

- Can you tell me two important cues to remember in hitting tennis serves?
- What is the main safety rule in floor hockey?
- What are two ways you can improve static balance?
- When (in the music) do you begin this dance step?

If students know that the teacher will regularly check for their understanding, they will be more likely to pay attention during task presentations and will try to retain information in anticipation of being asked for it.

Written in-class assignments. Teachers can design brief, written assignments for students to complete as they go through a physical education class. These assignments should serve to complement the movement components of class—not to become the major learning activity in physical education. Some examples of in-class assignments for different grade levels are:

Elementary:	Students circle a smiley face on a task sheet after completing each station.
Middle/junior high:	Students list the key elements that made them successful in class that day.
High school:	Students exercise for three minutes and record if they are in or out of their target heart-rate zone.

Homework assignments. Physical education does not have a strong tradition of assigning student homework. While we might think of "PE homework" as out-of-class physical activity, some kinds of assignments can be given to help students learn in the cognitive domain. Teachers might give homework instructions such as these:

- Keep an activity log or journal.
- Watch a ballet on TV, and list all the locomotor skills used by the dancers.
- Ask one of your parents what PE was like for them in school. How is yours different?
- Watch a game on TV, and write an article about it for the morning newspaper.
- Locate and critique PE-related sites online.

Videos for self-analysis of key elements. Students can make short videos of themselves performing learning tasks in class and then use a checklist of key elements to analyze their skills. This develops their ability to observe movement and promote analytical knowledge.

Performance analysis of peers. Students can develop their movement-observation skills and analytical knowledge by observing the performance of their peers in class. Using a checklist of key performance elements, they can observe other students in "live" practice or by reviewing videos, as in the previous self-analysis strategy.

Individual and group projects. Students can learn physical education content by completing outside projects, either individually or in an assigned group. The project might develop skills in locating resources, organizing thoughts, selecting materials, and making a presentation (oral, written, multimedia, and so forth).

Student-designed activities and games. Most often, the teacher determines which learning activities will be practiced, which games will be played, and what game rules will be followed. Yet a teacher can foster students' creativity and cooperation by allowing them to design their own learning tasks, games, and game rules. They can be given the opportunity to explore variations on familiar activities and games and allowed the needed time to experiment with their ideas until they create a new form of activity or game.

Curriculum integration. In recent years there has been a noticeable attempt to combine physical education with other content areas in the school curriculum. Curriculum integration occurs when both areas are developed with equal emphasis and students learn by using knowledge from both areas. When designing and implementing integrated learning activities, teachers must be careful that real integration is occurring—not just *coincidental* learning in two areas. Exhibit 4.8 describes some examples of coincidental and actual curriculum integration.

Strategies for Task Progression

All physical education content units include a series of learning tasks for students to practice or otherwise be engaged in. The teacher will need to make decisions about when to move from one task to the next. Task progression decisions can be based on two factors: mastery and time.

Mastery-based progression. Mastery-based task progression occurs when students must complete the current learning task to a stated criterion before moving on to the next task in the series. Performance criteria are given to students, along with an open-ended time to demonstrate proficiency or "mastery" of each task.

Time-based progression. Most task progression decisions in physical education are based on a teacher's planned time allotment for each learning task. The teacher estimates how much time it will take for the majority of students to learn a task; he then moves to the next task when that time elapses. Some adjustments can be made, but most task progressions are determined by the teacher's planned schedule.

EXHIBIT 4.8	Coincidental and actual curriculum integration with physical education.		
INTEGRATED AREAS	LEARNING CONTENT OR ACTIVITY	COINCIDENTAL INTEGRATION	ACTUAL INTEGRATION
Physical education and social studies	International dance	Point out that the dance is from Spain	1. Inform students of the dance's origin 2. Explain the meaning of the dance to the Spanish people 3. Explain when and why (significance) it is danced 4. Use authentic music (with Spanish lyrics) 5. Students translate words/calls from Spanish (from Spanish/English dictionary, or by a Spanish-speaking student) 6. Students look up the dance online
Physical education and math	Finding target heart rate (THR)	Use software to determine one's THR zone	1. Explain the major components of THR 2. Students enter their own values and perform the math operations to get THR 3. Students exercise and calculate HR every 10 minutes

Both types of task progression schemes have strengths and weaknesses. Mastery-based progressions ensure that students have demonstrated a readiness before moving to more difficult and complex tasks in a series, but it is not always possible that all students can master a task in a reasonable amount of time, if ever. Time-based progressions are efficient and orderly, due to their predictability, but if a group of students falls behind the rest of the class on early tasks, those same students will likely get further behind as the unit moves along.

Strategies for Maximizing Student Safety in Physical Education

One of the main functions of teaching in physical education entails planning and maintaining a safe learning environment for students. The most obvious reason for this is to prevent students from getting injured; that almost goes without saying. In addition, if students are aware of any existing safety problems, they are likely to choose not to participate fully or refuse to participate at all. So students must not only have a safe environment, they must *feel safe* as well. Instructors can use a few preventive strategies to improve and maintain safety in physical education.

Develop and post gym safety rules. Students need to know that the gymnasium is no different from any other classroom in the school and that some basic safety rules apply in that setting. Most gym rules will involve ways to move in relation to others in that space, proper use of equipment, and identification of potentially unsafe areas or situations. Teachers need to communicate all safety rules to students early in the school year and post those rules in a visible part of the gym.

Review rules. As the school year progresses, it is likely that some students will forget safety rules, especially if a rule has not been violated for a long time. It is often helpful just to remind students of safety rules from time to time, even when no infractions have occurred. This keeps safety as a regular part of your class routine and can reduce some types of accidents that happen when students simply forget.

Establish contingency management. Behavior modification techniques can be put in place that systematically reward students for safe behavior in the gym or punish them for being unsafe according to your posted rules. As discussed earlier in this chapter, this is called contingency management because there is a known relationship between student behavior and its consequences; students are either rewarded or punished, depending on how they follow the teacher's safety rules.

Use a student buddy system. Accidents in physical education can sometimes occur when a student gets caught up in the excitement of the moment and does not pay attention to potential hazards in the gym—even those the teacher has pointed out and reviewed. If students are in pairs or small groups, the teacher could ask members of the group to watch out for their "buddies" as they practice and warn them of any safety problems (e.g., balls rolling into the practice space, other students inadvertently coming into the area).

Watch students. One of the easiest and best strategies is for the teacher to simply monitor students when a new practice task or game begins. The teacher should pay attention to proper spacing among students, check for the correct use of equipment, and examine the potential for groups to interfere with each other. If a practice task gets off to a safe start, it will be more likely to stay that way.

Strategies for Lesson Review and Closure

In nearly all instructional models, a well-planned physical education class will end with a brief review of the lesson and a defined closure. The purpose of this segment is to bring the lesson to "full cycle" by tying together set induction, task presentation, instructional activities, and observed student learning. It can also be used to preview the next lesson in the unit. Good lesson review and closure includes the elements featured below.

Quick transition to closure. Since time is short, it is essential that the teacher get students out of the last learning activity and into closure quickly. A quick transition allows adequate time for that purpose and avoids doing it hurriedly or "on the run" to the exit door or locker room. A key decision at this juncture is whether the teacher should bring the students back to one group or conduct the review with students dispersed around the gym. If there is enough time, bring the students into one group in a convenient place. That decision can be based on the amount of time left and the need to put equipment away. If time is short and equipment must be put up, conduct the review with students remaining in place, and ask them to put up the equipment after the closure is complete.

Review of class organization and structure. The teacher should ask students general questions like, "Who can tell me what kinds of things we did in class today?" or "Was there anything special about the way we did those things today?" or "From now on, that's the way we will enter the gym and line up. Can you remember that until next class?" This allows students to realize that the class had a definite organization and plan and that they should remember that plan in the future.

Review of learning cues. During the course of the lesson, students can often forget the learning cues and key elements covered in the task presentation segment. This is a good time to get them to review those cues or to ask them analytical questions like, "Which of the cues were the most important ones to remember while you practiced?" It is important to make this review interactive by asking students questions rather than just telling them the cues once again.

Review of student conduct, rules, and safety procedures. Be sure to compliment students when they were well behaved and followed the rules.

Informal assessment of learning. One of the best uses of this segment is to assess informally what students learned in the lesson. This can be accomplished with a few brief questions like, "How many of you were able to . . ." or "How many completed their goal at every station?" or "If you know all three cues we learned today, please raise your hand."

Preview of next lesson. The last part of the closure should give students a preview of their next lesson to spark their interest and let them know what they can expect next time in physical education.

Dismissal. The class should end just as it began, in an orderly fashion. The teacher can give a verbal signal to students that class is over and that they should walk to the locker room or to the exit door.

That is a lot to do within a lesson segment that should last no more than three minutes! However, most parts of the review/closure last only a few seconds. The greatest amount of time should be given to the review of actual lesson content so that students leave the gym with an understanding of what and how they learned in physical education.

SUMMARY

Teaching strategies work as a bridge between a teacher's declarative and procedural knowledge. The general declarative knowledge becomes a bit more focused when it is applied to planning managerial and instructional strategies in physical education. Each instructional model will call for a unique set of strategies that gives it a large part of its identity because these strategies determine "how things will look" for the teacher and students in that unit. With its many content areas and student developmental levels, the number of teaching strategies needed for physical education is very large. However, in a model-based approach, each model will call for a specific set of strategies, so a teacher will need to use far fewer strategies with any given model. The actual implementation of teaching strategies—the conditional knowledge link in this chain—occurs through the use of effective teaching skills, featured in the next chapter.

LEARNING ACTIVITIES

1. If you are not now teaching, select a content area and grade level that you are likely to teach in the future; make a list of the preventive and interactive managerial strategies that you would use in that unit. If you are presently teaching, make a list of the preventive and interactive managerial strategies you use in your teaching; mention why you use each one, and explain how effective it is for your intended purpose.

2. Make a list of every way you can think of to get students into random groups for physical education. (No fair using the examples given in this chapter!)

3. Make a task presentation to a group of students—either actual students or your peers/colleagues—that satisfies all the elements of a set induction, listed on page 86. Ask them to rate you on each element.

4. Now make that same task presentation by using someone other than yourself as the model.

5. Select a content unit and a grade level. Now identify your primary learning domain. Then list and explain at least five learning activities that could be used to promote student achievement in that domain. Finally, select another primary domain and make another list of five activities for that domain.

TOPICS FOR REFLECTION & SMALL-GROUP DISCUSSION

1. What is the difference between an instructional strategy and an effective teaching skill?

2. Why do you think physical education teachers need to know so many different strategies?

3. What is the most important reason for using a particular instructional strategy at a given time?

4. What is the relationship between an instructional strategy and student learning preference? That is, why do some students like certain kinds of strategies but not others?

5. What is the relationship between an instructional strategy and a teacher's intended learning outcomes for students?

SUGGESTED READING

Lavay, B. W., French, R., & Henderson, H. L. (2001). *Positive behavior management for physical education* (2nd ed.). Champaign, IL: Human Kinetics.

EFFECTIVE TEACHING SKILLS FOR MODEL-BASED INSTRUCTION

Discrete teaching skills are defined here as individual, situation-specific teacher and/or student behaviors carried out before and during class. Forming the next tier of building blocks for instructional models, discrete teaching skills determine the moment-to-moment decisions and actions that teachers and students carry out within instructional strategies. Many discrete teaching skills can be applied generally within all strategies and models. However, each strategy and model will call for certain skills to be used more often than others. Every teacher possesses a *repertoire* of such skills, which are then implemented at key times within instructional strategies to facilitate the functioning of each model. Teaching skills can be decisions and actions either carried out solely by the teacher or used by the teacher to promote desired student behaviors in class. These skills represent conditional knowledge that is applied in specific situations within the teaching strategies presented in Chapter 4.

While teachers and students do many things in a physical education class, not all of these actions fall under the definition of a *teaching skill,* which is characterized by intentional decisions and actions carried out before and during class. These decisions and actions become *effective teaching skills* when they contribute to the achievement of stated learning goals in a lesson or unit of instruction. Research on teaching has identified many teacher and student behaviors that correlate strongly with increased levels of student achievement. Most of this research has been carried out in subjects like math, science, and reading, but there is a similar body of evidence from the study of physical education instruction (Silverman & Ennis, 2003).

A *correlation* means that a relationship exists between two variables, so that when one of those variables changes, we can make good predictions about what will happen to the other variable. Effective teaching skills are those teacher decisions and actions that correlate with higher levels of student learning. By doing certain things and getting students to do certain things, teachers increase the possibility of student learning. Those "certain things" are labeled effective teaching skills.

Effective teaching skills begin with *declarative knowledge,* when teachers become aware of things they can do to increase the likelihood that students will achieve the lesson or unit goals. *Procedural knowledge* helps the teacher know how to successfully carry out each effective teaching skill when it is called for. But perhaps the most important type of knowledge for effective teaching skills is *conditional knowledge*—knowing exactly when and why each decision and/or action is needed. It is essential that teachers know how to do "the right thing, in the right way, at the right time, and for the right reason(s)."

The many effective discrete teaching skills used by physical education teachers before and during class can be grouped into seven areas of related decisions and actions: (1) planning for instruction, (2) time and class management, (3) task presentation and task structure, (4) communication, (5) instructional information, (6) use of questions, and (7) lesson review and closure. Refer to Exhibit 5.1 to see how these effective teaching skills for model-based instruction in physical education are built upon both knowledge areas, featured in Chapter 3, and instructional strategies, presented in Chapter 4.

AREA 1: PLANNING FOR INSTRUCTION

I t can be said that a teacher determines the effectiveness of any lesson before it even begins by how well she plans for it. Good planning facilitates the flow of the lesson and leads to a more efficient use of time and other instructional resources. This, in turn, leads to higher levels of student learning in the lesson and content unit.

Effective teaching does not happen by accident. Teachers who are better prepared before class use class time and other resources more efficiently, increase appropriate student engagement, and promote higher levels of student learning (Clark, 1983; Stroot & Morton, 1989). Novice and expert teachers may differ in the amount of written planning they will need to be ready for a lesson (Housner & Griffey, 1985; Graham, Holt/Hale, & Parker, 2009). But

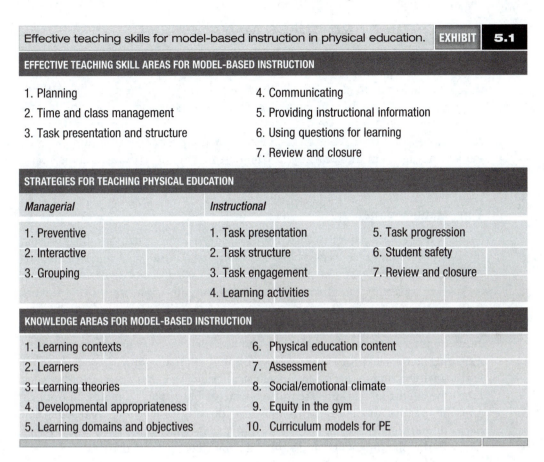

Effective teaching skills for model-based instruction in physical education.   **EXHIBIT   5.1**

EFFECTIVE TEACHING SKILL AREAS FOR MODEL-BASED INSTRUCTION

1. Planning
2. Time and class management
3. Task presentation and structure
4. Communicating
5. Providing instructional information
6. Using questions for learning
7. Review and closure

STRATEGIES FOR TEACHING PHYSICAL EDUCATION

Managerial	*Instructional*	
1. Preventive	1. Task presentation	5. Task progression
2. Interactive	2. Task structure	6. Student safety
3. Grouping	3. Task engagement	7. Review and closure
	4. Learning activities	

KNOWLEDGE AREAS FOR MODEL-BASED INSTRUCTION

1. Learning contexts	6. Physical education content
2. Learners	7. Assessment
3. Learning theories	8. Social/emotional climate
4. Developmental appropriateness	9. Equity in the gym
5. Learning domains and objectives	10. Curriculum models for PE

written preparation is not really the most critical factor. It is more important that the teacher be *sufficiently prepared* when the lesson begins, regardless of whether the lesson plan is detailed on paper, on a smartphone, or kept "in one's head" from past experience. Once the instructional model has been selected, unit and lesson planning should contain:

1. Learning goals for the unit and each lesson
2. An overall managerial plan
3. Task presentation and learning cues
4. Needed equipment and facilities
5. A list of learning activities and a content-development plan
6. A floor/space plan for activities
7. An estimated "time budget" and transitions between class segments
8. Safety plans
9. Learning-assessment procedures
10. Lesson review and closure plans

These components of a lesson plan for physical education will be discussed further in Chapter 6.

AREA 2: TIME AND CLASS MANAGEMENT

P erhaps the most consistent findings from research on teaching physical education show that there is a strong relationship between how students spend time in PE class and how much they achieve (Metzler, 1989). Early descriptive research indicated that students in physical education classes were more likely to be listening or waiting than actively engaged in learning tasks. Process-product research then established a positive correlation between student engagement and learning, meaning that the more time students spend in appropriate tasks, the more they are likely to achieve (Rink, 2003).

Time Management

Time management refers to a teacher's ability to maximize one of the most important learning resources available to him—the number of minutes allocated for each lesson. A lesson will consist of several segments or blocks of time, each given to certain operations: management/organization, transition (moving students between segments), task presentation, learning activities, and closure/review. Since it is not possible to extend class beyond its scheduled length, extra minutes used in one segment must be taken away from other segments, including active learning time. Some amount of management, organization, and transition time is necessary in physical education, but teachers who keep that time as low as possible are more effective. They thereby maintain optimal amounts of time in the segments that lead directly to learning. A teacher can perform many actions to maximize available class time; some of these decisions occur in the planning stage and others during the course of the lesson.

Set out equipment before class. Instructional time can be lost when the teacher must arrange equipment and materials during a class. This decrease in instructional time comes not only from the actual arranging process but also from lost momentum as students wait for the next activity to be organized (Siedentop & Tannehill, 2000). When safe and possible, the teaching area should be organized before students arrive for class. If that is not possible, the teacher can have equipment and materials near the spot where they will be set up and ask students to assist when it is time to arrange equipment for use.

Use an alternative roll call method. The traditional method of taking attendance by calling out each student's name wastes time and gets class off to a "sitting start"—not a good way to begin physical education class. If roll must be taken before class can begin, it should be completed in the most efficient method possible, such as having squad captains identify absent students or using a sign-in sheet posted in the gym. If attendance can wait for a few minutes, the teacher can take roll while students warm up or perform their "instant activity" before the main lesson begins.

Use attention and start/stop signals. Physical education teachers often hold class in large, open spaces and noisy gymnasiums with many students. It can sometimes be difficult to get students' attention and to let them know it is OK to proceed. An attention signal gets students to stop what they are doing at the moment, put down their equipment, be silent, and pay attention to the teacher. These signals help the teacher maintain a safe and orderly class and bring activity to a quick stop. Signals can be audible ("3, 2, 1, stop"; a whistle; a shout), be silent (a raised hand, a finger over the mouth, waved arms), or involve a combination of both.

Start signals ensure that activity starts correctly and safely for all students at the same time. These signals indicate that the teacher is satisfied that "all is ready," and they provide students with a cue that activity can begin. The teacher can tell students, "When I say 'go,' you may begin to practice." After seeing that all is quiet and ready, the teacher then says "Go" to start the segment. Instructors may also use nonverbal start signals, such as a hand clap or a "starter's motion." Stop signals are used to get students to end an activity quickly and in an orderly fashion. Start and stop signals should remain consistent so that students always know what they need to do.

Practice and review classroom management routines. At times, it will be useful to ask students to practice and review classroom management routines such as getting in lines, finding self-space, and putting equipment away properly. Young children in particular can benefit from several rehearsals of management directions so that they will be more likely to remember them when needed and complete the routine more efficiently. This practice does take some time in the beginning, but those minutes can be made up when the routines are completed quickly and correctly in the future.

Teachers may find it helpful to review a managerial routine when it has not been used for a while. First, remind students or ask them to recall the correct procedure before the start signal is given. Once again, although this process will take a few minutes, that time will be saved when students complete the routine quickly and correctly in the future.

Post class rules in public. A good way to teach students class rules, and to let students review them, is to post the rules in a public place, such as the locker room or entry into the gymnasium. Rather than reading or presenting rules to the class, the teacher can save time by assigning students to read them on their own.

Post and use an "instant activity" to start class. Too many physical education classes begin with students remaining inactive while the teacher takes roll or waits for the entire class to get to the gym. That early inactivity can set the tone for the rest of the lesson, and it can lead to excessive time spent in management as the teacher tries to overcome that initial inertia. In most cases, the students are inactive because they simply don't have anything to do when they enter the gym. Instead, an *instant activity* can be planned to get the lesson off to an energetic, movement-based start. The activity should last only about three to five minutes or until all students are present. It can be a general warm-up activity or one that will lead into the main part of the lesson content. The instant activity can be posted in the locker room or near the entry to the gym so that students can read it as they arrive and can begin to participate immediately. Rauschenbach and Vanoer (1998) mention eight characteristics of instant activities:

1. Require little setup
2. Take just five minutes to complete
3. Are easy to learn
4. Can begin with little help from the teacher
5. Get students moving quickly
6. Are large-muscle activities
7. Are designed for maximum success
8. Are modifiable for different ability levels (p. 7)

Some examples of instant activities include:

- throwing and catching a ball
- jogging or walking laps to music
- stretching
- non-elimination tag games
- mini games (one on one, two on two, and the like)
- cooperative games
- practicing with equipment to be used later in class

Class Management

Class management has a broader scope than time management, and its contribution to effective teaching is just as important. It refers to the decisions and teaching skills that provide an underlying structure to facilitate student learning and to establish a positive environment for the teacher and students. A good classroom manager can be likened to an orchestra conductor who must coordinate many musicians with the written music in order to achieve the desired harmony—although in the teacher's case, some conditional factors cannot be predicted before the class begins! Regardless, there are many discrete teaching skills that contribute to classroom management and good harmony.

Establishing the learning environment

Students need to understand that class time in physical education is *learning time* and that the gymnasium or other physical education settings are *places for learning*—just like all other classrooms in the school. It is the teacher's responsibility to establish the learning environment by making students aware of particular expectations, rules, conduct, and routines that apply in physical education. Effective teachers take extra time and effort to establish the learning environment in the first two weeks of school and then maintain that environment throughout the school year. Since the learning environment is typically complex, the teacher will have to establish it in several ways:

1. Have and enforce class rules about student safety, conduct, and responsibility.
2. Use a set induction (see Chapter 4) to set the stage for each lesson.
3. Establish physical boundaries within which students must practice.
4. Use and enforce attention and start/stop signals.
5. Instruct students to practice listening skills.
6. Set rules for the care and use of equipment.
7. Have and use a plan for student discipline.
8. Be sure not to talk until *all* students are quiet and ready to listen.

Manage facilities and equipment

Teaching most physical education content requires the use of much equipment and large instructional spaces. Effective teachers must plan ahead and during classes to maximize equipment use by facilitating the distribution of equipment and the allocation of space, thereby increasing student engagement time and safety. Exhibit 5.2 presents several considerations for the management of space and equipment.

Managing facilities and equipment.	EXHIBIT	5.2

FACILITIES:

- Allocate activity space for safe participation.
- Check the teaching area for safety hazards.
- Remind students of "out of bounds" areas.
- Make students aware of temporary hazards (e.g., wet grass, water on floor).
- Determine the number and location of learning centers and how many students can use each center at one time.

EQUIPMENT:

- Check condition, repair, and safety of equipment.
- Ensure that equipment is sized correctly for student safety and developmental readiness.
- Check for the needed number of objects and implements for planned learning tasks.
- Color-code and match equipment when possible.
- Teach and remind students of safety rules.
- Use modified/adapted equipment when called for.
- Have enough equipment to reduce or avoid student waiting.

Monitor during learning activities

When the task presentation is complete and students are actively participating, it is important for the teacher to observe, or monitor, students. Ideally, the teacher would give the students a few minutes to organize themselves in the activity and get going. While all the students are active, the teacher should monitor to make sure that they are participating safely and according to the intended task structure.

Even the best-made plans do not guarantee that classes will run smoothly and that students will always behave appropriately during managerial and learning tasks. Teachers must constantly monitor students to make sure they are doing what is expected of them in class. Some of the following discrete teaching skills can be used for effective monitoring during class.

Circulating while monitoring. Physical education teachers usually have many students spread out in large activity areas. It is not convenient to interact with students across the gym or field, so the teacher should be prepared to monitor by circulating around the area while students practice. This allows the teacher to more easily observe student practice and to quietly interact with one or a few students when needed.

"Back to the wall." If a teacher monitors only from the middle of the gym or field (even while circulating), it is likely that many students will remain out of sight behind the teacher's back. When the situation allows, the teacher should circulate and monitor with her "back to the wall" as she moves around the activity area, thereby keeping all students in front of her and in sight (Graham, 2001).

Proximity control. Given the number of students in a physical education class and the typically large activity area, some students will choose to take advantage of the momentary distance between themselves and the teacher and become off-task. Many times it is possible to get a student back on task simply by moving closer to him, to let him know the teacher is paying attention. At other times it might be necessary to move the student to where the teacher is standing so he will be under direct supervision. Called *proximity control,* both methods can be very effective in getting a student back on task without having to single him out or stop class to discipline him.

"With-it-ness." Jacob Kounin (1970) developed a description of an educational monitoring skill that can be quite useful for physical education teachers. The idea of *with-it-ness* means that a teacher can discern class events by keenly listening rather than actually seeing them happen. We have all heard of the teacher who has eyes "in the back of her head" and seems to be aware of everything that goes on in the classroom or gym—even when students think she is not paying attention. That teacher is said to have good with-it-ness and is able to monitor class events while doing other things at the same time. With-it-ness requires that the teacher know the typical patterns and sounds of events in the gym, so she will be aware when something is just not right.

AREA 3: TASK PRESENTATION AND TASK STRUCTURE

One of the main functions of teaching is to provide students with information about learning activities they will engage in during class. For many types of learning in physical education, it is essential that students become familiar with the skill or learning task, what the desired performance standard looks like (how well to do it), and how they will participate in the learning activity. The *task presentation* addresses the first two types of information by showing or telling students what the next skill or task will be and how to perform it correctly. Information about how the learning task will be managed determines the *task structure* for the upcoming activity. The discussions of task presentation and task structure will be separated for clarity, but often a teacher will include both in a single episode. That is, the teacher's demonstration of the skill and its key performance elements occurs within a simulation of the task structure for the upcoming activity. Task presentation and task structure represent both strategy and teaching skills in physical education. The strategic part, discussed in Chapter 4, is determined by how each one is designed and organized. The skill part depends on how the teacher communicates and interacts with students to facilitate each selected presentation and structure.

Task Presentation

Teachers plan for a variety of learning tasks in physical education. A *learning task* is the specific activity that students will engage in to acquire a motor skill, cognitive knowledge or concept, or affective outcome. Most learning tasks in physical education are activity-based, so students must understand what the task entails and how it should be performed correctly before they can attempt the task. As discussed in Chapter 4, the process of providing that information to students is called task presentation (Rink, 2009). In a task presentation, the teacher will furnish students with learning cues—specific pieces of information about how to perform key elements of the task correctly. A full and complete task presentation requires the use of all the effective teaching skills described below.

Get and keep student attention. Even the best-planned task presentation will not be effective if students are not paying attention when the teacher gives the information. The presentation should be conducted in a location that is comfortable for students and that has the fewest possible distractions. Attention signals can help get students ready to listen and watch. Students should be organized around the teacher so that all of them can see and hear easily. The teacher can do some things to keep student attention once he has it:

- Ask questions often.
- Check for understanding during and after each task presentation.
- Make frequent eye contact with students.
- Avoid repeating information too often.

- Use proximity control by moving nearer to students who are not paying attention.
- Make the task presentation interesting and "snappy."

Present information clearly to students. Most task presentation information is given to students verbally and visually. Effective communications include a well-paced, orderly flow of information to students, so it is important that the teacher carefully plan this part of class. When speaking, the teacher should check that all students are paying attention and able to hear all that is said without her having to raise her voice to strenuous levels. When presenting visual information—usually modeled examples of how to perform skills—the teacher should display the model from the best viewing angle to give all students a good line of sight.

Provide a full and correct model. When demonstrating tasks that involve implements and/or objects, the teacher should provide students with a full example of the skill or task, using the correct form and desired result. It is not a good idea to model the skill/task with an imaginary implement or object or by saying something like, "You get the picture, even though I did not have a bat in my hand when I showed you."

Provide verbal and visual information together. Students always benefit when they get information in two modalities, typically verbal and visual. A powerful connection occurs when a student can see and hear information at the same time. In addition, the teacher should accurately give both kinds of information and alert students that what is being said goes with what is being modeled. Therefore it is more effective to *overlay* the modeled information with the verbal information (i.e., deliver both at once) and not separate them (i.e., tell them, then show them).

Use an active task presentation when possible. An active task presentation occurs when the students hear and see the key elements of the task while performing those elements at the same time. This allows students to see, hear, and move in "real time" so that they employ all three sensory modalities at once. For instance, if the teacher is showing students the key elements of the golf grip, the students could have a club in their hands and follow along as the teacher says, "This is the overlapping grip. Put your right hand at the bottom of the club's grip, and move your left hand just on top of your right. Then, tuck your left thumb into your right hand—like this. Now show me what your grip looks like, and I will come around to check." When students have successfully completed that part of the task, the teacher resumes the rest of the instructions on the grip, again by having the students follow along on each key element.

It is not always possible to use an active task presentation—sometimes because it is not safe and sometimes because the performance of the skill needs too much room. However, when possible to use, active task presentations effectively give students task information and allow the teacher to check directly whether students have comprehended before dispersing for practice. It is also helpful to give a visual demonstration in slow motion the first few times, while matching the verbal cues with the physical movements. Pairing each verbal cue with its movement counterpart allows students to comprehend better. As student comprehension increases, so too can the speed of the demonstration.

Use a vocabulary that students understand. The physical education teacher will have a greater understanding of the skill/task and a more advanced technical vocabulary than students, especially younger or novice students. It is not sufficient that a teacher understand what he is telling students; the task presentation must be communicated with words and terms at the students' comprehension level. Sometimes the teacher must translate complex terms and concepts into words that are simpler and more familiar to students. Some examples would be using the word "speed" instead of "velocity" or a descriptor like "snap your wrist" (on the tennis serve follow-through) rather than "hard pronation."

Determine the best model for the presentation. Because the teacher has the skill and experience to provide an accurate and time-efficient demonstration, she is most often the one to show or model skill performances in task presentations. However, a teacher will typically demonstrate a more mature version of the performance than most students are capable of understanding, much less duplicating. When feasible, a teacher can ask one student in the class to serve as the model, to demonstrate a more age-appropriate example for the other students to follow.

There are other ways to provide students with models during task presentations. Teachers can use videos, CDs, DVDs, books, drawings, and photographs to give students the needed information about a skill and how to perform it. Perhaps the greatest advantage of these media is that students can use them independently from the teacher, whenever each student is ready to get that information. Students rely less on the teacher as the only source of skill information, allowing for more options in delivering task presentations.

Provide appropriate and accurate information. Regardless of how the teacher delivers the task presentation, it is essential that students get appropriate and accurate information about the upcoming task. The *appropriateness* of task information can refer to the *amount* of information given to students at one time. If students receive too little information, they cannot achieve to their fullest potential. If students receive too much information or too many cues at once, they are likely to be confused and overwhelmed. Appropriateness can also refer to *how much of the task/skill* students get in one presentation. Some skills can be acquired better when people learn component parts one at a time; other skills are acquired best when the learner practices the entire sequence of movements in one series. Whether to use part- or whole-task learning will depend on the specific task, the students' readiness, and the teacher's expertise with that task.

The *accuracy* of task presentation information refers to how *correct* it is relative to some standard for performance. Proper technique is essential for many skills in physical education. Teachers must not only know the proper technique for the skill being explained but also be able to communicate that information correctly to students. Teachers should remember that most students they instruct are novices and will follow any cues given to them—correct or incorrect. So it is important that teachers provide accurate cues at all times so that the worst-case scenario of teaching does not occur—students practicing and learning the *wrong* techniques well!

Task Structure

Task presentation refers to what will be learned or practiced; *task structure* tells students how the practice segment will be organized. As used in this book, task structure includes three components from what Jones (1992) called a task system (task presentation and task structure combined): (1) a set of operations or procedures used to pursue the learning task, (2) resources and conditions available to accomplish the task, and (3) a means of accountability that indicates the importance or significance of the task (p. 412). Operations include the location and organization of the learning environment and directions for safe participation. Resources and conditions include equipment and the number of minutes allocated for the task. Accountability includes expectations for student behavior, a proficiency goal, or an explanation of how the task relates to subsequent learning activities in the lesson or unit. According to Jones, when students become engaged in a learning task they can respond in one of five ways:

1. Pursue the stated task with success.
2. Pursue the stated task with little or no success.
3. Self-modify the task to make it more difficult and challenging.
4. Self-modify the task to make it easier.
5. Become off-task. (p. 418)

You will note that only the first of these five ways of engaging indicates student achievement of the learning task. This underscores how important it is that the teacher plan the structure and supervise the students to actively engage them in interesting tasks at a moderate to high success rate. Otherwise, students might choose to engage in ways that reduce their opportunity to learn and increase inappropriate behavior in class. Teachers should be sure to include in each task structure some important elements described below.

Explanation of the task's duration. If students do not know how long each task will last, they cannot properly pace themselves to complete it within the allocated time. Some students might hurry to finish the task and then have to wait several minutes for the next task to begin. This leads to boredom. Other students might be too deliberate at the start of the segment and then run out of time at the end. This leads to anxiety and frustration. For each task, students should know the exact time allotted ("Practice your shooting for 15 minutes") or at least an estimated time ("Practice for about 10 minutes, and I will give you a 2-minute warning before we stop").

Explanation of performance criteria. Performance criteria can provide students with information about how well they should complete a given task and also help them make performance evaluations while they are practicing the task. Performance criteria can also be used to help students know when they have completed a task to a desired standard ("Do this until you can make 7 out of 10") or to signal the end of one task and student readiness for the next ("When you can complete five sets in a row, raise your hand, and we'll move on to something else"). Criteria can be established from several metrics: time, distance, accuracy, height, weight, form, consistency, percent correct or completed, average score, or ability to beat one's previous "personal best" performance (see Exhibit 5.3). Whatever metric is used, the

Metrics for determining task performance criteria.		EXHIBIT	5.3

PERFORMANCE CRITERION METRIC	EXAMPLES
Time	1. Complete an obstacle course in under 3 minutes. 2. Juggle three balls for at least 15 seconds. 3. Dribble a soccer ball through eight cones in less than 30 seconds.
Distance	1. Throw a softball 50 feet. 2. Run three laps around the track. 3. Hit the ball to the outfield.
Accuracy	1. Hit the smallest target. 2. Kick the soccer ball into the left side of the goal. 3. Throw to your partner so she does not have to move to catch the ball. 4. Make legal serves (tennis, badminton, pickleball).
Height	1. Jump over the lowest bar. 2. Toss the ball 3 feet over your head and catch it. 3. Walk at a low level.
Weight	1. Lift 25 pounds with a bench press. 2. Use the heaviest ball.
Form	1. Use the correct technique. 2. Balance on two body parts. 3. "Do it just the way I showed you."
Consistency	1. Complete 25 rope jumps in a row. 2. Get five serves in the target in a row before you move back.
Percent completed	1. Score higher than 75 percent on the test. 2. Get 60 percent of your first serves in play.
Average score	1. Try it four times. Your average score should be 8 or better. 2. A good bowling average is around 75 for middle schoolers.
Personal best	1. Try it once, then try it again. Try to beat your first score the second time. 2. Look in your fitness log for your best time. Try to beat that today.

teacher should state the metric and the standard for performance as part of the task structure.

Designation of task space configuration. Every learning task will take place in a designated location in the gym, on a field, or in some other area. Sometimes the entire class will be using one location (as in a game situation), a few locations (grouped practice), or multiple locations (station teaching). Students will need to know the exact space plan for the upcoming task and how each space has been set up for that task. Advanced learners will need very little such information, but novices and young children must get explicit directions and even be shown how each learning area is set up. It is sometimes a good idea to draw up a floor/field space "map" as part of the lesson plan; this picture can help a teacher organize the space more efficiently and safely.

Expectations for student conduct and responsibility. Students are rarely passive participants in learning tasks. Except in the most direct teaching strategies, students will have some degree of choice and responsibility for their behavior. Sometimes their responsibility is to other students, as spotters, partners, team members, or assistants (e.g., tossing and retrieving balls, playing defense in an offensive drill). The task structure should communicate to students what is expected of them during each task regarding proper engagement, safety, waiting time, team/group participation, or assisting other students.

Explanation of intra-task variations. Many times a teacher will plan several versions of a learning task, typically set up as different centers. This intra-task variation (Graham, 2001) is designed to give students different ways to practice the same or related skills. For instance, five centers could be set up for kicking practice, with each one using a different kind of ball to be kicked or requiring a slightly different kicking technique—all at about the same level of difficulty. As part of the task structure, the teacher should inform students of the different organization, criteria, and safety points for each center. Instructors must not assume that students, especially young ones or novices, will be able to detect the differences as they move from center to center.

Explanation of options to change task or its difficulty. Graham, Holt/Hale, and Parker (2009) use a technique called *teaching by invitation,* in which multiple centers or tasks allow students to practice the same skill with varying degrees of difficulty. The teacher explains the key elements for each center/task in the task presentation and then permits ("invites") students to pick which level of difficulty they wish to attempt. Task structure information helps students determine the requirements for each center/task, select where they will begin, and know if the level of difficulty is inappropriate for them. Some restrictions might need to be made on the number of students who can work at one center or task, again communicated as part of the task structure.

Use of attention, start, and stop signals. An important part of the task structure is to inform students when they can begin and what signal will indicate when to stop and pay attention. Any familiar signal will work, but it is a good idea to remind students of it during the task structure briefing. See the discussion earlier in this chapter for some examples of signals.

Check for understanding. Just as a teacher should check for understanding of the task presentation content, she should also check for understanding of the task structure before students disperse for practice. Some simple questions can be used, such as these examples: "When I say 'go,' where will squad 1 line up?" "How long will we be practicing this task?" "What should you do when I give the 'stop' signal?" "How can you tell when you are in a safe area of the gym?" or "What should you do when you have finished?"

Monitor task structure and engagement. The teacher should also monitor task structure early and regularly. Once students are dispersed for practice, the teacher should take a moment to check that students are engaged according to the directions just given. Immediate and appropriate engagement are indicators of good task structure information. Delayed or incorrect task engagement can mean that some students did not understand the task structure, and it should alert the teacher to stop the class and make things clear to students before more time is lost. The teacher should also monitor for appropriate task engagement periodically during the activity segment, making adjustments as needed.

AREA 4: COMMUNICATION

Effective teachers communicate in ways that allow students to understand instructional information and questions well, using the least amount of class time possible. There are many aspects to effective class communications.

Get students' attention. Communication will not be effective if the listeners are not ready to receive it. Physical education teachers can increase students' attention by using an attention signal, getting students in close proximity, getting them quiet, and eliminating distractions—all before beginning to speak.

Be clear. Information must be presented in a manner that all students can comprehend. The teacher should face the students directly, be articulate, and speak at a rate that students can follow.

Use an appropriate vocabulary level. The words and terms of a teacher's speech should be at the appropriate vocabulary level for students. This means that the teacher will need to use different words for different grade levels, even for the same task or content. There is one precaution to keep in mind—just because *the teacher* understands what is said does not mean that students understand it!

Use voice inflections. Students will pay less attention to verbal information given in a monotone delivery. Teachers should use voice inflections to keep students alert and to help them discern the most important pieces of information they receive.

Check for understanding. As mentioned previously, it is important for the teacher to know that students have heard and understood verbal information before letting them follow those directions or engage in the learning task. If, when monitoring an activity, the teacher realizes that students did not understand, additional time must be taken to stop class, get the students' attention again, and repeat the directions. This process wastes time and breaks the flow of the lesson—and it can be annoying to the teacher. Teachers should develop the habit of checking for understanding every time students receive information.

AREA 5: PROVIDING INSTRUCTIONAL INFORMATION

Most of the information that teachers provide to students serves the purpose of enhancing learning. Such information can be provided before, during, and after learning activities. *Cues* are pieces of information communicated before practice and intended to facilitate the upcoming learning trials. *Guides* are given to students during a practice trial. Performance *feedback* is provided to students after the trial is completed and pertains directly to the attempted trial.

Cues

During task presentations, teachers provide students with many "bits" of learning information called *cues*. Cues alert students to key performance elements in the upcoming task, serving as tips on how to perform with greater proficiency. Although most cues are given during the task presentation, they can occur at any time in a lesson, and they may be directed to one student, a group, or the entire class. Cues can take a variety of forms:

1. *Verbal:* Spoken information about how to perform better
2. *Nonverbal:* Gestures and modeled examples of correct or incorrect movements
3. *Combination:* Simultaneous verbal and nonverbal information
4. *Manipulative:* Hands-on cues in which the teacher moves the student's body to make the communication (e.g., moving the student's hand into the correct tennis grip, turning the student's shoulders into the proper alignment in the golf setup, moving a dancer's foot into the proper position)
5. *Mediated:* Cues provided through audiovisual media, such as videos, CDs, DVDs, drawings, and photographs

Guides

Students often need performance information while they are still attempting a skill or involved in a dynamic task, such as a lead-up or full-game setting. This type of instructional information is called a *guide*. It is typically delivered verbally but could also come from nonverbal and manipulated information. The following list illustrates some examples of guides:

- Students are in a full-court basketball game, and a fast break develops. The teacher yells, "Get the ball to the middle, and fill the passing lanes. Defense, get back, get back!"
- Students are practicing a square dance. As the music plays, the teacher says, "OK, now get ready for the next call. Keep with the music; keep your head up, and find your partner."
- Children are dribbling soccer balls. Phil is looking down at the ball on each contact. The teacher reaches and gently lifts his head at the chin, to get him to stop looking down.
- Students are following the teacher's modeling of the tennis stroke in slow motion, while the teacher verbally prompts each part of the stroke.
- Students are stretching. The teacher moves one student's legs into the correct position for the quad stretch.

Feedback

One of a teacher's most essential instructional functions is to provide students with information about the adequacy of completed task performances. This feedback is crucial to the learning process. Interestingly, while we have known for many years about the importance of performance feedback in physical education, recent research has raised some questions about the exact role it plays in this process (Silverman, Tyson, & Krampitz, 1993). Researchers are confident that learners need performance feedback, but they are less so about when and how feedback becomes most effective (Rink, 2003). Feedback is multidimensional, and there are many different aspects involved in the type of performance feedback a student receives at any given moment in class (see Exhibit 5.4).

We know that feedback represents an important part of the learning process, but we don't yet know the best way to use it in every situation (Rink, 2003). However, research from motor learning and pedagogy provides some rules of thumb that teachers can keep in mind for this important teaching skill:

1. More feedback is usually better than less feedback.
2. Specific feedback is more effective than general feedback.
3. Immediate feedback is more effective than delayed feedback.
4. Corrective feedback helps the learner more than non-corrective feedback.
5. Combination feedback is more helpful than verbal or nonverbal alone.
6. Advanced learners can get by with less feedback, but it should be more specific.
7. Novice learners need all the feedback they can get, including feedback that motivates and acknowledges effort.

EXHIBIT 5.4 Dimensions of performance feedback.

DIMENSION	TYPES	EXAMPLES
Origin or feedback agent (refers to the source of feedback information)	1. *Task intrinsic* Feedback information that a student can ascertain for herself by observing the result of a skill attempt. That general information provides the student with some degree of feedback about performance, typically on its success or nonsuccess. 2. *Task extrinsic (or augmented)* Performance information provided by another person or agent that is not part of the task itself. That person is usually the teacher, but it could also be another student. Task extrinsic feedback can refer to any part of the completed skill attempt, including the performance result, form, technique, effort, or quality.	1. Student sees a ball hit its intended target. Student hears and feels solid contact on a swing. 2. Teacher says, "I liked your follow-through that time." A classmate tells another student, "Way to go!"
Congruency of feedback (refers to how well the feedback matches the key elements being practiced at the moment)	1. *Congruent* Includes a reference to the specific learning cue(s) emphasized during the task presentation. 2. *Incongruent* Does not include a reference to the specific learning cue(s) of the moment.	1. If the teacher told students in his task presentation to "really concentrate on making a nice, long follow-through on your tennis backhand swing," then any feedback that pertains to the follow-through is considered congruent. 2. If, after that same task presentation, the teacher directs feedback toward a student's service form, forehand shot, or *some other part* of the backhand shot, that feedback is considered incongruent at the moment.
Feedback content (refers to the reference point of the feedback information)	1. *General* Contains no mention of which part of the completed skill attempt is being referred to by the teacher. It makes only a general indication that the attempt was satisfactory or not. 2. *Specific* Includes a reference to which part of the completed skill attempt is being described by the teacher. Specific feedback provides the learner with more useful information and is preferred over general feedback in nearly all situations.	1. "That was good." "Way to go." "That wasn't right." "Nice." 2. "You really followed through that time." "Your wrist was not in the right position." "You were not quick enough to cover the base." "You really had good balance that time."

EXHIBIT 5.4 Continued.		
DIMENSION	**TYPES**	**EXAMPLES**
Accuracy of feedback (refers to the correctness of the feedback: does the information communicated to the student really describe the performance?)	1. *Accurate* The performance information is a correct description of the skill attempt. 2. *Inaccurate* The performance information is not a correct description of the skill attempt.	(Self-explanatory)
Timing (refers to the span between the end of the skill attempt and the delivery of the feedback information to the learner)	1. *Immediate* Feedback is provided to the learner right after the skill attempt is completed or at least before the next skill attempt occurs. 2. *Delayed* Feedback is not provided immediately or soon after the skill attempt, or not until more skill attempts have been completed.	1. Student finishes a high jump, and the teacher tells her right away, "You really had good form on that jump." 2. Twenty minutes later, as the class is ending, the teacher says to the same student, "It looked like you were not extending your kick leg fully enough in your jumps today."
Modality (refers to how augmented feedback is provided to students)	1. *Verbal* Provided to students in the form of spoken words or phrases. It is what the teacher says to students about the completed skill attempt. 2. *Nonverbal* Provided in the form of gestures made to students. 3. *Combination* Verbal and nonverbal information given at the same time.	1. "You really did a nice job that time." "I liked your effort." "You did not run fast enough." 2. Giving the "OK" signal. Hand clapping. A pat on the back. A re-enactment of part or all of the skill attempt. 3. Saying "Way to go" while patting a student on the back. Saying, "You gave a really nice fake on the defender" while modeling the faking move for the student at the same time.

(continued)

EXHIBIT 5.4 Continued.

DIMENSION	TYPES	EXAMPLES
Evaluation (indicates whether or not the teacher is expressing approval/agreement or disapproval/disagreement to the student about the adequacy of the completed performance)	1. *Positive* Approval or agreement with the completed performance.	1. "I really liked that." "I think you made the right decision on that play." "Nice try."
	2. *Negative* Disapproval or disagreement with the completed performance.	2. "That was the wrong play by the goalkeeper." "Team 2 is not trying very hard." "You gave up that time." "Your balance was way off on that last swing."
	3. *Neutral* It is not clear if the teacher is stating a positive or negative indication.	3. "Not bad." "You had some of it correct that time."
Corrective attributes (Is the feedback coupled with information about how to correct mistakes?)	1. *Non-corrective* Contains only information that the performance was incorrect or not approved of by the teacher.	1. "Your feet were in the wrong place." "You missed the ball." "You will never succeed that way."
	2. *Corrective* Provides feedback plus information (cues) about how to improve the next performance.	2. "That was better, but next time keep your head up." "Your elbow was extended too far; keep it tucked right next to your body."
Direction (refers to person to whom the feedback information is directed)	1. Individual feedback is directed to a single student.	1. "Donna was really trying hard in class today."
	2. Group feedback is directed to a recognized group of students in class.	2. "Squad 2 . . ." "Jerry's team . . ." "Everyone at this end of the gym . . ."
	3. Class feedback is directed to all students in the class.	3. "Everyone was really well behaved today." "This class showed great teamwork."

AREA 6: USING QUESTIONS FOR LEARNING

eachers' use of questions has been emphasized in classroom subjects for many years. Only recently has this skill become an integral part of the effective physical education teacher's repertoire. The increased need for effective questioning skills in physical education has come about because of the expanded use of interactive teaching strategies for content areas such as movement education, skill themes, concept learning, and affective outcomes. Questions can be categorized according to their focus and type.

Question Focus

The focus of a question depends on the aspect of class to which it pertains. *Managerial questions* focus on noninstructional parts of the lesson, such as class organization, preparation of the learning environment, class procedures, and routines. Typical managerial questions include: "Where does the equipment go when you are finished with it?" "What time is class supposed to begin?" or "Can I have three volunteers to help me set up the nets?" *Behavioral questions* focus on student in-class conduct, such as class rules or safety. Some examples include: "Who can tell me two things to keep in mind about safety in this next drill?" "What is our rule about improper language?" or "Marie, do you know it's not OK to get a drink of water without my permission?" "What do you do when I give the attention signal?" *Content questions* help develop student learning of the subject matter. They can promote learning in all three domains, depending on the type of response students give to the question.

Types of Content Questions

Benjamin Bloom and his colleagues (Bloom, Englehart, Furst, Hill, & Krathwohl, 1956) developed a classification system for content questions, based on their classic taxonomy of the cognitive domain. Because of the strong link between the cognitive and psychomotor domains, it is possible for physical educators to use each type of question to promote learning in both domains. From the same or similar questions, a student can develop two kinds of responses: a verbal response in the cognitive domain and a motor response in the psychomotor domain. Exhibit 5.5 shows examples of questions for these two domains, based on the taxonomy levels defined by Bloom and colleagues.

Knowledge, comprehension, and application questions in this taxonomy (Bloom et al., 1956) are referred to as *lower-order questions* because they appear on the bottom half of the original taxonomic scheme. Typically they require less knowledge and ability for responses. Analysis, synthesis, and evaluation questions are considered *higher-order questions* because they are positioned on the top half of the taxonomic scheme. Because they build on knowledge from the lower order and involve the creation of new knowledge, they are more complex and difficult to answer—in both the cognitive and psychomotor domains. The best question at any given moment depends on the teacher's purpose for asking it and student readiness to make a successful response.

EXHIBIT 5.5 Levels of content questions for physical education.

CONTENT QUESTION TYPE	PURPOSE	FOR COGNITIVE RESPONSE	FOR MOTOR RESPONSE
A. Knowledge	Asks students to recall previously learned facts, simple ideas, or concepts	"Can you tell me three key elements for the batter's stance we discussed last time?" "Can you tell me where the server stands in badminton singles?"	"Can you show me the correct batting stance we learned yesterday?" "Terry, would you please walk to the best place to make your badminton serve, and show the class the proper stance and aiming direction?"
B. Comprehension	Requires students to translate, interpret, or compare facts or ideas	"What is a double dribble?" "What is a hop? What is a jump? How are they different?"	"Who can show me two moves that can be called 'double dribble'?" "Who can show me a hop, then a jump, then another hop?"
C. Application	Asks students to solve problems that are based on previously learned facts or ideas	"When you are spotting for the bench press, when do you give the lifter assistance?" "What is the best formation for receiving a 'floater' volleyball serve?"	Teacher demonstrates a bench press and asks Scott to show proper spotting technique and timing. "Team 1, can you get yourselves into correct position and receive the 'floater' serve I am sending to you?"
D. Analysis	Asks students to break down the elements of complex concepts, to examine relationships, and to detect organizational patterns and principles	"When do you run a fast break and when do you go into your half-court offense?" "Who can tell me when you should toss a ball and when you should throw a ball?"	In a drill, the teacher directs point guards to either make a fast break or "slow it up" when they get an outlet pass. Teacher sets up a tossing/throwing station and asks students to use the right skill for hitting the target most often.
E. Synthesis	Asks students to generate new knowledge by putting together two or more facts, ideas, or concepts	"How do you know when you have reached your optimal heart rate zone for exercise?" "What do you think will happen when you put more spin on the ball?"	"Can you practice an exercise that will place you in your target zone within 5 minutes of starting it?" "Can you show me how to make the ball curve more when it is kicked?"

		EXHIBIT 5.5
Continued.

CONTENT QUESTION TYPE	PURPOSE	FOR COGNITIVE RESPONSE	FOR MOTOR RESPONSE
F. Evaluation	Asks students to make judgments based on personal knowledge and feelings, or knowledge generated by other people	"What makes the difference between a 6.7 and 7.0 on a floor exercise routine?" "Which do you like more, square dancing or line dancing?"	"Can you perform two floor exercise routines, with one that would be judged higher than the other?" "Pick a square dance or a line dance, and practice it for the next 10 minutes."

Convergent questions most often lead to one correct answer, whether the response is made in the cognitive or psychomotor domain. They are sometimes called *closed-ended* questions because the teacher will have one correct answer in mind and ask a convergent question to prompt that single response. Examples are: "How many positions are there in soccer?" or "Can you show me the sideline boundary for tennis singles?" or "Who can use a compass to find and point to due north from here?" *Divergent,* or *open-ended,* questions allow several correct or feasible answers to a single question—usually a higher-order question. Again, responses can be made primarily in either the cognitive or psychomotor domain. Some examples are: "Can you show me how many ways you can hold a static balance with your partner?" or "When would you use the high, deep serve in badminton?" or "Under what conditions might a compound bow not be the best kind for you to use?" The choice of a convergent or divergent question will depend on what the teacher is trying to teach students, their level of ability/knowledge, and their experience with the content.

Using Questions for Learning

It is not enough for a teacher to know the focus and types of question to use in class. There are some specific skills that teachers can use to make questioning a more effective part of the instructional process.

Use wait time. *Wait time* refers to the amount of time that passes from the end of the teacher's question to the moment he designates a student to answer (Rowe, 1986). It is generally best for the teacher to give about three seconds of wait time, which allows more students to develop an answer and keeps students who develop answers fastest from getting called on more often than others (Tobin, 1987). Adequate wait time lets every student come up with her own answer and then privately compare the answer to that of the student called on by the teacher.

Use divergent questions whenever possible. Convergent questions lead students to one or a few possible answers. When students have that one answer, they stop considering more possible answers. Divergent questions require students to consider many possibilities and thus keep the intellectual process going.

Establish rules for responding to questions. Effective teachers develop rules for students to follow when answering questions. These rules make the process more orderly and provide students with the best opportunity to learn from questions asked in class. Some rules might include:

- Students must raise a hand to be called on.
- Students cannot say the answer out loud until called on.
- Students cannot use inappropriate gestures to get the teacher's attention.
- Teacher and students should not criticize other students' answers (especially for divergent and personal responses).
- Teacher and students should allow complete answers. Don't cut off students who answer slowly.

Respond appropriately to incorrect answers. Students who get called on to say or show their answer to a teacher's question will give an incorrect answer at times. Since that moment is very public for the student, the teacher must be sensitive and careful when providing comments and feedback. Consider the following guidelines for such situations:

- Do not ignore the answer and quickly call on another student.
- Give the student a chance to clarify by asking a "redirect" question.
- Be sensitive in your reply. Say, "That was not the answer I was looking for," not "That was wrong, sit down—next."
- Give the student more time if you think she is close to the correct answer.

Ask for clarification and reasons. There is a tendency for teachers to stop asking questions when the students have provided an answer. But getting the initial answer is only a part of the learning process. Teachers can probe students to find out how they arrived at an answer or ask their reason(s) for their answer. Questions like "How did you figure that out?" or "Where did you learn that?" or "What made you think of that?" allow students an opportunity to reflect on an answer, providing a deeper level of learning and good information for other students.

Call for group answers. Much of the time, students think about questions privately and individually. They do not get the benefit of other students' views and knowledge. Sometimes a teacher can ask a question to a group of students and direct them to formulate an answer "by committee." This strategy will work only with higher-order questions.

Ask verbal questions to get a movement response. Answers to a teacher's questions are not limited to the cognitive domain and verbal responses. Some teaching models are based on questions that students must think about and then answer by showing a movement response. The cognitive domain is initially engaged to formulate an answer, but students must then transfer that knowledge to the psychomotor domain to demonstrate their knowledge to the teacher. For example, a teacher could ask a group of third graders, "Think of your favorite animal, and move around the room to look like that animal. Be sure to make that animal's sound, too."

AREA 7: LESSON REVIEW AND CLOSURE

It is a good idea to end lessons with a review and closure segment. This part of the lesson should be planned like all other segments and have an intended learning purpose for students. It is not just a quick review of what was done in class that day; it should allow students to reflect on completed learning tasks, remind themselves of key performance cues, and make the connection between those concepts covered in class. The brief closure in the review should bring the lesson to a logical and complete ending to ensure that the intended learning goals were reached and that students have no unanswered questions. The closure then leads directly to the final management directions (lining up, going to the locker rooms, and so forth) and dismissal of class.

Transitioning to the review. Because time is usually short at the end of class, teachers must use quick and simple ways to get students organized for the review segment. It is best to get students to one location with no equipment in their hands, so the teacher should stop the final activity, direct students to quickly put away their equipment, and meet in a place near the equipment collection area. If the teaching area is small, the teacher can use a signal to get students to stop the activity and conduct the review while students are standing in place; the students can then put the equipment away afterward.

Getting attention. Like any other time when the teacher will talk to the entire class, it is important to get students in a close formation and to have them pay quiet attention. Since this is "listening and thinking" time, the teacher should not proceed with the review until students are quiet and attentive. This is a good time to use an attention signal.

Using interactive communications. The best reviews will require students to reflect on the lesson—to think, not just listen. Teachers can do this by checking for understanding or with an "ask, don't tell" strategy that prompts students to provide answers to review questions. This will make the review interactive, not just a passive listening time for students.

INTERACTIVE (ASK)	PASSIVE (TELL)
"Who can tell me three things we learned in class today?"	"Today in class we learned how to balance on one foot, on two body parts, and with a partner."
"Why did we need to have a no-high-stick rule today?"	"We had a no-high-stick rule today because I saw several of you with your hockey sticks in a dangerous position in our drills."

"How do you think you could apply the skills we learned today?"

"Once you know how to strike objects with short-handled implements, you could use that in sports like racquetball and table tennis."

SUMMARY

The lists of effective teaching skills and their component parts in this chapter can be intimidating to read, especially for novice teachers. You might ask, "Do effective teachers really do all of those things in class?" Yes and no. Effective physical education teachers will have the complete repertoire of those skills, along with good procedural and conditional knowledge for each one. However, the instructional model in place and its accompanying strategies will call for a smaller number of teaching skills to be used in any given lesson. As this book has emphasized many times, the teacher who can successfully apply situation-specific decisions and actions will be more effective more often. That use of effective teaching skills comes from good planning, experience, and regular updates of one's instructional abilities.

LEARNING ACTIVITIES

1. Select one of the seven application areas for effective teaching skills in physical education presented in this chapter. Conduct a brief literature review of the research findings for that area in physical education. Make a list of "what we know" and "what we still need to learn" about that area. (You might need to ask your instructor for a list of sources for your review.)

2. Using the same sources from Activity 1, explain what an effective physical education teacher would do, or not do, in that area of instruction. How does research inform practice in that area?

3. The next time you teach a lesson, provide a self-assessment of your own skills in each of the seven areas of effective teaching presented in this chapter. What evidence did you use to make your assessment?

4. Assume you are a mentor teacher, trying to help a novice physical educator improve in each of the seven areas of effective teaching. What advice would you give that novice teacher for learning how to be effective in each area? Be sure to write out your answers as if you were talking to this teacher in person.

TOPICS FOR REFLECTION & SMALL-GROUP DISCUSSION

1. Respond to this statement: "Physical education teachers either have effective instructional skills, or they don't. These skills cannot be practiced and learned much beyond a teacher's 'natural ability.'"

2. If you do not agree with the statement in Topic 1, that means you think teachers can learn, practice, and improve their instructional skills. Talk about some ways you think that learning can happen.

SUGGESTED READINGS

Rink, J. (2009). *Teaching physical education for learning* (3rd ed.). Boston: McGraw-Hill.

Siedentop, D., & Tannehill, D. (2000). *Developing teaching skills in physical education* (4th ed.). Mountain View, CA: Mayfield.

Silverman, S., & Ennis, C. (2003). *Student learning in physical education: Applying research to enhance instruction* (2nd ed.). Champaign, IL: Human Kinetics.

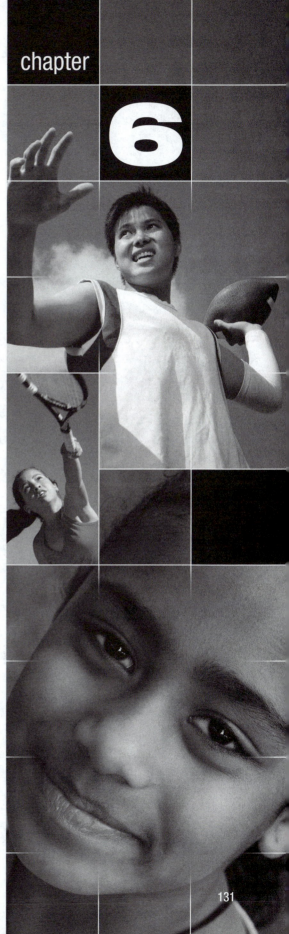

PLANNING FOR MODEL-BASED INSTRUCTION

O ne of the most important contributions to effective physical education instruction is planning. Research on teaching has demonstrated that effective instruction is intentional and purposeful. Well-organized units and lessons have a greater chance of leading to student achievement of the intended learning goals. Planning needs to take place before the unit begins and regularly during the length of the unit. You will notice that I did not say "daily," because some instructional models use *modular planning,* which covers two or three consecutive lessons, or *unified planning,* which covers the entire unit. Both eliminate the need for daily lesson planning. Now, that does not mean the teacher does no planning from day to day. Rather, the teacher completes the majority of planning before the unit begins, and the model operates from a "flowing" plan that carries over from lesson to lesson.

Exhibit 6.1 shows the relationship between planning and other aspects of a teacher's knowledge of teaching physical education. Planning serves to facilitate the transfer of content knowledge and general pedagogical knowledge into pedagogical content knowledge (Shulman, 1987)—the ability to teach effectively a specified content to a certain group of learners.

EXHIBIT 6.1 The role of planning in model-based instruction.

PLANNING FOR MODEL-BASED INSTRUCTION

Unit Planning		Lesson Planning	
Context analysis	Learning activities	Context description	Learning activities
Content analysis	Assessment/grading	Learning objectives	Task presentation and structure
Learning objectives	Teacher functions	Time and space management	Assessment
Selection of model	Student functions		Review and closure
Management plan			

EFFECTIVE TEACHING SKILL AREAS FOR MODEL-BASED INSTRUCTION

1. Planning
2. Time and class management
3. Task presentation and structure
4. Communication
5. Providing instructional information
6. Using questions for learning
7. Review and closure

STRATEGIES FOR TEACHING PHYSICAL EDUCATION

Managerial	Instructional	
1. Preventive	1. Task presentation	5. Task progression
2. Interactive	2. Task structure	6. Student safety
3. Grouping	3. Task engagement	7. Review and closure
	4. Learning activities	

KNOWLEDGE AREAS FOR MODEL-BASED INSTRUCTION

1. Learning contexts
2. Learners
3. Learning theories
4. Developmental appropriateness
5. Learning domains and objectives
6. Physical education content
7. Assessment
8. Social/emotional climate
9. Equity in the gym
10. Curriculum models for PE

OVERVIEW OF PLANNING

Instructional planning ties together the context, learning goals, learning activities, classroom management, and assessment within the model being used for each unit. It requires the teacher to consider many factors that will interact in a dynamic setting and take place in a predetermined (and usually restricted) span of time. Planning and anticipation are essential skills that allow a teacher to efficiently organize herself, students, facilities, and available resources to lead students toward stated instructional goals in the shortest amount of time. Teachers may plan so they feel more comfortable in front of class, because the planning process lets them review the content ahead of time, or because it allows others to see how well they are organized. In my opinion, the single most important reason for planning is to improve the likelihood that students will learn the intended instructional outcomes with the most efficient expenditure of time, effort, and resources. In other words, planning should occur for no other reason than to increase the teacher's effectiveness within each unit and lesson. This clearly puts planning's *function* well ahead of its *form*.

Novice teachers soon discover the difference between *planning* and *being prepared*. Planning is the process of making decisions and producing a written document for each unit and lesson to be taught. However, *having planned* does not always mean a teacher is actually *prepared and properly organized* for effective instruction. The catch is that you can plan but not be prepared; but if you are prepared, you have planned well enough! That also answers the question, how much planning should a teacher do? Enough to be prepared! Sometimes planning time will be quite short, particularly when a teacher has instructed the same content to the same grade level in the same context several times in the past. When the teacher is not familiar with the students, the content, or the context, much more planning time should be expected in order to become prepared.

Guidelines for Planning

It is easy for a novice teacher to underestimate or overestimate the planning process in physical education. To underestimate the planning process means that the teacher will not be prepared and that the instruction will not be as effective as it could have been. There is also a tendency for underprepared teachers to become anxious and confused in the midst of poorly planned lessons, a reaction that is apparent to students. To overestimate the planning process means that the teacher spends more time and energy than necessary to get ready—time that could be given to other aspects of one's professional and personal life.

Planning for effective instruction in physical education operates on two levels: the unit and the lesson. Unit planning includes all of the decisions and readiness actions that take place before the unit begins. It provides the "big picture" of learning goals, content to be taught, learning activities, needed resources, and class management—all within the instructional model selected for the unit. Lesson planning includes many of the same types of decisions and readiness actions as they are made right before and during each lesson in the unit. Let me emphasize that both levels of planning are essential for effective teaching and learning. In order to approach the planning process realistically at both levels, consider the following guidelines.

Make firm but flexible plans. *Firm* plans give the teacher a good idea of how the instruction will proceed before it begins. This allows the teacher to anticipate many of the key factors and events that will affect the conduct, management, and outcomes of instruction. *Flexible* plans give the teacher a few reasonable options when unforeseen conditions or events force changes to the original plan.

Write the plan primarily for your own use. It is the teacher who must use the plan to promote effective classroom management and learning. Therefore, the plan should be written in a way that the teacher can understand and implement. The teacher chooses the plan's specific form to match the needs of his situation. Some teachers have a "personal shorthand" for making notes to themselves; this is a good practice, especially for lesson plans. Plans should be as detailed and functional as the teacher needs them to be.

When in doubt, overplan. It is sometimes difficult to project how long it will take the majority of students to progress through content. Thus teachers should prepare more in each unit and lesson than they expect to cover, just in case students move along faster than anticipated.

Have a related alternate plan. Physical education units and lessons often depend on factors that are out of the teacher's control: prolonged bad weather during outdoor units, equipment breakage or failure, changes in the school's schedule, availability of facilities, and excessive student absences. When these and other situations arise, the teacher must be able to provide students with learning activities that are directly related to the present content—and not from a makeshift plan. To maintain continuity in the instruction, a teacher can plan ahead for a "fail-safe" lesson on unit content that can be implemented in nearly any circumstance. Good fail-safe lessons might focus on rules and strategy, officiating, selection and purchase of equipment, history and background of the content, group projects, modified games, Internet searches, media presentations, or group discussions.

Keep all written planning records. Most content units have a short useful life within a school year. They last anywhere from a few days to several weeks and are then not taught again until the next year. Lesson plans have an even shorter useful life. Most are used just once, then not again until the next time the unit is offered. Diligent teachers will increase the "shelf life" of planning records by filing them after each use and then referring to them in the planning stage the next time the unit is offered.

Reflect on completed units and lessons. Because units and each lesson in them are usually taught only one time each year, it is important for teachers to take time to reflect on, evaluate, and make notes for modifying plans that have just been used. Those notes can then be filed with the plan to serve as reminders the next time the plan is used.

Planning as a Guide for Action

Whether it addresses a single lesson or an entire unit, the written plan serves as a guide for the teacher and students. The planning process allows the teacher to think about, decide, and visualize a series of steps that will promote more effective and efficient instruction. This becomes a tangible picture of how events will happen and a source for making well-informed modifications as the unit progresses. A good plan gives the teacher several advantages:

1. Predetermined starting and ending points are made for the unit and each lesson.

2. The plan can be referred to along the way to check for progress.

3. The plan provides reference points for making long- and short-term decisions.

4. The plan can be used as the basis for making modifications along the way.

5. The plan allows for better evaluations of teaching effectiveness by comparing what was planned with what actually happened.

6. The teacher can use the plan to verify that he is teaching according to the design of the instructional model.

UNIT PLANNING

Physical education instructional units can last from a few days to several weeks. Regardless of the unit's length, instruction is more likely to be effective when the teacher has made a clear and coherent plan before the unit begins. When the unit plan is in place, the planning for daily lessons becomes much easier as the unit progresses. A complete unit plan should contain nine components: (1) a contextual analysis, (2) a content analysis and listing, (3) learning objectives, (4) selection of the instructional model to be used, (5) a management plan, (6) student learning activities, (7) assessment and/or grading, (8) a description of the teacher's role in the unit, and (9) a description of the students' roles in the unit.

It should be noted that all the models in this book have unique formats for unit planning. The plans will be based on the intended learning outcomes and how the model should be implemented most effectively. For example, Direct Instruction (Chapter 8) has a planning format that all teachers have used and will recognize—one that breaks the unit content into small steps that students progress through under close teacher guidance. This format calls for the unit to be planned in a clearly sequential manner, with distinct lessons for each class led by the teacher. The Personalized System for Instruction (Chapter 9) has a unified planning format in which the entire unit content progression is presented to students at the start, and they move through the content at an individual pace. There are no daily lesson plans—students come to class and "pick up where they left off the last time," moving through as much content as they can. They then do the same for each subsequent lesson. No one unit planning format will work for all the models you will learn in this book. All unit plans should include the nine components just listed, but those components will look different for each model.

The IMPE website provides many samples of unit and lesson plans for each model presented in Part Two. As you will see, the sample for each model varies somewhat, most often due to differences in specific learning outcomes and contextual factors present in these teachers' actual setting. Although they differ, all the samples for each model reflect the most important elements needed to make that model effective. It is my advice that you use these samples as "starting points" in planning your own units of model-based instruction, and do not attempt to use them exactly as they were implemented by the teachers who designed them.

Contextual Analysis

Playing an extremely important role in teaching, *context* refers to the sum of all the factors that influence what is taught, how it is taught, and what students will learn in the unit. Some contextual factors will facilitate instruction and learning by providing the teacher with many ways to be effective (e.g., sufficient space and equipment, manageable class size, and adequate scheduled time). Other contextual factors will inhibit the teacher's decision making by reducing options for effective instruction. Typical inhibiting factors in physical education are large classes, inadequate equipment and facilities, and limited instruction time. Most contextual factors are fixed; that is, they simply "are there" and cannot be altered by the teacher to any significant extent during the unit. The four main determinants of context are the teacher, the students, the content, and available resources. Exhibit 6.2 shows those determinants, along with some key questions that must be asked to analyze the context for any unit of instruction.

Content Analysis and Listing

A content analysis determines what will be included in the unit and the order in which students will learn it. The results of the content analysis will have a strong bearing on what can be taught and learned in the unit, so it must take place immediately after the contextual analysis. The teacher begins the content analysis by listing the developmentally appropriate psychomotor skills, cognitive knowledge areas, and affective dispositions essential to the activity, sport, or dance. The teacher then considers the students' current abilities, knowledge, and attitudes, using those as the starting point for the unit content. The ending point is determined by estimating how long it will take most students to learn each part of the content and by considering the number of lessons in the unit. That ratio will help the teacher decide how much progress (and content) is reasonable for that unit and determine the *amount* of content to be taught and learned. The content areas to be taught are then placed in a logical order of progression, which completes the content analysis and listing. Some sample content lists are shown in Exhibit 6.3.

Learning Objectives

A key part of the planning process is the determination of student learning objectives in the unit. The stated objectives must reflect the results of the

Major contextual determinants for unit planning.		EXHIBIT 6.2
DETERMINANT	**KEY QUESTIONS FOR CONTEXT ANALYSIS**	
The teacher	1. What do I know about this content?	
	2. What experience do I have teaching this content to this grade level?	
	3. Where can I go (e.g., books, colleagues, clinics) to gain content knowledge?	
The students	1. How many will be in this class each time?	
	2. How many and which students have special learning needs?	
	3. What are those needs, and what do I know about teaching those students?	
	4. What is the typical developmental stage in this class?	
	5. What is the students' motivation to learn this content?	
The content	1. What is the expected range of ability in, and knowledge of, this content?	
	2. What do students at this age/stage need to know about this content?	
	3. What specific content should be covered in this unit?	
	4. In what order should the content be learned? Does it matter?	
	5. Will I need to modify the content to meet students' abilities?	
	6. How long should it take most students to learn each part of the unit?	
	7. What learning goals should students pursue?	
	8. How can I assess that learning?	
Available resources	1. How many lessons will the unit include?	
	2. How many actual minutes are available for instruction in each class?	
	3. How much content can students reasonably learn in that amount of time?	
	4. What is my teaching area for the unit?	
	5. How many stations, courts, fields, etc. can the area accommodate?	
	6. What equipment do I have for this unit?	
	7. What is the ratio of equipment/implements/objects to students?	
	8. Do I have to modify equipment for safe and effective usage?	
	9. Will I have any assistance (e.g., team teacher, teacher's aide)?	

contextual analysis and the content selected for the unit. Objectives can be stated at two levels: general and behavioral. *General objectives* are just what the term implies—global areas of intended student learning within each domain. *Behavioral objectives* describe specific performance criteria that students will demonstrate within each general objective area. Exhibit 6.4 provides some examples of how general objectives lead to behavioral objectives in physical education.

Note that the behavioral objectives have three main parts: (1) the setting or conditions for performance, (2) the behavior, skill, or knowledge to be demonstrated, and (3) established performance criteria. These kinds of objectives are called Mager objectives, after the person who first developed them

EXHIBIT 6.3	Content listings for some physical education units.		
GRADE LEVEL	**CONTENT UNIT**	**LESSONS**	**CONTENT LISTING**
1st	Movement concepts	First 8 of the year	1. PE class rules 2. Safety in PE class 3. Self-space, general space, scatter space 4. Pathways 5. Levels 6. Balancing 7. Twisting 8. Leaping 9. Hopping 10. Dodging 11. Low-organization movement games
5th	Soccer	10	1. Dribbling 2. Trapping 3. Passing 4. Shooting on goal 5. Goal keeping 6. Basic rules and strategies 7. Offensive positions 8. Basic offensive plays 9. Modified games (four vs. four, smaller field)
11th	Personal fitness	20	1. Concepts of personal fitness 2. Planning a safe fitness program 3. Safe stretching 4. Introduction to workout options 5. Guided instruction on workout machines 6. Pre-assessment 7. Design and complete a personal fitness program 8. Post-assessment

(Mager, 1984). The setting or condition describes the context or situation in which the learning will be demonstrated. Some of the conditions can occur before the performance ("Given 10 minutes of practice time . . .") or be in place during the performance (". . . in a badminton match"). The behavior/ skill/knowledge states exactly what will be demonstrated ("tennis etiquette" or "moving in pathways and levels"). The performance criterion states in objective terms how proficient, correct, consistent, accurate, and so on the

	General and behavioral objectives for physical education.		EXHIBIT 6.4
DOMAIN	**GENERAL OBJECTIVE**	**BEHAVIORAL OBJECTIVE**	
Cognitive	1. Students will learn rules and strategies for soccer.	1. Student will score at least 80 percent on a soccer-game strategy and rules test.	
	2. Students will know common square dance calls.	2. Student will correctly recite the five most commonly used square-dance calls.	
	3. Students will learn how to design their own new games.	3. Given 10 minutes of individual time, student will write three major rules for a self-designed new game.	
Affective	1. Students will learn the proper etiquette for tennis.	1. During a three-set match, student will display no more than two violations of tennis etiquette.	
	2. Students will be good team members in a cooperative game.	2. Student will participate in a cooperative game without arguing with teammates.	
	3. Students will be good sports-persons.	3. Student will demonstrate three instances of good sport behavior in a flag football game.	
Psychomotor	1. Students will learn the basic skills for golf.	1. Student will make three of five putts from on the green from a distance of 6 feet.	
	2. Students will learn badminton serves.	2. Student will have 75 percent serving accuracy in a badminton match.	
	3. Students will learn pathways and levels.	3. Student will correctly demonstrate how to move in three different pathways at two different levels in scatter space.	

performance must be to indicate that learning has occurred ("score at least 80 percent correct" or "no [zero] arguing"). The three parts of a Mager objective will not necessarily appear in the same order, but they must always be present for objectives to be considered good for most types of learning. Refer to Chapter 3 for a more complete explanation and examples of learning objectives for physical education.

Selection of the Instructional Model

Once the teacher has analyzed the context, determined the content listing, and stated the intended learning objectives for the unit, he can then make a well-informed decision about which instructional model (or models) most effectively help students learn in the unit. Two things must be kept in mind when selecting a model for a unit. First, selection is a *deductive* process; the decision is made after consideration of context, content, and objectives. The stated learning objectives will indicate the domain priorities and domain interactions that directly influence the selection. Second, student learning will be maximized if the entire unit uses one model. It is not advisable to change models after the unit has started or to freely combine the components of two or more models.

Because each model has unique characteristics and patterns for teacher and student behavior, it is important to maintain consistency from start to finish.

Management Plan

The management plan serves to identify important rules, routines, and procedures that will make the learning environment safe and efficient in the unit. The plan will also inform the teacher and students of each one's responsibilities in class. A typical management plan should include:

1. Determination and communication of class rules.
2. Procedures for entering and leaving the gym or teaching area.
3. Procedures for the distribution, care, and collection of equipment.
4. Safety rules.
5. Procedures for taking class roll.
6. Designation of a signal for attention and start/stop.

Learning Activities

All instructional units include a series of planned learning activities that allow students to interact with the content and learn the stated objectives. Chapter 4 described learning activities that can be used in physical education for each of the three major domains: cognitive, psychomotor, and affective. Before the unit begins, the teacher should make a list of the activities for the unit and the order in which they will be presented to students. She can then make plans for the management, task presentation, task structure, and assessment of each activity. This allows the teacher to plan ahead for equipment and other resources needed for each activity.

Assessment and/or Grading

Before the unit begins, the teacher must plan for assessing student learning. That plan will also include policies, procedures, and criteria for determining grades when they will be assigned at the end of a unit. Assessment and grading decisions must consider:

1. Which goals and outcomes are to be assessed or graded.
2. What kind of assessment(s) will be used (e.g., traditional, alternative, authentic).
3. When assessment will take place (e.g., formative, summative, or both).
4. How assessments will be planned and conducted.

It is not necessary to prepare specific assessment materials before the unit begins, but the teacher should have a general assessment plan in place at that time—so he can be looking ahead and getting ready. Chapter 7 includes more detailed information about assessment types and procedures for physical education.

Teacher's Role and Functions in the Unit

Each instructional model will designate a unique pattern of decision making and behavior for the teacher. That will transfer into certain roles the teacher will assume and certain operations the teacher will carry out in the unit. It is important that the instructor recognize the role she is expected to play and how she is to function within each unit and make plans to execute them accordingly. A teacher can prepare for her role by reviewing the characteristics of each model before it is implemented, as a preview or reminder of "how to teach" during the upcoming unit.

Students' Roles and Functions in the Unit

Just like the teacher, students will have patterns of decisions, behavior, and responsibility within the model selected for each unit. Teacher control models will call for students to be more passive, while interactive and student control models will require them to take an active role in the unit. Some models will demand very little responsibility on their part; others will give students control of many class decisions and operations. When the teacher begins a unit with a new model, she will need to help students learn how things will work during that unit and give students some time to acclimate to a new pattern of class participation. It is the teacher's responsibility to make plans for initially *teaching the model* as well as the content, until students accept and take on new roles and responsibilities in class.

LESSON PLANNING

G ood planning at the unit level greatly facilitates the planning for each lesson in the unit. The unit and lesson plans should be strongly aligned. If the unit plan is viewed as the outline for overall action in the unit, then the lesson plan provides the specific instructions and details to guide the teacher in each class meeting. The main task now is to "fill in" that part of the unit plan to be implemented in each lesson. There are many ways to format and write a lesson plan for physical education, but most plans will include seven common components: (1) a brief contextual description, (2) learning objectives, (3) time and space management procedures, (4) learning activities, (5) task presentation and task structure, (6) assessment, and (7) review and closure.

Some instructional models will require specialized planning formats, but most models use lesson plans that share several common characteristics. This allows teachers to use a generic *template* for lesson planning. A template functions well in most instances and can be based on the lesson-plan components presented below. Refer to Exhibit 6.5 for a generic lesson-planning template (also available on the IMPE website) that describes many of the components needed for effective instruction; *the numbers assigned to sections of the template correspond to the numbered components discussed on the following pages.* You will notice that the form is very open, with each section address-

EXHIBIT 6.5 Physical education lesson plan.

①

Teacher: _____ Date: _____

Grade(s): _____ Number of students: _____

Lesson Content: _____ Lesson # ___ of ___

Skills and knowledge already developed by students: _____

What happened during last lesson? _____

②

Lesson objective(s):

	DOMAIN	PERFORMANCE	SITUATION	CRITERIA
1				
2				
3				

NASPE or state standard(s) targeted. Indicate standard(s) and number(s), and write out standard(s).

_____

_____

_____

③

Assessment for measuring lesson objectives _____

My goal for improving my teaching in this lesson _____

Equipment and resources needed _____

Inclusion or alternative activities for students with special needs _____

Instructional / practice time / organization (see other side)

Continued.   EXHIBIT   6.5

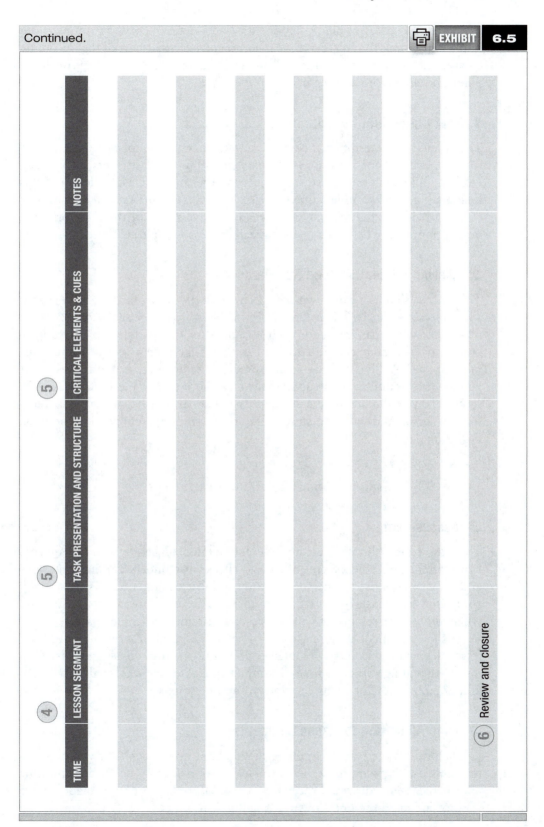

TIME	LESSON SEGMENT	TASK PRESENTATION AND STRUCTURE	CRITICAL ELEMENTS & CUES	NOTES
④		⑤	⑤	
	⑥ Review and closure			

ing one or more lesson-plan components. Each section acts as a prompt, or an implied question, that directs the teacher to consider that part of the upcoming lesson. The openness of the form allows the teacher ample room to write down plans and notes for each segment.

1 Brief Contextual Description

The contextual description includes a summary of the major factors that need to be considered for the lesson: students (the number of students, their grade level[s], and which ones have special needs), the time or class period, and this lesson's place in the unit sequence (e.g., first class, fourth of 10 classes, last class). Obviously the teacher will already be aware of all these factors—the description simply helps the teacher recall the lesson the next time it is taught.

2 Learning Objectives and Standards

The teacher should write down the specific objectives for the upcoming lesson. The objectives can be taken directly from the unit plan. Usually one to three objectives will be sufficient for each lesson. After the learning objectives have been stated for the lesson, the teacher can then align each objective with one or more of the NASPE national or state standards being addressed in the lesson. If you are attempting to get your students to achieve one or more of the NASPE standards, you should specifically identify which standard(s) you have targeted for that lesson and write the standard(s) in this section. Abbreviations are OK. For example:

- NASPE 1. Motor skill competency
- NASPE 2. Concepts, principles, strategies and tactics

3 Assessment

The lesson plan should indicate how each stated objective will be assessed. Most often, assessments are informal—checks for understanding, question-and-answer periods, teacher observation, or just asking students how many completed each task to a certain standard. The lesson plan should indicate when and how assessments will be made, as a reminder to the teacher.

If the assessment is more formal, the plan will need to show it as a defined lesson segment, with its own managerial and procedural considerations. That means allocating sufficient time to complete the assessment, planning its setup, and organizing the necessary equipment and materials.

4 Time Allocation for Class Segments

It is helpful for the teacher to think ahead about how much time will be given to each class segment, how the learning environment will be set up, and how management episodes will proceed. A time allocation plan can be made for the lesson, similar to the one shown in Exhibit 6.6.

Sample time plan for a physical education lesson.	EXHIBIT 6.6

LESSON: FITNESS STATIONS FOR SEVENTH GRADERS

9:15 – 9:20	Students in locker room.
9:20 – 9:24	Warm up and stretch. (Take roll.)
9:24 – 9:25	Set induction.
9:25 – 9:30	Task presentation and station descriptions.
9:30 – 9:40	Rotate through first three stations.
9:40 – 9:43	Review first three stations.
9:43 – 9:53	Rotate through last three stations.
9:53 – 9:55	Review last three stations.
9:55 – 10:00	Walk to cool down.
10:00 – 10:05	Lesson review, closure, and dismissal.

The time allocation plan is mostly an estimate and does not have to be followed to the minute. It serves as a series of starting and ending points that can be adjusted as the lesson progresses. After class, the teacher should make notes about how long each segment actually took, for use when the lesson is taught again. After a few repetitions, a teacher can become very accurate in making these allocations.

The space allocation plan can be a simple diagram that allows the teacher to see how the learning environment will be set up for each activity. This helps to show where learning stations will be and if they are too close together, too far apart, unsafe, or might result in a "bottleneck" that causes excessive waiting in class.

5 Task Presentation and Task Structure

Plans will need to be made to prepare for each learning task included in the lesson. That preparation will have two parts: task presentation and task structure. Chapter 4 provides a complete description of both these components. In general, the lesson plan should include the following elements relating to task presentation and structure:

1. Set induction to gain the students' interest.
2. Models and cues to be used for task presentation.
3. Description of task structure, including directions for students.
4. A check for understanding.
5. The sequence and progression of various tasks within one lesson.

6 Review and Closure

A well-planned lesson will end with a review segment and an orderly closure, giving students one more chance to engage with the content. The lesson plan should include a brief segment at the end that permits teacher and student interaction and any final comments or observations. In the best review segments, the teacher brings the students' attention back to the start of the lesson by recalling performance cues and asking what they learned and why it was important. If the closure is planned and completed in an orderly way, it will allow students to be dismissed quietly, giving the entire lesson a sense of purpose and accomplishment for the teacher and students alike.

Adapting Lesson Planning to Various Instructional Models

Although Exhibit 6.5 provides a generic template for lesson planning, be aware that no generic planning template will suit all of the instructional models presented in this book. Like unit planning discussed previously, each lesson plan will contain unique features based on the specific model chosen by the teacher. And like unit plans, no single lesson plan format can fit all models. The generic template in Exhibit 6.5 works well for models that call for much teacher-directed instruction (Direct Instruction, Inquiry Teaching, Peer Teaching, and Tactical Games) but is not suited for interactive models (Cooperative Learning, Teaching Personal and Social Responsibility, Sport Education) or a student-directed model (Personalized System for Instruction). Therefore, each of the chapters in Part Two will present more details about lesson planning within each model, showing you how to custom-fit your plans to the model you have chosen.

A specific lesson plan template for each model in Part Two can be found on the IMPE website. These templates can be downloaded to your computer and used to help you plan better as you learn each model. Note that you will sometimes need to make slight revisions in these templates when your lesson structures reflect creative variations in the use of each model.

LESSON PLANNING AS QUESTION-ASKING

T eachers have many useful ways to prepare a lesson plan and commit it to writing and memory. Remember, though, that the primary purpose of the plan is to facilitate effective instruction by maximizing students' learning opportunities in class. In my work with teachers, I have encouraged them to think of lesson planning as a series of questions that need to be asked—and answered—before a lesson begins. The question-asking process itself leads directly to the formulation of a plan. After key questions have been addressed, the teacher should be adequately prepared for the lesson. Exhibit 6.7 lists some key questions.

Just by answering those key questions, the teacher can have a good head start on a functional and effective lesson plan for every class, whether or not the plan is written down on paper. I strongly suggest that novice teachers write out their lesson plans every time, until those key questions become

Key questions for lesson planning in physical education.	🖨 **EXHIBIT** 6.7

LESSON CONTEXT OR SEGMENT	KEY QUESTIONS TO ASK
Students	1. How many will I be teaching? 2. Which of them have special learning needs? 3. What is the typical developmental stage for this class? 4. What do they already know about this content?
Place in the unit	1. What have we covered already? 2. What comes next? 3. Are we on schedule to finish the unit?
Learning objectives and assessment	1. What objective(s) from the unit plan need to be learned today? 2. What can assessments tell me if the objectives have been learned?
Learning activities	1. What learning activities are scheduled for this time in the unit? 2. How many activities can be completed in this lesson?
Space and equipment	1. Where will each activity take place? What is my floor plan? 2. What equipment do I need for each activity? 3. Can I set out equipment before class? If not, how will students get it and return it? 4. How can I maximize equipment usage for the highest amount of student practice time?
Task presentation and task structure	1. Where will each task presentation take place? 2. What key cues will be given for each task? 3. How will I demonstrate the task to students? 4. How will each task be structured? 5. How long will each task be given? When will the students change tasks? 6. Where will each activity happen in the gym? 7. What are the performance criteria for each task?
Classroom management	1. How will class get started? 2. How will transitions be organized? 3. Do I need special rules for this lesson? 4. What are some potential safety hazards? 5. What is my time allocation for each class segment?
Teaching "jobs"	1. What special conditions exist that I need to alert students to? 2. What will I be doing while they are practicing? 3. Will some students need extra attention from me? 4. What might go wrong, and how will I handle it if it happens?
Review and closure	1. How much time will I need for it? 2. Where will it take place? 3. What needs to be reviewed? 4. Should I make any last minute announcements? 5. How do I dismiss the class in an orderly way?

automatic from experience. Let me state one precaution here. Even when those key questions have been answered, there is always the possibility that things will change as the class proceeds and that the teacher will need to make new plans "on her feet" during class. *Interactive planning* denotes that the teacher is making decisions and taking actions by responding to unanticipated events in the lesson as they occur in "real time." Graham and colleagues (1993) found that expert teachers needed to use less interactive planning than novice teachers because the experts were better able to anticipate and plan for class events ahead of time. In effect, they asked and answered more and better key questions in their pre-lesson planning.

THE UNWRITTEN PARTS OF A LESSON PLAN— BEING COMPLETELY PREPARED

Physical education classes can be very complex and dynamic. Several things can be going on at any moment, and any one of them can change instantly to force the teacher to make a new decision or action. A *pedagogical move* occurs anytime the teacher makes and carries out an instructional decision in class. Research on teaching suggests that physical education teachers make about 15 pedagogical moves *each minute* of class (Anderson, 1980). That means in a 30-minute class the teacher will make and act on about 450 decisions; in a 45-minute lesson that means nearly 700 pedagogical moves could happen! The number of decisions and different actions underscores the importance of planning well, being prepared, and anticipating what must be done within each class segment—the "jobs" of teaching, so to speak. Most of those jobs do not appear in the written plan, but they must be on the teacher's mind as class progresses. The well-prepared teacher not only will know what's in the written plan but also will anticipate what she and her students will be doing at all times in class. Some common anticipation questions are presented in Exhibit 6.8.

As you can see, most of the unwritten plan comes from questions the teacher should ask himself before the lesson starts, to anticipate and prepare for possible events in each class segment. Other elements of the plan represent reminders of what to do or say as class progresses—reminders that will reduce the chance of forgetting important functions during the lesson.

SUMMARY

Good unit and lesson planning provide the best opportunities for effective teaching and learning to occur in physical education. As you now know, an instructional model can be likened to a blueprint that provides the builder with a schematic picture of the project's end product and guides the entire building process to completion. The unit and lesson plans work to put the model's blueprint into action to "get the job done." Even with a good blueprint, poor planning can prevent something from getting built. Models and plans must work together.

Common anticipation questions.   🖶 **EXHIBIT**   **6.8**

BEFORE CLASS BEGINS:

- What is my students' motivation? Why should they want to learn this?
- What in my lesson is interesting, educational, and fun?
- What if this "bombs"?
- Reminder: Make sure to tell the class how well they did last time.

AS STUDENTS ENTER THE GYM:

- Where do I want them to stand or sit while I take roll?
- Is all equipment out and ready? If not, how will students get it?
- Do I have any special announcements to make before class begins?
- Reminder: Be sure to check for proper footwear on all students.

AS STUDENTS MOVE TO THE FIRST TASK PRESENTATION:

- Where will they go to get the task presentation?
- Reminder: Be sure to speak clearly and slowly. This is new content for them.
- What are the cues I will tell them, and what is the best way to explain them to students?
- How do I get and keep every student's attention?
- How will I check for understanding?
- How will I get them into groups and moved to the first activity?

WHILE STUDENTS ARE PRACTICING:

- Are they on task? If not, what is the problem?
- Are they doing the task as I requested?
- Are too many students waiting?
- Are they practicing safely?
- Are most students successful at the task? If not, how do I modify it for them?
- How will I know when it's time to go to the next task?

AS THE LESSON COMES TO A CLOSE:

- How do I get them to stop and pay attention?
- Can I do the closure while students are spread out, or do I need to bring them together?
- Reminder: Make the closure interactive. Do not just review what we did in class.
- Reminder: Be sure to allow "wait time" after each question.
- If several students raise their hands to answer, how do I decide whom to call on?
- What is the best way to dismiss students to the locker room or to their classroom teacher?

The early part of this chapter featured two key concepts about planning. First, the purpose of planning is to promote the most effective instruction possible in any content unit. Second, the idea is not just to plan, but to *be as prepared as possible* for each unit and lesson. If a teacher approaches planning as a series of key questions to ask before each unit and lesson, the answers will help that teacher be prepared most of the time. With experience, those questions, along with their answers, will arise automatically, greatly reducing preparation time and giving the teacher greater confidence as units and lessons begin—and, most important, greater effectiveness in reaching intended learning goals for students.

LEARNING ACTIVITIES

1. Select a class of students at any grade level along with a physical activity content area. Using the printer-friendly version of Exhibit 6.2 on the IMPE website, conduct a complete contextual analysis in anticipation of teaching a 10-lesson instructional unit to that class.

2. Using that same class and content area, complete a content analysis and listing using the printer-friendly version of Exhibit 6.3 on the IMPE website. What will you include in the unit, and why did you choose each part of the content?

3. Now make a complete outline for that unit of instruction.

4. Write an annotated lesson plan using the generic lesson plan available on the IMPE website for the first day of the unit, the fifth day of the unit, and the last day of the unit. Annotating involves making notes on the lesson plans that explain your decisions for each part of the lesson.

5. Share your unit and lesson plans with another physical education teacher, getting her comments and feedback.

TOPICS FOR REFLECTION & SMALL-GROUP DISCUSSION

1. Why can it be said that effective teaching is *not accidental?*

2. What factors might contribute to a teacher's willingness and ability to spend time in unit and lesson planning?

3. How do unit and lesson planning lead to the achievement of the NASPE standards for physical education?

4. How should assessment information from the previous lesson be used to plan the next lesson?

7

ASSESSING STUDENT LEARNING IN MODEL-BASED INSTRUCTION

A s you know by now, quality physical education programs are based on standards of learning or other outcomes determined by a school's teaching staff. But standards alone are not enough. Teachers must be able to document that students are meeting the standards to a satisfactory level. In order to provide that documentation, teachers will need to assess student learning on a regular basis. Teachers also should use assessment to inform their instruction. If the assessment indicates that some or all of the students failed to meet a lesson's objectives, a teacher should modify her instruction accordingly. This chapter will describe the many things to consider in making good assessments in physical education within a model-based instruction approach. Assessment in physical education is done for three important reasons:

1. To describe how much learning has taken place within a given amount of instructional time (a lesson, a unit, a year, or the entire program) and to use that information to plan future lessons and units.

2. To judge or evaluate the quality of that learning (usually for grading).

3. To make decisions for improving instruction when one or more standards are not being met to a satisfactory level.

ALIGNING ASSESSMENT WITH STANDARDS

Assessment provides the crucial link between standards or other defined outcomes for a program and the program's success. As you recall from Chapter 1, the NASPE standards for physical education (NASPE, 2004) are widely accepted as the best and most comprehensive list of the key learning outcomes for contemporary physical education programs. Because standards express "what should be learned," they also provide the best starting point for conducting assessment to answer the next key question: "How can teachers document that the standards have been learned?" If a school, district, or entire state has adopted the NASPE standards, for example, the standards should guide the assessment process from start to finish. Because of the wide acceptance of the NASPE standards, these standards will guide this chapter. When you begin your teaching career, your school or district may have adopted a different set of standards. However, this chapter's example of the NASPE standards will help you understand how standards can be used to guide and assess instruction. This chapter will also give you an abundant set of resources and examples to draw on beyond this book. Many of those resources will be listed at the end of the chapter.

KEY ASSESSMENT CONCEPTS AND TERMS

The first step in learning about assessment in physical education is to become familiar with the various concepts and terms used in that process.

Assessment and Evaluation

Two terms are commonly used to describe the process of documenting what students have learned. Be aware that the terms do have different meanings, but they are often used interchangeably, and this can be confusing. *Assessment* includes those processes used to gather and analyze information to document what students have learned in a lesson, unit, or program. Assessment describes or measures what has been learned and uses that information to plan for future lessons and units. The next—but different—step, *evaluation,* involves a determination of the worth or value of that information. That evaluation is done by the teacher, a student, or some other person who can judge "how good" the learning was. Let me give you a common example to show the difference between these concepts. You are a player on a softball team, and your team scores five runs in the game. "Five runs" is an assessment to *describe* your total for the game. However, it does not tell you if scoring five runs was good enough to win. To evaluate *how well* your team met its goal of winning the game, you must know the other team's score. If it is more than five, your team did not play well enough to win; if it is less than five, your team played well enough to win.

Grading starts with assessment and leads to evaluation. The assessment step includes determining how many correct answers a student gave, how many points she earned, or what percentage score she got. The evaluation step happens when the teacher converts those answers, points, or scores to letters indicating whether a student passed or failed and, if he passed, to what degree (i.e., "D," "C," "B," or "A").

So, if a teacher gathers information about students' knowledge, performance, or behavior related to a standard, that is assessment. If the teacher uses that information to make a judgment about the worth or quality of that knowledge, performance, or behavior, he has taken the next step of evaluation. In reality, most of what is done in physical education today is assessment; most teachers want to know what their students have learned in order to make better decisions for their instruction and their programs. What little evaluation takes place usually measures non-performance criteria such as dressing out, class participation, effort, and behavior. To reduce the potential for confusion, *assessment* will be used as the key operating term in this chapter and the rest of the book.

Timing of Assessments

Assessment information can be gathered according to three time plans in a unit of instruction: (1) continuous, (2) formative, and (3) summative. See Exhibit 7.1 for examples. Each time plan will give the teacher different amounts of information and determine what can be done with that information.

1. *Continuous assessment* occurs automatically during each learning task in the unit. It provides the teacher with "up-to-the-minute" information that can be used to make decisions about task progression—whether to keep students on the present task longer or advance them to the next task. Continuous assessment produces smaller amounts of information, but the timeliness allows the teacher to make changes for the next lesson or even within the current one. One model in Part Two, Personalized System for Instruction (PSI), uses only

Examples of three time plans for assessment.		EXHIBIT 7.1
CONTINUOUS	**FORMATIVE**	**SUMMATIVE**
Self-check performance tasks each day	Short weekly quizzes	Written final exam
Checking for understanding after task presentation	Partner-checked tasks after each skill component	Skills test at the end of the unit
Checking for target heart rate several times in class	Weekly log of fitness activity	Fitness testing at the end of the unit

continuous assessment techniques to provide information about every student in every lesson.

2. *Formative assessments* are conducted periodically during the unit of instruction, perhaps every second or third lesson. They provide the teacher with "midstream" feedback on student learning, so that changes can be made during the unit—before it is too late. Formative assessments can be of short or medium duration, giving the teacher enough information to make changes without forcing him to sacrifice instructional time.

3. *Summative assessments* are conducted at the end of the unit and allow the teacher to determine how much learning occurred during the entire time of instruction. They usually generate larger amounts of information because they cover most or all of the intended learning outcomes. Summative assessments typically require more student preparation time (e.g., studying for tests) and more teacher organization time. Although summative assessments provide more information than continuous or formative techniques, they come at the end of the unit, so the teacher cannot use that information until the next time she teaches that unit.

Norm-Based and Criterion-Based Assessments

All assessments generate a score or other indicator of student performance, and all scores need some level of interpretation by the teacher to be understood. How that interpretation is made will depend on whether the assessment technique used was norm-based or criterion-based.

Norm-based assessments require the collection of a large number of scores on standardized tests, such as fitness tests or skills tests. Scores are then compiled into subgroups according to some common factors of test takers, usually age and gender (e.g., 10-year-old boys, 14-year-old girls). The large number of scores for each group will generate a *normal distribution* of scores that allows any one student's score to be compared with the scores of other students of the same age and gender. Raw scores can be determined and reported, but normed test scores are usually reported as a percentage of students who scored above and below each individual student. For example, being in the 85th percentile of 10-year-old boys means that 84 percent of all other similar test takers scored lower and 15 percent of all other similar test takers scored the same or higher. If a teacher uses a norm-based test, she can then compare her students' performance to all other similar students who have taken the test. Some normed tests can help determine if a student is developing at or near the expected maturation rate in areas like motor skills, fitness, and social development.

Criterion-based assessments compare a student's performance to standards (the criteria) deemed appropriate for mastery in a particular area. Scores from these assessments usually offer a number, or percentage, for the amount of material each student has mastered. The performance standards are determined by the person who uses the assessment technique and reflect one's professional judgment about the quality of each score. A teacher who makes her own tests and sets the passing grade for a written test on volleyball rules at 75 percent, or who determines that students must score 45 out of 50 possible points to get an A on a tennis skills test, is using criterion-based assessment. The value of criterion-based tests is that they can be written to include only what the teacher wants covered in them, thus reflecting the specific kinds of outcomes most sought by the teacher.

Organizational Plans for Assessment

All assessment techniques require the teacher to make an organizational plan to implement them. Assessment doesn't just happen; it must be thought out in advance and implemented in a way that matches the amount and complexity of needed information.

Informal assessments are those that require little advance planning and little class time. Many informal assessments can actually happen in the regular flow of class in a way that is almost undetectable by students and outside observers. Of course, the teacher is well aware of the assessments and controls when and how they occur. The teacher can use many informal techniques on the spot to make decisions about task progression or to gauge student enjoyment of the current activity. One effective informal assessment strategy called *checking for understanding* is used to determine how much information students have retained during a short period of class time, such as a task presentation or explanation of game rules. The teacher simply asks students to recall what was just said or shown to them, which lets the teacher know if they are ready to go on from there.

Formal assessments require more planning and implementation time both for the teacher and the students. Students are typically given advance notice of these assessments and often extra time to prepare for them. Formal assessments include fitness tests, skills tests, or group projects. Formal assessments often count in students' grades or other performance reports. Exhibit 7.2 lists some examples of formal and informal assessments.

Examples of informal and formal assessment plans.	EXHIBIT 7.2
INFORMAL	**FORMAL**
Checking for understanding after a task presentation	Giving a written quiz on key elements of a skill
Asking for a show of hands of those who were able to make five shots on goal in this drill	Giving a skills test on soccer shooting, with the teacher counting makes and misses
Asking students, "How many of you feel your heart pounding hard right now?"	Directing students to take their pulse and calculate to see if they were in their target zone
Asking students, "How many of you like skateboarding?"	Asking students to write five things they like about skateboarding

TRADITIONAL ASSESSMENTS IN PHYSICAL EDUCATION

There are many techniques for assessing learning in physical education, regardless of whether they are designed to be formative or summative, norm-based or criterion-based, formal or informal. Assessments can be divided into two broad categories: traditional and alternative. Traditional assessments have been used in physical education for many years, as their label indicates. Alternative assessments have been recently developed to provide information about learning that is quite different from that provided by traditional techniques. Keep in mind that neither type of assessment is inherently better than the other—they simply produce different kinds of information about learning. It is up to the teacher to decide the best type of assessment to use in individual situations.

Traditional assessments in physical education follow three primary principles, derived from the subdiscipline of measurement and evaluation (Wood, 1996):

1. Establish (and formally state) appropriate instructional objectives.
2. Use appropriate (validated and reliable) tests to measure characteristics related to the instructional objectives.
3. Develop an evaluation (grading) scheme that reflects attainment of instructional objectives. (pp. 202–203)

This traditional assessment process involves an approach that resembles data collection and analysis for research purposes. It typically involves rigorous standards in all parts of the process, to ensure that the data can be used with confidence. As will be discussed below, this kind of rigor can make for a "double-edged sword" for teachers who wish to use these traditional assessments.

Some of the most common forms of traditional assessment used in physical education are:

1. *Informal teacher observation.* Probably the most common type of assessment in physical education occurs when the teacher observes students as they practice skills, play games, and answer questions in class. When asked how they know when their students have learned to throw a Frisbee, the majority of teachers will respond by saying that they saw or heard evidence of that learning in class. This is not truly assessment, but it does provide the teacher with some level of confidence that learning has occurred.

2. *Standardized skills tests.* Many sports in the physical education curriculum have standardized skills tests that assess student performance abilities (Strand & Wilson, 1993). Most of these involve static tests that measure a limited range of skills needed to play each sport. A static test uses a mostly artificial display of skills that determine the student's ability to perform in nongame situations. The front-wall volley tests in racquetball (Hensley, East, & Stillwell, 1979) and any test that calls for the student to hit a ball into a fixed target (such as tennis-serving accuracy tests) are static. Standardized skills tests are

not necessarily invalid, but teachers who use them must understand the tests' limitations for assessment purposes. That is, these tests measure only a small portion of the skills needed to play a game well, and those skills are measured in a nongame situation.

3. *Fitness tests.* Our field has a long history of testing children and youth on several parameters of physical fitness. Over the years, we have developed many standardized test batteries for school programs. The most prominent tests used today are the *Fitnessgram* protocol developed at The Cooper Institute for Aerobic Research and the *President's Challenge* test from the President's Council on Physical Fitness and Sports. With proper administration, these tests can provide students with results that help them determine their level of fitness relative to other students of the same gender and age (Safrit, 1995).

4. *Written tests.* Many teachers use written tests to assess students' cognitive knowledge in physical education. Nearly all of these tests are developed by individual teachers who use them in their own programs; we do not have standardized written tests in physical education like those developed nationally for subjects such as math, science, and reading. Written tests can include questions and problems in several formats: multiple-choice, short-answer, fill-in-the-blank, matching, diagramming, and open-ended. Each type of question or problem will prompt students to demonstrate their knowledge in a different way and to provide different types of assessment information to the teacher.

Advantages of Traditional Assessments

Within certain limits, skills tests, fitness tests, and written tests can provide useful assessment information. They usually measure learning in ways that are sufficiently objective, use accepted measuring techniques and instruments, and can be carried out with strong consistency. Standardized skills and fitness tests have met rigorous standards in their development and have been field-tested on many subjects who are similar in age, gender, and ability to those for whom the test is designed.

Most skills tests and fitness tests are normative, meaning that they have been used to measure many people in different age, gender, and ability groups, providing a large database for the test. Having that database allows a teacher to compare her students' results with those from similar test takers in other schools, states, and regions across the nation.

Traditional assessments also have the advantage of including content, procedures, and scoring developed by trained experts, so the teacher does not have to take the time to design, validate, field-test, and determine how to score the assessment. Many such tests today include software and data-entry procedures that simplify the tasks of scoring and reporting results to students. In addition, these types of assessments usually produce large amounts of numeric data that can undergo statistical treatment to generate many kinds of informative analyses, ranging from simple measures of central tendency to sophisticated tests of learning effects.

Disadvantages of Traditional Assessments

On the other hand, traditional assessments present some distinct disadvantages that have limited their use in school physical education programs. Some of the issues focus on the true validity of test design, relative to typical outcomes in physical education. For instance, does the serving accuracy test for tennis (AAHPERD, 1989) measure one's ability to play the game (a typical program outcome) or one's proficiency in a limited, controlled, and static aspect of tennis skill performance? Are health-related fitness tests good predictors of one's health risks or continued involvement in physical activity in later years, or are they one-time "snapshots" of a child's present condition with little relationship to the future? Most likely, the second answer is correct in both examples.

For a large number of teachers, the disadvantages of traditional assessments center on problems of practicality when they are used in large classes and with limited class time (Wood, 2003). The rigor with which most standardized tests generate data comes with a price; many of them must be administered by the teacher to individual students, taking time away from learning itself. This fact forces the teacher into a real trade-off—taking the extra time needed for the assessment away from instructional time—which in turn may result in lower performance scores on the assessment! Because of the time and effort needed to complete them, traditional assessments often limit the types of information they provide for the teacher and students; they tend to focus on a small portion of the intended learning outcomes, leaving many unanswered questions about student achievement.

In addition, traditional assessments often require that the data be transformed in ways that are difficult for teachers and students to understand. Statistical treatment can sometimes produce information that requires special expertise to interpret and communicate to learners. The final disadvantage of traditional assessments is that they tend to focus on identifying discrepancies between what was learned and what should have been learned, with little information for teachers and students about how to improve knowledge, performance, or fitness levels. A written test results in a score, or a percentage of items answered correctly. It does not help students improve their knowledge. Fitness tests and skills tests give students normative results, letting them know how they compare with others of the same age and gender, but there is nothing in those tests that teaches a student how to improve personal fitness levels for the next test or how to increase activity levels in daily life.

ALTERNATIVE ASSESSMENTS IN PHYSICAL EDUCATION

Educational assessment has undergone much reform in recent years. Some of that reform has been driven by professionals who believe that the disadvantages of traditional assessment outweigh its advantages. A second factor has been the expanded scope and variety of new learning outcomes in physical education that cannot be assessed with traditional techniques (Lambert, 2007). This growing movement is called *alternative assessment,* to indicate that it was developed, in large part, as a direct contrast with traditional assessment in physical education. So, in the most simplistic sense, *alternative* means "something other" than the traditional assessments just discussed. But it really is much more than just an opposition movement. Proponents of alternative assessment techniques point out that these methods have a sound theoretical foundation and sufficiently rigorous procedures. They represent logical ways to assess students on the diverse types of learning pursued in many contemporary physical education programs—such as the types of learning included in the NASPE (2004) K–12 physical education standards discussed in Chapter 1.

Alternative assessments are based on four principles:

1. Knowledge can be demonstrated in a variety of ways, all of which can be valid indicators of student learning.
2. The process of learning is as important to assess as the outcomes themselves.
3. Diverse types of learning goals require diverse types of assessment.
4. Higher-order learning, particularly in the cognitive domain, requires inventive assessment that is not possible with traditional techniques.

Many kinds of alternative assessments have been developed for physical education. Because these assessments are designed by teachers, and not test-making experts, they are customized to allow each teacher to assess learning outcomes specific to his own instruction. Some common types of alternative assessment used in physical education include:

1. *Group projects.* Students are placed into learning teams of three to five members and given an assignment to complete. That assignment could ask them to develop a report, make a photo collage to represent a certain theme or event, or complete an extended motor skill "problem" (e.g., learn how to use a zone defense in ultimate Frisbee).

2. *Multimedia presentations.* Individual students or learning teams make a presentation to the class that incorporates two or more types of media, or students could be asked to make a video to show other students how to play a position such as goalie in field hockey.

3. *Activity logs.* Students keep a log of all physical activity they do for a week to monitor their levels of fitness-promoting activity. The log would include all the activities, the amount of time spent in each one, and the level of exertion needed for each.

4. *Personal journals.* Students keep a record of how they felt and what they thought during physical education class or some other physical activity event in which they participated.

5. *Role-playing.* Students assume a nonplaying role for an extended period of time to learn the decisions, responsibilities, and knowledge needed for that role. Some examples are coaching, officiating, or serving on a league board of directors.

6. *Oral examinations.* Students receive questions that require a high level of knowledge and are expected to give and explain their answers. Example questions could be: "What are the advantages and disadvantages of playing zone defenses in football?" or "Why is it important to drink fluids before, during, and after exercise?"

7. *"Show and tell" presentations.* Students do some research or practice outside of class and then present what they have learned to the class.

8. *Interviews.* Students interview other students, family members, or community members about what physical education was like when they were in school.

9. *Teacher, peer, and self-observations with performance checklists.* A set of correct performance cues is taught to students and listed on a checklist. The teacher or a classmate observes a student practicing and "checks off" those parts that were performed correctly. Or a student can be recorded while practicing and then watch the video to check herself.

10. *Portfolios.* Students collect and organize various kinds of artifacts (photographs, videos, drawings, newspaper articles, and the like) that demonstrate their knowledge of a certain topic or concept (e.g., the Olympics, Title IX). The process of identifying an organizing theme for the portfolio and gathering artifacts becomes just as important as the final contents of the portfolio itself.

Rubrics

The cornerstone of alternative assessment is the scoring *rubric,* which is used to determine the quality of the learning demonstrated by students (Lund, 2000). Rubrics inform students of the performance criteria on the assessment ahead of time and serve as the basis of the teacher's review of the completed work. The rubric translates the quality of the demonstrated learning into a descriptor (e.g., "novice," "intermediate," "advanced," or "incomplete," "almost complete," "complete") or a numeric/value rating (e.g., 1/poor, 2/fair, 3/good, 4/excellent) based on criteria stated in advance.

Goodrich (1996–97) highlights seven steps in the process of creating good rubrics:

1. *Look at models.* Show students examples of good and not-so-good work from previous assessments.

2. *List and discuss criteria.* Use the models to help students make a list of what counts as quality work.

3. *Articulate gradations of quality.* Present and discuss what separates each level of quality from the others.

4. *Practice on models.* Have the students use the rubric on the models.

5. *Use self- and peer assessments.* Allow for periodic assessments as the task is being completed. Provide students with formative feedback.

6. *Revise.* Allow students time to make revisions based on the feedback given in step 5.
7. *Use teacher assessment.* Apply the rubric in the same way that students have learned it.

Exhibits 7.3–7.5 present three examples of alternative assessment tasks in physical education and the scoring rubric for each one.

Example of alternative assessment and rubric for Newcomb rules lesson.	EXHIBIT 7.3

Grade levels: 3–4 (at the end of a 4-week Newcomb unit)

Knowledge assessed: Newcomb rules

Assessment task: Three teams are made at each court. Two of those teams will play, while the third team will watch the action from the sideline and record the results and score after each volley. Teams rotate after every 10 volleys, regardless of the score. The teacher also keeps a score sheet for assessing students' answers when the teams change (this constitutes the rubric for assessing students' accuracy).

	POINT SCORED BY TEAM A OR B?	HOW?*	WHAT IS THE SCORE NOW?	DOES ANYONE ROTATE?**
Volley #1 (A serves)	A	5	1–0	N
Volley #2	A	3	2–0	N
Volley #3	B	1	2–1	Y
Volley #4	B	4	2–2	N
Volley #5	B	5	2–3	N
Volley #6	B	3	2–4	N
Volley #7	A	1	3–4	Y
Volley #8	A	3	4–4	N
Volley #9	B	1	4–5	Y
Volley #10	B	4	4–6	N

* How?

1. Foot fault
2. Net serve
3. Out of bounds
4. Ball touched too many players' hands
5. Other team did not return the ball over the net

** Does anyone rotate?

Y = YES
N = NO

Developed by Donna Hicks, physical education teacher at Hickory Flat Elementary School, McDonough, GA. Used with permission.

EXHIBIT	7.4	Example of alternative assessment and scoring rubric for Olympic Oath and Spirit lesson.

Grade levels: Middle school

Knowledge assessed: The Olympic Oath and Spirit

Assessment task: Following a unit on Summer Olympic sports, make a multimedia collage that shows athletes competing and displaying the "Olympic Spirit."

Time allowed: Out of class, due in one week

Scoring rubric:

MEDAL LEVEL	ASSESSMENT CRITERIA
Gold medal	1. Your collage uses three or more types of media.
	2. Your collage shows at least five different sports.
	3. Your collage shows many types of sports, athletes, and five countries.
	4. Your collage shows athletes displaying the Olympic spirit in many ways.
Silver medal	1. Your collage uses two types of media.
	2. Your collage shows three or four different sports.
	3. Your collage shows a few types of sports, athletes, and countries.
	4. Your collage shows just a few examples of the Olympic spirit.
Bronze medal	1. One type of media is used.
	2. One or two sports are displayed.
	3. Only competition is shown.
Future Olympian	1. Collage includes non-Olympic examples.
	2. Collage does not fill up the poster you selected.
	3. Incorrect examples of the Olympic spirit are included.

Advantages of Alternative Assessments

Just as with traditional techniques, alternative assessments have advantages that teachers need to understand. Perhaps the greatest advantage of alternative assessments is their ability to be designed to monitor the specific learning standards or outcomes planned by the teacher. The teacher can feel more confident that the assessment targets what she really wanted her students to learn. Another strong advantage is that alternative assessments allow students to demonstrate their learning in a variety of ways—not just through the recall of information or through skill performance on standardized tests. Because we know that students are engaged in diverse kinds of learning activities, it makes sense that they should be able to demonstrate their knowledge in a way that matches how they actually gained it.

Example of alternative assessment and rubric for golf swing lesson.   **EXHIBIT   7.5**

Grade levels: High school

Knowledge assessed: Ability to analyze key elements of the golf swing

Assessment task: Get a partner. One partner will take 10 swings with a "driver" while the other partner observes each trial. The observer will evaluate each key element on the checklist to reflect how well his/her partner performed that component each time. The observer's checks will be compared with those made by the teacher, who will also watch the practicing student. Switch roles after every 10 tries.

KEY ELEMENT	1	2	3	4	5	6	7	8	9	10
1. Stance and alignment										
2. Grip										
3. Back swing										
4. Point of contact										
5. Follow-through										

After each shot, score: 3 if element was fully correct

2 if element was almost fully correct

1 if element was incorrect

Scoring rubric for the observer (1 point for each analysis that matches the teacher's; possible 50 points):

45–50	Teaching professional
40–44	"Scratch" player
35–39	Low handicapper
25–34	High handicapper
24 or lower	Novice

By using a scoring rubric, students know the performance expectations for the assessment task ahead of time. They are then able to make choices and devise strategies for the *process* of completing the assessment as well as the final demonstration of their knowledge. In other words, the rubric fosters the ability to *learn how to learn*. Rubrics provide another advantage. They include a common set of criteria used by the teacher to assess student work. Rubrics lend a sufficient degree of objectivity to the review process and make for more consistent assessments within and among classes.

Finally, alternative assessment, particularly through the rubric, has the ability to provide students with feedback about their learning and to identify ways for them to improve performance.

Disadvantages of Alternative Assessments

Although alternative assessments provide unique, creative, and diverse ways to assess student learning in physical education, they are not without disadvantages. Because they are customized, it takes time for a teacher to design each one for her class. The examples shown earlier can give a teacher some ideas for assessment, but unless those examples are perfect matches, they will need to be adapted or completely redesigned for use by other teachers. The design stage may also require some trial-and-error time to get the assessment just right for its intended use.

Alternative assessments typically take longer for students to complete and for the teacher to review. Many of these tasks require extended time for students to plan their work, conceptualize answers, organize materials, and develop the final product. All these steps contribute to the learning process itself, but they do take time to accomplish. Similarly, the teacher will need some time to review each completed assessment—usually more time than it would take to score written tests and skills tests.

AUTHENTIC ASSESSMENT
FOR PHYSICAL EDUCATION

A *uthentic assessment,* sometimes called *performance assessment,* refers to the practice of making assessments that involve, or simulate, the real-life settings in which knowledge taught in school will be applied (Lambert, 2007). Some examples will help to clarify this concept. Health-related fitness tests (e.g., Fitnessgram, President's Council) measure student abilities on several parameters that are *indicators* of present fitness levels. They do not assess health-related *behaviors and choices* made at other times during the school day, after school, and at home that more accurately determine patterns of healthy living. If a stated goal of the physical education program is to promote active and healthy lifestyles, then an authentic assessment of that learning would occur at the times and places that students make health-related choices for their behavior. Student logs that record the foods they eat and the moderate to vigorous activity they engage in would be an appropriate authentic assessment of physical fitness behavior and choices.

If the goal is to teach students how to play the game of softball, then an authentic assessment would take place during an actual game, not with a skills test in a nongame context. In this case, an authentic assessment could be based on students' game statistics or a performance checklist completed as the game is played. The Game Performance Assessment Instrument (GPAI softball version) developed by Griffin, Mitchell, and Oslin (1997) does precisely that by analyzing players' performance in several categories of involvement, skills, strategies, and decision making during game play. The GPAI will be explained in much more detail in Chapter 14.

If the goal is to assess junior high students' dance performance ability, then an authentic assessment could be designed during their participation in a class dance production at the school. Asking students to demonstrate their cognitive knowledge or their appreciation for dance with a multimedia collage would be an alternative assessment technique, but that is not nearly as authentic as performing in a production. I emphasize that authenticity is determined by the *degree* to which the assessment calls for students to demonstrate real-life applications of their knowledge. Rarely is any assessment technique totally non-authentic or entirely authentic.

Physical education teachers need to know that all assessments, traditional or alternative, and at whatever degree of authenticity, are essentially tools used to understand what students have learned from instruction in a content unit or program. The key here is to understand what each assessment tool can do and when it is appropriate to use it. Teachers should not start by saying, "I am going to use an alternative, authentic assessment in this upcoming dance unit." Rather, the teacher should follow a deductive process that starts with "What and how will students learn in this unit?" which leads to "How do I want them to demonstrate that new knowledge for me?" and then "Which assessment technique will provide the best demonstration of their knowledge?" From that, the teacher will select the right assessment tool for the right assessment job.

ASSESSMENT IN MODEL-BASED INSTRUCTION

All of the assessment concepts and techniques described so far in this chapter have been presented as declarative knowledge, key things that all teachers should know *about* assessment. Effective teachers who use instructional models will need to have that kind of knowledge as well as good procedural and conditional knowledge in order to select and carry out the best assessment strategies within the model used for a unit. Exhibit 7.6 shows some assessment strategies for each of the models in Part Two of this book, along with suggested times to implement those strategies. These assessment techniques will be explained in more detail in the assessment section of each model described in Part Two.

Documenting Learning with Assessments

Assessment techniques will provide the teacher with a description of students' current learning, but how can the teacher know *how much* learning has occurred over the course of the unit? Summative assessments give a good picture of what students know and can do at the end of a unit but furnish no information about what students knew or could do when the unit started. Teachers can do two things to document the amount of student learning that occurs in a unit. They can give pre-assessments that cover the major learning outcomes in the unit and then compare the pre-assessments with summative assessments. Learning can then be defined as the difference in those scores, commonly called *gain*. Second, teachers can use continuous assessments to monitor student progress over the course of the unit, placing

EXHIBIT 7.6	Assessment strategies and timing with instructional models.			
MODEL	**MAJOR LEARNING OUTCOMES**	**TRADITIONAL ASSESSMENTS**	**ALTERNATIVE ASSESSMENTS**	**TIMING**
Direct Instruction	1. Motor performance 2. Knowledge of rules 3. Fitness	Skills tests Written tests Fitness tests	Performance checklists	Formative Summative
Personalized System for Instruction	1. Motor performance 2. Knowledge of rules 3. Fitness	Skills "quizzes" Written tests Fitness tests	Performance checklists Logs	Continuous
Cooperative Learning	1. Knowledge of concepts 2. Team participation 3. Social development	Skills "quizzes" Written tests	Group projects Multimedia projects Portfolios Journals	Continuous Formative Summative
Sport Education	1. Game performance and strategy 2. Team participation 3. "Duty role" performance	Written tests	Role-playing checklists Team projects Game performance summaries GPAI Journals	Formative Summative
Peer Teaching	1. Motor performance 2. Cognitive knowledge (to teach) 3. Social development	Skills tests Written tests	Performance checklists Journals	Continuous Formative
Inquiry Teaching	1. Higher-order knowledge, combined with 2. Movement skills	Written tests	Oral examinations Interviews Journals	Continuous Formative Summative
Tactical Games	1. Tactical knowledge, combined with 2. Motor performance	Written tests	GPAI Performance checklists Oral examinations	Continuous Formative Summative
Teaching Responsibility	1. Social development 2. Motor performance	Skills tests	Performance checklists Journals	Continuous Formative Summative

students' performance scores in the many assessments on a chart to show the amount and the rate of learning.

Teachers can use individual or grouped information to document how much learning has occurred. Since each student will have her own set of scores over time, the teacher can examine those scores to determine if progress is being made. Teachers can group assessment data by calculating mean scores for subgroups of students (e.g., boys and girls, less skilled and more skilled) to note if any group shows a different amount of learning. If one group is found to be learning less, the teacher can change instructional strategies to help that group catch up. Assessment data can also be grouped for all students in the class by calculating a mean class score. Although class mean scores give the teacher an overall description of learning, they can often hide differences among individual students in the class.

Using Assessment for Planning and Teaching

Formative assessments can be used to monitor student learning as a unit progresses and to help teachers make informed decisions about changes that could be needed right away to increase the amount and rate of student learning. A performance assessment taken at the end of one day's lesson can provide a teacher with important information about whether students have learned the content well enough to move ahead in the sequence of learning activities, or whether students need more time and practice before moving on to new content, to more advanced content, or to playing competitive games. For example, if most students in a class score very low on a test of speedball rules and etiquette, it would not be a good decision to advance them to actual game play in the next lesson—even if the schedule calls for that to happen. This should clue teachers that further review of the rules and etiquette are needed and that they should conduct that review and a follow-up assessment in the next lesson, before students move on to game play.

Making Assessment Practical

Assessments give teachers valuable information about what students have learned in physical education. Teachers really need to know what students have learned, how much they have learned, and how well students have achieved stated standards and outcomes. As noted earlier, however, good assessments take time for teachers to prepare, for students to complete, and for teachers to review. And there is a catch—the time it takes a teacher to gather assessment information can take time away from student engagement with the content, actually reducing the amount of time available for learning.

Physical education teachers can use several strategies for gathering assessment information in a practical manner:

1. Do not attempt to assess all the potential learning outcomes in a unit. Identify the three or four most important outcomes, and assess only those.

2. Use assessments that have been successful for other teachers. Good examples of assessments can be found in many places, including the suggested readings listed at the end of this chapter.

3. Teach students to do self- and peer assessments when possible. Sometimes the teacher's main task is to watch students perform and count successful tries. Students from the middle grades and up can learn the key elements to look for and how to measure and quantify them; then they can watch and score their peers.

4. Use worksheets and scoring sheets to reduce paperwork. Many scores can be entered on one page rather than one score per page. This will help the teacher to be more organized and also allow for faster scoring of the results later.

5. Use small, continuous assessments as much as possible. Simply asking students to raise their hands if they have performed a learning task to a certain level can supply quick and valuable information.

6. Build assessment into learning tasks whenever possible. Rather than just asking students to practice for five minutes, direct them to count the number of "good" tries they make during those five minutes. Similarly, scoring sheets can be placed at learning stations, with students directed to fill in their scores before they move to the next station.

7. Use technology to gather, store, and analyze assessment information. Many physical education teachers are now using desktop computers, laptops, tablets, and even smartphones to enter assessments and store assessment data. This technology allows for convenient data entry and storage and facilitates generation and distribution of assessment reports to students, parents, and school administrators.

SUMMARY

Good physical education programs today must have standards for student learning, whether they are the NASPE standards or other stated goals and outcomes. Those standards represent the essential kinds of knowledge, skills, behaviors, and dispositions that students will achieve by participating in regular, quality physical education instruction. But having standards is not enough; good programs must be able to document the degree to which students have achieved those standards, based on relevant performance criteria—not just a teacher's opinion that learning has taken place. The key operation in documenting student achievement involves gathering assessment data and other information that can be used to establish a program's success or the need for improvement in certain areas. Because contemporary physical education programs strive for many and different outcomes and also because teachers want to help students to achieve in and out of school, assessment must take many forms and happen in many settings. The most effective teachers and programs are those that link standards, assessment, student learning, and continuous program improvement.

LEARNING ACTIVITIES

1. Go to the website of your state's department of education, and follow the links to its standards or other learning outcomes for physical education. (Your professor may need to assist you with this search.) For each standard/outcome, do two things. First, make a copy of the exact statement of that standard/outcome as it appears on the website. Second, use your own words to express the standard/outcome, as if you were trying to explain it to your students. That is, what would you tell students you are trying to teach that relates to this standard/outcome?

2. Select one standard/outcome in your state's list, and identify a grade level (preschool/lower elementary, upper elementary, middle school, high school). Next, identify a content unit you might teach for that grade level in order to address that standard/outcome (e.g., dance, fitness, team sports, basic throwing and catching). Explain how your content unit can lead students toward achieving that standard/outcome. What is the alignment between that unit and the standard/outcome you wish students to achieve?

3. Following up on the previous learning activity, state and explain three ways that students could demonstrate they have achieved the standard/outcome. One of those ways must occur *outside* the physical education program (e.g., in school, at home, in youth sports). Design an assessment strategy for each of those three ways of demonstrating the standard/outcome. Your strategy must include a description of the assessment task to be given to students, how it will be implemented, and how it will be scored. Finally, explain how you will use that assessment information to determine the degree to which your students have met the standard/outcome.

4. Select another standard/outcome, and repeat Activities 2 and 3.

TOPICS FOR REFLECTION & SMALL-GROUP DISCUSSION

1. Schools in the United States today are being held more accountable for student learning. Why do you think this is happening? What factors are contributing to this?

2. What is the relationship between learning standards (e.g., NASPE standards or your own state's standards) and assessment?

3. What kind of assessments did you have in physical education as a P–12 student? What was assessed, and how was that information used?

4. What are some of the reasons why meaningful assessments are difficult for physical education teachers to complete?

5. Pick any physical education content area that you know well (e.g., dance, team sports, fitness). What do you think is the best way to show that you have *really* learned that content?

SUGGESTED READINGS

Lambert, L. T. (2007). *Standards-based assessment of student learning* (2nd ed.) Reston, VA: National Association for Sport and Physical Education.

Lund, J. L., & Kirk, M. K. (2010). *Performance-based assessment for middle and high school physical education* (2nd ed.). Champaign, IL: Human Kinetics.

Mitchell, S. A., & Oslin, J. L. (1999). *Assessment in games teaching.* Reston, VA: National Association for Sport and Physical Education.

National Association for Sport and Physical Education. (2004). *Moving into the future: National standards for physical education* (2nd ed.). Reston, VA: Author.

O'Sullivan, M. O., & Henniger, M. (2000). *Assessing student responsibility and teamwork.* Reston, VA: National Association for Sport and Physical Education.

Schiemer, S. (2000). *Assessment strategies for elementary physical education.* Champaign, IL: Human Kinetics.

EIGHT INSTRUCTIONAL MODELS FOR PHYSICAL EDUCATION

part two

B y now you should have a good understanding of what an instructional model is and why model-based teaching can promote a wide range of standards and learning outcomes in physical education programs at all grade levels and for all kinds of content units. But you still might not have a good idea of what any one instructional model looks like, how to select a model for a content unit, how to implement a model the way in which it was designed, and how to know if a model is leading to the learning goals you have for your students. Part Two will give you an extensive description of eight models that have been shown to be effective in teaching physical education, along with some examples of how each model can be used for unit and lesson planning. This will take you from the sometimes abstract discussions in Part One to a clear picture of what a model actually looks like and how to use it in your teaching.

You will be reminded many times in Part Two of the two most important things to understand about every instructional model in this book. First, each model is designed to promote certain types of student learning outcomes. No model "does it all." If that were true, we would need only one model! A teacher who wishes to have students become truly "physically educated persons" will have to use more than one model in her program. Second, the effectiveness of a model depends heavily on the teacher's using the model as it was designed, as measured by "bench-marks" that verify how well the model was implemented. Very simply, if the model is not followed according to its design, it will not work for its intended purpose.

Examples of unit and lesson planning for each model will be found on the IMPE website. It is a good idea to refer to those examples as you read each chapter. At some point, you will need to understand each model well enough to use it in your teaching, as part of a methods course, during a field experience, or with your own students. That's when you will really learn model-based instruction. At that time, be sure to use the appropriate chapter in this book and the suggested readings for each model as good resources. All these models have been field-tested, and you can use others' experience to learn model-based instruction.

DIRECT INSTRUCTION
Teacher as Instructional Leader

Even though they may not identify it formally as model-based teaching, the vast majority of physical education teachers today probably use some recognizable version of what is known as *direct instruction.* For many years this was the most dominant teaching approach in physical education—although not under that label. If you will recall from Chapter 1, there was a distinct "method" of teaching physical education that was dominant from around 1890 well into the 1970s. Oberteuffer and Ulrich (1962) refer to it as the *direct method,* characterized by the "teacher saying" and the "students doing." This method is not to be confused with the Direct Instruction model, but it does bear enough resemblance that the uninformed observer can misinterpret it as such.

It must therefore be emphasized that the Direct Instruction *model* is not the same as the wide range of *direct teaching strategies* used in physical education today. Although the model incorporates many direct teaching strategies, it is based on a series of defined steps, teacher decisions, and student engagement patterns that form the model's design. Any number of direct teaching strategies might also be used in other models presented in this book, but they become

Direct Instruction only when a teacher plans and implements instruction according to the intentional design of the Direct Instruction model.

As Baumann (1988) correctly notes, the Direct Instruction model was not developed by a single designer at a readily identifiable point in time. In reality, the model evolved from a number of classroom practices that teaching research correlated with increased levels of student achievement, practices that shared some similar instructional operations. Baumann notes that the model had at least three other labels (explicit instruction, active teaching, and teacher-directed instruction) until Rosenshine's (1979) label of *direct instruction* became the most common name for it. It was Rosenshine in 1983 who also delineated what would become the most widely accepted design of and operations for this model. The ideas presented in this chapter are derived primarily from Rosenshine's (1983) conceptualization and design.

OVERVIEW

Direct Instruction is characterized by teacher-controlled decisions and teacher-directed engagement patterns for learners. Teachers will have a distinct set of learning goals in mind; present students with a model of the desired movement, skill, or concept; and then organize student learning activities into segmented blocks of time, providing high rates of augmented feedback and encouragement as learners practice each task or skill. Given only a few decisions to make, students mostly follow the teacher's directions in class and respond to the teacher's questions when asked. The purpose of this pattern is to provide the most efficient use of class time and resources in order to promote very high rates of student engagement in practice tasks and skills. The essence of the model is to give students as many supervised practice attempts as possible, so that the teacher can observe those attempts and deliver high rates of positive and corrective feedback.

The unit content in Direct Instruction is divided into a series of sequential performance skills and areas of knowledge. This is accomplished through a task analysis, leading to a list of content areas to be covered, much as you learned in Part One. Each skill and knowledge area will contain a set of specific performance tasks for students to practice and learn. According to Rosenshine (1983), Direct Instruction teachers perform a set of prescribed operations to promote student achievement (p. 336):

1. They structure the learning.
2. They proceed in small steps but at a brisk pace.
3. They give detailed and repeated instructions and explanations.
4. They ask a large number of questions and provide overt, active practice.
5. They provide feedback and corrections, particularly at the initial stages of learning.
6. They ensure a student success rate of 80 percent or higher on initial learning tasks.

7. They divide large academic tasks into smaller tasks.

8. They provide for continued student practice with a success rate of 90 to 100 percent, so that students' responses become rapid, confident, and firm.

A class lesson can include anywhere from one to several learning tasks planned by the teacher. It is at the level of the lesson that Direct Instruction takes on its unique (but definitely recognizable) pattern for the teaching/ learning process. Rosenshine (1983) identifies six key operations in a Direct Instruction lesson (p. 338), all described in detail below.

1. Review of previously learned material. Each Direct Instruction lesson should begin with a brief review of the previous lesson. This forms part of the teacher's *set induction,* or what the Hunter version of the model calls the *anticipatory set.* This review should cover the most essential skills and concepts learned before and preview the content for the upcoming lesson. The review serves four functions: (1) it helps the teacher understand how much students retained from the previous lesson(s), (2) it allows students to bring that previously learned material into more recent memory, (3) it immediately establishes a learning environment by getting students to think, and (4) it provides a link between the previous and upcoming learning tasks.

2. Presentation of new content/skills. Typically, right after the set induction, the teacher presents the new content (skills, knowledge, or concepts) that students will learn in the lesson. The new content is shown or "modeled" (refer to discussion of modeling on p. 178) to students in a task presentation segment led by the teacher. The task presentation provides students with a verbal and/or visual description of what the new content is and how it should be performed. This gives students the "picture" or "idea" of what proficient performance looks like. Of course, that picture or idea must be a developmentally appropriate one for the students' age/stage.

3. Initial student practice. The task presentation leads directly into a practice segment, during which students take their initial steps toward proficiency. The practice task should allow for very high rates of student responses, with the teacher using direct monitoring in order to provide high rates of corrective feedback. The initial practice task should continue until students reach a success rate of at least 80 percent on their attempts.

4. Feedback and correctives. The teacher's delivery of augmented feedback and corrective statements to students can be done concurrently with the early learning task(s), or between each task in a practice sequence. The teacher may choose to reteach some of the key performance cues and even repeat some of the earlier learning tasks to ensure that students are ready to move on.

5. Independent practice. After the teacher is confident that students have become proficient in the basic, supervised practice tasks, she can then plan for students to practice more independently. The teacher still designs the learning activities and leads the task presentations for them, but she allows students to make their own decisions about pacing. This promotes even higher rates of student response, since students do not wait for the teacher to cue and supervise their practice attempts. The goal is for students to achieve about a 90 percent success rate on each independent task before the teacher moves on to a new task or content.

6. Periodic reviews. Direct Instruction teachers will often plan to repeat previously learned tasks. Such reviews help the teacher check for student retention and alert the students that new content is built from earlier content in the unit.

Even though Direct Instruction is still the predominant instructional model in U.S. schools in all grades and subject areas, it has come under recent criticism as other learning models have received increased attention—some because they have been designed in contrast to Direct Instruction (Baumann, 1988). Some of that criticism is legitimate, pointing out a few of the well-recognized limitations of Direct Instruction—particularly its emphasis on lower learning domain outcomes. On the other hand, some of the opposition is not valid, especially when opponents point to misuses of Direct Instruction and then attribute low student achievement to flaws in the model itself (Baumann, 1988). Morine-Dershimer (1985) gives well-stated support for Direct Instruction:

> Students are reinforced for correct responses, and incorrect responses are followed by corrective feedback, probing questions, or redirecting questions. Although the term Direct Instruction has suggested pupil passivity to some educators, the effectiveness of this [model] is in fact associated with the very active participation of students. The communication patterns in Direct Instruction clearly delineate both the content task and the participation task confronting pupils, and they place an obvious emphasis on the content-learning task. When the participation task is clear and fairly well routinized, as in Direct Instruction, then pupils can concentrate on learning content rather than on trying to draw inferences about shifting requirements for participation. (p. 179)

Although it has been said many times, the following statement bears repeating once again: Every instructional model (in this book and elsewhere) is designed to promote certain kinds of student learning outcomes by following a well-defined set of teaching and learning operations. As with all models, Direct Instruction will be effective when it is used for its intended purposes and implemented according to its prescribed plan. When a teacher has other purposes for instruction or can't implement the Direct Instruction model faithfully, he should look for a different model to use in that content unit.

ALIGNMENT WITH NASPE NATIONAL STANDARDS

Exhibit 8.1 shows the alignment of Direct Instruction with the NASPE standards. This model is most strongly aligned with those standards that focus on competency with skill and movement patterns and those that focus on movement concepts, principles, strategies, and tactics. It should be emphasized

Alignment of direct instruction with NASPE National Standards.		🖶 EXHIBIT 8.1
NASPE STANDARD	**ALIGNMENT RATING**	**COMMENTS**
1. Demonstrates competency in motor skills and movement patterns needed to perform a variety of physical activities	1	One of the best models for learning movement skills
2. Demonstrates understanding of movement concepts, principles, strategies, and tactics as they apply to the learning and performance of physical activities	1	Achieved by the teacher telling and showing these outcomes to students
3. Participates regularly in physical activity	2	Will vary according to the learning task of the moment
4. Achieves and maintains a health-enhancing level of physical fitness	3	With focus on skill, moderate-to-vigorous-physical activity is usually limited
5. Exhibits responsible personal and social behavior that respects self and others in physical activity settings	3	Students follow what the teacher says or asks, so personal decision making is limited
6. Values physical activity for health, enjoyment, challenge, self-expression, and/or social interaction	1–3	Strongly aligned for enjoyment and challenge; moderate alignment for self expression and social interaction; weakly aligned for health.

Ratings categories:

1. Strong alignment
2. Moderate alignment
3. Weak alignment

that the ability of Direct Instruction to address each of the NASPE standards will be affected by the way a teacher designs specific learning tasks within a unit of instruction, so the ratings shown here should be viewed as typical, not definitive.

FOUNDATIONS

Theory and Rationale

The teaching and learning strategies that evolved into Direct Instruction were derived from the operant conditioning theories of B. F. Skinner, the noted experimental behavioral psychologist. Many of the operations in Direct Instruction were extrapolated from his research on laboratory animals, which demonstrated a clear relationship between learned behavior and its consequences. Essentially, responses that were followed by certain consequences, called *reinforcers*, increased the probability that the behavior would be emitted when the environmental stimulus was present again. Responses that were followed by other consequences, called *punishers*, would tend to decrease or not occur at all when the environmental stimulus was present again. Skinner and his colleagues used this simple set of relationships as the basis of several operations that could get animals (and subsequently humans) to acquire long and complex sequences of learned behaviors. In the terminology of behavioral psychology, this process was called *behavior training* and included five main concepts: shaping, modeling, practice, feedback, and reinforcement.

The process of *shaping* occurs by determining the final outcome for the training procedure and then taking the learner through a series of small learning steps, or successive approximations, that lead to the eventual goal. At the start of the shaping process, the form of the skill to be learned might bear only a small resemblance to the final form. However, as the process goes on, the learner will acquire skilled movement patterns that look more and more like the final desired outcome.

The use of *modeling* provides the learner with a tangible, proficient example of the desired skill or movement. Having seen or heard the modeled performance, the learner has a clearer frame of reference—an image of what her practice attempts should look like or result in. Of course, it is essential that the modeled performance be appropriate for the students' current developmental stage and readiness for the task.

Practice segments in Direct Instruction are highly structured and always have a mastery criterion with them. Having structure does not indicate that they are dull or rigid; it means that the teacher makes explicit plans for every aspect of the learning task, including the task structure, the materials to be used, the time allocation, and student engagement patterns. Practice segments in Direct Instruction should be designed for very high rates of opportunities to respond (OTR), providing students with many repetitions of correct performance. The stated mastery criterion informs the students as to how proficient they should become at the present skill or task.

The high rates of OTR are matched by similar rates of *augmented feedback* provided by the teacher. Two kinds of feedback are preferred in Direct Instruction: positive and corrective. Positive feedback serves the dual purpose of reinforcing correct learning trials and giving the learner motivation to maintain task engagement. When the teacher does observe mistakes, he should be sure to tell the student not only that a mistake was made (negative feedback) but how to correct that mistake on the next try. A teacher might offer corrective feedback for a tennis serve by saying, "You made contact with the ball below its highest point; that's why it went into the net [negative feedback]. Next time, hit the ball at its highest point, right at the very top of your reach" [teacher models the high reach; corrective]. This performance cue for the next serve turns negative feedback into corrective feedback that the learner can better use.

Reinforcement is a strong feature of Direct Instruction and is used not only for correct performance trials but also to reward many kinds of student behaviors: listening, good effort, staying on task, following directions, and paying attention to class rules and routines.

The basic rationale for Direct Instruction is quite straightforward, as described earlier by Morine-Dershimer (1985). The teacher makes explicit plans for a series of class events that will give the students a clear picture (model) of the desired performance outcome; that modeling then leads into one or more teacher-directed learning activities that promote high levels of student engagement, coupled with high rates of positive and corrective feedback. Each learning task must be performed to a stated level of mastery and brings the students one step closer (shaping) to the larger learning goals in the content unit. That rationale has proven to be highly effective in many grade levels and nearly all school subject areas, including physical education.

Assumptions About Teaching and Learning

The Direct Instruction model assumes certain principles about teaching and about learning; these principles are listed separately below.

Assumptions about teaching

1. The teacher is the main source of instructional content and decisions and should take a pronounced leadership role in planning and implementing classroom events.
2. The teacher should determine the unit content and place that content into a series of learning tasks through which students progress.
3. The teacher is viewed as one who possesses the content knowledge that must be transferred to students by the most efficient and effective means possible. Based on this assumption, teachers must have high levels of expertise in physical education content and strong class-management skills.
4. The teacher should use her expertise to efficiently manage the complex learning environment in ways that make the best use of class time and resources and that maximize student engagement with the lesson and unit content.

Assumptions about learning

1. Learning occurs when students make incremental progress on small tasks that leads to the acquisition of larger and more complex skills/knowledge.
2. Learners must have a clear understanding of the learning task and its performance criteria prior to being engaged in any of the learning activities.
3. Learning is a function of the consequences that immediately follow emitted behaviors. Behaviors that are followed by reinforcers will tend to be maintained or emitted at higher rates; behaviors that are followed by no reinforcer or a punisher will tend to decrease or desist over time.
4. Learners need a very high rate of OTR in order to shape their learning into the desired performance form or outcome. This necessity effectively counters the criticism that Direct Instruction is a passive model for students; in fact, students need to have very high rates of engagement for movement patterns to become proficient and be retained.

5. The high rates of OTR must be coupled with equally high rates of augmented positive feedback and corrective feedback that inform the learner about the adequacy of learning trials.

The Major Theme of the Direct Instruction Model: Teacher as Instructional Leader

"Teacher as instructional leader" accurately describes the most essential operations of the Direct Instruction model. Some precautions must be given along with that concept so that the teacher's actual role in this model is not misinterpreted. The teacher is the source of nearly all decisions made about content, management, and student engagement. There is a definite leadership function for the teacher; however, the purpose of that leadership is to allow students to have high OTR, to receive high rates of needed feedback, and to make steady and positive steps toward learning the intended content. The teacher is a leader, not an authoritarian; he gives structure to the learning setting and the content progression, but it is the students who benefit from that structure because much of the trial and error has been eliminated from the learning process.

Learning Domain Priorities and Domain Interactions

Domain priorities

Direct Instruction is an achievement-based educational model, used most often for teaching movement patterns and concepts. While it was developed initially to foster cognitive learning in other subjects (e.g., reading and mathematics), it has been used in physical education primarily for learning outcomes in the psychomotor domain. For physical education, the learning domain priorities in Direct Instruction will most often be:

First priority: Psychomotor learning

Second priority: Cognitive learning

Third priority: Affective learning

At times, the cognitive domain will have the highest priority, as in the learning of rules and concepts, but most often learning in that domain serves to facilitate what is being learned in the psychomotor domain. Students' cognition is developed to help them learn motor skill patterns more quickly and proficiently.

Domain interactions

As just explained, in order to become proficient in learning tasks in the psychomotor domain, students must have some engagement in the cognitive domain. They must recognize, process, and learn concepts and strategies that are prerequisite to and concurrent with desired movement patterns. However, the teacher first alerts the learners to those cognitive aspects, rather than making students sometimes struggle through a trial-and-error period. This model does not directly address the affective domain. It is assumed that students will achieve positive affective outcomes through the processes of working diligently, experiencing regular success, and making steady progress toward learning goals.

Student Developmental Requirements

Student readiness for learning. Students' readiness for Direct Instruction depends on their levels of motor and cognitive development. They must possess the prerequisite physical attributes that upcoming learning tasks will call for. Some of those motor attributes might be strength (to handle an implement or object), perceptual–motor abilities (e.g., being able to track an object coming at them, being able to judge speed), and stamina (for repetitive practice). Cognitive prerequisites would include the ability to understand verbal, written, or modeled information given to them by the teacher in task presentations and the ability to use feedback to guide their next practice trial.

Student receptivity to the model. Using the Reichmann and Grasha (1974) profile for student learning preferences, those students who are classified as avoidant, competitive, and dependent will be particularly receptive to Direct Instruction. As mentioned in Chapter 2, those labels should not be interpreted negatively. They are used to describe how some students would prefer the instructional environment to be designed. Within Direct Instruction, the selection of content and the learning tasks are strongly teacher-controlled and provide students with little personal choice regarding what and how they learn in physical education.

Validation of the Model

As stated at the beginning of this chapter, many people often mistake the Direct Instruction model with any number of direct teaching strategies. A teacher using the Direct Instruction *model* would follow most or all of Rosenshine's (1983) six operations presented earlier, in approximately that same order. A teacher using a direct instruction *strategy* might use only a task structure that places her in control of the learning activity for the moment, without implementing the other components of the model described by Rosenshine. The tendency for misinterpretation makes it difficult at times to provide an accurate validation for the Direct Instruction model. The following section on validation will be based as much as possible on discussions, research, and other evidence taken from sources that refer to either the Direct Instruction model or an adequate simulation of it.

Research validation

The Direct Instruction model has been the object of much research in classroom-based teaching, particularly in reading and mathematics. Those studies reported consistent, if modest, gains in student achievement when various forms of the Direct Instruction model were used as the primary teaching/learning process. It should be noted that those gains occurred most often in basic academic skills; the research in support of Direct Instruction's effectiveness with higher-order outcomes and with advanced students is somewhat less convincing. Still, studies demonstrate the model to be very effective when used to teach certain academic content to students at certain stages of the learning process.

Research support for Direct Instruction in physical education is a bit more difficult to document, mainly due to the model/strategy problem discussed above. While many studies have focused on direct teaching strategies, very few of them reported to have focused on Direct Instruction in the more formal sense of the model's definition and design. Even so, the large number of studies in physical education that looked at direct strategies does allow us to make some valid statements about the effectiveness of that approach to teaching (Rink, 2003).

Descriptive research. The first descriptive studies on Direct Instruction in physical education indicated that students were likely to spend more time in class receiving information and waiting than practicing motor skills (Metzler, 1989). Also, physical education teachers typically gave very low amounts of performance feedback to students. Both findings, of course, are contrary to the model's design. To support the use of direct instruction strategies, interaction analysis research with the Cheffers Adaptation of the Flanders Interaction Analysis System (CAFIAS) instrument (Cheffers, Mancini, & Martinek, 1980) verified that many physical education teachers were able to fulfill the role of instructional leader by maintaining control of the flow of information in classes. The descriptive research was not always complimentary of physical education teachers, but it did draw attention to some teaching/learning process variables that showed promising links to student achievement. Foremost among those variables was *academic learning time* (ALT), defined as the amount of time a student spends in class engaged in appropriate learning activities with a high level of success (Metzler, 1979). Many studies in physical education helped to substantiate the link between ALT and achievement, and many teachers now try to design instruction that maximizes the amount of ALT in classes. Most of those instructional strategies are based on some version of the Direct Instruction model.

Rink (2003) identified several other connections between teacher/student process and student achievement in physical education within Direct Instruction (pp. 167–179):

1. Students who spend more time in good practice learn more.
2. Practice should be appropriate to the goal of learning and the individual student.
3. Students who practice at a reasonably high success level learn more.
4. Students who practice at a higher level of processing learn more.
5. Effective teachers create an environment for learning.

6. Effective teachers are good communicators.

7. Good content development can increase learning.

Again, these relationships are important because they have all been established with teachers who used some form of Direct Instruction in physical education, thus providing strong research validation for direct teaching strategies, if not the model itself.

Experimental research. Experimental research has yielded many promising results related to Direct Instruction in physical education. Intervention studies have shown that it is possible to successfully change many process variables that increase the likelihood of student learning in physical education. For instance, it is possible, and relatively easy, to increase the rate of teacher feedback, to improve class and time management, to increase student OTR, and to raise levels of ALT within the Direct Instruction model (Metzler, 1989). So, while the descriptive phase of research on Direct Instruction showed that many physical education teachers did not apply the model as designed, the experimental phase demonstrated that improvements were fairly simple to make and easy to generalize.

Craft knowledge validation

Physical education teachers have been using some form of Direct Instruction for more than a hundred years, attesting to its ability to help students acquire skills and knowledge efficiently and effectively. The model's longevity and its current widespread usage are further evidence that teachers consider it to be one of the tried-and-true ways to teach movement skills and concepts to students of all ages and skill levels. Although it is no longer the "only way" to teach physical education, the fact that so many teachers continue to use direct strategies (if not the Direct Instruction model itself) provides strong validation for this approach to teaching and learning.

Intuitive validation

The basic operations of the Direct Instruction model make a strong case for why it makes sense to instruct that way: (1) content is broken into a series of small steps that students master on their way to the eventual, larger learning goals; (2) the teacher provides the students with a model of how the skilled movement should look, along with key performance cues to increase proficiency; (3) students get very high rates of OTR and ALT, along with high rates of teacher feedback; and (4) students must demonstrate mastery of learning tasks before they can pursue subsequent tasks on the content list. If you were to ask physical education teachers what makes for good teaching, many of them would cite any number of these operations without hesitation. When the goal is to learn movement skills and concepts, this approach makes good sense to teachers, providing strong intuitive validation for the use of Direct Instruction in physical education.

TEACHING AND LEARNING FEATURES

Control

Exhibit 8.2 shows the teacher–student control profile for Direct Instruction as it is used for physical education. Each element of the profile is explained below.

1. Content selection. The teacher maintains complete control of content decisions in the Direct Instruction model. He decides what will be included in the unit, the order of the learning tasks, and the performance criteria for students' mastery of the content. The students receive that information from the teacher and follow along during the unit.

2. Managerial control. The teacher determines the managerial plan, class policies/rules, and specific routines for the instructional unit. She maintains managerial control in order to provide maximum efficiency for class operations.

3. Task presentations. The teacher plans and controls all task presentations in Direct Instruction. However, this does not mean that the teacher always acts as the model; other students or audiovisual materials can give learners visual and verbal explanations of the upcoming skill or learning task.

4. Engagement patterns. A wide variety of student engagement patterns can be used in Direct Instruction for physical education: individual practice, partner practice, groups of all sizes, stations, and whole-class instruction. However, it is the teacher who decides which pattern will be used for each learning task.

5. Instructional interactions. Nearly all instruction interactions are initiated and therefore controlled by the teacher in Direct Instruction. The teacher is

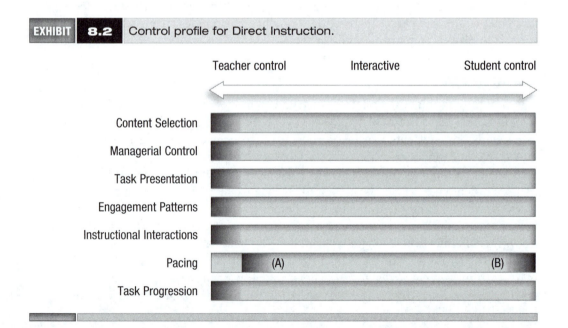

EXHIBIT 8.2 Control profile for Direct Instruction.

the major source of augmented feedback and directs all the question-and-answer class segments. This does not mean that students are forbidden to ask questions—only that the teacher will set predetermined times to solicit student questions.

6. Pacing. The teacher maintains firm control of the pacing of student practice trials, especially for initial learning tasks. The teacher might even choose to deliberately cue each practice trial at the beginning of a learning sequence by telling students when to start and stop each attempt (see A in Exhibit 8.2). This allows the teacher to monitor every trial in order to provide a better analysis of students' skill attempts. A bit later the teacher might say, "Practice your overhand serves 10 times" or "Practice only overhand serves for the next 5 minutes," letting students determine when to start each trial (see B in Exhibit 8.2). Note that the teacher still decides how many tries or how long students will get to practice.

7. Task progression. The teacher makes all determinations about when students will move from one learning task to the next. Those determinations can be made according to the teacher's criterion for task mastery (e.g., 80 percent correct trials). When most or all of the students have met that criterion, the teacher moves the class to the next learning task. Or, the teacher may decide how much time will be given to each task and then direct students to change tasks when the allocated time has elapsed, regardless of how many students have reached mastery.

Inclusiveness

When used according to the model's design (Rosenshine, 1983), the Direct Instruction model is inherently inclusive. All students see the same task presentation; practice the same learning tasks; get high rates of OTR, ALT, and augmented feedback; and progress to the next learning activity together. However, since task progression is often determined for the whole class, it is possible that less-skilled or slower learners will not have mastered one learning task before they must move along with the rest of the class to the next task. They are included, but their need for more practice at the current task is not met by the teacher's decision to move all students to the next task in the unit. Direct Instruction teachers can plan for multiple groups in class, based on learning rate, but this occurs less often than is desired in physical education. Teaching by invitation is a good strategy for promoting more inclusiveness in planned learning activities in classes with a wide range of learner aptitude and experience. For example, a teacher could set up four different stations that focus on passing a soccer ball at different degrees of difficulty. The skill is the same (e.g., passing to a target), but each one presents a different level of challenge. The teacher explains each station, identifies the degree of difficulty for each one, and then "invites" students to self-select the station at which they wish to work.

Learning Tasks

Task presentation

Because the task presentation provides students with key information about how to perform the skill/task proficiently, it is essential that the presentation give a clear "picture" of how to perform the task successfully. While it is possible to use instructional media such as videos for task presentations, the Direct Instruction teacher will most often serve as the model in order to better control the flow of information to students. Student models can also serve this function, but it is important that their modeled performances represent exactly what the teacher wants the other students to see. The Direct Instruction model promotes very high rates of OTR, so it is important that students not practice the wrong performance cues and later have to "undo" their learning and replace it with correct performance patterns. To prevent this costly mistake, a Direct Instruction teacher will most often act as the model in task presentations.

Task presentations are given to all students in a class at one time. The teacher must be sure to check for understanding frequently, in order to be confident that students comprehend the model and performance cues they are given. It is also possible to use the *active demonstration strategy* that calls for students to move along with the teacher's model as performance cues are stated. The teacher can then see if students really do comprehend the task presentation before they begin to practice.

Task structure

As mentioned earlier, Direct Instruction can use a wide variety of learning activities with different task structures planned for them. Regardless of which task structure the teacher selects, it is essential that students understand the activity's organization and the accountability system in place for it. If students do not understand the task structure, the teacher will need to repeat the directions, resulting in lost momentum and engagement time in the lesson. Structures that can be used for learning tasks and independent practicing are shown in Exhibit 8.3.

Learning tasks in Direct Instruction can use any number of visual aids and markers to help students practice the task as designed and to increase OTR as much as possible. Lines drawn on the floor to denote proper spacing, cones used as path markers, targets on the wall that indicate accuracy, and mechanical devices that return balls all help students maintain the desired performance parameters and get more OTR in physical education.

Content progression

In Direct Instruction, progression through a unit's content is based on the teacher's content list and sequence, determined before the unit begins. The teacher identifies each skill and knowledge area in the unit and places them in an order to be learned by students. Students then move through that content by practicing in progressively difficult ways, like those shown in the lists of initial and advanced structures in Exhibit 8.3. If the teacher closely follows the design of the Direct Instruction

Direct Instruction task structures.	EXHIBIT	8.3

INITIAL LEARNING TASKS

1. Individual practice in self-space
2. Individual practice in repetitive drills
3. Teacher-led practice (e.g., following along on dance steps, slow-motion practice of skills)
4. Low organizational games (e.g., tag games)

ADVANCED LEARNING TASKS AND INDEPENDENT PRACTICING

1. Partner practice (e.g., throwing back and forth, kicking to each other)
2. Station tasks
3. Circuits and obstacle courses
4. Complex drills
5. Lead-up games
6. Mini games

model, students should achieve a mastery rate of 80 percent on their current learning task before moving to the next task in the sequence. Because students learn at different speeds, the teacher will often have to place students in learning groups that include peers with similar learning rates. In addition, learning tasks should have specific performance criteria so that the success rate can be determined.

In physical education, teachers frequently base content progressions on time allocations. The teacher estimates how much time most students should need to master the planned learning task and then moves to the next task when that amount of time has elapsed. Yet this practice goes against the design of the Direct Instruction model, as it may cause the slower learners to get further behind with each content progression change.

Engagement Patterns for Learning

Direct Instruction uses many types of student engagement patterns, determined by the task structure the teacher chooses for each learning activity. Students can practice alone, with partners, in small groups, in large groups, or as a whole class. Stations are often used as well. The only common feature here is that the teacher is the one who decides the engagement pattern and then gives students directions for how to organize and maintain that pattern.

Teacher and Student Roles and Responsibilities

Each instructional model will have certain operations that need to be completed to allow the model to function according to its design. Some of the operations are carried out by the teacher; others are carried out by one or more students. Exhibit 8.4 shows the major operations within the Direct Instruction model and indicates who is responsible for completing them during each lesson.

EXHIBIT 8.4	Teacher and student roles and responsibilities in Direct Instruction.
OPERATION OR RESPONSIBILITY	PERSON/PEOPLE RESPONSIBLE IN DIRECT INSTRUCTION
Starting class	The **teacher** begins class by calling all students together for the set induction.
Bringing equipment to class	The **teacher** makes a list of needed equipment and brings it to class. Students can assist in setting up the equipment.
Dispersing and returning equipment	The **teacher** gives students directions for how and where to set up equipment. Students can assist by returning the equipment to a designated place at the end of class.
Roll call (if needed)	The **teacher** can call the roll or use an alternative method to save time.
Task presentation	Presentations are planned and implemented by the **teacher,** who most often provides the performance model for students to observe.
Task structure	Task structure is planned and directed by the **teacher.** Students get instructions from the teacher and carry them out.
Assessment	The **teacher** determines the performance criteria for each learning task and monitors student achievement. Assessment can happen in a variety of ways but should include formative and summative assessment of each student.
Content progression	By monitoring student performance, the **teacher** determines when a learning activity ends and when students move to the next one.

Verification of Instructional Processes

Teachers who use Direct Instruction can learn the benchmarks for the teaching and learning patterns that should be consistently evident in the model. Monitoring and adhering to these benchmarks ensure that the teacher is using the Direct Instruction *model,* and not simply groupings of *direct teaching strategies* in physical education. The teacher and student benchmarks for Direct Instruction are shown in Exhibits 8.5 and 8.6.

Assessment of Learning

The Direct Instruction model calls for frequent assessment of student learning, usually done for each planned learning task. Rosenshine (1983) recommends that students achieve a success rate of 80 percent on initial learning tasks and 90 to 100 percent on the later learning tasks in a content unit. This means that students do not necessarily take quizzes or skills tests in physical education; rather, they practice a task until they have achieved the criterion success rate set by the teacher for that task. After they reach that rate, students then move to the next learning task. Success rates can be monitored with formal and informal assessment techniques, both described in detail below.

Direct Instruction teacher benchmarks.	🖶 **EXHIBIT** **8.5**	
BENCHMARK	**HOW TO VERIFY**	
Teacher breaks unit content into a series of small learning tasks, leading to larger learning goals.	Review the teacher's task analysis, content listing, and content progression prior to the start of the unit.	
Teacher reviews previous day's content.	Ensure that the teacher's lesson plan includes a review of the previous lesson and a set induction.	
Teacher makes a clear and effective task presentation.	Observe students as they begin to practice. Are they doing the task correctly? Did the teacher check for understanding?	
Teacher presents a clear task structure.	Observe students as they begin to practice. Are they engaged in the way described by the teacher? Did the teacher check for understanding?	
Teacher uses a brisk pace through content progression.	1. Teacher plans a series of small learning tasks. 2. Teacher has quick transitions between planned class segments.	
Teacher provides high rates of positive and corrective feedback.	Record the frequency and types of augmented feedback given to students by the teacher.	
Teacher provides a mastery criterion for each learning task.	1. Check lesson plan. 2. Verify that 80–100 percent of students have mastered the previous task.	
Teacher conducts regular content reviews.	1. Check the unit plan. 2. Record the timing and focus of each review.	

Informal assessment

A Direct Instruction teacher can informally monitor student success rates with some practical strategies that take very little time and record keeping:

1. Students practice in "blocks" of task trials and then stop when all students have finished one block. If each block contains five trials and the criterion success rate is 80 percent (four out of five), the teacher can ask, "How many of you were able to get four or five correct that time?" If not enough students reached that success rate, the task continues. If all or nearly all students got four or five correct, the teacher then moves to the next task.

2. The teacher can monitor a sampling of students as the class practices a task and count the number of successful and unsuccessful trials each selected student completes. When all or nearly all of the sampled students have reached the criterion rate, the teacher then moves to the next task. It is important that the sampled students are representative of the entire class, meaning that the sample should include more than one student from various skill ability groupings in the class and a number of boys and girls proportionate to the numbers in class.

EXHIBIT 8.6	Direct Instruction student benchmarks.
BENCHMARK	**HOW TO VERIFY**
Students understand task presentation.	Count the number of students who are practicing the skill/movement/concept as it was described by the teacher.
Students understand task structure.	Count the number of students who: a. Are engaged according to the teacher's direction b. Have modified the task c. Have withdrawn from the task
Students have high rates of OTR.	1. Count the number of practice attempts (if frequency is the best indicator of OTR). 2. Measure how much actual practice time students get (if time is the best indicator of OTR).
Students have high rates of ALT.	Monitor a sampling of students with an ALT-PE recording instrument.
Students get high rates of positive and corrective feedback.	When counting the teacher's feedback, note which student(s) receive it, and which type. The feedback should be distributed to all students in the class.
Initial student practice is directed by teacher.	Check task structure and content progression.
Later student practice includes some independent practice.	Check task structure and content progression.
Students have mastered content.	Students complete and pass regular assessments that match the teacher's stated learning goals.

Formal assessment

Informal strategies are typically very practical, but they run the risk of providing the teacher with potentially misleading information about student success rates in learning tasks. Although they present some feasibility problems for physical education, formal strategies tend to be more systematic, objective, and rigorous. Formal strategies include:

1. Students are given cards on which to record successful and unsuccessful skill attempts for each learning task. When students have reached the criterion rate, they turn the card in to the teacher for his records. When enough students have turned in their cards, the teacher moves to the next task.

2. The teacher gives students periodic, brief performance quizzes and immediately scores them. These quizzes can be written, oral, or skill-based. When all or nearly all students reach the criterion score, the teacher moves to the next task.

3. The teacher can observe students' skills with a checklist of key performance cues. When all or nearly all students have demonstrated proficiency, the teacher moves to the next task.

4. In place of the teacher, student peer observers can use the previous assessment strategy.

Because Direct Instruction involves a mastery approach, it is essential for the teacher to document that students have achieved the criterion success rate or performance score before progressing to the next learning task. The behavioral shaping feature of Direct Instruction will not work if students do not master each successive approximation to the eventual performance outcome. If allowed to proceed without mastery, students will at some point "get stuck" on a new learning task because they have not demonstrated adequate proficiency in lead-up tasks.

IMPLEMENTATION NEEDS AND MODIFICATIONS

Teacher Expertise

Direct Instruction teachers will need to have several particular areas of expertise to use this model to its fullest capacity.

Task analysis and content listing. Direct Instruction features learning content that is broken into small units and sequenced into a series of progressive learning tasks. Teachers will need to be able to complete detailed task analyses that are used to construct the learning task sequences through which students progress. When the task analyses are complete, the teacher must decide how much content can be learned in a unit, which determines the content listing. This process requires knowledge of content and students' learning abilities.

Learning objectives. Direct Instruction strives for student achievement of stated learning goals, written in the form of performance objectives. Teachers should be able to write objectives that include challenging yet attainable performance criteria for students. The first time a teacher uses Direct Instruction for a certain content and context, he will have to make a "good guess" at determining performance criteria for specific learning tasks. After its first use, adjustments can be made for the next time Direct Instruction is used in that same situation.

Physical education content. In order to provide effective task presentations and give students usable performance feedback, Direct Instruction teachers must know the content being taught to students. That knowledge takes two forms: the ability to describe and model proficient skill performances in a task presentation and the ability to observe students' movement skills in order to provide high rates of specific, corrective feedback. Because the Direct Instruction teacher serves as the source for nearly all unit content, there is no substitute for strong content expertise in the unit being taught.

Developmentally appropriate instruction. To lead students through a series of learning tasks with performance criteria, the Direct Instruction teacher must know the cognitive and psychomotor performance abilities of her students. Teachers must be able to communicate task presentations at a level that matches students' cognitive level, and they must provide clear directions for task structure—not only before the lesson begins but also as the teacher observes students during practice. The teacher must know the range of developmentally appropriate responses that students can make at that stage so that expectations for performance match student abilities.

Key Teaching Skills

Much of the research on effective teaching in physical education has been derived from teachers using some version of the Direct Instruction model. Therefore the link between teacher and student in-class behaviors and student achievement has more substantiation with Direct Instruction than with any other model presented in this book. In fact, the model itself was originally built on process-product research's repeated findings in numerous subject areas, including physical education (Rink, 2003).

If you will recall, one of the most important variables in effective teaching is *academic learning time* (ALT), the amount of time students spend engaged in appropriate learning tasks with high levels of success. Very simply, students who accrue higher rates of ALT are more likely to acquire the stated learning objectives of the moment. Therefore, if ALT is observed and measured, it gives a good approximation of how much student learning is happening in a lesson. All the effective teaching skills discussed in this section have a known effect on ALT rates in physical education, so we can be more confident about their contribution to student achievement in Direct Instruction than in other teaching models. Teachers who make decisions and instruct in ways that raise student ALT are considered to be more effective Direct Instruction teachers.

Planning. Because the teacher maintains control of nearly all instructional operations in Direct Instruction, a premium is placed on detailed unit and lesson planning. At the unit level, the teacher will need to determine the content listing and make plans for every learning task students will pursue. This involves task presentation, task structure, time allocation, space and equipment needs, content progression, and assessment. At the lesson level, Direct Instruction depends heavily on the maximum use of class time and other learning resources, facilitated by careful and detailed planning for each lesson.

Time and class management. The most effective Direct Instruction teachers maximize allocated time in class to provide students with high rates of OTR and ALT. The Direct Instruction teacher must be able to orchestrate many aspects of the learning environment—aspects that are always complex and sometimes at odds with one another. Class events and planned segments must flow smoothly from one to the next, and students must become engaged in learning activities quickly and correctly—all under the teacher's direction.

Task presentation and structure. Task presentations are key segments in every Direct Instruction lesson. Students must be given a clear picture of the upcoming skill, movement, or concept so they can try to perform it correctly in the learning activity. The same principle holds true for the task structure. When students understand the organization of the learning task they can become engaged in it quickly and correctly, which promotes high rates of OTR.

Graham (1988) identifies eight attributes of an effective task presentation and structure for physical education:

1. Making instructions explicit
2. Emphasizing the usefulness of the content being presented
3. Structuring new content
4. Signaling for students' attention
5. Summarizing and repeating information
6. Checking for understanding
7. Creating a productive climate for learning
8. Presenting accountability measures

Teachers can monitor their task presentation skills by using the Qualitative Measure of Teaching Performance Scale (QMTPS) (Rink & Werner, 1989). The QMTPS rates a teacher on seven aspects of task presentation: clarity, demonstration, appropriate number of cues, accuracy of cues, quality of cues, appropriate focus, and specific congruent feedback. The resulting total QMTPS score indicates a teacher's ability to plan for and present effective task descriptions to students. Gusthart, Kelly, and Rink (1997) validated the QMTPS instrument for use with Direct Instruction teaching, linking total QMTPS scores with increased levels of student achievement.

Communication. Clarity is the key communication skill for Direct Instruction teachers. Teachers must give task presentations, task structures, and feedback to students in ways that are comprehensible and useful to students. An instructor can facilitate good communication by checking for understanding frequently and repeating information students did not understand the first time.

Instructional information. The flow of instructional information in Direct Instruction is most often one-way. The teacher initiates the communication, and students listen or watch. The teacher can ask questions, but these are used mostly to have students clarify previous information. The most essential kinds of instructional information are verbal and modeled cues given in the task presentation and two types of augmented feedback (positive and corrective) given during learning activities.

Review and closure. A good Direct Instruction lesson will be "bookended" at the start and finish. The class begins with a review of the previous lesson and a set induction. It ends with a well-planned review and closure. The opening review and set induction allow the students to get focused on the lesson content; the culminating review and closure tie together what was learned in that lesson and end the lesson in an orderly manner. During the closing review, the teacher can reinforce learning cues, highlight aspects of student performance, ask questions, and preview the next lesson's content. The closure alerts students that "PE is over for the day" and brings them to the exit routine.

Contextual Requirements

Direct Instruction has been used in every conceivable physical education context. It can teach virtually all kinds of movement content to students at any age and developmental level. The main contextual consideration concerns the ability to provide students with very high rates of OTR, so it is necessary to have sufficient amounts of equipment and enough activity space to reduce or eliminate student waiting time in class.

Selecting and Modifying Direct Instruction

As mentioned at the start of this chapter, physical education teachers have used Direct Instruction for many years to teach nearly all content to all grade levels of students. The selection of Direct Instruction depends more on the teacher's learning goals for a content unit than on any other factor. Direct Instruction is designed to teach basic movement skills and concepts, and it does that more effectively than any other model in this book. However, when the teacher wants student learning to occur at higher cognitive or psychomotor levels, or primarily in the affective domain, then Direct Instruction will not be the ideal model. Direct Instruction seems best suited for certain types of content units in physical education:

1. Individual sports (beginning and intermediate levels)
2. Team sports (beginning and intermediate levels)
3. Recreational activities (e.g., bowling, horseshoes, darts)
4. Dances with prescribed steps (e.g., line, square, folk)
5. Aerobics (all kinds that require teacher cuing for students)
6. Repetitive exercises (e.g., calisthenics, stretching, weight training)
7. Martial arts (noncompetitive)

Grade-level adaptations

As just explained, the most effective use of Direct Instruction will depend more on the stated learning goals for a content unit than on the grade level of students. If the Direct Instruction teacher correctly selects unit goals that are fostered through Direct Instruction, then she needs only to make the instruction developmentally appropriate for the students she will teach. Exhibit 8.7 provides examples of ways to adapt the Direct Instruction model to various grade levels.

| | Grade-level adaptations for Direct Instruction in physical education. | **EXHIBIT 8.7** |

GRADE LEVELS	SELECT DIRECT INSTRUCTION?	POSSIBLE ADAPTATIONS
Preschool	Yes	1. Reduce verbal cues in task presentations. Use more modeling and have students mimic. 2. Use only teacher-led tasks. 3. Provide feedback as encouragement—not corrective information. 4. Make questions very simple—yes/no answers. 5. Use more general performance criteria.
Elementary	Yes	1. Simplify task presentation and structures. 2. Use mostly teacher-led tasks. 3. Make questions simple. 4. Repeat instructions, and check for understanding every time. 5. Use less stringent performance criteria, but do expect some proficiency before moving to new tasks. 6. Cover less content by giving students more time on each task.
Middle school/ junior high	Yes	1. Couple verbal information with teacher demonstrations in task presentations. 2. Use a combination of teacher-led and independent practice tasks. 3. Teach for developmentally appropriate performance proficiency. 4. Increase corrective feedback. 5. Use higher-order questions to help students learn underlying concepts.
High school	Yes	Use the full Direct Instruction model.
College/adult	Yes	Use the full Direct Instruction model.

Adaptations to accommodate diverse groups of learners

Direct Instruction can be a highly inclusive model for physical education if the teacher uses strategies to help all students understand the task presentation, task structure, and managerial directions. Exhibit 8.8 lists some strategies that address a variety of special learning needs found in many schools today.

PLANNING TIPS FOR DIRECT INSTRUCTION

Refer to the Direct Instruction unit plan on the IMPE website. Teachers using the full Direct Instruction model for the first time can benefit by following a few additional planning tips for that model:

1. Plan the whole unit content ahead of time, and make an outline of the scope and sequence. Then make a good estimate of how long it will take students

> **EXHIBIT 8.8** Strategies to adapt Direct Instruction for diverse groups of learners.

FOR STUDENTS WITH HEARING IMPAIRMENTS:
1. Use a microphone to amplify the teacher's voice.
2. Move students closer during task presentations.
3. Use visual signals for start/stop (e.g., raised hand, flashing light).
4. Use task cards that can be read by students.

FOR STUDENTS WITH SIGHT IMPAIRMENTS:
1. Use larger font for task cards.
2. Modify equipment (by color or size, or use "beeper balls").

FOR STUDENTS WITH PHYSICAL DISABILITIES:
1. Provide appropriate versions of tasks (e.g., lower volleyball net for students in wheelchairs).
2. Modify equipment according to their needs.
3. Adjust learning goals according to student ability.

FOR STUDENTS WHO DO NOT SPEAK ENGLISH:
1. Use student translators, when available.
2. Provide written directions in appropriate language.
3. Use body gestures and manipulative (hands-on) cues.

FOR LOWER-SKILL STUDENTS:
1. Have multiple levels of difficulty, and "teach by invitation."
2. Use appropriate skill-level models for task presentation.
3. Place students in ability groups.
4. Allow lower-skill students more time to complete learning tasks.
5. Provide extra encouragement and praise.

to learn each skill or knowledge area. Remember that they will not likely learn as fast as you, so don't base your estimate on *your* ability! Adjust the content (add more, delete some) before the unit starts, not as it goes along.

2. If you plan the unit ahead of time, you can then adjust each lesson according to the amount of time and content left to learn in the unit.

3. Provide several ways for students to get the task presentation, and use instructional media (e.g., videos, smartphones, task cards) whenever possible.

4. Use student-based assessments whenever possible—preferably by building them into the learning tasks themselves.

5. Be sure to plan for enough learning stations so that students have little or no waiting time.

6. Don't cover only content: make sure that you have provided some way for students to demonstrate mastery of each skill or knowledge area in the unit.

UNIT AND LESSON PLAN EXAMPLES
FOR DIRECT INSTRUCTION

Y ou will find several complete unit plans with lesson plans for Direct Instruction on the IMPE website. It is not recommended that you follow these examples exactly as they are presented. The context, specific learning objectives, and content of your own unit will require you to make changes in these examples to allow the Direct Instruction model to lead to the most effective instruction in your situation.

SUMMARY

Even though physical education teachers do not often use the full and formal model of Direct Instruction described in this chapter, the use of several forms of directed instruction has been common in our field for more than a hundred years. That longevity, along with the strong research evidence of Direct Instruction's effectiveness, supports its continued use in many settings, grade levels, and movement content areas for physical education. However, we must recognize that Direct Instruction has received criticism in the past decade or so, as other contrasting models have been developed for our field. To be fair, we should note that the Direct Instruction model will be less than effective when employed to pursue student learning that is incongruent with the model's foundational learning theories and when applied in ways that do not match its intended design. But that observation applies to every instructional model—something you should keep in mind as you learn the other models in the remainder of this book.

It is also important that you do not interpret the amount of control retained by the teacher in this model to mean that this is a rigid or authoritarian approach. Good Direct Instruction is highly flexible, supportive, and positive. It provides students with increased time to learn lesson and unit content, along with high rates of teacher monitoring and instructional interaction, particularly in performance feedback. All of those elements contribute to higher levels of student achievement in physical education—one of our most valued learning outcomes.

LEARNING ACTIVITIES

1. Make a list of five activity units (e.g., movement skills, fitness, softball, tennis, golf) that might be taught in a physical education program. Next, determine an appropriate grade level (P, K–2, 3–5, 6–8, 9–12) for teaching each of those activity units. Now, write two major learning outcomes for those units. Then, go through the process of selecting an instructional model, shown in Chapter 2, to determine if Direct Instruction would be an appropriate model for teaching that activity to children at that grade level.
2. If Direct Instruction is appropriate for that activity, grade, and goals, mention three things that make it appropriate. If Direct Instruction is not

appropriate for that activity, grade, and goals, mention three things that make it inappropriate.

3. For one activity unit at one grade level (e.g., K–2 movement skills, high school tennis), write a complete list of content to be taught in that unit with Direct Instruction.

4. Pick one of the major goals identified in Activity 1, and design an assessment strategy for monitoring student learning.

5. Write a lesson plan for each of the first three lessons of this unit, including notes that explain your decisions in each part of the lesson.

TOPICS FOR REFLECTION & SMALL-GROUP DISCUSSION

1. I have suggested in this chapter how the Direct Instruction model is aligned to achieve one or more of the NASPE standards. Take a moment to review those alignments (refer back to Exhibit 8.1). After that, make some notes about whether you agree with those alignments, and then share them in your small group. After you have reached your final thoughts, please share them on the IMPE website Forum for others to review, and check back for replies.

2. Direct Instruction is the most widely used model in physical education today. Why do you think that is so?

3. Why does the basic pattern of Direct Instruction make so much sense at an intuitive level?

4. Why do you think most teachers are so comfortable using Direct Instruction?

5. In general, which types of students are placed at an advantage in this model, and which students are at a disadvantage?

6. Since Direct Instruction is the most common model in physical education today, why shouldn't every teacher be using it?

SUGGESTED READINGS FOR DIRECT INSTRUCTION

Baumann, J. F. (1988). Direct Instruction reconsidered. *Journal of Reading Behavior, 31,* 714.

Rosenshine, B. (1983). Teaching functions in instructional programs. *Elementary School Journal, 83,* 335–350.

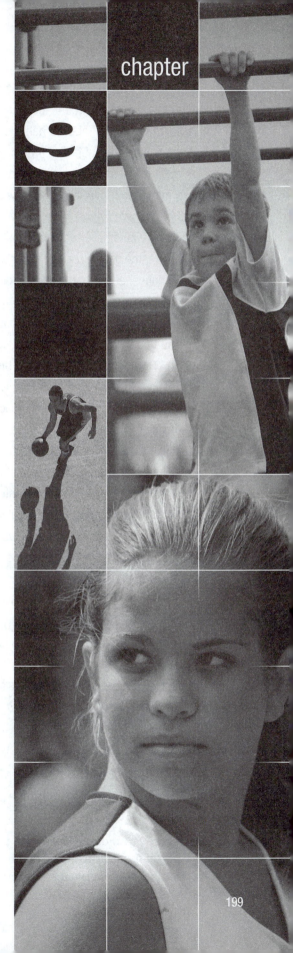

PERSONALIZED SYSTEM FOR INSTRUCTION
Students Progress as Fast as They Can or as Slowly as They Need

Providing individual instruction to every student in the class is one of the most frequently mentioned goals of teaching. It is also one of the least frequently achieved goals of teaching. Large classes, inadequate time, limited equipment and facilities, and a typically wide range of student abilities all work against a teacher who attempts to plan and implement individualized learning for students. From another perspective, it should be noted that nearly all instructional strategies and models are simply not designed for individual instruction, and they are able to give only well-intended but unsuccessful attempts at personalizing instruction in physical education. Some models are more successful than others, but only one model is designed to provide truly individualized instruction. That model is called the Personalized System for Instruction (PSI). It is also known as the *Keller Plan,* after its developer, Fred Keller.

PSI was developed by Keller and his graduate students at the University of Sao Paulo, Brazil, in the early 1960s and refined a few years later at Arizona State University (Keller & Sherman, 1974). Faced with teaching Introductory Psychology to sections of over 300 students, Keller immediately realized that the traditional lecture approach would not meet the needs of those students. Keller had come from the research tradition of applied behavior analysis, which focused on observing and teaching as few as one subject at a time, so he set out to design an instructional model that would provide an individual learning program for all students. The educational world was introduced to PSI in the provocative article "Goodbye, Teacher!" (Keller, 1968) in the *Journal of Applied Behavior Analysis.* You can imagine how readers, especially teachers, would have reacted to just the title of the article. Now imagine the reactions of those same people reading Keller's design for instruction, which placed the teacher at the periphery of the instructional process and suggested that students could learn more if the teacher were less involved in the direct transmission of content!

After the initial article (Keller, 1968), Keller modified his plan a bit, recognizing that he had underestimated the role of context and student motivation (Keller & Sherman, 1974). The biggest problem with his original plan was that he considered time (for instruction) to be unbounded. That is, the PSI plan was first designed to give students unlimited time to learn. Eventually accepting that time is rarely unlimited in education, he modified some of the radical claims for PSI's learning effects. Notice that he did not change his claim for PSI's ability to provide individualized instruction for every learner— he acknowledged only that some students would simply "run out of time" in the term before they achieved all that was intended. The very strong research history examining the effectiveness of PSI in every subject among nearly all age groups of learners bears this out. Lowry and Thornburg (1988) published a summary of research on PSI that included more than 1,500 references just from 1968 to 1988.

Though the use of PSI in physical education has been limited, it has great promise as an effective instructional model for nearly all movement content and across most grades, particularly at the secondary levels. Siedentop (1973) was the first to suggest the possibility of using PSI as an instructional model for physical education, although his suggestion referred mostly to cognitive content for college students. The most complete implementation of PSI in physical education for activity instruction appears in the *Personalized Sport Instruction Series,* edited by Metzler (2000). That series contains complete PSI units for badminton, golf, tennis, racquetball, soccer, and volleyball. Although designed for college-level activity courses, such PSI courses can easily be adapted for use in any grade from middle school upward, as I will show later in this chapter.

OVERVIEW

he PSI model is designed to allow each student to progress at his or her own pace through a sequence of prescribed learning tasks. The learning tasks are derived from a task analysis for each of the skills and knowledge areas to be covered in the content unit, determining the content listing for the entire unit. Every learning module includes information on task presentation, task structure, error analyses, and performance criteria given to students in a written and/or mediated format. The key here is that teachers do not provide this information to students in person; students read prepared materials or view video samples instead. This method frees the teacher from having to spend class time on those functions, allowing her to have much more instructional interaction with students. As each student completes a learning task to its stated performance criteria, he then moves to the next task on the list, without depending on the teacher for permission or directions.

When used in very large classes in which the teacher has designated assistants, PSI as it was designed by Keller relies on proctors to review unit exams, assist students with logistics, and provide one-on-one tutoring (Keller & Sherman, 1974). Those proctors could be teaching assistants, teacher's aides, or advanced students. In most applications for physical education in schools, the availability of proctors is limited. But there are other ways to provide that function for students, which this chapter will discuss. Because there are few, if any, teacher-directed task presentations, PSI instructors use interactions with students to furnish motivation and instructional information (e.g., feedback and one-on-one tutoring).

The PSI model is based on a *unified plan* for the content unit; there are no daily lesson plans. Students progress individually through the sequence of learning tasks, simply beginning each lesson where they left off in the previous one. The teacher need only be aware of which tasks will be attempted in the upcoming lesson so that he can provide the necessary equipment for student engagement with them. The responsibilities of providing students with information about class management, learning tasks, and assessment are carried out with a course workbook and instructional media (videos, DVDs, or online sources). Students read and follow the course workbook as much as possible; the teacher offers only needed clarification and details not covered in the workbook. (Refer to the sample workbook on the IMPE website.)

The basic design goal of PSI encourages students to be independent learners and, at the same time, allows the teacher to use high rates of interaction with students who need it. It has proven to be a highly effective model for student achievement in the psychomotor and cognitive domains.

ALIGNMENT WITH NASPE NATIONAL STANDARDS

Exhibit 9.1 shows the alignment of the PSI model with the NASPE standards. This model is most strongly aligned with those standards that focus on competency with skill and movement patterns and those that focus on movement concepts, principles, strategies, and tactics. Due to the specific wording of some standards, PSI is strongly aligned for some outcomes in certain standards but weakly aligned for other outcomes in those same standards. It should be emphasized that the ability of PSI to address each of the national standards will be affected by the way a teacher designs specific learn-

EXHIBIT 9.1	Alignment of PSI with NASPE National Standards.	
NASPE STANDARD	**ALIGNMENT RATING**	**COMMENTS**
1. Demonstrates competency in motor skills and movement patterns needed to perform a variety of physical activities	1	One of the best models for learning movement skills
2. Demonstrates understanding of movement concepts, principles, strategies, and tactics as they apply to the learning and performance of physical activities	1–2	Can be better aligned if cognitive content is added to motor skill competency tasks
3. Participates regularly in physical activity	2	Will vary according to the content unit
4. Achieves and maintains a health-enhancing level of physical fitness	1	Very effective model for teaching personal fitness concepts and performance
5. Exhibits responsible personal and social behavior that respects self and others in physical activity settings	1–3	Strong for personal responsibility; weak alignment for social learning outcomes
6. Values physical activity for health, enjoyment, challenge, self-expression, and/or social interaction	1–3	Strong alignment for enjoyment (through mastery) and challenge; moderate alignment for health; weak alignment for self-expression and social interaction

Ratings categories:

1. Strong alignment
2. Moderate alignment
3. Weak alignment

ing tasks within a unit of instruction, so the ratings shown here should be viewed as typical, not definitive.

FOUNDATIONS

Theory and Rationale

The first ideas for PSI were developed within the field of applied behavior analysis. That branch of psychology holds that human learning occurs as a result of interactions between a person and the external environment. Certain consequences of behavior, called *reinforcers,* increase the likelihood that a behavior will be emitted again. Other consequences, called *punishers,* tend to decrease the likelihood that the behavior will be emitted again. A science of human behavior is based on these and other relationships between a person and her environment. B. F. Skinner was among the first psychologists to use behavioral theory in the design of instruction for school subjects. His "teaching machines" delivered positive reinforcement to learners who made correct answers by pressing buttons, touching screens, or pulling levers. This rudimentary design allowed the teacher to determine the questions and correct answers but gave the key functions of delivering content presentation, feedback, and reinforcement to the machines. That important step led to the development of a larger role for the entire teaching environment (besides the teacher) in the teaching/learning process.

Keller was Skinner's colleague and an experimental behavioral psychologist who shared that same theory about the environment's crucial role in the teaching/learning process. If the complete environment—not just the teacher—leads to human learning, then it would be possible to design environments that could promote student learning with or without a direct role for the teacher. Keller and Sherman (1974) acknowledge that PSI has four features that provide students with a rich schedule of reinforcement not often available within other models:

1. The ability to view creative and interesting learning materials
2. Regular, tangible progress toward the course goals
3. Immediate assessment of learning
4. Individual attention from the instructor

Assumptions About Teaching and Learning

The PSI model assumes certain principles about teaching and about learning; these principles are listed separately below.

Assumptions about teaching

1. Many teaching functions, especially task presentation and task structure, can be provided through printed, visual, and audio media (that is, not by the teacher).
2. The teacher's primary function is to interact with students for learning and motivation, not to manage the class. Class management operations can be communicated to students in print or video and carried out by students with little teacher direction.
3. Student engagement and learning are most effective when they remain largely independent of the teacher.
4. Planning decisions are made from data collected on student learning.
5. It is not only desirable but also possible to design truly individualized instruction.

Assumptions about learning

1. Student learning can occur with little dependence on the teacher.
2. Students learn content at different rates.
3. Students have differing aptitudes for learning content.
4. If given enough time and/or trials, nearly all students can achieve the stated goals of instruction.
5. Students will be highly motivated and responsible as independent learners.

The Major Theme of PSI: Students Progress as Fast as They Can or as Slowly as They Need

The basic design in PSI provides each student with a complete set of instructional materials that includes management information, task presentations, task structures, learning activities with performance criteria, and assessments (see the sample student workbook on the IMPE website). Students then proceed through the sequence of learning activities, completing each one according to the stated performance criterion before moving to the next activity. Students are allowed to progress at their own pace, according to their aptitude of learning for each unit content. Students with higher skills, more experience, and better aptitude are allowed to progress as quickly as they can through the content. Students with lower skill, less experience, and lower aptitude can take the time needed to complete each activity, since there are no group- or class-level progressions. Therefore, the theme for PSI is *"Students progress as fast as they can or as slowly as they need"* (Metzler, 2000).

Learning Domain Priorities and Domain Interactions

Domain priorities

PSI is a decidedly mastery- and achievement-based instructional model. *Mastery-based instruction* means that students must meet the performance criterion for the current learning task before they can proceed to the next task in the sequence. *Achievement-based instruction* focuses strongly on student learning outcomes that are demonstrated through overt student performance, either in the cognitive or psychomotor domain. For physical education, student learning is most often demonstrated in the psychomotor domain. Therefore, the learning domain priorities for the Personalized System for Instruction are typically:

> *First priority:* Psychomotor learning
> *Second priority:* Cognitive learning
> *Third priority:* Affective learning

Domain interactions

The domain interactions for PSI work in the following manner. Students must use their cognitive abilities to comprehend the written, visual, and electronic media used for task presentations and task structures. They must also use those abilities to devise some learning strategies for completing learning tasks. However, cognitive learning occurs in order to facilitate performance in the psychomotor domain, in which most performance criteria are stated. Some learning tasks are designed for performance in the cognitive domain—such as comprehension quizzes, strategy tests, and rules tests—but the majority of performance criteria are written for the psychomotor domain. The domain interactions in PSI do not ignore affective learning, but this domain is not directly addressed in the PSI model. Students who are able to progress at their own pace enjoy this feature and feel a strong sense of accomplishment as they move from one mastered task to the next. This promotes high levels of independence and student self-efficacy, both desired outcomes in the affective domain.

Student Developmental Requirements

Student readiness for learning. Students in PSI can remain independent of the teacher because most of the key managerial and instructional information is presented to them in written and visual form. Therefore, students must be able to read (or view) and comprehend that information in order to be ready for this kind of teaching and learning. The large degree of independence in PSI also requires that students be personally responsible, as they will need to stay on-task without constant managerial supervision from the teacher. Students who are not able to assume this level of responsibility are not ready to learn with PSI.

Student receptivity to the model. Using the Reichmann and Grasha (1974) profile for student learning preferences, PSI will appeal most to those students who are classified as avoidant, competitive, and dependent. As mentioned in Chapter 2, those labels should not be interpreted negatively. They are used to describe how some students would prefer the instructional environment to be designed. Although PSI offers students much independence in how they progress through learning tasks, the list of tasks is determined solely by the teacher, giving students little latitude on what and how they learn in physical education.

Validation of the Model

Research validation

Perhaps more than any other model presented in this book, PSI has received extensive and mostly consistent research support as an effective instructional model. Over 20 years ago, Lowry and Thornburg (1988) cited more than 1,500 research articles that described how to implement PSI and how effective it could be in a wide variety of content areas: earth science, mathematics, writing, physics, chemistry, health, psychology, and many others. Most of the completed research has focused on grades from middle school through college. Some research has also been completed on the effectiveness of PSI for teaching physical education. In a summary of the literature in personalized instructional materials, Annarino (1976) reported results from several studies in which personalized instruction was compared with other approaches in teaching physical education. The key point in his review was that the PSI and PSI-like techniques were always shown to be at least as effective as other teaching methods, and often more effective. Metzler and graduate students at Virginia Tech completed a series of studies on the effectiveness of authentic PSI materials used in college Basic Instruction Programs. Metzler (1984) compared how students spent time in tennis classes while using PSI and Direct Instruction. The PSI students had higher rates of content engagement, skill practice time, Academic Learning Time, and success at learning tasks. In a follow-up study,

Metzler (1986) reported the same positive results for student process, along with a more important finding that the PSI students had significantly higher learning gains over the students who had Direct Instruction. In an analysis of teacher processes in PSI, Metzler, Eddleman, Treanor, and Cregger (1989) reported that PSI teachers spend less than 1 percent of class time managing and giving task presentations and provide almost three times as much verbal and nonverbal feedback as non-PSI teachers.

Cregger (1994) designed an animated PSI-Computer Assisted Instruction (CAI) module for students learning spare conversion in a college bowling course. Students who used the PSI-CAI module showed increased learning gains over another group that received a traditional Direct Instruction approach. Interestingly, the CAI group did not show significant gains over a group of students who received that same PSI information on spare conversion from a packet of written text and graphics—suggesting that the format of the PSI media is a less important factor than the model itself.

Research on PSI has consistently demonstrated the model's effectiveness in promoting high levels of student achievement, but support has not been unanimous. A few reports suggest that PSI will work better for students who are self-disciplined and independent learners; the lack of task progression structure allows students to procrastinate if they wish, thereby reducing achievement and risking lower grades (Sherman, 1974a). Indeed, most of the research that does not support the effectiveness of PSI points to factors that are not design flaws; they consist typically of errors made by the teacher when implementing PSI and of contextual factors that cause the model not to work for some students, while others who apply themselves are showing large learning gains (Sherman, 1974b).

Craft knowledge validation

The fact that PSI has been used in almost every content area and has generated much literature about how to implement it provides good evidence for craft knowledge validation. If the model was not effective and not adaptable to so many content areas, it would not have received so much attention in the educational literature. Its continued use for nearly 40 years is strong evidence that many kinds of teachers like it, use it, and see demonstrable gains in student learning. PSI was never a fad!

I have used PSI in my teaching of physical education activity courses for more than 20 years. After becoming familiar with this model in a graduate instructional design course, I soon faced the "PE version" of Fred Keller's dilemma: how to provide personalized tennis instruction in classes with sections of more than 50 students of varying ability (and with five teaching courts)! I designed some rudimentary PSI materials that have evolved over the years into the six-course PSI series for physical education described earlier (Metzler, 2000). During that same time, many of my students have designed and used PSI units for middle school, junior high, and high school instruction—demonstrating that PSI can be adapted for many grades and for much of the movement content in physical education programs.

Intuitive validation

This chapter began by stating that individualized instruction has been a long-standing goal for physical education teachers. All teachers know that some students learn faster than others, that students come to physical education with varying levels of skill and experience with the unit's content, and that the most effective teaching occurs one-on-one with a student. All of those realizations provide strong intuitive evidence that PSI can effectively teach physical education in many settings. In addition, PSI's strong emphasis on achievement-based learning in the psychomotor domain matches many teachers' expressed domain priorities in a large number of physical education units.

TEACHING AND LEARNING FEATURES

Control

The following list describes each part of the control profile for PSI as it is used for physical education (see also Exhibit 9.2).

1. Content selection. The teacher maintains complete control of the content and its sequencing in PSI. She decides what will be included in the unit, the order in which learning tasks will be sequenced, and the performance criteria used to determine mastery of each task. Students simply receive the content and task listing from the teacher (in the course workbook) and pursue them in the order given.

2. Managerial control. The teacher determines the managerial plan, class policies, and specific procedures in the PSI model. However, after those are determined, students assume a large degree of responsibility in implementing class management within each lesson.

Control profile for PSI.	EXHIBIT 9.2

3. Task presentations. In a true PSI design, the task presentations are given to students via written and/or video displays prepared by the teacher. The teacher produces or adopts instructional media that show students how to do each task, how to correct errors, and how to set up each task for engagement. This allows students to work independently of the instructor and progress individually through the content. Students read or view the task presentation information on their own, when they are ready for it.

Some PSI designs use one whole-class task presentation by the teacher to start the unit, then they call for small-group presentations by the teacher as students begin each new skill or knowledge area in the unit. In these cases, the teacher's control of the task presentation process is stronger than is usual in PSI.

4. Engagement patterns. Students practice independently of the teacher and other students nearly all the time in PSI. Most learning tasks are designed for individual practice; a few are designed for partner- or small-group engagement. Regardless of the design, students are typically engaged independently of the teacher's direction.

5. Instructional interactions. Because a PSI teacher has very few managerial responsibilities in class, he is able to provide students with high levels of instructional interaction, especially relating to content. Metzler et al. (1989) observed rates of teacher feedback at over three per minute during PSI units—more than three times the rates typically reported in physical education research. But increased feedback is not the only benefit; PSI teachers are also freed from most managerial operations to provide "tutoring time" with students who need more of their attention in class.

6. Pacing. In the PSI design, each student determines the pace at which she engages in learning tasks and progresses through the unit content. Students make their own choices about when to start and stop practicing, how many trials they attempt, and how long to take between trials. They are held accountable for achieving each task's performance criterion but not for the process of getting there.

7. Task progression. In a different way, students also control their own pace through the unit content according to how fast their ability and effort allow them to move through the task sequence. They can go "as fast as they can or as slowly as they need." Admittedly, some students cannot progress as fast as they wish, but by and large it is the student, not the teacher, who controls task progression.

Inclusiveness

PSI's focus on individual student achievement makes it a highly inclusive model for teaching physical education. All students are able to participate and progress through the sequence of learning activities according to their own abilities, so no one is excluded by being "left behind" as when teachers base task progressions on a time allocation plan. Lower-ability learners can take the time they need to demonstrate mastery on each task. Higher-ability students can progress according to their own pacing as well.

PSI also allows the teacher time to identify and work one-on-one with those students who need more extensive instructional interaction. Since students know what they are supposed to be doing at all times, the teacher can spend several minutes with one or a few students who want extra attention—without losing managerial control of the class.

Learning Tasks

Task presentation

The most important feature of PSI is that it allows students to be largely independent of the teacher in the management of class operations and progression through learning activities. The idea is not to have the teacher carry out the many routine operations that take away from instructional time with students or reduce students' active engagement. In PSI, information about learning tasks that is typically provided to students by a teacher's lecture and/or demonstration (as in Direct Instruction) is instead given to students via written and visual media. Recall the most important functions of task presentation: (1) to give students a "picture" of the correct way to perform a task or skill, (2) to provide learning cues on key elements of the skill, and (3) to alert students to common errors that occur when practicing that skill. In most instances, this information is communicated to the entire class, with the teacher serving as the model. In PSI, the modeling operation of task presentation is most often performed by instructional media—some combination of written text, photographs, illustrations, videos, and DVDs. Separately from other students in class, each student reads/views a presentation when she is ready to begin a new learning task. She informs the teacher that she is ready, gets and reviews the media presentation of the task and structure, and then proceeds to practice the task on her own.

Written text. Most students cannot get sufficient task information from reading text only. The transfer from reading to a "mind's picture" of a psychomotor skill is too abstract for all but a few learners, so text must be supplemented with visual displays.

Photographs. Pictures and other images of models performing a skill can be helpful for many learners. These images can show good detail and can be superimposed with text and graphics for added information. The limitation of still images is that they are just snapshots that portray one brief instant of skill performance in each frame.

Animation. These are like photographs when used as single frames, but they have the added potential to show movement through animation of body parts and sequential motions. Superimposing text and graphics also enhances the amount of information that animations can provide to learners.

Videos. One of the best ways to show task presentations is a video that has both visual and audio elements. It is quite simple for a teacher to record a task presentation for each learning task and then let students view the video when they begin a new skill or task in the PSI sequence. Teachers should not worry about achieving professional-quality production on these videos—they are meant to be "homemade" and will work fine as long as they give students the needed information. Many commercial instructional videos and websites are available but must be carefully selected to provide the exact task presentation desired by the teacher. Cost may also be a prohibitive factor.

A modified task strategy. If none of those kinds of media is available, the teacher can use a modified approach for PSI task presentation by having one whole-class, live task presentation for *only* the very first skill in the course (e.g., forehand drive in tennis). All students then progress individually through the forehand task sequence. When a small group of students has finished that sequence, the teacher then gives them the second task presentation (e.g., backhand drive), and they move on while the rest of the class is still working on the forehand. That scenario is repeated as small groups finish one skill sequence and need a new task presentation. Teachers should be aware that this approach has the potential to undermine the PSI model by taking up time with many "mini presentations" at the cost of spending time with students who are practicing. But it can be a practical alternative to producing or purchasing instructional media.

Task structure

PSI uses a list of sequenced learning activities within each of the skill and knowledge areas in the unit's content listing. For example, a tennis course would have a list of learning activities under each area to be included in the unit: forehand drive, backhand drive, serving, returning serve, volleying, rules, scoring, and strategy. Each learning task includes the needed task presentation information, error analyses, performance criteria, and details about task structure. The task structure information should include:

1. Needed equipment
2. Practice space requirements or specific location
3. Arrangement for the task (e. g., where to place targets, where to hit from, needed assistance from partners)
4. Performance criteria for accuracy, consistency, time, and so forth
5. Directions for pursuing the task, including safety
6. Procedures for verifying completion of the task (self-check, partner check, instructor check)
7. Information that can be easily read by students about how to correct common performance errors

As mentioned, students can get task presentation information from a variety of sources; task structure information comes from written and visual directions. Exhibit 9.3 shows an example of a PSI learning task for badminton.

Task presentation and task structure for a badminton skill.	**EXHIBIT**	**9.3**

HIGH, DEEP SERVE FOR BADMINTON

1. View the DVD segment for the high, deep serve. Be sure to note the applicable rules and the key elements for this important badminton skill.

2. Equipment: racquet, 10 shuttles, 2 small cones, pencil for recording scores

3. Mark off a line 8 feet from the back boundary of the opposite service return box, and put one cone there on each side. The resulting rectangle is your aiming area for this task—purple for serves from the right side, yellow for serves from the left side. Set up for your serves in the proper position in the service court. Practice your high, deep serves in blocks of 10 shots, keeping a record of how many shots in each group have a high trajectory and land in the aiming area. When you are ready, your partner witnesses and scores your mastery attempt. When you reach the criterion, your partner puts initials and dates in the designated areas.

   1. Position: Serving position in appropriate box
   2. Aiming area: Marked rectangle in opposite service return box
   3. Trajectory: High
   4. Shuttle: Self-tossed, with legal contact
   5. Performance criterion: 7 of 10 in aiming area; two sets from both service sides

From the Right Service Side (Purple target area)

Practice this task in blocks of 10 serves. Record the number of successful high, deep serves for each block on the Personal Recording Form below. When two block scores reach or exceed 7 out of 10, your partner puts initials and dates in the space provided.

Block 1	Block 2	Block 3	Block 4	Block 5	Block 6	Block 7	Block 8	Block 9	Block 10
__/10	__/10	__/10	__/10	__/10	__/10	__/10	__/10	__/10	__/10

Your partner's initials and date go here: _____

From the Left Service Side (Yellow target area)

Practice this task in blocks of 10 serves. Record the number of successful high, deep serves for each block on the Personal Recording Form below. When two block scores reach or exceed 7 out of 10, your partner puts initials and dates in the space provided.

Block 1	Block 2	Block 3	Block 4	Block 5	Block 6	Block 7	Block 8	Block 9	Block 10
__/10	__/10	__/10	/10	__/10	__/10	__/10	__/10	__/10	__/10

Your partner's initials and date go here: _____

Common Errors on the High, Deep Serve and Their Correction

1. *The serve does not go straight.*
   - Make sure your footwork is correct on setup. (Point your front foot to the target.)
   - Change your swing path to be more vertical (straight up in the air).

(continued)

EXHIBIT 9.3 Continued.

2. *The serve goes too long.*
   - Use a little less power and wrist action.
   - Increase lifting action on the serve to get higher trajectory.
3. *You have inconsistent shots, with no set pattern for errors.*
   - Recheck all key elements by yourself without striking the shuttle.
   - Practice this serve with no target until you gain more consistency.

The example contains directions telling students how to get all the needed task presentation and task structure information. When a student is ready for this task, he reads the directions, watches the task presentation, gathers the needed equipment and proceeds—with no dependence on the teacher.

Six different kinds of tasks can be written for PSI units: (1) readiness drills, (2) comprehension tasks, (3) criterion tasks, (4) challenge tasks, (5) quizzes, and (6) game or match play. Each type of task has a different structure.

1. *Readiness drills.* Students receive the task presentation, complete the comprehension task, and then spend a short period of time in non-criterion engagement to get the feel of objects, implements, and movement patterns. They just hit, throw, catch, run, jump, or shoot for a few minutes to become familiar with space, objects, and equipment.

2. *Comprehension tasks.* Students demonstrate that they have understood the key elements of the task presentation by making a brief display for the teacher. Examples include showing the correct grip in golf, using the proper form for soccer trapping, and performing the correct stance and swing for a badminton serve. The teacher observes each student's display with a short checklist of key elements; when those elements have been correctly demonstrated, the student proceeds to independent practice. A sample checklist for the overhead volleyball serve is shown in Exhibit 9.4.

EXHIBIT 9.4 Sample checklist for key elements of the overhead volleyball serve.

KEY ELEMENT	DEMONSTRATED	NEED MORE PRACTICE
1. Proper stance, 2 feet behind the baseline	✓	
2. High and accurate toss	✓	
3. Contact ball at nearly full extension	✓	
4. Proper arm speed at contact		✓
5. Proper follow-through, one step onto court	✓	

3. *Criterion tasks.* Most tasks in PSI are criterion tasks in which students must demonstrate mastery of the current skill to meet the standards established by the teacher. Students practice these tasks until they are ready to be monitored for mastery. Criteria can be set for accuracy, consistency, time, distance, speed, or attained score. More will be presented on these tasks later in this chapter.

4. *Challenge tasks.* Since proficiency for most criterion tasks is demonstrated in isolated and sometimes static drills, there is a need for students to extend their mastery to the next level of complexity. Challenge tasks are lead-up and modified games that allow students to practice combinations of newly acquired skills in two or more criterion tasks. Some examples of challenge tasks are:

- Tennis: Serving and returning games (no volleying)
- Soccer: "Keep away" or three vs. three in a small area and with a small goal
- Basketball: Two-on-two half-court games
- Volleyball: Three vs. three with a "no spiking" rule

5. *Quizzes.* Some content areas will develop students' knowledge of game history, rules, scoring, and strategy. In PSI, students typically learn that kind of content by reading it or viewing videos. After they have studied the material, they must pass a quiz to demonstrate a stated performance criterion.

6. *Game or match play.* Once students have completed all the content areas in the unit, they progress to playing games or matches. Students who finish all of a unit's content areas faster get more class days of play. Students who take longer often appreciate the extra time to develop their skills, knowing they will be more prepared for competition when that time comes. Getting to the game stage is a motivating factor for many students, regardless of their skill levels.

Mastery/non-mastery attempts. As mentioned previously, a student practices a task or studies content (e.g., reads a chapter) until she thinks she is ready to be checked for mastery. At that time, either the instructor or a peer will watch as she attempts to meet the criterion stated in the task structure. If the criterion is met, she moves to the next task. If the criterion is not met, she resumes practice until she once again feels confident enough to make a second mastery attempt. The same process applies to non-mastery attempts on tests and quizzes—they can be retaken without penalty. *Mastery attempts can be repeated as many times as needed for the student to meet the performance criterion.*

Verifying proficiency. In small classes, it is possible for the teacher to be the witness for all mastery attempts. In larger classes, designated students or practice partners can serve as monitors for some of the lower-level tasks in a course content area. However, it is important that the teacher retain his role as witness for the final task demonstration in each content area, because completion of that task signals that the student is ready to move to new content in the unit.

PSI course workbook. All managerial operations, instructional materials, learning tasks, and assessments in a PSI unit are explained to students in a *course workbook* that they read as the unit begins and then refer to on an "as-needed" basis. The workbook should include the following kinds of information:

1. Attendance policies
2. Class rules and disciplinary plan
3. Dressing-out policies
4. Process for getting and returning equipment
5. Grading plan and applicable policies
6. Procedures for starting each class
7. Complete content list and all PSI learning tasks, with performance criteria
8. All required readings (rules, strategies, history, and so forth)
9. Student progress chart for completed tasks (refer to Exhibit 9.8 on p. 218)

See also the sample PSI workbook on the IMPE website.

Content progression

As you already know, each student progresses through the course content at an individual pace. The order of that progression is determined by the teacher and presented to students in sequential learning tasks via the workbook. The workbook makes the order very clear, so at no time does the teacher stop the whole class and move all students to the next task together.

Engagement Patterns for Learning

As the model's name would indicate, PSI uses individual practice engagement almost exclusively. Each student is on her own to get the task presentation information, set up the practice area, pace her practice, and monitor achievement. Some situations will call for paired practice, such as rallying in tennis, making and returning serves in badminton, or pitching to a batter in softball. Challenge tasks are modified games that focus on the skills learned previously and allow students to practice newly acquired skills in small-sided (e.g., four vs. four soccer) and simple games that develop tactical awareness and applications.

Teacher and Student Roles and Responsibilities

Each instructional model will require certain operations that allow the model to function according to its design. Some of the operations are carried out by the teacher; others are carried out by one or more students. Exhibit 9.5 shows the major operations within the PSI model and indicates who is responsible for completing them during each lesson.

Verification of Instructional Processes

Teachers who use PSI should learn the benchmarks for their own and student behavior patterns. These benchmarks, listed in Exhibits 9.6 and 9.7, verify that the PSI unit has been planned and implemented as closely as possible to the model's design, increasing the likelihood that the stated student learning outcomes will be achieved.

Assessment of Learning

Assessing student learning in PSI is mostly automatic and built into the design of the model. Continuous assessment occurs every time a student completes each learning task according to the specified performance criteria. If the task structure has directed students to record the number of successful trials in each practice block, then the teacher can easily know how many trials it took each

Teacher and student roles and responsibilities in PSI.	EXHIBIT 9.5
OPERATION OR RESPONSIBILITY	**PERSON/PEOPLE RESPONSIBLE IN PSI**
Starting class	Each student starts to practice when he/she arrives. There is no teacher-led starting procedure.
Bringing equipment to class	The teacher checks to see what tasks will be practiced in class and brings the needed equipment.
Dispersing and returning equipment	Students get the needed equipment for their next learning task and return it when finished.
Roll call (if needed)	Students keep their attendance in their workbook. The teacher verifies it after each class.
Task presentation	Students read or view the task presentation information as they begin each new task.
Task structure	Students set up each new task according to the directions in their workbook.
Assessment	Students verify mastery of each task in their workbook. Some tasks can be self-checked, some can be partner-checked, and some can be teacher-checked.
Monitoring learning progress	Students decide if they are going fast enough to complete the unit on time. The teacher monitors their progress periodically by checking workbooks.

EXHIBIT 9.6	PSI teacher benchmarks.
BENCHMARK	**HOW TO VERIFY**
Teacher ensures PSI course materials are clear to students.	Monitor the number and types of questions students ask after reading/viewing information in their workbooks.
Teacher has very low percentage of managerial time in class (less than 2 percent).	Use a stopwatch to measure how much management time teacher uses in class.
Teacher has very high rates of individualized instructional interactions in class.	Audiotape a lesson and count the number of cues, feedbacks, and questions directed to individual students.
Teacher sets performance criteria for tasks at appropriate levels of difficulty.	Direct students to practice tasks in blocks (e.g., 10 trials) and to record the number of successful tasks in each block. If most students reach mastery after one or two blocks, the task is too easy. If many students get "stuck" on a task, it is too difficult. Adjust the task or performance criteria accordingly.
Teacher does not spend too much time witnessing and verifying mastery attempts.	Count the number of times the teacher witnessed mastery attempts in each class. If that takes away from instructional time: (1) design more self- and partner-checked tasks or (2) appoint some dependable students as temporary witnesses until the backlog is gone.
Teacher makes few or no task presentations.	Count the number of task presentations made in class. If those presentations take away from instructional time with individual students, design and produce media-based task presentations.

student to reach mastery of every task. This built-in assessment feature can provide the teacher with a lot of useful information:

1. It lets the teacher know if tasks are too easy or too difficult. From this, the teacher can make adjustments, delete a task, add a task, or combine tasks.
2. It can be used to calculate the average number of trials students need on each task.
3. It can be used to determine the range of trials to mastery (the fewest and the most).
4. It lets the teacher identify students who are going too slow and need extra attention.

This continuous assessment feature is also beneficial to students:

1. They get regular knowledge of results and can tell when they need extra help from the teacher.

PSI student benchmarks.	🖶 **EXHIBIT** **9.7**
BENCHMARK	**HOW TO VERIFY**
Students have understood written or visual task presentation.	1. Check for understanding. 2. Monitor students on comprehension tasks that demonstrate key elements from the task presentation. 3. Note the number and pattern of students' questions.
Students are staying on-task.	Periodically monitor and count the number of students who are on-task in class.
Students can properly set up learning activities from the written task structure information.	Observe several students setting up learning stations. Note how long it takes each one to set up and how correctly it is done.
Students do not make "inappropriate progress" (i.e., cheat on verifying mastery).	Review students' progress charts each day, looking for faster than expected progress.
Students make self-paced progression.	Monitor the number of managerial questions students ask the teacher. Too much reliance on the teacher slows down students' progression.
Student progression is more or less even.	Review personal progress charts often.

2. They can see every day if they are on schedule to complete the course on time.
3. They experience frequent and predictable reinforcement for success.

Exhibit 9.8 shows an example of a student progress chart for a PSI badminton unit. As a student completes each listed task, he puts an X in the box across from that task in the column representing the class in which it was accomplished. Notice that the sequence of learning activities starts at the bottom of the page, so if all the Xs were connected they would form a line graph that represents that student's learning pace in the unit. The student and teacher can then see with one glance if the student is making satisfactory progress in the unit.

IMPLEMENTATION NEEDS AND MODIFICATIONS

Teacher Expertise

Teachers using PSI will need to have several particular areas of expertise to use this model to its fullest capacity.

Implementing developmentally appropriate instruction. The main building blocks for PSI are the individualized learning tasks pursued by students. From a

| EXHIBIT | 9.8 | Student's personal progress chart for badminton. |

| STUDENT'S NAME: ROBERT WEIR | CLASS PERIOD FOR PE: 3RD |

	1	2	3	4	5	6	7	8	9	10	11	12	13
Match play										X	X	X	X
Pass rules and scoring quiz										X			
Final challenge task										X			
Backhand drop									X				
Forehand drop									X				
Overhead smash									X				
Backhand drives								X					
Forehand drives								X					
Challenge task for clears							X						
Overhead clears						X							
Backhand drive clear						X							
Forehand drive clear					X								
Serving challenge				X									
High, deep serve			X										
Short, low serve		X											
Stretching	X												
CLASS DAY	1	2	3	4	5	6	7	8	9	10	11	12	13

managerial standpoint, students must be able to comprehend written and media-based task presentation and task structure directions with little teacher guidance, so the teacher must know the appropriate level at which to design those tasks. From an instructional standpoint, the teacher must be knowledge-able about students' ability in the cognitive and psychomotor domains so that the performance criteria for tasks can be set at levels that are challenging—not too easy or too difficult.

Learning objectives. Because PSI relies so much on the sequence of mastery-based learning tasks, teachers must be able to write clear and concise learning objectives—often in the Mager (1984) format, as discussed in Chapter 3. Good learning objectives will have three parts: (1) a description of the setting or conditions in which the learning activity will occur, (2) clear descriptions of the behavior to be learned, and (3) performance criteria that indicate the level of proficiency needed to demonstrate mastery of the task.

Task analysis and content progression. Each content area in a PSI unit will contain a sequence of learning tasks, progressing from simple to complex. Teachers using PSI must know how to analyze skills into component parts and then sequence those parts into a coherent learning progression.

Assessment. As shown in the example in Exhibit 9.3, each PSI learning task contains an assessment component, most often expressed as a performance criterion. Teachers will need to know how to establish the criterion for each task and how best to assess performance abilities in an ongoing *formative* plan. It is possible to write authentic assessments for PSI tasks, such as the Game Performance Assessment Instrument (Griffin, Mitchell, & Oslin, 1997) discussed in Chapter 14, but most tend to be static assessments of discrete student knowledge in the cognitive and psychomotor domains. The key here is that a teacher who uses PSI must know how to write performance assessments into the task structure itself.

Key Teaching Skills

A teacher will apply his effective teaching skills in unique ways while using PSI for physical education.

Planning. PSI requires a substantial amount of advance planning for each unit. The managerial plans, content listing, task analyses, learning activities, task presentation materials, and performance criteria must all be designed and produced for the student workbook before the unit can begin. A PSI teacher must have the unit's "big picture" clearly in mind throughout the planning process. On the other hand, daily lesson planning is very simple in PSI. Since the unit plan contains all the plans for each learning activity, the teacher needs only to know what tasks students will be working on in the upcoming lesson and bring the necessary equipment for that class.

Time and class management. Time management is easy and efficient in PSI. Because students know exactly what they are to do in every class and all the task information appears in their workbooks, the teacher does not have to monitor tasks or make managerial decisions in class. The same goes for class management, as students have all necessary information at their disposal in the workbook. Essentially, the information in the student workbook runs the class for the teacher, so the teacher's skill in designing and writing the student workbook is vital to the success of PSI.

Task presentation and structure. Most or all task presentation and structure information is provided through instructional media or written in the student workbook. A PSI teacher needs to know how to select and/or produce these materials so that students can use them without asking the teacher for clarification or added information. Designing the student workbook is greatly facilitated by a teacher's skill in and knowledge of word processing and other information technologies.

Communication. Writing is the key communication mode in PSI. The teacher decides what information students will need in the unit and writes that information into the students' workbook. Therefore, PSI demands good writing skills *at the student level of comprehension.*

Instructional interactions. Because the teacher is free from nearly all managerial operations in PSI, she has much more time in class to interact with students on skill development, strategy, and game/match performance. Metzler et al. (1989) found that PSI teachers give more than three times the amount of teaching cues and feedback to students as teachers who use Direct Instruction. This interaction is possible because PSI can lower class-management time to around only 1 percent of total class time—the rest of class time can be used to interact with students for their learning. So PSI teachers must have good skills in observing student performance and providing many different kinds of feedback in order to prevent interaction from becoming stale and ineffective. The increased opportunity for interaction also calls for good questioning skills so that a PSI teacher can get students to think independently when they are practicing individualized learning tasks. Students will benefit more from PSI if they can reach a point of *knowing how to learn* without regular dependence on the teacher.

Contextual Requirements

PSI can work in any physical education setting. It is not limited by facility or environmental factors. The main contextual requirement is that there be enough instructional space for all students to practice individually without having to wait. There should also be enough equipment so that all students can practice their current learning task. PSI can actually require fewer of each object or implement in many instances. For example, in a PSI golf unit, some students might be putting, some might be chipping, some might be hitting short irons, and others might be using drivers—all at one time—so it is not necessary to have each type of club for every student in the class. However, it is important to have a sufficient number of objects (e.g., balls, shuttlecocks, bean bags) because the individualized practice structure will require students to perform a large number of practice trials.

Student reading level. PSI students must be able to read (or view) and comprehend the written and visual task presentation and structure information in their personal workbook. The teacher can write that information for the average reading ability of the class, but the below-average readers or those for whom English is not their primary language will be challenged greatly in this model. PSI should not be used with students who have poor reading skills or who are not fluent in English, regardless of their grade level. Using the latest word processing technology, it is now possible to translate the workbook into many languages.

Technology. There are many technologies that can present PSI task and structure information besides printed media. Videos, DVDs, YouTube, and other online sources can all be used for that purpose. Students will need to be able to operate any such technology used in a PSI unit.

Personal responsibility. As you know by now, the key design feature of PSI is individual student learning, with very little direct guidance by the teacher. PSI students must be mature enough to make good decisions about how they spend their time in class. They must also be able to assume the responsibility of monitoring their own practice and verifying their own task mastery when self-checks are allowed. Teachers should not select PSI for classes with too many students who cannot take on these responsibilities.

Contextual modifications. PSI requires that all students have the opportunity to engage independently, without having to wait for activity space or equipment. Thus, the teacher will have to find ways to eliminate student waiting. Some practical modifications include maximizing practice space by getting students to share courts, nets, areas, and so on, even if they are not on the same task. Other modifications can be made by periodically allowing some students to monitor instructor-checked tasks when the teacher gets behind in those assessments. The teacher can also allow higher-skilled students to make task presentations to students who follow them in the sequence.

Selecting and Modifying PSI

PSI can be used in many physical education settings for a wide variety of content. It is particularly effective for activities that can be broken into discrete skills or knowledge areas that should be learned in a definite sequence. It can be designed for units that have a strong emphasis on learning outcomes in the psychomotor domain, along with some outcomes in the cognitive domain. I recommend the following types of content for PSI use in physical education:

1. Individual sports
2. Team sports
3. Recreational activities (e.g., bowling, horseshoes, Frisbee)
4. Dances with prescribed steps (e.g., line, square, folk)
5. Personal fitness concepts
6. Personal fitness programs

PSI will be more effective with students who have the prerequisite abilities discussed earlier in this chapter. Students must be able to read and follow directions and to make responsible decisions about pacing, engagement, and asking for help when they need it. Exhibit 9.9 presents an analysis to be used in selecting PSI and adapting it to different grade levels.

EXHIBIT 9.9	Grade-level adaptations for PSI in physical education.	
GRADE LEVELS	**SELECT PSI?**	**POSSIBLE ADAPTATIONS**
Preschool	No	
Elementary	No	
Middle school/ junior high	Yes	1. Reduce the number of learning tasks. 2. Simplify the task presentations or designate the teacher to make them. 3. Make performance criteria simple and attainable but still at an appropriate mastery level. 4. Set up learning stations for students. 5. Use task cards with pictures at each station. 6. Simplify the management system.
High school	Yes	1. Designate higher-skilled and dependable students to assist novices or slow readers. 2. Use video-based media for task presentations. 3. Use more teacher-checked tasks.
College/adult	Yes	None needed. The full PSI design can be implemented.

Adaptations to accommodate diverse groups of learners

PSI can be a highly inclusive model for physical education if the teacher uses strategies to help all students receive task presentations and move through the content at their own pace. Exhibit 9.10 lists some strategies that address a variety of special learning needs found in many schools today.

PLANNING TIPS FOR PSI

Teachers who will use the PSI model can benefit by following a few additional planning tips:

1. Plan the entire unit content ahead of time, and make an outline of the scope and sequence. Then, make a good estimate of how long it will take students to learn each skill or knowledge area. Be sure to remember that they are not likely to learn as fast as you, so don't base your estimate on *your* ability!

2. Be careful not to respond to students' questions that they could answer by looking in the workbook. This takes your time from other students.

3. Provide several ways for students to get the task presentation, and use instructional media (e.g., DVDs, task cards) whenever possible.

Strategies to adapt PSI for diverse groups of learners.	EXHIBIT 9.10

FOR STUDENTS WITH HEARING IMPAIRMENTS:

1. Use a microphone to amplify the teacher's voice.
2. Move students closer during task presentations.
3. When using media-based task presentations, use the closed-caption feature to allow students to read along with the demonstration.

FOR STUDENTS WITH SIGHT IMPAIRMENTS:

1. Use a larger font for task cards.
2. Modify equipment (by color or size, or use "beeper balls").
3. Make targets more highly visible for them.
4. Use spotters at targets to determine success.

FOR STUDENTS WITH PHYSICAL DISABILITIES:

1. Provide appropriate versions of tasks for them (e.g., allow low-ambulatory students to practice stationary tasks when possible).
2. Modify equipment according to their needs.
3. Adjust learning goals and criterion tasks according to student ability (e.g., lower mastery levels or larger targets).

FOR STUDENTS WHO DO NOT SPEAK ENGLISH:

1. Use student translators when available.
2. Provide the PSI workbook in appropriate languages, or use translated closed-caption media when possible.
3. Use body gestures and hands-on cues.

FOR LOWER-SKILLED STUDENTS:

1. Use appropriate skill-level models for task presentation.
2. Adjust criteria for tasks or grades that match student abilities.
3. Provide extra encouragement and praise.

---

4. Have enough learning stations so that students have little or no waiting time.
5. Collect student workbooks after each lesson. This prevents them from losing the workbook or forgetting it the next time.
6. Review each student's learning progress after every lesson so that you can know which learning tasks they will practice next class and can plan accordingly.
7. At the end of each PSI unit, look back at the criterion tasks to see how long, on average, it took students to complete each one. Adjust accordingly for the next time you teach the PSI unit with that content.

UNIT AND LESSON PLAN EXAMPLES FOR PSI

Y ou will find several complete unit plans with lesson plans for PSI on the IMPE website. It is not recommended that you follow these examples exactly as they are presented. The context, specific learning objectives, and content of your own unit will require you to make changes in these examples to allow the PSI model to lead to the most effective instruction in your situation.

SUMMARY

Perhaps the biggest problem with the PSI model arises when a teacher wishes to implement individualized instruction but fails to follow the PSI model faithfully. Because of PSI's uniqueness, it is important that physical education teachers do not compromise its design. Siedentop (1973) cautioned physical educators about ways in which the PSI model could be compromised, causing it to (1) violate Keller's design enough to make it something other than PSI and (2) result in reduced student achievement:

1. Reducing performance criteria to non-mastery levels (e.g., 5 successful out of 10, rather than 7)
2. Extended delay of students' attempts at mastery due to "backlogs"
3. Reducing the number of tasks (and performance assessments)
4. Attempting to limit cheating by structuring group performance assessments (pp. 118–119)

The PSI courses mentioned earlier (Metzler, 2000) offer some field-tested versions of PSI for physical education. Cregger and Metzler (1992) analyzed an earlier version of the PSI volleyball course in this series and determined that its few modifications fully complied with the key PSI design features. Teachers were using faithful versions of PSI, and students were engaged in a manner consistent with PSI learning processes. Only when this happens can the full potential of PSI be realized for students in physical education.

LEARNING ACTIVITIES

1. Make a list of five activity units (e.g., movement skills, fitness, softball, tennis, golf) that might be taught in a physical education program. Next, determine an appropriate grade level (P, K–2, 3–5, 6–8, 9–12) for teaching each of those activity units. Now, write two major learning outcomes for those units. Then, go through the process of selecting an instructional model, shown in Chapter 2, to determine if PSI would be an appropriate model for teaching that activity to children at that grade level.
2. If PSI is appropriate for that activity, grade, and goals, mention three things that make it appropriate. If PSI is not appropriate for that activity, grade, and goals, mention three things that make it inappropriate.

3. For one activity unit at one grade level (e.g., K–2 movement skills, high school tennis), write a complete list of content to be taught in that unit with PSI.

4. Write one complete learning module using the PSI design for your activity unit. Be sure to include all of the types of learning tasks and assessments shown in this chapter.

TOPICS FOR REFLECTION & SMALL-GROUP DISCUSSION

1. I have suggested in this chapter how the PSI model is aligned to achieve one or more of the NASPE standards. Take a moment to review those alignments (refer back to Exhibit 9.1). After that, make some notes about whether you agree with those alignments, and then share them in your small group. When you have arrived at your final thoughts, please share them on the IMPE website Forum for others to review, and check back for replies.

2. PSI has a long and impressive record of research to support it as a highly effective instructional model in many different content areas and contexts, yet it is not widely used in physical education today. Why do you think that is so?

3. Mention three ways the PSI model is similar to Direct Instruction and three ways it is different.

4. In general, which types of students are placed at an advantage in this model, and which students are at a disadvantage?

5. If you were to use PSI, how much would you be afraid that students will take advantage of their greatly increased independence in your classes? What could you do to reduce that possibility?

SUGGESTED READING FOR PSI

Metzler, M. (2000). *Instructor's manual for the Personalized Sport Instruction Series*. Boston: Allyn and Bacon. (This series includes PSI courses for college-level instruction in badminton, golf, racquetball, soccer, tennis, and volleyball. All student workbooks can easily be adapted for use in middle/junior and high schools.)

COOPERATIVE LEARNING
Students Learning With, By, and For Each Other

O ne of the major dilemmas all teachers face is how to engage every student in the learning process at the same time, without allowing one or a few to dominate the interaction and reduce the learning opportunities for others. Consider this scenario: Mrs. Prusak asks her fifth-grade class, "Who can show me three important things to do when you are throwing a ball?" Several students who have answers immediately raise their hands. Mrs. Prusak calls on Roberto, who says, "Make sure you step with your opposite foot," and he shows the rest of the class how to do that part of the throw. The teacher then calls on Mara, who says, "You need to follow through to your target," while she demonstrates the proper technique. Finally, Mrs. Prusak calls on Madison, who adds, "You should turn your opposite shoulder toward your target when you start, like this," as she also shows the other students the correct movement. Acknowledging all three as good answers, Mrs. Prusak continues to the next part of her task presentation. This is a very common scenario that could take place in almost any physical education lesson at any grade level. But, on a closer look, this approach to teaching raises a few important

chapter

10

questions. First, it becomes competitive because students who have answers raise their hands to get the teacher's attention and the chance to be "in the spotlight" for a moment. Second, when those students raise their hands, the other students are likely to stop trying to come up with answers of their own, in effect becoming passive learners for the moment. As a result, students who do not have an answer right away do not learn for themselves—they are actually taught by those students who do have answers. Third, this approach does not allow students to interact with each other, promoting a kind of isolation among them even while they are very close to each other. That is not to say this approach is bad—only that it contains some features that open the door to other possible ways to structure the learning environment. One such way is represented by the Cooperative Learning model, developed in the early 1970s and now used in many schools, at all grade levels, and for every subject area in the curriculum, including physical education.

Cooperative Learning is not really a model by itself. It encompasses a set of teaching strategies that share key attributes, the most important being the grouping of students into *learning teams* for set amounts of time or assignments, with the expectation that all students will contribute to the learning process and outcomes. Here the word *team* takes on the same meaning as it does in sport—all members work to achieve a common goal. In this model, that common goal is the completion of a learning task given to the team by the teacher. The task can require them to base their achievement on intra-group performance (trying to be the best team they can be), on inter-group performance (competing with other teams), or shared-group performance (learning content so that they can teach it to the rest of the class).

The Cooperative Learning model was developed and initially researched at Johns Hopkins University in the mid-1970s. Led by Robert Slavin, this development was first reported in a series of research and topical articles in educational journals. It is now one of the most recognized instructional models in education worldwide. Slavin's early label for the model was Student Team Learning (STL). Slavin (1983) stated that STL is based on three concepts: team rewards, individual accountability, and equal opportunities for success.

1. Team rewards. The main building block in STL is a task the teacher gives to each team (made up of 4 to 6 students). All teams can be working on the same task or different but related tasks. Either way, the teacher includes one or more stated performance criteria that teams must meet, along with the reward to be received by those teams who meet the standard. Rewards can be cumulative points, classroom privileges, public recognition, or grades.

2. Individual accountability. Another key part of the learning task is the specification that all team members' performance is included in the team score or assessment. Therefore, all students must contribute to the team's effort, so it is important that all members learn and achieve to their fullest potential. This requirement leads to regular peer teaching within groups as higher-ability students interact with lower-ability students to enhance the whole team's performance. In turn, peer teaching becomes a large factor in the model's ability to promote high levels of social learning within teams.

3. Equal opportunities for success. The process of selecting student teams is critical in STL. The model calls for groups of 4 to 6 students who are as heterogeneous as possible and for all teams to be equal in their total performance abilities. Student learning teams should be established for a mixture of gender, skill levels, previous experience with the content, cognitive ability, and motivation. This diversity within teams promotes social learning outcomes within the model. Balancing teams on performance ability allows fair competition and increases student motivation. Once that balance is achieved, and with the stipulation that all team members' performances count, there is a greater likelihood that all students will have an equal chance to be successful and that each one's contribution will be valued by other team members.

As more techniques developed under these three main concepts, a more inclusive name was given to the model: Cooperative Learning (Slavin, 1983). The Cooperative Learning label is the one now used most often by Slavin and many other proponents worldwide, so it will be used in this book, even in reference to developments prior to 1983.

It is important to note the difference between Cooperative Learning (the model) and collaborative learning (various group-learning strategies). To live up to its name, the Cooperative Learning model stipulates that all three major design concepts must be present. The model also includes a finite number of recognized learning task structures that adhere to those concepts and have been validated by research. In addition, six procedural elements give the model much of its identity and uniqueness (Cuseo, 1992):

1. Intentional group formation
2. Continuity of group interaction
3. Interdependence among group members
4. Individual accountability
5. Explicit attention to the development of social skills
6. Instructor as facilitator

By contrast, collaborative learning techniques represent a much less formal and less enduring structure. They feature small groups that are together usually for only a short time, most often for reasons related to management, not to social and performance learning. Collaborative structures can be characterized as "students learning alongside or assisting one another," while cooperative techniques can be characterized as "students learning with, by, and for each other."

OVERVIEW

As mentioned, Cooperative Learning is a set of related instructional strategies that share three common attributes: team rewards, individual accountability, and equal opportunities for success for all students. However, given that all the strategies used in Cooperative Learning have those common attributes as well as established procedures for instruction, it is possible to regard them as a formal instructional model, as this book does. Again, it is those attributes and procedures that differentiate Cooperative Learning from other collaborative or small-group instruction.

Eileen Hilke (1990) lists the major instructional goals for Cooperative Learning: (1) to foster academic cooperation among students, (2) to encourage positive group relationships, (3) to develop students' self-esteem, and (4) to enhance academic achievement (p. 8). From those goals it is clear that Cooperative Learning is both achievement-oriented and process-oriented. *Achievement-oriented* means that the model is designed to foster student mastery of the instructional unit's content, whatever it may be. The model places a strong emphasis on student learning. *Process-oriented* means that the way students interact with each other in order to learn the content is equally important and, in fact, facilitates each student's achievement. It is not that "students must learn to cooperate" but that "students must cooperate to learn."

Five essential elements of Cooperative Learning promote the process of learning, according to Johnson, Johnson, and Holubec (1994, pp. 27–34):

1. Positive interdependence among students. Students must understand that all members of the cooperative team help the whole team achieve its goals. Each team member brings to the group unique talents, knowledge, experience, and skills that can aid the team. This array of talent might also lead to intellectual conflict within a group, which then provides even more opportunities for social learning to occur. This model, then, makes it possible to turn a seemingly negative situation into one that gives rise to other kinds of learning.

2. Face-to-face promotive interaction. The team structure can cause students to support, facilitate, and reinforce the work of teammates—to "root them on" as sport team members do for each other. Students soon realize that all members of the team must achieve to their fullest potential for the team to reach its shared goals, so it is best for the group to pull together and take a genuine interest in the achievement of all members.

3. Individual accountability/personal responsibility. Cooperative Learning works best when all students in the group contribute their fair share. That does not mean all students get the same score on assessments. Rather, all students should participate fully in the group process and learn as much as their own abilities allow. In order to make this happen, the teacher must set expectations for students' participation in their groups and find ways to assess each student's contribution. In addition, all performance assessments must include some form of individual student scoring so that every student's learning counts. This type of accountability promotes increased levels of personal responsibility in students.

4. Interpersonal and small-group skills. Student achievement in Cooperative Learning is highly valued. Of equal value is the learning of interpersonal skills displayed in the team dynamics. The model emphasizes knowing and trusting team members, good communication, mutual acceptance and support, and conflict resolution. What social learning students don't bring to their team as the process begins must be learned as the cooperative process unfolds.

5. Group processing. To further stress the value of social learning, the teacher must regularly get students to reflect on, or process, their shared team experience. This processing should be a planned part of each lesson, particularly in the early part of a Cooperative Learning unit. At that time, the teacher takes an active role in teaching students how to work well in groups in order to reach their shared goals—both academic and social. The key strategy here is that the teacher should not directly tell students how to behave and interact with teammates. The processing should be more indirect, to foster thoughtful student reflection in this area of learning.

The formal Cooperative Learning model includes a recognized set of instructional strategies that can be used within it—once again, it is not just putting students in small groups to learn next to each other. A strategy can be used for a short learning task (one or two lessons), an extended learning task (three to five lessons), or an entire unit. Due to the time it takes to establish groups and to assign a Cooperative Learning task, using more than one strategy in a lesson is not recommended. Some Cooperative Learning strategies are designed specifically for subject areas other than physical education and will not be mentioned here. Those that would seem most effective for physical education are presented later in this chapter.

According to Johnson, Johnson, and Holubec (1994, pp. 37–48), the teacher who uses Cooperative Learning has six major role functions. As you can see, some teacher control is used to make groups and set the learning task in motion; from there, the students assume much of the control in this model. Here are the teacher's primary jobs:

1. Specify the instructional objectives. The teacher must delineate the academic objective(s) for the assigned task. What content is to be learned, and what are the stated performance criteria? The teacher must also specify the social skills objectives to tell students what it means to have good group interactions and process as they work together in teams.

2. Make pre-instructional decisions. Cooperative Learning teachers must make a number of planning decisions before units and lessons begin, in order to facilitate student interaction on teams. These decisions: allow each team to have a clear understanding of its assignment, inform teams of the performance criteria in place, announce how much time they will have to complete each assignment, and let them know what instructional resources (equipment, space, and so forth) they will have to work with. The teacher must also decide how teams will be selected, how learning will be assessed, and how social skills will be monitored. Undoubtedly, this model requires a lot of pre-unit planning that eventually allows the teacher to set the cooperative process in motion.

3. Communicate task presentation and task structure. There must be a delicate balance between the amount of information students need to get going on the assigned task and the amount of performance or background information the teacher gives about how to complete the task. Many cooperative tasks will emphasize task structure (space, equipment, time, teams, and criteria) over task presentation. When in doubt about the amount of information to give about task presentation, give less than one might suspect, as a general rule. This encourages teams to be a bit more resourceful and to figure out on their own when they need more information from the teacher—and then ask for it.

4. Set the cooperative assignment in motion. After the teacher has selected teams, informed the class of the upcoming assignment, and provided the task structure, she will simply tell students to "get going" on the assignment. Students should be given only enough information to allow them to understand the assignment, without any indication of how to complete it. When teams are first engaged in the task, it will take some time for them to grasp the problem embedded in the assignment and to get organized for its solution. The teacher needs to monitor this period closely to see that teams begin to move in the right direction.

5. Monitor the cooperative learning groups and intervene as necessary. As teams engage in the assignment, the teacher will monitor to see if the teams are working cooperatively. Note that this does not mean the teacher monitors for progress on the assignment; that will take care of itself if teams are using all of their resources and if all team members are contributing to the best of their ability. Interventions by the teacher should happen only when a team is not working cooperatively. Those instances then become "teaching moments" for the development of social skills and teamwork and provide the topics to be processed at the end of each class.

6. Evaluate learning and processing interaction. Assessment in Cooperative Learning takes place in two areas: (1) the quality and quantity of student learning and (2) the effectiveness of team interactions. The teacher establishes assessments and criteria for both outcomes. The assessment of achievement is likely to be more summative, once teams complete each assignment. The assessment of team interaction must be formative, and quite regular, so that periods of ineffective interaction will be fewer and shorter.

Cooperative Learning has received an enormous amount of attention, both from supporters and critics. That attention has resulted in the discussion of the advantages and disadvantages of Cooperative Learning strategies as they are used in the formal sense of the model described in this chapter. McCaslin and

Good (1996) summarize both sides of the debate over Cooperative Learning as follows.

ADVANTAGES

1. Cooperative assignments simulate the way most people work outside of school, by sharing work to "get the job done."
2. Subject matter knowledge increases because the sum of a group's abilities is always greater than that of any single member.
3. Students learn dispositions about shared tasks and group challenges.
4. Group members serve as developmentally appropriate models for each other.
5. Students learn to manage and use human resources.
6. Students come to value shared academic work more than working in isolation.
7. Students develop a greater understanding of self and others from the shared work.
8. Students can make choices that regulate the pace and process of learning.

DISADVANTAGES

1. If group members focus too much on the product of the assignment instead of the process, they become too product-oriented and miss the other major point of the model.
2. When more emphasis is placed on process than achievement, students can value "getting along with others" more than "working with others to achieve a stated goal."
3. When all students in a group share misconceptions, there is no way to change those misconceptions, because there is little content interaction with the teacher.
4. There is a danger of one or more students in each group becoming authority figures in place of the teacher.
5. Higher achievers can come to feel pressure to make disproportionately more contributions than other students.
6. There is a risk of some students learning to be "social loafers," either intentionally or unintentionally.
7. Students who try hard but make a lesser contribution to the team's achievement may feel ashamed or become defensive.
8. Some students may limit their own contributions (and learning) to allow other students a greater chance to contribute.

Read over the advantages and disadvantages once again. You will note that the advantages are part of the model's design; the disadvantages occur when the model is not applied correctly, and these can all be avoided or reduced by careful teacher planning and monitoring of the group process. In that sense, Cooperative Learning is no different from any of the other models in this book: when implemented according to its design, there is a strong likelihood that the model will promote the kinds of student learning it is designed for. If applied incorrectly, the model will not work as intended, but that should not be regarded as a design flaw and cause teachers not to use it when called for. Rather, teachers should be aware of those potential problems and plan accordingly to reduce or eliminate them from the model.

ALIGNMENT WITH NASPE NATIONAL STANDARDS

Exhibit 10.1 shows the alignment of the Cooperative Learning model with the NASPE standards. It should be emphasized that the ability of Cooperative Learning to address each of the national standards will be affected by the way a teacher designs specific learning tasks within a unit of instruction. For example, Cooperative Learning can be strongly aligned with

EXHIBIT 10.1 Alignment of Cooperative Learning with NASPE National Standards.

NASPE STANDARD	ALIGNMENT RATING	COMMENTS
1. Demonstrates competency in motor skills and movement patterns needed to perform a variety of physical activities	1–3	Depends on the degree to which these outcomes are intended in the assigned team learning tasks
2. Demonstrates understanding of movement concepts, principles, strategies, and tactics as they apply to the learning and performance of physical activities	1–3	Depends on the degree to which these outcomes are intended in the assigned team learning tasks
3. Participates regularly in physical activity	3	Moderate-to-vigorous physical activity not common, because many cooperative learning tasks involve team discussion
4. Achieves and maintains a health-enhancing level of physical fitness	3	Moderate-to-vigorous physical activity levels not high enough to promote fitness outcomes, because many cooperative learning tasks involve team discussion
5. Exhibits responsible personal and social behavior that respects self and others in physical activity settings	1	One of the best models for learning personal and social behavior in physical education
6. Values physical activity for health, enjoyment, challenge, self-expression, and/or social interaction	1	Strong alignment for all of these outcomes

Ratings categories:

1. Strong alignment
2. Moderate alignment
3. Weak alignment

standards 1 and 2 when the teacher designs team learning tasks that promote skill concepts and performance. This model is weakly aligned with those standards when the teacher designs team learning tasks that involve little or no motor performance or concept learning. However, the Cooperative Learning model is strongly and consistently aligned with standards 5 and 6.

FOUNDATIONS

Theory and Rationale

Deutsch (1949) suggested that there are three main goal structures in education: individualistic, competitive, and cooperative. Models like PSI (Chapter 9) are highly individualistic—students work on their own to achieve learning objectives and have very little interaction with others, including the teacher. Models like Direct Instruction (Chapter 8) are highly competitive because students must assert themselves to gain the teacher's attention and obtain resources needed to learn content, and they are sometimes assessed relative to other students' achievement. Cooperative models are well represented in this book by the one described in this chapter, by the Sport Education model (Chapter 11), and by the Peer Teaching model (Chapter 12). These models intend that students learn with and from each other through a structured interdependent relationship. The achievement of academic learning goals is a high priority but is no more important than social learning processes and skills. Clearly, the Cooperative Learning model has its foundation in Deutsch's third kind of structure.

The Cooperative Learning model's design is based on the convergence of four major sets of theories: motivation, cognition, social learning, and behaviorism. This is a distinguishing feature, because most other models are derived from only one or two theories about learning. However, all four theories play equally key roles in the design and operation of this particular model.

1. *Motivational theory* is used to create structures that get teams to recognize that the only way the team can achieve is for all its members to contribute and achieve. That prompts individual students to give their best and initiates group interactions to meet shared goals.

2. *Cognitive theory* is used to provide students with developmentally appropriate cooperative learning tasks that give teams the right amount of challenge to accomplish team goals. If the task is too easy, the team does not need to use all its resources to achieve the goal. If the task is too difficult, team members will become frustrated, leading to dissent and even withdrawal from the task.

3. *Social learning theories* figure into the model because much of the learning occurs by listening to and watching other team members. The process becomes reciprocal as one student makes progress and then shares that learning with others, most often by showing and explaining to them. Teachers contribute to the social learning agenda of the model when they watch for positive and negative instances of social skills and use them as "teaching moments" to highlight desired and undesired interaction skills.

4. *Behavioral theory* provides a relationship between cooperative processes, student on-task engagement, and the rewards of team achievement. Good cooperative tasks make clear to students the social skills (behaviors) that are needed in that situation, the learning goals, and the consequences for achieving or failing at the assigned task. Note that students are not directly informed about how to complete the task—only the parameters under which that task will be pursued.

The rationale behind the Cooperative Learning model is straightforward, as explained by its principal designer, Robert Slavin (1990):

> [C]ooperative structures create a situation in which the only way group members can attain their own personal goals is if the group is successful. Therefore, to meet their personal goals, group members must help their group mates to do what helps the group to succeed, and perhaps more important, encourage their group mates to exert maximum effort. (pp. 13–14)

The careful selection of groups that stay together for a longer period of time and the structuring of group tasks to promote academic and social learning outcomes are the major differences between Cooperative Learning as a model and the strategy of simply placing students in small groups for a single learning task in class. Keep this distinction in mind as you learn more about this model and as you use it to teach physical education.

Assumptions About Teaching and Learning

The Cooperative Learning model assumes certain principles about teaching and learning; these principles are listed separately below.

Assumptions about teaching

1. The teacher's main role is to serve as facilitator of students' academic and social learning.
2. The teacher can take on the role of facilitator only after he directly establishes the setting, structure, and parameters of group tasks. That is, the model begins with directed instruction and then becomes very indirect after teams are engaged in their assigned task.
3. The teacher is the key person to teach students the reflective processes for social learning and monitor for the application of those processes.
4. The teacher must seek a balance between social and academic learning goals. The process of social learning is just as important as the academic product(s) of learning.

Assumptions about learning

1. Cooperative structures promote higher levels of social and academic learning than individualistic or competitive structures.
2. Groups can, will, and *must* work cooperatively to achieve personal and shared objectives.

3. Team learning works best when groups are heterogeneous in all key factors and when the same groups are maintained over several class periods or an entire unit.

4. All group members have something to contribute to the achievement of the group's goals.

5. Learning tasks must specify criteria for individual accountability, and all members' performance must count in the team's assessment score.

6. "Social loafing" can be, but is not automatically, a part of the group process. Parameters must be stated to ensure that all team members contribute to the group's achievement.

7. Groups of students can organize themselves to pursue and complete an assigned task.

The Major Theme of Cooperative Learning: Students Learning With, By, and For Each Other

"Students learning with, by, and for each other" sums up the main design features of the Cooperative Learning model. It acknowledges that students will need to interact *with* each other in positive ways that lead to the achievement of academic and social outcomes in the model. It also recognizes that much of the teaching in the model will be done *by* students, in a peer-based process. Finally, the theme emphasizes that students must pull together *for* the team to succeed in accomplishing its academic and social learning goals.

Learning Domain Priorities and Domain Interactions

Domain priorities

Cooperative Learning is designed to promote increased levels of student achievement mediated by small-group interactions and social skills. The former cannot happen if the latter does not occur, making the acquisition of pro-group social skills a prerequisite to individual and group learning. That makes the *domain priorities* of Cooperative Learning a bit complex, considering that the affective domain will always share the highest priority with the major objective of the assigned learning task. For instance, if the assigned task has a primarily cognitive learning focus, the domain priority would be:

> *First priority (shared):*   Affective and cognitive learning
>
> *Third priority:*   Psychomotor learning

If the assigned task has a primarily psychomotor learning focus, then the domain priority would be:

> *First priority (shared):*   Affective and psychomotor learning
>
> *Third priority:*   Cognitive learning

To complicate matters even more, a good Cooperative Learning task in physical education will challenge students equally in all three domains, requiring good group interaction and reflection (affective), an appropriate degree of intellectual rigor (cognitive), and the eventual demonstration of skilled movement (psychomotor). When this happens, all three domains receive approximately the same level of emphasis and development. If students or groups cannot learn in all three domains equally well, they will not be successful at the assigned task.

Domain interactions

The domain interactions for Cooperative Learning tasks become equally complex when all three domains are shared. The interaction is not linear, with learning in one domain following from the other domains. Rather, all three domains take on a reciprocal relationship: learning in any one domain is dependent on learning in the other two. For instance, in order to achieve in the psychomotor domain, students in each small group must have good interpersonal skills (affective) and good problem-solving abilities (cognitive). This reciprocity must occur at all times within all domains, as Exhibit 10.2 illustrates.

This reciprocal relationship is the basis of the entire model and underscores the need for students to cooperate *not just to get along,* but to learn. It also emphasizes an important design feature in the model: the process of learning is just as important as the products of learning.

Student Developmental Requirements

Student readiness for learning. As the domain interactions indicate, the Cooperative Learning model will engage students in all three domains simultaneously much of the time. Student readiness in this model is then tied to their *potential* to contribute to the team's success by applying themselves to the best of their ability. If a student is not willing to apply herself in that way, then she is not ready to learn via Cooperative Learning. Because the process of selecting heterogeneous teams ensures that students will come to the team with different abilities, the model's most essential prerequisite is simply that each team member is actually ready to learn cooperatively. If too many students cannot or will not accept the shared responsibility for learning, then Cooperative Learning should not be selected for the upcoming unit in physical education.

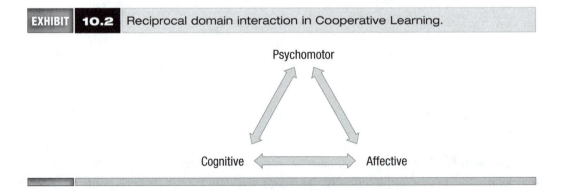

EXHIBIT 10.2   Reciprocal domain interaction in Cooperative Learning.

Psychomotor

Cognitive ⟷ Affective

Student receptivity to the model. Using the Reichmann and Grasha (1974) profile for student learning preferences, Cooperative Learning will most often work best for those students who are classified as participant, collaborative, competitive, and independent. The model requires that all students participate to the extent of their abilities as members of a learning team. Students who cannot participate effectively will not be receptive to this model. Collaboration is the key process needed for each team to succeed, so students who do not like to share work with others will be less open to Cooperative Learning. Competitive students will be receptive to this model and accept the challenge of completing sometimes difficult learning tasks and occasionally competing against other teams in class. The independent student will welcome Cooperative Learning because the model relies little on teacher direction. In this model, independence characterizes the team's relationship with the teacher.

Validation of the Model

Research validation

If you will recall, the Cooperative Learning model actually comprises a set of learning strategies that share some common attributes with, and a set of procedures that distinguish it from, simpler group-based learning activities. The Cooperative Learning strategies recognized as part of the model also share one other feature: they all started as experimental learning designs and were developed from systematic research in schools and school-simulation settings. With most other models presented in this book, the model was first designed and then researched. For Cooperative Learning, the strategies were shaped and developed from research findings until those findings began to validate each of the strategies over time. This is a very powerful way to validate an instructional model, because the research actually leads the development of the model, rather than being used to see how the model works after it has been designed "on paper."

Cooperative Learning has been the focus of an enormous number of research studies in the past two decades. In his review of more than 100 studies, Slavin (1995) summarized the major research findings about Cooperative Learning:

1. In 64 percent of the studies, the Cooperative Learning groups had significantly better achievement gains than counterparts who had some other form of instruction.

2. Students in Cooperative Learning groups improved cross-racial relationships significantly more often than students in control groups with traditional methods.

3. Students in Cooperative Learning groups improved cross-ability relationships significantly more often than students in control groups with traditional methods.

4. Cooperative Learning can be successful with students at every grade level and in all subject areas.

There is a wealth of research on Cooperative Learning in many subjects, including a growing amount of studies in physical education settings (see Dyson, Linehan & Hastie, 2010). The early results are generally supportive of Cooperative Learning's ability to promote fitness improvement and positive social interactions in young children and to reduce negative social interactions. An interesting study (Yoder, 1993) found that Cooperative Learning in a dance unit improved both social learning and achievement.

In a review of research on Cooperative Learning in physical education, Dyson (2005) cites a number of benefits for students in this model, despite the relatively little research available as yet:

1. Improved social reasoning
2. Increased interpersonal skills
3. Higher rates of active participation
4. Improved motor skills and game strategies
5. Increased tendency to help others improve their skills
6. Increased self-responsibility for learning
7. Increased willingness to hold each student accountable (in teams)

The effectiveness of the Cooperative Learning model has been validated in hundreds of studies in almost every school subject area. The fact that only a few studies have been completed in physical education probably reflects the newness of formal Cooperative Learning in our subject, and it should not call into question the model's potential in our field. In fact, the strong similarities between Cooperative Learning and the Sport Education model, which has its own early impressive research record, predict additional supportive findings on Cooperative Learning in physical education.

Craft knowledge validation

The record of craft knowledge validation for Cooperative Learning resembles that of its research validation. That is, the model has an extensive and impressive record of use in many school subject areas in every grade level from elementary to college. Thousands of teachers have used the model and refined its instructional strategies for many situationally specific applications (Slavin, 1995). This history validates not only the model's effectiveness but also its adaptability for many settings and subject areas. A study by Stevens and Slavin (1995) focused on five entire elementary schools that used Cooperative Learning in several subject areas for two years, with positive results for many types of students. The key point here is that the teachers at each of those schools voted unanimously to be trained in Cooperative Learning and to implement the model for two full school years. That is strong evidence that those teachers were familiar enough with Cooperative Learning before the study began to commit to its use for an extended period of time.

Craft knowledge validation for Cooperative Learning in physical education has started to grow. Grineski (1996) stated that very few physical education teachers use the formal Cooperative Learning model; they instead use some form of small group-based learning activity that they might misconstrue as Cooperative Learning. However, since the publication of Grineski's book, the use of faithful versions of Cooperative Learning has increased rapidly in physical education (Dyson, Linehan & Hastie, 2010; Hannon & Ratliffe, 2004). More teachers have become familiar with the kinds of learning tasks used in this model, in part attributable to the online sharing of lesson and unit plans on sites such as PECentral (www.pecentral.org/) and PELINKS4U (www.pelinks4u.org/).

Intuitive validation

Considering the team-sport background of so many physical education teachers, this model makes sense for physical education. Nearly all of us have experienced and recognized the role of team effort in the achievement of shared and individual goals in sport settings. We have all rooted on teammates, let our own success hinge on the success of others, and pulled together for the common good of the team. We also know that the team is only as strong as its weakest player—so we all try to help every other member perform to his fullest potential. If those reasons explain why sport-team members need to work together in assigned group tasks in physical education, it is easy to come up with a strong rationale for the Cooperative Learning model. It makes sense that any group of students will achieve more when they work together than when they work individually and that their social development is greatly enhanced by that process—giving strong intuitive validation for the use of Cooperative Learning in physical education.

TEACHING AND LEARNING FEATURES

Control

The control profile for Cooperative Learning is based on three different patterns that occur during lessons. The teacher controls decisions about the assigned task, team selection, and determining the parameters for completing the task (e.g., available time and other resources), and the criteria for performance and social skill behaviors. After that, students control how they will go about completing the task. It then becomes highly interactive as the teacher processes the learning of social skills with students during class and at the end of class. These three major structures in a cooperative lesson determine the control profile for Cooperative Learning. Exhibit 10.3 indicates how each component of the profile can change according to the different structures. More complete explanations of the profile's components follow.

1. Content selection. This component of the Cooperative Learning model is very much under teacher control. The teacher determines the series of tasks that teams will pursue in the unit and communicates them to students. A formal content listing is difficult to determine ahead of time because the teacher cannot often predict the needed social learning skills in advance. Those needs

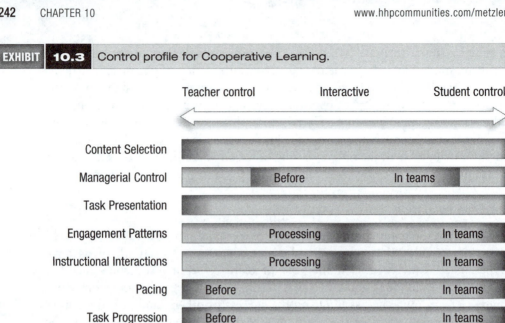

EXHIBIT 10.3 Control profile for Cooperative Learning.

will become apparent as teams work on the assigned tasks. The academic content is also difficult to list ahead of time because each task will probably be large enough to contain many outcomes within it. Given that, the content listing is usually represented by the series of learning tasks the teacher will assign to groups as the unit progresses. That process is almost always teacher-controlled.

2. Managerial control. Teachers maintain strong managerial control before the teams start to engage their learning tasks. The teacher selects the teams, decides what resources will be available, determines the amount of time to be allocated for each task, and decides the parameters within which teams must remain. Once the teams begin to pursue the task, this control shifts quickly to the students within each cooperative group. They make decisions about how to organize themselves, how to divide the work to be done, and how to use their available time and resources.

3. Task presentations. There are no task presentations by the teacher in Cooperative Learning. However, the teacher "frames a problem" by explaining the assigned task and the ground rules teams must follow in their pursuit of it. After that, it is up to students, in their groups, to explain to each other what needs to be done and how to do it. It is expected that students will use peer teaching as their main mode of instructing.

4. Engagement patterns. There are two primary engagement patterns in this model. One of the patterns is strongly student-controlled, occurring among students in each of the cooperative teams. They decide who takes the lead at any given time, and they establish their own engagement plans for completing the task. The other pattern is interactive: the teacher uses questions to develop students' social skills when problems occur and in the post-lesson review. To be most effective, this processing should allow students time to reflect on their current behavior patterns and to come up with their own solutions when they are not working cooperatively in groups.

5. Instructional interactions. As with the two distinct engagement patterns, there will be two types of instructional interactions with Cooperative Learning. The interactions will be the same two types as the engagement patterns: almost totally student-controlled as teams work on the assigned tasks; interactive when the teacher is attempting to develop students' social skills. While students work in their teams, the teacher takes on the roles of facilitator and primary resource person. The teacher facilitates the cooperative processes, getting teams to work to their fullest capacity; the teacher also serves as the "resident expert" when teams need advice or want someone to listen to their ideas. The most effective Cooperative Learning teachers are those who can facilitate the learning process without providing teams with too much information or assistance.

6. Pacing. The pacing of class is controlled by the teacher as teams are selected and the learning problem is framed. After the teacher has introduced the learning task and informed teams about how long they will have to complete the task, the pacing of instruction becomes strongly student-controlled. In their teams, the students decide how much work needs to be done and how long they plan to spend on each part of the task. The teacher intervenes only when a team's plan will obviously not allow that team to finish on time.

7. Task progression. The teacher decides when a new task will be assigned and how long students will have to work on it. As with pacing, once the teams are working together, each team determines the steps needed to complete the task and when to consider each part of the task finished. Having a work plan and evaluating it regularly is a key part of student participation in the Cooperative Learning process.

Inclusiveness

The Cooperative Learning model is designed to include every student in the team process. This inclusion is achieved in three ways. First, the team selection process ensures that all teams are heterogeneous, comprised of students with diverse abilities, motivation, and personalities. That diversity promotes interaction among all types of students. Second, all members are accountable for making a contribution to the team's success, so there is strong motivation for students to support, encourage, and teach each other to meet the team's goal. This promotes fuller participation by all team members. Third, the team's success is more likely when it recognizes and uses the full range of talent among its members, promoting an appreciation for any contribution that helps the team achieve its goal. Therefore, it is in the team's best interest to find ways to include, not exclude or isolate, students with unique abilities and talents.

Slavin (1995) cites several studies that support the potential for Cooperative Learning to promote greater awareness, appreciation, and inclusion for diverse student groups: "Cooperative Learning increases contact between students, gives them a shared basis of similarity (group membership), engages them in pleasant activities together, and has them work toward common goals" (p. 66). This statement highlights one of the strengths of the Cooperative Learning model—it is specifically designed to be inclusive and to make every student's contribution count. The teacher's group-processing procedures can teach students how to include all team members, taking inclusion one large step beyond just "learning next to one another" to "learning with, by, and for each other."

Learning Tasks

As previously explained, the Cooperative Learning model constitutes a group of related teaching strategies that share a common purpose, procedures, and student engagement patterns. This section will describe the major learning strategies and explain how each one can be structured for physical education instruction.

Framing the task (Task presentation)

Cooperative Learning involves no task presentation in which the teacher shows students how to set up and perform learning tasks. Instead, it is up to each team of students to organize themselves for the assigned task and to determine their own solutions to the learning challenges present in the task. In that way, this model is very different from nearly all other models in this book. The teacher does take time to *frame* the learning task in a manner that allows students to understand what the task is without informing them how to complete the task (that is, without teaching them). When framing the task, the teacher should do a number of things:

1. Announce membership for all teams and explain how teams were selected
2. Announce how long teams will have to complete the task
3. Announce which Cooperative Learning strategy will be used for the task (e.g., "We are going to be using the 'Jigsaw' approach for the next five classes. Each group will learn one tennis skill and then teach it to the rest of the class when it's their turn.")
4. Inform teams of any ground rules to be in effect
5. Let teams know what resources will be available to them and how shared resources will be divided among teams
6. Explain the learning objectives and how they will be assessed
7. Explain objectives for social learning and how they will be assessed
8. Explain the teacher's role as facilitator
9. Inform teams of any products that should be generated in the task (e.g., posters, portfolios, team records)
10. Explain the rules for team competitions when used with some strategies

After the teacher has framed the task, she should provide students with an opportunity to ask her to clarify the directions and parameters for completing the task. When students have no more questions, the teacher simply says, "OK, go to it," and the Cooperative Learning process is set in motion.

Task structure

There are many recognized organizing strategies that can be considered part of the formal Cooperative Learning model. Five of these strategies can be adopted for the kinds of content and outcomes typically taught in physical education. Each strategy has its own unique task structure that teachers should explain to students as part of the task presentation.

1. Student Teams–Achievement Divisions (STAD). First developed by Robert Slavin (1980), this strategy requires students in a class to be placed in noncompeting teams. All teams are given the same assigned learning task and needed resources for it. The teacher allocates a set time period for teams to learn and practice initially, typically 15 to 20 minutes. The teacher is available during this time to clarify the task or to serve as another resource for teams. At the end of the time period, all members of each team complete an assessment task on the knowledge or skill just learned. That assessment could take the form of a short quiz, a skills test, or any type of performance test that covers the content just practiced. The scores for all team members are added together to get a team score. Team scores are announced, and the teacher interacts with the class to discuss the cooperative process and make suggestions for improved group interactions. Teams are then directed to return to practicing the same task again, with an added emphasis on cooperation, peer teaching, and improving the scores of every team member. A second time period is allocated, after which all team members complete the assessment task again. Two goals are stated for the second practice period: all individual members and the team as a whole should beat their first score. Obviously, succeeding at the first goal as individuals automatically achieves the second goal for the team. The teacher assigns team grades based on the amount of improvement in the total team score from the first to second assessment. Only a "team grade" is given, so that students who improve between assessments will be motivated to help (teach) other students do the same. (See the Cooperative Learning unit plan on the IMPE website.)

Orlick (1982) uses two variations of STAD in physical education, called Collective Score. Scores can be totaled for entire classes or for entire schools. Both variations expand the scope of Cooperative Learning so that more students are working for and supporting each other.

2. Team Games Tournament (TGT). The initial structure of TGT resembles that of STAD. Students are placed in teams, presented with the assigned learning task, and given a set period for the initial practice or knowledge acquisition. All members of every team complete an assessment at the end of the practice period. At this point, TGT departs from STAD. In TGT, scores of individuals on each team are compared with the corresponding ranked scores from all other teams—first against first, second against second, and so on. Each winning score earns the team a predetermined number of points, which allows all students to contribute to their team's success, regardless of ranking. A second round of practice takes place, which usually results in increased interaction and support on each team. The assessment is given again, and ranked scores are compared again with points awarded in the same way. The team with the most points at the end of the game wins the TGT. (See the unit plan for Cooperative Learning on the IMPE website for a scoring example.) It is possible to keep teams intact for many assigned tasks and to make the tasks progressively more difficult over time. It is not necessary to keep students on the same task for more than two practice and assessment periods.

3. Team-Assisted Instruction (TAI). This strategy combines the Cooperative Learning and PSI (Chapter 9) approaches. After teams are selected, a list of learning tasks with performance criteria is given to all students. The list contains a progression for one or more skills and knowledge areas, going from easy to more difficult. Team members may practice the tasks individually or with assistance from other members. When a student has completed a task to its criterion performance level, another team member checks that off, and the first student moves to the next task. Team performance can be assessed in one of two ways: (1) the teacher can give points for the number of tasks each team completes each class or week or (2) a final assessment task can be given to all team members independently, with the totaled scores used to award points and derive the team grade.

4. Jigsaw. Students are placed in teams and assigned to learn one part of a skill, knowledge area, or game. For instance, in a tennis unit, one team can be assigned to learn the components and cues for the forehand drive, another team can be assigned to learn the backhand drive, another team can be assigned to learn game rules and scoring, and so on. All teams are given a set period of time to learn their component and then take the role of teacher when the whole class moves to that segment of the unit. Teachers base their assessment on the quality of a team's instruction to the class, which is determined by how well the whole class learns that part of the jigsaw.

In a variation of the Jigsaw strategy, members of each team can be assigned to learn different components, so that each member becomes an "expert" on a particular topic or skill. "Expert groups" are formed by having students from different teams who learned the same topic/skill meet to share what they have learned individually. After the meeting, each "expert" goes back to his original group to teach his own teammates what he has learned. (See the Cooperative Learning unit plan on the IMPE website.) The Jigsaw strategy and its variations share one key feature: at some point in time students will instruct other students through peer teaching.

5. Group Investigation. This strategy asks teams to cooperate to produce and share the results of their learning. Teams are selected, and the task is assigned. The time period for Group Investigation is typically longer, perhaps as long as three weeks, with the expectation that students will work on the task in class and outside of class. The teacher presents the task as a group project, part of which requires each team to share what they learned via some form of media: posters, collages, a video, computer-generated graphics, a website page, or a written report. The media production serves two purposes: it represents the self-contained evidence of each team's learning, and it is shared with other teams to help them learn. Assessment is completed from a scoring rubric presented to students before the Group Investigation begins, and it results in a single grade for each team.

Content progression

Because most learning tasks in Cooperative Learning are larger and longer than those used in other models, content progression is different in this model. The Cooperative Learning unit consists of a series of learning problems, or tasks, which progress from simple to more difficult as the unit goes along. The time given to each task reflects this progression, with shorter tasks in the beginning and longer tasks toward the middle and end. This structure allows students to practice their interaction and teamwork skills early with tasks they are likely to have much success on. As the teams get used to working together, they are able to take on longer and more difficult tasks.

Engagement Patterns for Learning

Except when the teacher is introducing a learning task or processing for social skill development, the Cooperative Learning model uses only one engagement pattern: groups of four to six students working in teams for an extended period of time. All the strategies used in Cooperative Learning are initially based on that configuration; at times two or more groups will merge—but only temporarily.

Selecting team members. Placing students into teams is one of the most important functions for the teacher in the Cooperative Learning model. Notice that I labeled it as a teacher function, not to be delegated to students. That is because the team-selection process must serve several key purposes in the model in order to promote the most effective academic and social learning possible. The primary considerations are to promote diversity within teams and fairness between competing teams (when teams compete with each other). Having diversity within a team not only fosters the awareness of others' talents, personalities, and perspectives but also provides students with a wider range of resources with which to work on the assigned task. The major criteria for achieving diversity should include previous experience in the content area, gender, skill ability, cognitive ability, learning style, race, ethnicity, tendency to lead or to follow, and student behavior. Each teacher might have other criteria that influence decisions.

The process of assigning students to teams should be done privately by the teacher and then announced in class or posted. Because some students might misunderstand the larger purposes being served by the selection process, it is not a good idea to make team selection a public event or to liken it in any way to picking sides for a game. We are all aware of the potential harm that can occur with that type of selection process. Once the teams are formed, the teacher should inform students of the human resources and talent on their team and not allow students to focus on perceived shortcomings of team members or to over-analyze the composition of other teams. Therefore, it is helpful for the teacher to begin the cooperative process right away by explaining how and why teams were selected and by getting teams working together as soon as possible.

Teacher and Student Roles and Responsibilities

Each instructional model will have certain operations that need to be completed to allow the model to function according to its design. Some of the operations are carried out by the teacher; others are carried out by one or more students. Exhibit 10.4 shows the major operations within the Cooperative Learning model and indicates who is responsible for completing them during each lesson.

EXHIBIT 10.4 Teacher and student roles and responsibilities in Cooperative Learning.

OPERATION OR RESPONSIBILITY	PERSON/PEOPLE RESPONSIBLE IN COOPERATIVE LEARNING
Content listing	The **teacher** decides what is to be learned, in the form of assigned tasks given to student teams.
Team selection	The **teacher** selects teams to ensure the maximum amount of diversity and heterogeneity on all teams.
Task "framing" and problem setting	The **teacher** explains the assigned task to all teams, based on the formulation of a problem that student teams will need to pursue or solve.
Bringing equipment to class	The **teacher** brings to class what each team states it needs for the assigned task.
Task structure	The **teacher** decides the task structure, in the form of a defined Cooperative Learning strategy that provides the ground rules for student engagement.
Engagement patterns	**Students** on each team decide how they will organize themselves to complete the assigned task.
Problem mediation	Initially, problems are mediated within teams by **students.** If that is not successful, the **teacher** mediates through a reflective process.
Assessment of performance	The **teacher** designs all performance assessments, typically in the form of a scoring rubric. **Students** on each team decide how their team will work to achieve the best possible score on each assessment.
Social skill assessment	The **teacher** decides the criteria for group interactions and monitors students as they work in their teams.
Instructional processes	**Students** on each team decide and implement their own peer-teaching plan as they pursue the assigned learning task.

Verification of Instructional Processes

Teachers who use Cooperative Learning should learn the benchmarks for their own and student behavior patterns (see Exhibits 10.5 and 10.6). These benchmarks verify that the unit has been planned and implemented as closely as possible to the model's design, increasing the likelihood that the stated student learning outcomes will be achieved.

Cooperative Learning teacher benchmarks.	🖨 EXHIBIT 10.5
BENCHMARK	**HOW TO VERIFY**
Teacher selects heterogeneous and equitable teams.	1. The teacher lists the criteria used for making selections. 2. The teacher shows a plan for how each student was assigned. 3. The teacher asks students for their feedback on selections.
Teacher selects an appropriate assigned learning task.	1. The task has stated time limits and procedures. 2. The task can be completed by all teams in the allocated time. 3. The task requires a contribution by all team members. 4. The task challenges teams in all three domains.
Teacher selects an appropriate Cooperative Learning strategy.	1. The task is one of the recognized Cooperative Learning strategies, and not simply "grouped learning." 2. The task challenges students to learn in all three domains.
Teacher frames the assigned learning tasks.	1. The teacher provides sufficient information about the task without giving clues for completing the task. 2. Teams become engaged right away, indicating that they understand the task and its structure.
Teacher serves as a facilitator during tasks.	1. The teacher monitors the number and types of interactions he or she initiates. 2. The teacher should use indirect statements and questions—and only when interaction is initiated by students.
Teacher monitors and processes for social learning outcomes.	1. The teacher includes a planned segment to process for social learning outcomes. 2. The teacher uses few, if any, direct statements in this segment.
Teacher designs assessments for performance and social learning.	1. Check the teacher's plan for these components. 2. Assessments should be designed for team achievement, with each team member having individual accountability. 3. Assessment should include specific social learning goals.

EXHIBIT 10.6 Cooperative Learning student benchmarks.	
BENCHMARK	**HOW TO VERIFY**
Students view teams as being fair.	Students are asked for their comments on the selection process and indicate no objections.
Students understand the assigned task.	1. Teams begin right away to work on the task. 2. Teams ask few clarification questions of the teacher.
Students understand the cooperative strategy in place.	1. Teams begin right away to allocate time and other resources for the task. 2. Teams quickly formulate a "plan of attack." 3. Teams follow the procedures given for completing the task.
Teams share the work and the accountability of all members.	1. Teams assign individual members to specific "jobs." 2. Teams chart the contributions of each member. 3. Teams complete peer evaluations of other members.
Teams use peer teaching to improve performance and publicly support each member's efforts.	Monitor the type and frequency of interactions within teams.
Teams show improvement on performance assessments.	Compare assessment scores over time.
Teams show evidence of social learning.	Teacher or peers use critical incident reports or checklists to identify instances of positive and negative social behaviors.

Assessment of Learning

Because the learning domain priorities in the Cooperative Learning model are typically shared among all three major domains, the teacher should assess student learning in ways that give equal attention to all those kinds of outcomes. The authenticity of assessments in the Cooperative Learning model will reflect the nature of the assigned learning task given to students. If the task is designed to develop rather standard kinds of psychomotor skills and content knowledge, then the assessment can be mostly traditional (e.g., a skills test or a written test). If the assigned task strives for more complex and applied outcomes, then the assessment should be more authentic and alternative. Either way, the assessment is likely to be "homemade" by the teacher because the assigned learning task will be that way as well—designed by the teacher to match the specific student abilities, content, and context of the unit.

Assessing learning in the psychomotor domain

The Cooperative Learning teacher has several options for assessing outcomes in the psychomotor domain:

1. Short skills tests that require students to complete a certain number of trials to a stated criterion (e.g., the number of successful shots to a target, the number of made foul shots, the number of completed passes)

2. Timed completion of an event or task (e.g., elapsed time for the 200-meter run, time taken to complete an obstacle course, time needed to achieve a certain number of successful trials)

3. Accuracy tests (e.g., score on an end of arrows, percent of made shots, distance from a target)

4. Consistency (e.g., number of made shots in a row)

5. Standardized skills tests (e.g., tennis serving test, racquetball wall volley test, basketball shooting test)

Recall that strategies like STAD and TGT require teams to practice for a set amount of time and then complete an assessment of that learning. Those assessments should be directly related to the task just practiced, and they are to be completed very quickly. Most often the teacher can simply ask each member of all teams to make a certain number of attempts (shots, kicks, throws) and to record the number of successful attempts. Each team score is the sum of all members' scores. These little tests can be used to monitor each student's progress (remember that the model calls for individual student accountability) and to assess the effectiveness of teams' peer teaching.

Assessing learning in the cognitive domain

Assessment in the cognitive domain is similar to that in the psychomotor domain when the assigned task focuses on a relatively simple outcome such as recall knowledge. The teacher can use homemade quizzes to assess students' knowledge on such things as game rules, procedures, and strategy. Such assessments are most likely to be used in STAD and TGT. Again, the quiz should focus on the content just studied, and students should be able to complete it in a few minutes. Quizzes can consist of several kinds of questions and items:

1. Multiple-choice

2. Fill-in-the-blanks

3. "What if . . ." questions

4. Definitions and terminology

Teachers will need to use more sophisticated assessment techniques when the cooperative strategy is more complex and strives for higher-order learning outcomes. Such strategies include Jigsaw and Group Investigation, in which student learning is multidimensional, representing several types of knowledge. Because these strategies are more likely to lead to authentic learning experiences, they should then be assessed with alternative and more authentic techniques. This typically leads the teacher to develop a scoring rubric that he gives to the teams at the same time he assigns the learning task. The scoring rubric should include:

1. Parameters for what the learning should produce (a portfolio, video, collage, or lesson to be taught to other students)

2. A delineation of each level of quality for the completed work, and a clear description of the features that make up each level (for example, a Group Investigation on the history of the Olympic Games will be assessed at four levels: Olympian [lowest], Bronze Medalist, Silver Medalist, and Gold Medalist [highest]. The teacher then describes the characteristics of each category so that teams can know what it will take to reach each level of quality in the product they generate.) (See the Cooperative Learning unit plan on the IMPE website.)

3. A scoring sheet and written report that the teacher completes for each team's work and gives to them for their review

Assessing learning in the affective domain

The Cooperative Learning model also calls for assessing student learning in the affective domain, represented by intra-team interactions such as peer teaching, verbal support for teammates' efforts, cooperation, leadership/"followership," and problem solving. Assessing those kinds of processes can be a bit tricky, but it is possible for the teacher to use several strategies to get a handle on the development of students' social skills:

1. Regularly monitor each team as it works together, making notes on positive and negative instances of social interactions. This is called *critical incident reporting*. For example, a peer observer (not on the team) could write down every time she hears a team member support a player on that team or another team. She could also write down every time she hears a player scold, taunt, or reprimand a player on that team or another team. At the end of class, the teacher can use these statements to ask the whole class, "What would you have done in that situation?"

2. Use a checklist of positive and negative social interaction items to monitor the frequency and patterns of those interactions. Similar to the first example, a simple checklist can be made to tally "good sport" and "bad sport" behaviors seen or heard from each team in class. Points can then be added or subtracted to game scores based on those tallies.

3. Instruct each team to compile a log of its work, listing who did which part(s). The log for a task to make a multimedia report on the Negro Baseball Leagues might include:

Whole team	Met to make a work plan
José	Did the initial online search
Diane	Contacted local baseball historians
Paul	Interviewed two former Negro League players
LaTanya	Scanned pictures for the collage
Janice	Collated Randy's, Diane's, and Paul's notes

Whole team	Met to discuss content and format for the presentation
Paul, LaTanya	Wrote first draft of presentation
Whole team	Reviewed draft and recommended changes
José	Put the multimedia presentation together
LaTanya, Diane	Made the multimedia presentation to the class

4. Instruct each team to complete a daily journal of its group work, noting positive and negative instances of group process. This would be similar to the process in number 1, except the instances would be recorded by each team member.

5. Use the end-of-class processing time to allow students to make comments on the group process.

Teachers who use the Cooperative Learning model will need to keep in mind that, because the process of team learning is just as important as the academic outcomes of team learning, social learning skills must always be monitored in some way, either formally or informally.

IMPLEMENTATION NEEDS AND MODIFICATIONS

Teacher Expertise

Cooperative Learning teachers need to possess several particular areas of expertise to use the model to its fullest capacity.

Learners. One of this model's key functions is the selection of heterogeneous teams that are mixed in several ways: by skill level, previous experience, gender, race/ethnicity, communication skills, leadership abilities, and willingness to contribute to the team's efforts. As a result, the teacher will have to know each student in all these ways and be able to select teams that reflect diversity in talent and team dynamics. It is not possible to balance all teams in every way, but the goal is to provide all teams with an equitable chance of succeeding at the assigned task.

Learning theories. The Cooperative Learning model combines four major learning theories: cognitive (during team problem solving), behavioral (in meeting performance criteria), motivational (in mutual support among teammates), and social (learning by observing and interacting with team members). The teacher will need to recognize which theory is most prominently at work within each part of the model and to facilitate that kind of learning at the appropriate time.

Task analysis and content progression. The task analysis in Cooperative Learning must represent a learning progression in all three domains. Therefore, the teacher must be able to plan progressions for not only motor skill performance and cognitive learning but also the social/affective domain. The teacher will need to consider the progression from simple to complex learning in the affective domain just as she does for the other two domains. For example, the teacher should plan simple beginning tasks for each team—allowing teams to become acquainted, to succeed, and to practice working together. STAD tasks are good starters in a unit. After the teams are working well, longer and more challenging tasks, like Jigsaws and Group Investigations, can be assigned.

Developmentally appropriate instruction. It is possible that teams of students can be ready for the academic challenges of an assigned task in the psychomotor and cognitive domains but not be ready for the types of social and cooperative interactions necessary to make the team work successfully. As the teacher determines the task analysis and progression through assigned tasks, he must ask himself, "Are the students ready for the types of cooperative interactions needed to work well together on these tasks?" To design developmentally appropriate Cooperative Learning, the teacher must be quite certain that students can make good choices and assume the kinds of responsibilities needed to be contributing team members. Another key question to ask is, "What might happen if teams experience frustration, conflict, and failure?" Those experiences can and will happen in challenging Cooperative Learning tasks, so the teacher must be ready to turn them into positive "teaching moments."

Assessment. All assigned Cooperative Learning tasks are assessed for performance and cooperative team processes. Performance assessments occur regularly during and after assigned tasks. Teachers must know how to design interim assessments during tasks that directly target the key performance outcomes and that can be completed and scored quickly to determine team points and new objectives. Performance assessments must also be designed for the end of assigned tasks, to determine team points and grades. Even though cognitive and psychomotor performance are assessed, the cooperative model relies on alternative, authentic assessment techniques.

Teachers must also know how to design assessments for social skills observed within and between teams during cooperative tasks. The teacher should explain her expectations to students for team interactions and monitor (assess) those interactions during assigned tasks. This can be done by using checklists and critical incident reports, described earlier, that represent the types of social learning outcomes the teacher seeks.

Establishing and maintaining a positive social climate on teams. The effectiveness of the Cooperative Learning model depends largely on the regularity and quality of student interactions on teams as they pursue assigned tasks. This requires teacher expertise in three related areas: establishing a positive environment, detecting ineffective patterns that lead to a negative environment, and teaching students how to change a negative climate into one that is positive. The tricky part is that the teacher should not dictate to students how they should act toward each other and thus influence students to behave well just to avoid being punished by the teacher. The teacher should establish some ground rules and select teams in a way that will set the cooperative process in motion—then allow students to discover how they can best work in their teams to meet their goals. The teacher monitors as teams work on tasks, noting interactions that lead toward a positive or negative climate in class. Positive interactions are noted and reinforced through public recognition at the end of class (e.g., "Today's Honor Roll," applause from the class, points for rewards). Negative interactions are *processed* at the end of class through a reflective analysis led by the teacher. The purpose of processing is to locate the source of the problems ("What happens when teammates criticize each other?") and to get students to reach solutions on their own in their respective teams ("If a teammate says something negative to you, what should you do?").

Physical education content. The indirect, facilitative type of instruction used for Cooperative Learning tasks calls for a knowledge of physical education content that differs from the knowledge required in more direct kinds of instruction. In direct instruction, the teacher demonstrates content expertise by modeling proper techniques (during task presentations) and analyzing students' practice attempts. In the Cooperative Learning model, the teacher demonstrates expertise by framing appropriate, challenging, and creative assigned learning tasks and by recognizing diverse ways in which teams can reach solutions to the problems embedded in those tasks. "Knowing your stuff" takes on a unique meaning in Cooperative Learning and other models that use facilitative approaches to student learning.

Equity in the gym. One of the founding principles of Cooperative Learning is to promote equal opportunities for success by all students (Slavin, 1995). The model assumes that all members of a team can contribute to the team's success if each one is allowed to let his or her unique talents be used in the team effort. The teacher's expertise is needed to select teams and design tasks in which individual students are held accountable in group work and on assessments, both for performance achievement and social learning outcomes. There is no expectation that all team members will contribute equal amounts of skill and knowledge, but there is every expectation that all team members will contribute their full effort to the team's success.

Key Teaching Skills

A teacher will need to develop a unique repertoire of effective teaching skills for use in the Cooperative Learning model.

Planning. Much of the planning in Cooperative Learning happens at the unit level, in determining the tasks given to teams and classes. The teacher will have to make several decisions ahead of time for each task:

1. What are the "problems" posed within each task? What cognitive, psychomotor, and social learning challenges will the task include?
2. Which Cooperative Learning strategy will work best for this task?
3. How will teams be selected? What factors will determine the size and heterogeneous mix of each team?
4. How long will teams have to complete the task?

5. What resources will be made available to teams for the task?

6. What performance outcomes or products will be produced by each team?

7. How will each team's performance and social learning be assessed?

8. What role will the teacher play as teams work on the task?

After all of those questions are answered, the teacher can select teams and present the learning task to them. At that time, planning becomes an interactive process as the teacher looks for things that need to be adjusted as teams work on the assigned task. When an assigned task will last for more than one class period, the teacher can plan a short briefing each day to give students feedback on their teamwork and to assess progress to that point.

Time and classroom management. The teacher's major time-management decision concerns how long to allocate for each assigned task. Some tasks will be brief, perhaps 10 to 15 minutes. Other tasks, such as those using Group Investigation, can last for several lessons, including time outside of the physical education period (library research, online research, writing reports).

Classroom management in Cooperative Learning is largely the responsibility of students once they are in teams and working on tasks. Each team can decide how to assign the needed work on the task, how to pace itself, and how to apportion the allocated time. The teacher does play a key, if indirect, role by monitoring student interactions within teams and by using the reflective process to help teams be more efficient and effective. The Cooperative Learning teacher will need to be skilled in recognizing poor team interactions and in knowing how to help teams become more productive without making direct interventions or taking punitive action.

Task framing and task structure. There is no task presentation, such as is used in many other models, whereby the teacher shows students how to perform the skill correctly. Instead, the teacher selects teams, frames the assigned task, and directs teams to start. The needed skill here involves giving teams enough information to start working on the task, without giving them clues on how to complete it.

Task structure in Cooperative Learning depends on which strategy is selected for each assigned task. All the strategies presented earlier in this chapter promote certain types of interactions and performance outcomes. The Cooperative Learning teacher should know the design and procedures for each strategy and then select the best strategy for each situation.

Communication. The Cooperative Learning teacher will need to give clear and specific information to teams when framing a task and explaining the strategy to be used for it. It will be helpful to check for understanding often during the explanation as well as in the first few minutes of team engagement.

Instructional information. The Cooperative Learning teacher must be skilled in providing two types of instructional information: explanations as tasks are framed, and questioning during reflective processing. As just mentioned, it is important that students (in teams) get a clear and detailed explanation of the assigned task and the cooperative strategy to be used for it. The better they understand the task, the more likely they are to become appropriately engaged right away.

Use of questions. The teacher's use of questions during times of reflection on the cooperative process is an essential skill. When the teacher observes that one or more teams are not working well together, she should not use directive statements to correct the situation. Instead, the teacher engages teams in a reflective exercise to get them to understand the nature of the problem and to devise their course of action. For example, the teacher could ask a series of questions such as these:

What is the specific problem your group is having?

Why do you think you are having this problem?

Can you give me three possible options for solving the problem?

Which option is best, and why?

What will it take to get going on this option?

If this works, what will I see in, say, 30 minutes?

How can your group keep this problem from happening again?

Use of questions is part of the social learning process, and fostering students' ability to make each team function to its maximum potential is one of the model's main goals.

Review and closure. Cooperative Learning lessons should end with the teacher leading an interactive reflection process to let teams know how well they worked together that day. The teacher prepares for this session by monitoring teams while they are engaged, noting instances of positive and negative interactions. Again, remember that the reflective process is indirect and interactive, with the teacher using questions rather than direct statements to get students to think about how well they worked as teams.

Contextual Requirements

Cooperative Learning can be used in any physical education setting in which students have the ability to learn how to work cooperatively. Notice that I did not say that students must *already* have good social learning skills. Since those skills are a major outcome in the model, it is necessary only that students are *ready to learn how* to contribute to a group's success. Once that condition is satisfied, Cooperative Learning can be used for its designed purposes in almost any physical education setting at any grade level. Equipment and facility needs are determined by the nature of the assigned task, so teachers can easily plan tasks that can be accomplished with existing resources. Perhaps the single greatest contextual requirement is having enough allocated time for groups to complete assigned tasks, especially when using strategies like Group Investigation. However, when that amount of time is not available, any of the other strategies can be used.

Selecting and Modifying Cooperative Learning

Because the Cooperative Learning model promotes outcomes in all three domains, it can work for a wide variety of goals and content in physical education. This model will be effective in many content areas of physical education:

1. Team sports
2. Dual- and small-team recreational activities
3. Dance (especially social dance)
4. Personal fitness
5. Personal fitness concepts
6. Sport history
7. Current trends and issues in sport and physical education
8. Group initiatives and Project Adventure
9. New games

Grade-level adaptations

Developmentally appropriate versions of Cooperative Learning can be used in many grade levels in physical education. Exhibit 10.7 shows possible ways to adapt this model for different grade levels.

EXHIBIT 10.7 Grade-level adaptations for Cooperative Learning in physical education.

GRADE LEVELS	SELECT COOPERATIVE LEARNING?	POSSIBLE ADAPTATIONS
Preschool	No	
Early elementary	Yes	1. Use teams of no more than three. 2. Do not use inter-team competitions. 3. Make tasks short and simple. 4. Do not use explicit performance assessments. Use simple checklists.
Upper elementary	Yes	1. Do not use inter-team competitions. 2. Make tasks short. 3. Use simple scoring rubrics for performance assessment.
Middle school/junior high	Yes	None needed if assigned tasks are developmentally appropriate.
High school	Yes	None needed if assigned tasks are developmentally appropriate.
College/adult	Yes	None needed.

Adaptations to accommodate diverse groups of learners

Cooperative Learning can be a highly inclusive model for physical education if the teacher makes the learning teams as diverse and fair as possible and if he stresses to students that *how* they learn is as important as *what* they learn. Exhibit 10.8 lists some strategies that address a variety of special learning needs found in many schools today.

Strategies to adapt Cooperative Learning for diverse groups of learners.	EXHIBIT	10.8

FOR STUDENTS WITH HEARING IMPAIRMENTS:

1. Use written and verbal directions to frame the learning task, and allow everyone in class enough time to read the directions.
2. Move students closer during any whole-class discussions.
3. Encourage teams (and the class) to think about and experiment with solutions to the task that involve all members of the team equally.

FOR STUDENTS WITH SIGHT IMPAIRMENTS:

1. Use larger font for written directions.
2. Encourage physically active student engagement—not engagement that requires a lot of reading, using the computer, or other visual activity.
3. Encourage teams (and the class) to think about and experiment with solutions to the task that involve all team members.

FOR STUDENTS WITH PHYSICAL DISABILITIES:

1. Encourage teams (and the class) to think about and experiment with solutions to the task that involve all team members.

FOR STUDENTS WHO DO NOT SPEAK ENGLISH:

1. Use student translators, when available.
2. Provide task presentations in the appropriate language, or use translated closed-caption media when possible.
3. Encourage teams (and the class) to think about and experiment with solutions to the task that involve all team members.

FOR LOWER-SKILLED STUDENTS:

1. Use assessment rubrics that allow students of all skill levels to contribute to the team's success.
2. Provide extra encouragement and praise.
3. Encourage teams (and the class) to think about and experiment with solutions to the task that involve all team members.

FOR STUDENTS WITH BEHAVIOR DISABILITIES:

1. Provide such students with extra encouragement for their participation.
2. Allow extra team points when everyone participates in a positive way.
3. Focus on the contribution to be made by such students, not their potential misbehavior.
4. Encourage teams (and the class) to think about and experiment with solutions to the task that involve all team members.

PLANNING TIPS FOR COOPERATIVE LEARNING

Teachers who choose to use the Cooperative Learning model can benefit by following a few additional planning tips:

1. Be sure to assign teams that are as mixed as possible in the key grouping factors: skill level, gender, race/ethnicity, cognitive development, creativity, leadership/followership, mastery of English, and so forth. When students view the teams as being fair, they will concentrate more on their own team's progress and be less concerned with other teams.

2. Once teams have been assigned, do not allow students to focus on what their team *lacks;* get them to focus on the unique abilities of each team member and to work with those to achieve the team's goals.

3. Carefully select the Cooperative Learning strategy (e.g., Team Games Tournament, Jigsaw) that is most likely to promote the kinds of development you seek in that unit. Remember, how students engage determines how and what they will learn.

4. Design learning tasks/problems that provide a high degree of challenge and that require a wide variety of student abilities (on each team) to achieve. Do not be afraid to adjust the task if you see that it is not promoting a high level of challenge and participation—with a reasonable chance of team success.

5. Frame the learning task/problem clearly, and offer ample opportunities for students to request clarification.

6. Include the rubric or other assessment strategy in the framing of the task/problem. Students and teams will become engaged faster and stay engaged longer when they know the teacher's expectations.

7. The rubric or assessment strategy must include a way to monitor student and team cooperation as well as performance.

8. A key "trick" is to provide teams with just enough information and directions to get them going, without letting them know how to complete the task/problem.

9. Be sure to look for good examples of student and team cooperation, and highlight those as part of the lesson closure and review.

UNIT AND LESSON PLAN EXAMPLES FOR COOPERATIVE LEARNING INSTRUCTION

You will find several complete unit plans with lesson plans for Cooperative Learning on the IMPE website. It is not recommended that you follow these examples exactly as they are presented. The context, specific learning objectives, and content of your own unit will require you to make changes in these examples to allow the Cooperative Learning model to lead to the most effective instruction in your situation.

SUMMARY

Although the field of physical education has been a bit slower than some others to adopt the theory and practice of Cooperative Learning, it would appear that this model can be invaluable in the process of promoting the multidimensional outcomes expressed in the NASPE (2004) standards for P–12 programs. It strives for a true balance among outcomes in all three major learning domains and, when implemented correctly, can accomplish that very well. The key is that physical education teachers must recognize the difference between "students learning alongside each other" (i.e., grouped learning) and "students learning with, by, and for each other" (Cooperative Learning). The Cooperative Learning model begins with an emphasis on teacher-centered decisions in the planning stage and the presentation of assigned learning tasks. However, once a task is framed and assigned, the model becomes very much student-centered as they negotiate the dynamics of team learning and pursue their common goals. The model changes to an interactive mode at the end of each lesson, as the teacher guides students toward a better understanding of the group process. Cooperative Learning, perhaps more than any other model in this book, requires a teacher to use a broad range of real-time communication, observation, and decision-making skills to promote the types of learning intended in the model.

As more physical education teachers at all levels adopt the broad learning goals reflected in the NASPE (2004) standards, Cooperative Learning is becoming one of the most widely used instructional models in physical education. That is due to Cooperative Learning's expanding record of promoting social and cognitive learning outcomes in physical education. It seems to be very much a model for the times.

LEARNING ACTIVITIES

1. Make a list of five activity units (e.g., movement skills, fitness, softball, tennis, golf) that might be taught in a physical education program. Next, determine an appropriate grade level (P, K–2, 3–5, 6–8, 9–12) for teaching each of those activity units. Now, write two major learning outcomes for those units. Then, go through the process of selecting an instructional model, shown in Chapter 2, to determine if Cooperative Learning would be an appropriate model for teaching that activity to children at that grade level.

2. If Cooperative Learning is appropriate for that activity, grade, and goals, mention three things that make it appropriate. If Cooperative Learning is not appropriate for that activity, grade, and goals, mention three things that make it inappropriate.

3. Write an annotated plan for one complete learning task/problem in this unit. Be sure to include all of the directions to be given to students, the parameters for their engagement (time, resources, and so forth), and your assessment plan.

TOPICS FOR REFLECTION & SMALL-GROUP DISCUSSION

1. I have suggested in this chapter how the Cooperative Learning model is aligned to achieve one or more of the NASPE standards. Take a moment to review those alignments (refer to Exhibit 10.1). After that, make some notes about whether you agree with those alignments and then share them in your small group. After you have arrived at your final thoughts, please share them on the IMPE website Forum for others to review, and check back for replies.

2. Mention three ways Cooperative Learning is similar to Direct Instruction and three ways it is different.

3. In general, which types of students are placed at an advantage in this model, and which students are placed at a disadvantage?

4. Why is it so important to have heterogeneous teams?

5. Why is it important to give equal attention to process (how teams work together) *and* outcomes (what teams produce or accomplish)?

SUGGESTED READINGS FOR COOPERATIVE LEARNING

Dyson, B. (2005). Integrating cooperative learning and tactical games models: Focusing on social interactions and decision-making. In J. Butler and L. Griffin, eds. *Introduction to teaching games for understanding* (pp. 149–168). Champaign, IL: Human Kinetics.

Dyson, B. P., Linehan, N. R., & Hastie, P. A. (2010). The ecology of cooperative learning in physical education. *Journal of Teaching in Physical Education, 29,* 113–130.

Grineski, S. (1996). *Cooperative learning in physical education.* Champaign, IL: Human Kinetics.

Hannon, J. C., & Ratliffe, T. (2004). Cooperative learning in physical education. *Strategies, (17)5,* 29–32.

11

SPORT EDUCATION
Learning to Become Competent, Literate, and Enthusiastic Sportspersons

Teaching and learning the many forms of institutionalized sport have been central to physical education in the United States for more than 100 years. Many of the earliest school programs started on a sport foundation, stemming from the huge popularity of sport in American culture, with both participants and spectators. The traditional benefits of participation in sport—skill, strategy, cooperation, and healthy competition—were often used as the curricular objectives for teaching sport at all grade levels. America loves sporting activity in all its many new forms, so our schools were quick to use that as the primary vehicle for achieving three key goals of the 1918 Seven Cardinal Principles of Education: worthy use of leisure time, health and safety, and ethical character (Van Dalen & Bennett, 1971). The pursuit of those goals through sport remained the cornerstone of U.S. physical education for more than 50 years afterward.

It is evident that the place of sport in the physical education curriculum is being reduced today, at the same time that sport participation is still showing steady growth in our society. The continuing growth among population groups that had typically been denied access to sport participation—girls, women, people with disabilities, and older adults—is nothing short of phenomenal. Concurrent with that expansion was the growth of familiar sport organizations (such as youth sports, interscholastic sports, community leagues) and structures (such as private clubs, community recreation centers, and instruction-for-pay) that provide participation opportunities for anyone who wants to and can afford the costs. It is still clear that Americans love to participate in sport, yet they are turning less often to physical education programs to get a positive sport experience. That is a sad reality for the many physical educators who grew up and started their careers in the sport model. However, there is a curriculum and instruction model that can provide students of nearly all ages with positive, educational, and lasting sport experiences as part of the school physical education program. Sport Education, an approach developed by Daryl Siedentop (1998), is "designed to provide authentic, educationally rich, sport experiences for girls and boys in the context of school physical education" (p. 18). According to Siedentop, the Sport Education model has strong implications for curriculum and instruction—so it represents a dual-level model. On the curricular level, it puts sport at the organizing center for the physical education program: everything that is taught and learned is accomplished in the context of developmentally appropriate forms of sport. As an instructional model, "its purposes are best achieved through combinations of direct instruction, cooperative small-group work, and peer teaching" (Siedentop, 1998, p. 18), all designed within a comprehensive approach to teaching and learning sport.

You should be aware that the model presented in this chapter (which will sometimes be referred to simply as Sport Education) is not used to teach *sports, per se* (such as flag football, basketball, soccer, and tennis), although students will certainly learn much about each sport form offered within this model. Rather, it is designed to teach the concept and conduct of *sport,* a much broader set of goals that includes team affiliation, fairness, etiquette, traditions, appreciation, strategy, values, structure, and, of course, the inherent movement patterns that are part of every sport form included in the physical education program. These lofty goals separate Sport Education from simply *learning to play* flag football, basketball, soccer, tennis, and so forth. These goals and the processes that teachers use to accomplish them within the model give Sport Education a unique look as it is carried out in physical education, allowing students to learn about sport from many perspectives through authentic participation.

OVERVIEW

The basic structure of Sport Education is adapted from the familiar model of organized sport leagues. Think for a moment about what you would need if you were starting a competitive youth or interscholastic sport league. What roles and jobs must be carried out? You would need players, coaches, officials/referees, scorekeepers, trainers, administrators, and support staff (managers, groundskeepers, and the like). You would also need practice time, a schedule (with play-offs), league rules, equipment, and facilities. All these features and others provide the structure that allows students to experience and learn from their participation in youth and interscholastic sport.

Yet there is one major exception that distinguishes the Sport Education model from the sport league structure. In the youth or interscholastic league structures just described, children and youth most often learn sport from only one perspective—that of player and, typically, that of a single-position player. They rarely get a broader sport experience from which they can learn the many other facets of each sport and thus reach a fuller understanding of, and greater appreciation for, the entire scope of our sport culture. In addition, their experience is very strongly controlled by the coach, who makes nearly all the decisions, and the players are expected to comply with the coach's directions. In Sport Education, all students are players, but they also learn one or more of the other roles needed to make the league operate. Their experience base broadens as they learn the skills, decisions, customs, and responsibilities that go with those roles in the league structure. For example, a student does not just "call balls and strikes" in a baseball game to fill a need for that role at the moment. Rather, she *becomes an umpire* in the fullest sense of that term, by learning all the things needed to do that job well for an entire sport season.

Students in the Sport Education model take active roles in making decisions that determine the structure and operation of the league—they are not passive participants. For instance, students who become part of the "league council" are given autonomy in deciding things like rules modifications, team selection procedures, scheduling, and conflict resolution. Students who become coaches are responsible for team selection, position assignments, practice planning, and game strategy. Students who act as the support staff make sure that the playing area is set up properly and that the required equipment and gear are ready. In effect, students are not merely *in a league* for a season. They *become part of the league* in many ways that can provide a deeper, broader, and more positive educational sport experience.

Siedentop (1994) cites three major goals for the Sport Education model: to develop competent, literate, and enthusiastic sportspersons (p. 4):

1. A *competent* sportsperson has sufficient skills to participate in games satisfactorily, understands and can execute strategies appropriate to the complexity of play, and is a knowledgeable games player.

2. A *literate* sportsperson understands and values the rules, rituals, and traditions of sport and distinguishes between good and bad sport practices, whether in children's or professional sport. A literate sportsperson is both a more able participant and a more discerning consumer, whether fan or spectator.

3. An *enthusiastic* sportsperson participates and behaves in ways that preserve, protect, and enhance the sport culture, whether it is a local youth sport culture or a national sport culture. As members of sporting groups, such

enthusiasts are involved, participating in further developing sport at the local, national, or international levels.

Siedentop (1994) cites 10 specific learning objectives for students in the Sport Education model (pp. 4–5):

1. Develop skill and fitness specific to particular sports
2. Appreciate and be able to execute strategic plays in sports
3. Participate at a level appropriate to student development
4. Share in the planning and administration of sport experiences
5. Provide responsible leadership
6. Work effectively within a group toward common goals
7. Appreciate the rituals and conventions that give particular sports their unique meanings
8. Develop the capacity to make reasoned decisions about sport issues
9. Develop and apply knowledge about umpiring, refereeing, and training
10. Decide voluntarily to become involved in after-school sport

As you can see, the Sport Education model attempts to educate students in all aspects of each sport by assigning them more than one active role (player, plus one or more "duty roles"). Once students have had positive sport experiences in physical education, it is hoped that they will extend their participation and involvement beyond the physical education program.

Sport Education has six key features that give it its unique identity (Siedentop, 1994). As you will discover, each of these features is an adaptation of a characteristic of organized sport:

1. *Seasons.* Sport Education uses seasons as an organizational structure, rather than the more traditional content units of physical education. A season implies a longer time period that includes an organization and practice period, a preseason, a regular season, and a postseason or culminating event. Sport Education seasons should be a minimum of 20 lessons when possible (Grant, 1992).

2. *Affiliation.* Students remain members of the same team for the entire season. This extended affiliation promotes many of the affective and social development objectives within the model by allowing team members the opportunity to work toward common goals, make group decisions, experience success and failure as a group, and fashion a group identity for the team.

3. *Formal competition.* Students make many of the decisions that determine the structure and operation of the season. They can modify game rules to promote fairness and better participation. A formal schedule of competition lets each team and its players make short-term and long-term decisions for the season. The competition schedule provides teams and players with an ongoing focal point for their practices and preparation.

4. *Culminating event.* The season ends with a culminating event that could take many forms: a round-robin tournament, a team competition, or individual competition. This event should be festive and permit all students to participate in some capacity (except as spectators).

5. *Record keeping.* Games provide a lot of opportunities to make records of performance that can be used to teach strategy, increase interest within and among teams, publicize results, and assess student learning. Records can be simple or complex, depending on students' ability to keep and comprehend them. Because the records are public, they help provide a backdrop to the competition schedule (e.g., when the top defensive team is getting ready to play the top offensive team). Coaches and players can use game statistics to analyze their own team strengths and those of their opponents.

6. *Festivity.* Sporting events are known for being festive. Teams have names that become part of their tradition and add to the lore of the sport. Playing venues are colorful and often decorated with signs and banners. Although on a somewhat smaller scale—so as not to detract from the event itself—Sport Education teachers try to make their seasons and competitions as festive and celebratory as possible.

Sport Education makes a direct effort to reduce and eliminate some of the negative characteristics that have become associated with sport in our society:

1. Competition represents a means of getting students to develop their skills, knowledge, and strategy. It is used as an educational tool.
2. Everyone participates—both as a player and in an assigned role. Sport Education is not exclusionary, as are many sport experiences that allow only the best players an opportunity to participate.
3. Students are given an active, not passive, role in determining the context and structure of sport. They learn to make decisions that normally belong to adults in sport settings.
4. Students can decide to design and play developmentally appropriate versions of sport—not necessarily the adult versions often imposed on them.
5. Because physical education occurs in an educational setting, the teacher has the ultimate responsibility to keep the goals and conduct of Sport Education in line with the school's and program's most important mission—to teach children. There should be no mixed messages or misplaced priorities, as there sometimes are in interscholastic and youth sport leagues.

The Sport Education model relies heavily on cooperative learning strategies, in which teams (coaches and players together) hold much of the responsibility to get prepared for the season. The teacher and the league council (made up of students) decide the basic structure for the season, and teams are determined. Once in teams, students use cooperative learning to determine their needs for the season, how their team will be organized, and how they will prepare for the season. They work out practice schedules, position assignments, substitution plans, and game strategy. Even though one student is designated as "coach," his role is to *coordinate* the team's efforts, not *run* the team. Much of the teaching on a team takes the form of peer teaching, as teammates help each other learn the skills and strategies needed for the team's success. The amount of cooperative learning responsibility and peer teaching given to students will depend on their developmental readiness for their nonplaying roles. The Sport Education model can be modified for students as young as fourth graders and still maintain many of the model's key features.

ALIGNMENT WITH NASPE NATIONAL STANDARDS

Exhibit 11.1 shows the alignment of the Sport Education model with the NASPE standards. As you can see, Sport Education is consistently and strongly aligned with standards 1, 2, 5, and 6. Its alignment with standards 3 and 4 will depend on the specific sport being played in each season. If the selected sport is one that involves high levels of moderate-to-vigorous physical activity (e.g., basketball, tennis, Ultimate), then this model is strongly aligned with those standards. If the selected sport involves lower levels of moderate-to-vigorous physical activity (e.g., softball, golf, archery), then the model has a weaker alignment with those two standards.

FOUNDATIONS

Theory and Rationale

The underpinnings of Sport Education can be found in some of Daryl Siedentop's earlier writings on philosophical issues in the field of physical education. *Physical Education: Teaching and Curriculum Strategies for Grades 5–12* (Siedentop, Mand, & Taggart, 1986) contains references to play theory that would eventually become the foundation of this curriculum and instruction model a few years later. In the tradition of Johan Huizinga and Roger Caillois, Siedentop recognizes sport as a form of play that has occupied a special place in societies throughout the world and throughout history. Because play is such a fundamental human endeavor, it is essential that societies pass down (through teaching) that activity from one generation to the next. Other forms of play include music, art, and drama, which share many of the same core characteristics as sporting activities in our culture.

The rationale for Sport Education is quite simple. If sport, as an accepted form of play, is a valued part of any society, it is the society's responsibility (and in its best interest) to find ways to formalize the process of how people come to learn and participate in the sport culture. Quite simply, we must teach each new generation our sport culture, and one of the best places to do that is within the school curriculum. Certainly, children and youth can and do learn the sport culture in many other ways and places (youth sport, church leagues, private tutoring, playgrounds, and home), but the best place to provide a broad-based, educational, and egalitarian sport experience is through

Alignment of Sport Education with NASPE National Standards.	🖨 EXHIBIT	11.1

NASPE STANDARD	ALIGNMENT RATING	COMMENTS
1. Demonstrates competency in motor skills and movement patterns needed to perform a variety of physical activities	1	Skills are practiced and developed for application in games.
2. Demonstrates understanding of movement concepts, principles, strategies, and tactics as they apply to the learning and performance of physical activities	1	These outcomes are achieved in the practices and games that are part of the Sport Education season.
3. Participates regularly in physical activity	1–3	The amount of physical activity will depend on the sport being played and the design of practices and games.
4. Achieves and maintains a health-enhancing level of physical fitness	1–3	The alignment will depend on the sport being played and the design of practices and games.
5. Exhibits responsible personal and social behavior that respects self and others in physical activity settings	1	This is one of the best models for learning personal and social behavior in physical education.
6. Values physical activity for health, enjoyment, challenge, self-expression, and/or social interaction	1	The model is strong in all of these outcomes.

Ratings categories:

1. Strong alignment

2. Moderate alignment

3. Weak alignment

our schooling system. Therefore, Sport Education is designed as a way to pass down our sport culture and promote sport's most positive characteristics.

Assumptions About Teaching and Learning

The Sport Education model assumes certain principles about teaching and about learning; these principles are listed separately below.

Assumptions about teaching

1. The teacher needs to use a combination of strategies to facilitate the varied learning goals in the Sport Education model. Those strategies include direct instruction, cooperative learning, and peer/small-group teaching.

2. The teacher should serve as the major resource person in Sport Education seasons, rather than be in direct control of every learning activity.

3. The teacher should guide students to make decisions that reflect the inherent values, traditions, and conduct of sporting activities.

4. The teacher should plan for and facilitate student opportunities to take on and learn the responsibilities within nonplaying roles in a Sport Education season.

Assumptions about learning

1. With proper guidance and facilitation, students can assume many decision-making and other responsibilities in the Sport Education season. Opportunities for student learning will occur as they engage in the processes of making and carrying out those decisions.

2. Students can work cooperatively within the team structure to set and reach group goals.

3. Active, rather than passive, participation is the preferred way to learn sport.

4. Students can determine developmentally appropriate forms of sport for themselves but sometimes need the teacher's guidance to do so.

5. The Sport Education structure provides a truly authentic sporting experience that can be generalized to participation in other settings.

The Major Theme of Sport Education: Learning to Become Competent, Literate, and Enthusiastic Sportspersons

The designer of the Sport Education model, Daryl Siedentop, succinctly states that he intends for the model to promote "the development of competent, literate, and enthusiastic sportspersons" (Siedentop, 1994, p. 4). He goes on to say that the model should teach students of all ages to become *players* in the fullest sense of that word. A player is someone who comes to know sport from a variety of perspectives, makes sport participation a central part of her life, and derives deep personal meaning from sporting activity. Think of something that you are really enthusiastic about in your own life. Perhaps you enjoy a hobby, can play music, have a favorite sport, or have come to know something "inside out." More than likely you got to that point through an initial interest that allowed you to become knowledgeable and proficient. Eventually the activity became a very important part of your life. That level of meaning is what Sport Education strives to instill in physical education students, and it is reflected as the major theme for the model. Students will not simply *play a game*—they will learn the sporting traditions embedded in the game and the structure of the sport itself, until they reach the point of being competent, literate, and enthusiastic sportspersons.

Learning Domain Priorities and Domain Interactions

Domain priorities

Sport Education promotes student learning outcomes that cut across all three major learning domains. Although from time to time learning in one domain will be the primary objective, there will generally be a balance among all three domains as the Sport Education season goes from beginning to end. The three-part theme of the model makes that point clearly: *competence* refers to the ability to discern and execute skilled strategic moves (psychomotor, with strong cognitive support); *literateness* refers to one's ability to comprehend and appreciate a sport form and culture (cognitive and affective); *enthusiasm* refers to making sport a central part of one's life and daily activity (affective). The teacher must address all of these domains when planning a Sport Education unit (called a "season"), so that ample learning opportunities are provided for each area of student development. Because students will have many different types of learning activities, with shifting domain priorities for each one, it is not appropriate to make a firm list of domain priorities as we have done with other models. Rather, teachers should understand what type(s) of learning are fostered in each part of the Sport Education model and should make sure that students get a balance of domain emphases during the season. Exhibit 11.2 shows how domain priorities can shift during various times and activities in the Sport Education season.

Domain priorities for the Sport Education model.	EXHIBIT 11.2
LEARNING ACTIVITY	**TEMPORARY DOMAIN PRIORITY**
Making organizational decisions	1. Cognitive 2. Affective
Preseason practice (as a player)	1. Psychomotor 2. Cognitive 3. Affective
Preseason practice (as a coach)	1. Cognitive 2. Affective 3. Psychomotor
Learning duty roles (umpire, scorekeeper, trainer, and so forth)	1. Cognitive 2. Affective 3. Psychomotor
Working as a member of a team	1. Affective 2. Cognitive 3. Psychomotor
During competitive games (as a player)	1. Psychomotor 2. Cognitive 3. Affective
During competitive games (as a coach)	1. Cognitive (strategy and tactics) 2. Affective (team leadership) 3. Psychomotor

Domain interactions

Determining domain interactions within the Sport Education model is even more complicated, due to the many unexpected events and "learning moments" that can occur during a sport season. For instance, as a team of students works cooperatively to prepare for the competitive part of the season, they will need to address all of the complex dynamics involved in getting the team ready: skill development, team cohesion, analysis of team strengths and weaknesses, position assignments, and assumption of leadership roles. The development of skills might be supported by the analysis of player abilities; the development of team cohesion might be fostered by negotiating clear role definitions and position assignments. And, because the teacher takes on a less direct role once the teams are in the preparation stage, it is difficult for the teacher always to recognize and change domain interactions for all teams in class.

Even though the teacher takes on a less direct role in Sport Education, she must still keenly observe the many complex events that will occur during the season and recognize the moments when domain interactions are not contributing to student development. For example, a team might be spending too much time on practicing skills (psychomotor domain) and not enough time on planning strategy (cognitive domain). This lack of planning could also limit the kinds of verbal interactions that promote learning in the social/affective domain. The team could become more highly skilled at the expense of development in other areas important in achieving its goals. When the teacher recognizes such situations, she can suggest that students look at the bigger picture to see that the team's success is more likely if they learn to approach sport from multiple perspectives.

Student Developmental Requirements

Student readiness for learning. Sport Education will be effective in a wide range of grade levels if the teacher matches the complexity of the season's organization with students' ability to assume the responsibilities of nonplaying roles (coaching and duty jobs). With lower grades, the teacher will need to retain more control of the managerial system and many of the instructional interactions. This can be accomplished with more direct instruction that does not place unrealistic demands on students as they learn the sometimes complex roles of coach and duty jobs. As students' maturity increases in higher grades, students can take on more responsibility for their own learning and that of others on their team. They can also assume a larger part of the managerial system in the Sport Education season.

Because Sport Education is new for so many teachers and their students, there are few guidelines to follow when determining student readiness. In elementary grades, it is best that a teacher experiment with Sport Education in increments, by increasing students' roles in the model and interacting with students often to get their feedback about the process. Secondary students should have no problems with the implementation of the full Sport Education model—although the teacher will have to acclimate them to this new form of physical education class.

Student receptivity to the model. Using the Reichmann and Grasha (1974) profile for student learning preferences, the Sport Education model will generally work best for those students who are classified as participant, collaborative (on their team), competitive (toward other teams), and independent. Participatory learners are naturally attracted to Sport Education because they enjoy the affiliation of team membership and the chance to contribute to the team's success. Students do need to be cooperative *and* competitive in the Sport Education model, although at first glance those attitudes appear a bit contradictory. Students must recognize times when the team needs to work cooperatively to achieve its goals, one of which is to compete well against opponents. The Sport Education model provides valuable opportunities for students to learn to be cooperative and competitive at the appropriate times and in appropriate ways. The independent learner will appreciate opportunities to learn new nonplaying roles and to take responsibility for the decisions in those roles. Some of the roles (e.g., coach, game official) require students to make important decisions on their own, again appealing to the independent learner.

Validation of the Model

Research validation

Because it relies on three different teaching models—Cooperative Learning, Direct Instruction, and Peer Teaching—the Sport Education model can draw general validation from the research base for each of those models. In addition, a growing body of research has been generated directly from the Sport Education model itself. This line of research has begun to provide descriptions of the model's effectiveness in many grade levels, sport content, and geographical locations.

Three major reviews of the research on Sport Education have been conducted in recent years. The first review included nearly thirty studies completed before 2004 (Wallhead & O'Sullivan, 2005). Overall, these authors concluded that the results were mixed or not supportive of Sport Education's ability to promote outcomes related to skill development, fitness, and the promotion of gender equity. However, they also concluded that the research on Sport Education documented a number of positive outcomes in physical education, mainly: strong team affiliation, good sport behavior, game play ability, leadership, responsibility, and increased engagement by students—regardless of skill, gender, or experience.

A second major review of the research on Sport Education was conducted by Kinchin (2006). Some of his findings are related to the implementation of Sport Education, indicating (1) a large increase in the amount of support materials now being generated from Sport Education teachers worldwide; (2) that Sport Education can be successfully implemented in elementary, middle, and high schools; (3) and that Sport Education units have been developed for use in a wide range of content units, including some that are novel (such as bicycle safety, dance, and outdoor/adventure activity). Kinchin also summarizes the research on the learning outcomes for Sport Education and concludes that there is strong evidence that (1) students are more attracted to the Sport Education approach than the approaches previously used for their instruction; (2) students value the affiliation that occurs with extended team membership; (3) students enjoy the peer-teaching component of sport education; (4) and students also learn from and enjoy the responsibilities they take on in their duty roles. There is conflicting evidence on outcomes related to skill development and the ability of sport education to fully promote equity and inclusion. Kinchin also reports findings on the perspective of teachers who use this model, citing their overall endorsement of the model—even with the difficulties encountered in moving to full implementation of the model in their schools.

The third major review of research on Sport Education was conducted by Peter Hastie (in press), one of the best experts on this model in the world, both as a teacher and researcher. Hastie's analysis included the time period from 2004 to 2010 and used 36 studies that were conducted in 8 different countries, on 16 different sports. Hastie summarized the findings from these studies around the three main themes of Sport Education and concluded that the evidence for skill competency is "burgeoning and developing," research support for literacy is "emerging," and enthusiastic responses by students have been "significantly substantiated."

Even though Wallhead and O'Sullivan (2005), Kinchin (2006), and Hastie (in press) all call for additional research on Sport Education, it is now one of the few instructional models in physical education that can be designed and implemented by teachers from a strong research base.

Craft knowledge validation

Developmentally appropriate versions of the Sport Education model are now becoming more common in physical education programs, attesting to the model's effectiveness in promoting its major goals in many situations. In the authoritative text on the model, Siedentop (1994) provides field-tested examples at elementary grades (soccer, gymnastics, basketball, volleyball, and track and field), middle schools (volleyball), and high schools (fitness, rugby, and tennis). In other adaptations, Hicks (1998) used Sport Education for a fourth-grade ultimate Frisbee season, and Watts (1998) designed a Sport Education unit for sixth-grade pickleball. Bennett and Hastie (1997) used the model within a collegiate physical activity course.

Sport Education has also been implemented in broader ways. Dugas (1994) described a Sport Education curricular track at the Louisiana School for Math and Sciences that included more than 20 different units spanning four distinct seasons. Many schools in Australia and New Zealand have adopted the Sport Education model as well. Grant (1994) reported that 21 schools in New

Zealand began to use the model on a trial basis. The trial was so successful that more than 150 schools had adopted the model for their entire programs just one year later. Similar growth was reported in western Australia by Alexander, Taggart, and Luckman (1998), starting with 53 teachers and growing to more than 100 teachers one year later. It should be mentioned that both the New Zealand and Australia implementations of Sport Education were endorsed and supported in part by their respective regional education agencies, allowing faster and more effective dissemination of the model, along with some funding for the necessary staff development.

Sport Education is now used by physical education teachers in a large number of countries and for units that include a wide range of individual and team sports, fitness, and dance. Much of that acceptance has come from the growing number of teachers who have used that model and who then "pass it on" to other teachers. The Internet has allowed Sport Education to become familiar to teachers in many countries outside the United States, making it a truly international instruction model for physical education.

The list of teachers, schools, and entire school districts that have now used the Sport Education model continues to grow at an impressive rate. Surely, part of that growth is attributable to demonstrable student learning observed by teachers who use Sport Education. Some evidence to that effect has been provided by published anecdotal records of teachers who have used the model. Alexander, Taggart, and Thorpe (1995), Carlson and Hastie (1997), and Grant (1992) all report strongly positive experiences by Sport Education teachers and their students.

Kinchin (2006) reported that a large amount of support materials have been developed for sport education, allowing more and more teachers to benefit from the experiences of those who have already used this model. Siedentop, Hastie, and van der Mars (2004) provide an excellent update on this model, with many resources for teachers to use. One resource (Bulger, Mohr, Rairigh, & Townsend, 2007) provides several dozen examples of field-tested Sport Education season plans that can be easily adopted by interested teachers.

Perhaps so many teachers have begun to use the Sport Education model in part because of their own experiences in sport and their familiarity with sport cultures and organization. It is probably safe to say that nearly every physical education teacher has a substantial history in one or more sport forms, as a player and/or coach. The shift from more formal and more competitive forms of sport to the Sport Education model is probably quite easy for teachers to make in their physical education classes and programs.

Intuitive validation

Sport has been used for over 100 years as a primary vehicle for achieving many of the standards and learning outcomes aimed for in physical education. The educational potential of the sporting experience is enormous if it can be structured and implemented at the appropriate developmental level for students and if the many positive features of sport are properly emphasized and learned. Perhaps this new model of something that physical educators have practiced for a century is so attractive because it allows teachers to get back to their roots and to revisit sport as an educational pursuit—without many of the negative practices that have come to pervade other sport settings (e.g., youth, interscholastic, and college sports).

TEACHING AND LEARNING FEATURES

Control

Exhibit 11.3 shows the control profile for the Sport Education model when used in physical education instruction. As you will note, control will change for most aspects depending on whether the students are in their teams or learning their duty roles. Each element of the profile is explained below.

1. Content selection. Teachers have two options for deciding which sport to offer in a Sport Education season. One option is direct; that is, the teacher makes the decision and informs students. The second option is to give students a range of choices and let them select the sport for each season. This option becomes interactive as teachers advise students about each possible choice while also taking contextual factors into consideration.

2. Managerial control. The teacher makes most of the initial managerial decisions that give the Sport Education season its overall structure: how teams will be selected, which nonplaying duties will be needed and how students get assigned to them, how long the season will last, how to prepare equipment

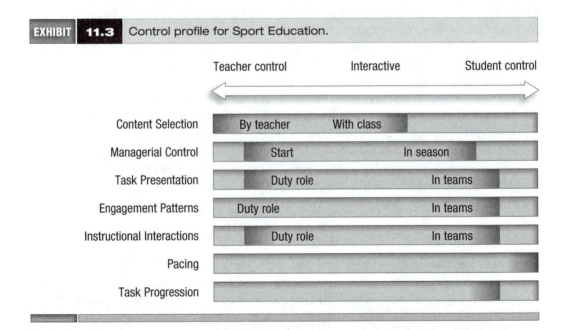

EXHIBIT 11.3 Control profile for Sport Education.

	Teacher control	Interactive	Student control
Content Selection	By teacher	With class	
Managerial Control	Start		In season
Task Presentation	Duty role		In teams
Engagement Patterns	Duty role		In teams
Instructional Interactions	Duty role		In teams
Pacing			
Task Progression			

and facilities, and overall ground rules for the season. (For example, refer to the unit/season plan on the IMPE website.) After those decisions are made and communicated to students, the students assume nearly all control for putting them into operation. Students will plan and carry out many of the day-to-day managerial tasks during the season.

3. Task presentations. Most of the task presentations for skill and strategy development will take place in the context of team practice sessions before and during the season. This is likely to take the form of peer teaching and group cooperative learning—both conducted by students. The teacher will perform task presentations for duty roles, in the form of mini workshops for each needed job (training officials, showing managers how to prepare the field, explaining scoring rules to statisticians, and the like). Because most students will have little or no experience in those roles and time will be short, teacher-directed instruction is usually the most effective way to teach roles to students at the start. Teachers can also invite guest speakers to conduct in-class "clinics" to teach students duty roles. Some examples of speakers would be licensed officials for officiating roles, the school athletic trainer for basic first aid, and local sportswriters for scoring and game reporting. These clinics are likely to use direct instruction, but the guest expert will command increased attention from students.

4. Engagement patterns. Like task presentations, student engagement patterns will differ between their playing and nonplaying roles. As members of a team, students will engage in peer and small-group cooperative learning tasks. Each team has the responsibility of getting ready for the season, so members must be able to make group decisions and take a very active role in teaching their teammates. In their nonplaying roles, students will engage as active participants as they learn the knowledge, skills, and procedures for each assignment. Initially, they are likely to get direct instruction from the teacher to become familiar with the rudiments of each job. After that, they will get a lot of on-the-job learning as they carry out their assigned duties during competitions. Most of their interaction will take place with other students in the game context.

5. Instructional interactions. Most of the instructional interactions will be controlled by students as they work on teams in peer and small-group cooperative learning activities. One or more students on each team will be designated as the captain or co-captains and will assume many of the teaching functions. The teacher will be available as a resource person, but most of the instruction is conducted through student-to-student interaction.

6. Pacing. Team members will decide what is needed to prepare for the competitive season and make up a preseason plan. They can also decide how much time they will need for preparation, giving them total control of pacing before and between games.

7. Task progression. As with pacing, teams make decisions about the order of practice tasks as they prepare before the season and between games. The content listing for each team in the class might be somewhat different, depending on the specific abilities of the players.

Inclusiveness

Sport Education is inherently designed for inclusive physical education instruction. Since all students must be players on a team, everyone is automatically included at that level. If the teacher has been careful to make sure that all teams are balanced as to skill levels, experience, and gender, then all teams must work equally well to ensure that members contribute to their potential, promoting inclusion at the most important level—among students themselves. According to Hastie (1998), three features of Sport Education directly benefit marginalized students: (1) small teams need everyone's contribution for success; (2) the affiliation with a continuing team promotes a sense of cohesion and belonging; and (3) the regular practice allows lower-skilled students to improve over the course of the season.

Not all students come to physical education with the same interest in and abilities to play the game in season. This can often be a source of student dissatisfaction and isolation that may work against an inclusive environment. However, because all students take a nonplaying role, they can be active sport participants from a second perspective and make valuable contributions to the season's operation. Each student must take on a duty job, so there is no playing of favorites in the assignment of these roles. All students must do their part, which also promotes an inclusive environment in physical education.

Learning Tasks

Task presentation

Due to the use of direct, cooperative, and peer teaching strategies, task presentation in Sport Education will vary according to grade level, depending on students' developmental readiness. In lower grades, the teacher is likely to assume a direct role more often than with older students. However, the design of the model supports student-controlled and cooperative learning activities to the highest degree possible for students in a given class. Sometimes the teacher will need to be very much in control; at other times the teacher can present tasks to students as learning problems, as in Cooperative Learning (Chapter 10). When in doubt, the teacher should start by giving students a reasonable amount of autonomy and then make adjustments as the situation allows.

Teaching players. In the full version of the Sport Education model, the teacher arranges for teams to be selected, oversees the organization of the season, and lets each team work cooperatively to determine what learning must take place and how it will get achieved. The task presentation function is left up to each team and its leaders to determine and carry out. In some situations, it might be necessary for the teacher to plan a short period of direct instruction tasks for the whole class before teams are selected (see Note 2 of the unit/season plan shown on the IMPE website). This ensures that all students have a basic level of proficiency, and it can facilitate the team selection process. After teams are selected and working together, the teacher can train one or more students on each team to plan and implement task presentations for other students. This will be the first step in the use of cooperative and peer-teaching strategies.

Teaching duty roles. The teacher is more likely to take a direct instruction approach when teaching students their assigned support duties for the season. There can be several "jobs" to teach and limited minutes in which to tell small groups of students about the skills, knowledge, and responsibilities of each job. The teacher can use a "clinic" model in which she gives students direct information and models task presentations for doing each job correctly. These are basically "how-to" mini sessions. This role can also be played by guest speakers—other teachers/coaches in the school, certified game officials and statisticians, or the school's trainer, just to mention a few. Instructional videos and other visual materials can also teach duty roles.

Task structure

Task structure will be greatly influenced by any modifications made in the sport itself—modifications decided by the students and the teacher before the season begins. For instance, a typical modification for soccer is to have reduced-side teams, such as three-person or four-person teams. Flag football can be played with four to six players per team, and three-on-three basketball works very well. These modifications greatly reduce the complexity of the games as well as the time needed to prepare for the season. These modifications will influence the kinds of learning tasks that players on teams need to master or refine before and during the season.

Teaching players. The structure of learning tasks in Sport Education will be similar to those used by sport coaches in practices and in game preparations. When together as a team, each group of students will essentially be practicing just like any other competitive team. The range of task structures could include warm-ups, "chalk talks," drills, conditioning exercises, run-throughs of plays and defenses, scrimmages, and strategy sessions—all designed by the team leaders and implemented with cooperative or peer-teaching strategies. Jones and Ward (1998) suggest that the teacher devise the general practice schedule and needed routines, then let students make specific plans within the teacher's time frame.

Teaching duty roles. The task structure for teaching students the various duty jobs can also have a familiar look, based on how people come to learn the important support roles in sport. Referees should first know the rules, and they can get that information from the teacher, videos, DVDs, or guest speakers. Taking and passing a rules test should be one requirement for that job. Next, they will need to learn procedures and techniques for refereeing the sport—typically by viewing correct models in a simple-to-complex progression. The student referees can then practice their own techniques under the supervision of the teacher while teams play preseason matches. Soon they will be ready to officiate a full competitive game, which then becomes the task structure for that learning progression—a quite authentic structure, at that! The teacher can plan similar task structures and progressions for all duty jobs in the Sport Education season.

Content progression

The unit for Sport Education is modeled after a season in competitive sport leagues. The teacher will have to plan before the season for the processes needed to get the league up and running; thus, he will list things to do in that regard, making an organizational progression of sorts. Most of the true content progression will take place at the team level, as coaches and players decide what they need to do to get ready for the season and as they make adjustments during the season. The teacher can provide some guidance, but this process will be decided mostly by students, so there is not a typical content progression for Sport Education.

Engagement Patterns for Learning

According to Siedentop (1994), there are three predominant engagement patterns for learning activities in the Sport Education model: direct instruction, cooperative learning, and peer teaching. *Direct instruction* is most often used by the teacher to train students for duty roles during games. This can be done in mini workshops that focus on each assigned role and teach students how to begin to carry out their responsibilities. Time is usually short for this, so a directed kind of engagement works quite effectively. After students are trained, they engage in authentic role assumption learning before, during, and after each duty time. That is, they learn what needs to be done to get ready for contests, how to carry out an active role during the contest, and to take on responsibility for any required post-contest work. They are not just temporary workers; they actually *assume* those roles when they are not playing on their team. *Cooperative learning* occurs regularly within each team as players and coaches make and carry out the many decisions needed to help the team reach its goals. This process tends to be very democratic because there is usually no central authority figure present. Conflict resolution may be needed from time to time, but that too becomes part of the cooperative learning process. *Peer teaching* is used frequently so that higher-skilled members of a team can help less-skilled members improve, facilitating the whole team's achievement. Students quickly recognize that a team is only as strong as its weakest link, so it is in everybody's interest to help less-skilled members improve by using the best resource for that improvement—other team members.

Teacher and Student Roles and Responsibilities

Each instructional model will have certain operations that need to be completed to allow the model to function according to its design. Some of the operations are carried out by the teacher; others are carried out by one or more students. Exhibit 11.4 shows the major operations within the Sport Education model and indicates who is responsible for completing them during each lesson.

Teacher and student roles and responsibilities in Sport Education.	**EXHIBIT 11.4**
OPERATION OR RESPONSIBILITY	**PERSON/PEOPLE RESPONSIBLE IN SPORT EDUCATION**
Decide on the sport for each season	The **teacher** can decide or give **students** a list of choices to select from.
Organize the season	The **teacher** provides the basic structure and then lets **students** determine specific rules and procedures. Typically, students elect a "sport council" that makes many of the rules for the season.
Select captains and teams	The **teacher** establishes some ground rules and lets students (or the sport council) determine procedures.
Determine rules and game modifications	**Students** (the sport council) can make suggestions for the teacher to approve.
Organize and conduct team practices	**Student coaches/captains** are responsible (**teacher** can be used as a resource).
Prepare teams for competitions and coach them during games	**Student coaches/captains** are responsible (**teacher** can be used as a resource).
Train students for duty jobs	The **teacher** serves as the key resource. Outside personnel (e.g., certified officials) can also be used.
Bring equipment, prepare the playing area, return equipment	**Student** managers are responsible.
Officiate games	**Student** referees are responsible.
Keep score and maintain season records	**Student** statisticians are responsible.
Assess learning	1. **Student coaches/captains** evaluate their players. 2. **Student** statisticians can analyze players' performance with game stats.

Verification of Instructional Processes

Since Sport Education uses a combination of direct instruction, cooperative learning, and peer teaching, it can be difficult at times to determine exactly what the teacher and/or students should be doing to implement the model according to its design. However, there are benchmarks within the general framework of the model that can be used to help Sport Education teachers know if they are staying within its parameters. Exhibits 11.5 and 11.6 list these benchmarks.

Because students take on the roles of player and a duty job, separate benchmarks are needed to verify each type of participation. The tables in Exhibit 11.6 show some useful benchmarks for each role.

EXHIBIT 11.5 Sport Education teacher benchmarks.

BENCHMARK	HOW TO VERIFY
Teacher provides the overall structure for the season.	1. Review the teacher's unit (season) plan. 2. Review the teacher's goals and objectives.
Teacher interacts with students to determine specific season structure, rules, and game modifications.	1. Review teacher's unit (season) plans. 2. Interview a small group of students to get their perspective.
Teacher assigns students to duty jobs or allows students to determine them.	1. Review teacher's unit (season) plans. 2. Interview a small group of students to get their perspective.
Teacher supervises the selection of teams for competitive balance.	1. Review teacher's unit (season) plans. 2. Interview a small group of students to get their perspective.
Teacher trains students to perform duty jobs proficiently.	1. Review teacher's unit (season) plans. 2. Teacher writes a "job description" for each duty role. 3. Teacher designs and implements assessments for all jobs.
Teacher promotes cooperative learning when teams are practicing and competing.	Observe the teacher's interactions with students. Are the interactions mostly indirect, with a problem-solving approach?
Teacher arbitrates disputes.	Observe teacher's interactions when disputes arise.
Teacher plans for player performance assessments.	1. Review teacher's unit (season) plans. 2. Teacher designs assessments for key performance objectives; assessments can be implemented by the teacher and/or student coaches.
Teacher promotes enthusiastic participation.	1. Review teacher's unit (season) plans. 2. Teacher maintains a list of plans and ideas for keeping students enthusiastic.

Sport Education student benchmarks.	EXHIBIT 11.6

PLAYER BENCHMARK	**HOW TO VERIFY**
Players are competent.	1. Monitor performance on teacher-designed assessments of game skills and knowledge. 2. Use the GPAI (Griffin, Mitchell, & Oslin, 1997) to assess game performance. (See Chapter 14.)
Players are literate.	1. Players can pass a test on rules, history, and game traditions. 2. Players demonstrate nuances of the game (clothing, selection of equipment, etiquette, appreciation of quality performance).
Players understand strategy.	1. Teams can plan and implement appropriate strategy and tactics from a cooperative approach. 2. Players can interpret a scouting report. 3. Players can correctly analyze game-summary statistics.
Players are enthusiastic.	Observe to monitor events that represent enthusiastic participation (cheering, celebrating, on-field hustling).
Players work cooperatively on their teams.	Monitor interactions on teams with event-recording systems.
Players display good sporting behavior.	1. Monitor games for examples of positive and negative sporting behavior. 2. Appoint students to duty jobs as "good sport checkers"; they record instances of good sporting behavior and make brief reports at the end of class.

DUTY JOB BENCHMARK	**HOW TO VERIFY**
Students can select their own duty jobs (or are informed why not).	Interview students after jobs have been assigned. Do they feel that they were given a chance to get the job they wanted?
Students are knowledgeable.	1. Students receive training in all duty jobs. 2. All students pass a written or oral test on their specific job.
Students can perform the skills of their duty job.	1. Students receive training in all duty jobs. 2. All students pass a practical/performance test on their specific job.
Students can carry out duty jobs with little supervision from the teacher.	1. Each duty job has a daily checklist for all responsibilities. 2. Teacher observes and records students as they complete each job (spot checks are OK). 3. Teacher monitors the number and types of questions students have about their jobs as the season progresses.
Students can resolve conflicts during duty jobs (e.g., officiating) independently.	Teacher monitors the number and types of disputes brought to him or the sport council.

Assessment of Learning

Assessment in Sport Education must include outcomes for both key roles that students perform during the season: as players and in their duty jobs. Assessment in both must reflect the major goals of the Sport Education model: to be competent, literate, and enthusiastic participants (Siedentop, 1994). In order to assess those goals properly, it will be necessary to use a variety of assessments, most of which should be authentic in nature.

Assessing players

Learning to be players in sport requires several types of knowledge and abilities: basic skills, knowledge of rules and strategies, game performance and tactics, team membership, and good sporting behavior. Some of these can be assessed in traditional ways, but most will require the teacher to design innovative, authentic assessments to monitor student learning.

1. *Basic skills* can be assessed with simple checklists implemented by student coaches and teammates. One player can perform the skill while another student observes for key performance cues completed to a stated level of proficiency.

2. *Knowledge of rules and strategies* can be assessed with short written tests or quizzes that cover the main rules to be used in the season. It is important that the rules being assessed match the way in which the rules will apply to the competition. It makes little sense to assess students on the official game rules when modified rules and competitions will be used in the season.

3. *Game performance and tactics* can be assessed in a few ways, but it is important that the assessments take place during actual games. Game statistics taken by the duty job scorekeepers can be used as one type of assessment when they accurately reflect the performance requirements of each player's position. Checklists can be made for each player (by position) that represent good performance, and other duty job scorekeepers can observe for checklist elements as the game progresses. A version of the Game Performance Assessment Instrument (GPAI) (Griffin, Mitchell, & Oslin, 1997) can be devised for the game being played and duty job students trained to use it. The GPAI is a checklist system that monitors a player's positioning, execution, decisions, and involvement to determine an overall Game Performance Index. Since it is used only during games, it is an authentic assessment technique. The GPAI is described fully in Chapter 14.

4. *Team membership* can be assessed by observing interactions between players and the student coach throughout the season. A checklist of behaviors that reflect positive participation on the team can be devised, with team members filling it out periodically on themselves and each other. The teacher can review these reports in order to head off potential problems and reinforce good team membership contributions.

5. *Good sporting behavior* can be assessed in at least three ways. The teacher and students can compile a list of good sporting behaviors for the particular sport before the season begins. Teams can complete the checklist during the preseason in much the same way as they do the team membership checklist— on themselves and on fellow team members. Teams can complete the checklist on other teams at the end of games during the season. Hicks (1998) trained students in the duty job role of "Good Sport Checkers" during games. The Good Sport Checkers watched from the sideline and recorded each instance of positive sporting behavior they saw or heard from either team. They would record things like, "The Bulldogs walked over right after the game to shake hands with the Eagles" or "Jimmy (Hawks) helped Paul (Yellowjackets) up when he fell during the game" or "Melissa told Danielle (teammates), 'good job, keep trying' when she missed her first three shots." The recorders would then make brief reports after each game was completed.

Assessing duty job roles

Students trained to do duty jobs must show adequate knowledge of how their job works, how to execute the necessary procedures and techniques, and, most important, how to fulfill decision-making responsibilities during actual competition. Each kind of knowledge will call for a different assessment technique.

1. *Job knowledge* should be assessed before the season begins to ensure that students have the rudimentary knowledge of their assigned job. Officials must know the rules and how to conduct a competition; scorekeepers must know the definitions of key performance statistics; managers must know how the playing area should be prepared (lined, measured, cleaned), what equipment is needed for a game, and how to check that the equipment is functioning properly. The student coaches must have the broadest scope of knowledge: how to evaluate players' abilities, how to assign positions, how to conduct practices, and how to devise game strategies. All of these areas of knowledge can be assessed with written and/or oral tests before the season begins. If students do not possess this fundamental knowledge when the season begins, things can get off to an uneven start and take several classes to be cleared up.

2. All jobs require students to *execute certain techniques* that reflect competent performance and make the game operate smoothly. Officials need to know how to signal calls; coaches need to know how to signal time-outs or plays to their team; scorekeepers need to know when and how to make accurate records; and managers need to know how to use tools and equipment safely and efficiently. This knowledge can be assessed by asking students to demonstrate techniques as the teacher uses a checklist to note key parameters of the task. These techniques can be assessed in static tasks (simply demonstrating for the teacher) and during preseason games (allowing the teacher to make corrections right on the spot).

3. In the final analysis, it is most important that students *fulfill decision-making responsibilities of their assigned duty jobs during actual games.* That

represents the most authentic assessment of their knowledge, techniques, and decision making in an assigned role. The teacher can devise a short checklist for each duty job and use it to monitor student performance during games. It would also be possible to have each student fill out the checklist after each match, for a self-assessment.

IMPLEMENTATION NEEDS AND MODIFICATIONS

Teacher Expertise

Sport Education teachers will need to have good expertise in many of the knowledge areas discussed in Chapter 3. The teacher's expertise is brought to bear on the delivery of what Knop and Pope (1998) call "educative sport" (p. 47) in physical education—a merging of the competitive sport structure and developmentally appropriate instruction.

Learners. Sport Education students must be able to learn three very different roles: player, teammate, and assigned duty job. Each role makes different demands on students' psychomotor, cognitive, and affective abilities. The Sport Education teacher must be well aware of how much students will be able to learn in each role, not letting expectations exceed those levels.

Developmentally appropriate instruction. Closely related to a teacher's knowledge about her learners is the ability to promote developmentally appropriate versions of sport for each physical education class. The Sport Education model rarely implies that students must learn "full" or "adult" versions of a sport (Siedentop, 1994). Game structures are simplified, rules are modified, record keeping is kept at a level students can follow and get down on paper, the teacher ensures a positive and safe environment, and duty assignments match student maturity levels—all so that students can learn the sport at their current stage of development.

Physical education (sport) content. Even though a teacher takes a more facilitative role in Sport Education, his knowledge of the season's sport form (game) is invaluable. The teacher must not only know the sport from a player's perspective but he must also know each of the various duty jobs, the sport's organizational structures, and its customs. Since most of the decisions will be made by students as the season progresses, the teacher must be able to see the big picture and anticipate potentially harmful situations before they occur. All of that comes from knowing the sport well and from many perspectives.

Equity. Sport does not work well when equity issues are not fully addressed and resolved. In fact, if inequities are left alone, sport will become miseducative and counterproductive to its own goals and objectives. Inequities arise when the sport environment allows one group of students more access to full participation than other groups of students. This inequity can be based on differences related to gender, ethnicity, or ability. The Sport Education teacher must be able to anticipate, recognize, and adjust inequitable situations so that all students get a similar chance to participate and learn through sport. Equity can be promoted by making rules and policies that give all students a fair chance to participate, such as:

1. All players must play every position (each game or on a set schedule).
2. Team rules are voted on by all members.
3. All players get to play the same amount of time each game.

Related to the issue of equity is fairness of competition. Once again, the teacher must use her knowledge of the students, the game, and the democratic process to select fair teams for the season. And the teacher must be ready to make adjustments when the teams are obviously not balanced for competition. Some suggestions for achieving fairness could be:

1. Make provisions that all teams must have the same number of boys and girls on them, according to how many of each gender are in the class.
2. Ask students to rate their own skill levels, and make provisions that teams will be balanced on that factor as well as on gender.
3. Allow all students to review the teams before they are finalized and to indicate if they think the teams are fair.
4. Conduct a limited "trading" procedure shortly after the season begins, allowing each team to change only one player from the current roster. All "trades" must be approved by a majority of members of both involved teams *and* the players to be traded.

Assessment. Sport Education relies heavily on authentic assessment of student performance, knowledge, and behaviors. In one sense, Sport Education is entirely authentic because it always provides students with a realistic context (a team and season) in which they prepare and apply their abilities. To monitor players' game play, teachers can design systems that the trained statisticians use to create records of each player's performance on key aspects. Keeping those records over the course of the season provides a clear picture for assessing each player's performance. Checklists can be made to assess student performance of duty jobs—much like a job description. The teacher can observe a student as she does her job and check off each completed part each time. Watts (1998) got students to check themselves each day after their jobs were completed, freeing the teacher to do other things as class ended.

The key source of assessment knowledge in Sport Education is the ability to recognize the most important aspects of playing and duty job performance. Once a teacher has identified those, she can then design self-made systems for monitoring performance in the most authentic way—as students apply their own knowledge and skills in the context of the season and competitive events.

Positive social climate. If you will recall, one of the key features of Sport Education cited by Siedentop (1994) is that it should be festive. The festive nature of sport should emphasize the positive, allow all students to participate and enjoy fully, strive for keen and fair competition, and promote the highest standards of good sport behavior. The Sport Education teacher must know how to arrange a social climate in the sport season to allow these things to happen—and to prevent the opposites from occurring. At various times, the teacher will find himself being mentor, arbitrator, coach, parent, sport psychologist, and cheerleader—all for the purpose of creating a positive climate in the Sport Education season.

Key Teaching Skills

With the combination of direct instruction, cooperative learning, and peer teaching, the Sport Education teacher will use a wide range of effective instructional skills in the model. The key point to understand is that each skill will be applied spontaneously—in most cases, as the teacher addresses situational needs during the season.

Planning. Most of the planning occurs once the teacher and/or students have decided which game will be played in the Sport Education season. That will lead to an intense period of formal planning for the teacher, followed by a longer period in which plans must be updated regularly as the season progresses. The initial planning period will determine the overall structure of the upcoming season and include many considerations:

1. How long will the season last?
2. What equipment and facilities will be needed?
3. What modifications, if any, will be made in the game?
4. What will be the competitive format?
5. How will teams be selected?
6. What duty jobs are needed, and how will students be selected for them?
7. How will students be trained for duty jobs?
8. If there is to be a "sport council," how will it be selected?
9. What is the season's schedule?
10. How will playing and duty job performance be assessed?
11. How will each lesson/practice be structured?
12. What kind of award system will be in place?

Once the overall structure has been determined and teams are preparing for the season, formal planning will shift to an as-needed and sometimes unpredictable kind of planning. Jones and Ward (1998) suggest that the teacher plan only an outline for each class and allow teams to make their own preseason and practice structure. The teacher's job is to know what teams will need each day and make sure those things are provided. Once the competitive schedule begins, the teacher's main planning responsibilities are to organize the duty students (some of whom bring the needed equipment and prepare the space), allocate time for games, and prepare assessment materials. Beyond that, little can be planned for; most of the teacher's decisions and actions will occur in real time as class events unfold.

Time and class management. The teacher needs to provide the overall plan for each class and competitive event, but most of the class management will be left to students after practices and the season begin. The teacher's main responsibility is to ensure that schedules are being met, so that the competitive season does not get behind.

Determining developmentally appropriate nonplaying roles. As mentioned earlier, most of the task presentations and structure will be determined by students as each team prepares for the season. However, the teacher still maintains the responsibility for training students for duty jobs that are essential to the season's operation. The key thing for the teacher to remember is that students are being trained for roles typically assumed by adults in most sport settings: coaches, managers, trainers, and scorekeepers. The teacher must understand how much of each role students can learn and the best way to teach it to them. Many times, tasks cannot be presented in "official" or adult versions; they must be presented to students in terms they can understand and relate to. Similarly, most students will not be able to perform the technical aspects of a job like a trained adult, so the teacher must show them developmentally acceptable ways to "get the job done."

Communication. Sport Education teachers need to be effective at both direct and indirect communications to students. Teachers will be more direct when they are explaining the organization of the season and when they are training students for duty job roles. Much of that communication resembles what is used in direct instruction.

Teachers will also need good indirect communication skills, most often in the form of questions. While teams are practicing and students are in duty jobs, it is better to encourage a problem-solving approach to learning, prompted more by questions than by direct statements or instructions.

Instructional information. As with task presentation and task structure, the operations for providing students with instructional information will differ between learning as players and learning duty job roles. For players, nearly all the instructional information will come through cooperative learning and peer teaching. Students (as coaches and teammates) will observe each other perform and provide the needed guidance and feedback to promote proficiency. For duty job roles, most of the instructional information will come from the teacher, who is typically both trainer and supervisor.

Review and closure. The review and closure segments serve familiar purposes in Sport Education lessons. In the preseason, the teacher can make general comments about how teams are progressing and answer questions from individual students and teams. The teacher can also preview the next day's lesson to allow teams to interact out of class if they wish to. During the competitive part of the season, the teacher uses the review and closure segment to summarize the major events and outcomes and to give deserving players and teams public recognition for good play and good sport behaviors. Hicks (1998) used "Good Sport

Checkers" in her fourth-grade ultimate Frisbee season, asking the monitors to make brief reports of positive and negative sport behaviors at the review. When entire teams went the whole lesson with no observations of negative sport behavior, a smiley face was placed on a poster, and they were given an extra point in the season's standings. The closure part of the lesson can allow the assigned duty students to gather up and store the equipment in its proper place while the rest of the students are dismissed or take a rest break.

Contextual Requirements

To implement Sport Education with an acceptable version of the model, three contextual factors must be considered: (1) resources, (2) students, and (3) competition format. At some point, all three become related and must be given an "OK" by the teacher before she decides if Sport Education is an appropriate way to instruct a content unit.

1. *Resources*. When considering resources, the teacher must be sure that sufficient time (lesson days), equipment, and space are available to allow the model to work properly. Grant (1992) suggests no fewer than 20 lessons be allocated for a Sport Education season. Although this seems excessive when compared with the current length of most physical education units, this model relies heavily on the cumulative benefits derived from extended practice, many scheduled competitions, and longer affiliation on teams. Teachers will need enough equipment and space to allow all teams to practice at one time and to hold concurrent games, as the number of teams warrants. Demands for these two types of resources can be reduced by using small-sided teams (e.g., three vs. three basketball, four vs. four soccer) and modified rules (e.g., four-inning softball games).

2. *Students*. Students are asked to assume some of the major managerial, instructional, and assessment operations in Sport Education. The teacher must be sure that the students can handle these responsibilities before selecting this model for physical education. The number of students in a class is also a consideration in determining which sport forms are possible in a season. Small classes will be limited to individual and small-team sports (e.g., tennis or racquetball doubles, or three vs. three volleyball or basketball), while larger classes can play full or larger-sided games (e.g., five vs. five basketball, six vs. six volleyball, flag football).

3. *Competition format*. The competition format refers to the kind of competition scheduled for the Sport Education season. Typical formats are single league, with all teams playing each other; divisions, with teams playing within their division until the play-offs; ladders, in which individuals/teams climb ahead of those they beat and stay there until they lose to a lower-ranked team; and "triangles," in which three teams compete at the same time (e.g., track and field meets). The possible formats will depend on the previous two factors, based on the number of teams and available space for competitions.

Selecting and Modifying Sport Education

Sport Education is one of the few instructional models presented in this book that was developed exclusively for physical education programs. Siedentop (1994) and others (Tannehill, 1998) describe many examples of how Sport Education has been implemented at every grade level from middle-elementary to college. It has proven a viable instructional model for a wide variety of sport forms, including:

1. Individual sports (regulation and modified)
2. Team sports (regulation and modified)
3. Fitness programs
4. Olympic-based festivals

Grade-level adaptation

Sport Education can work in any setting in which the students are able to assume a developmentally appropriate amount of decision making and other responsibilities in order to foster the many outcomes embedded in the model. Adaptations must be based on the students' abilities as players (performers and team members) and their ability to assume the duty job roles that are essential to the functioning of the Sport Education season. Sport Education will not be effective in reaching its overall goals if the teacher must take a direct role too often. Exhibit 11.7 shows possible ways to adapt this model for different grade levels.

Grade-level adaptations for Sport Education in physical education.		EXHIBIT 11.7
GRADE LEVELS	**SELECT SPORT EDUCATION?**	**POSSIBLE ADAPTATIONS**
Preschool	No	
Early elementary (1–3)	No	
Upper elementary (4–5)	Yes	1. Teacher decides much of the season's structure. 2. Game rules and procedures are modified (shorter games, small-sided games). 3. Teacher supervises team selections and the decisions of the sport council. 4. Student duty jobs are simple to learn and carry out. 5. Teacher organizes team or whole-class practice sessions each lesson.
Middle school/junior high	Yes	1. Game rules and procedures are modified. 2. Teacher monitors decisions of the sport council.
High school	Yes	None needed.
College/adult	Yes	None needed.

Adaptations to accommodate diverse groups of learners

Sport Education can be a highly inclusive model for physical education if the teacher clearly establishes the parameters for student decision making and responsibility and provides authentic ways for students to learn as players and in their duty roles. Exhibit 11.8 lists some strategies that address a variety of special learning needs found in many schools today.

PLANNING TIPS FOR SPORT EDUCATION

Teachers who choose to use the Sport Education model can benefit by following a few additional planning tips.

1. Allow students as much decision making and responsibility as they can handle. The more ownership they have in the season's success, the more they will be motivated to reach their goals. The same goes for deciding duty jobs. When students have more choice in selecting and performing a job, they will be more motivated to learn and do it well.

2. Provide students with clear parameters for their decision making and responsibility. Some decisions will remain with the teacher, and those are to be made clear to the students.

3. Do not allow team selection to be a public process; this has the potential to harm those same children who get harmed when "captains" choose teams in the traditional way.

4. Regardless of who chooses the teams, make sure they are as mixed and fair as possible in the key grouping factors: skill level, gender, race/ethnicity, cognitive development, creativity, leadership/followership, mastery of English, and so on. When students view the teams as being fair, they will concentrate more on their own team's progress and be less concerned with other teams.

5. After teams have been assigned, do not allow students to focus on what their team *lacks*; get them to focus on the unique abilities of each team member and to work with those to achieve the team's goals.

6. Allow students to determine age-appropriate versions of sport that allow them a better participatory experience (e.g., three-on-three basketball, reduced-field soccer).

7. Find ways to make the season look and feel like a true sport league season: planning structured practices, having team nicknames, announcing games in the school newspaper or on a website, posting results for all students to see, and, most importantly, keeping a festive atmosphere.

8. Keep the responsibilities of the duty roles authentic so that students experience the full range of learning, decisions, problems, and rewards inherent to those jobs.

| Strategies adapting Sport Education for diverse groups of learners. | EXHIBIT | 11.8 |

FOR STUDENTS WITH HEARING AND/OR SPEECH IMPAIRMENTS:

1. Select season content that will not put such students at a disadvantage as players or subject them to potential harm in a duty role responsibility.
2. Encourage students with speech impairments to devise creative ways to carry out their duty roles effectively (e.g., using a red flag to indicate a "strike" and a green flag to indicate a "ball" when umpiring softball).
3. Encourage teams to develop hand signals to call plays on the field or court.

FOR STUDENTS WITH SIGHT IMPAIRMENTS:

1. Encourage physically active duty role assignments, not those that require keen vision, such as entering game statistics on a small scorecard.
2. Use modified equipment (e.g., "beeper" soccer balls) that can be tracked by students with impaired sight.
3. Encourage teams to develop creative verbal signals to call plays on the field or court.

FOR STUDENTS WITH PHYSICAL DISABILITIES:

1. Adapt rules and/or equipment to promote higher levels of performance for all students.
2. Encourage less physically active duty role assignments, such as team coach or trainer.

FOR STUDENTS WHO DO NOT SPEAK ENGLISH:

1. Use student translators, when available. Put matching bilingual students on the same team with non-English speakers.
2. Provide task presentations in appropriate language, or use translated closed-caption media when possible.
3. Select season content that reflects the interests of students from many cultures, not just traditional American sports.

FOR LOWER-SKILLED STUDENTS:

1. Enact rules that allow all players to assume key positions during the course of the season.
2. Allow for extra points to be scored when all members of the team contribute to success (e.g., adding one point to a basket that has been scored after all five players touched the ball on that possession).
3. Provide extra encouragement and praise.
4. Encourage teams to think about ways to involve all members.

FOR STUDENTS WITH BEHAVIOR DISABILITIES:

1. Provide students with behavior disabilities with extra encouragement for their participation.
2. Allow for extra team points when everyone participates in a positive way (e.g., every five "good behavior points" earned by a team count as one more "win" for their season's record).
3. Focus on the contribution to be made by students with behavior disabilities, not the potential for misbehavior.

UNIT AND LESSON PLAN EXAMPLES FOR SPORT EDUCATION INSTRUCTION

Y ou will find several complete season unit/lesson plans for Sport Education on the IMPE website. It is not recommended that you follow these examples exactly as they are presented. The context, specific learning objectives, and content of your own unit will require you to make changes in these examples to allow the Sport Education model to lead to the most effective instruction in your situation.

SUMMARY

The effectiveness of the Sport Education model can often be a "moving target," as it requires the teacher to make many on-the-spot decisions that cannot necessarily be anticipated—very much like sport competition itself. This model calls for a complex balancing act of the teacher facilitating student responsibility and learning without inadvertently allowing some of the miseducative aspects of sport to emerge during the season. The teacher can guide and monitor the structure of the season, but much of the Sport Education process happens in the minute-to-minute interactions between team members and opponents, leaving the teacher to make an instant judgment as to whether those interactions promote or inhibit competent, literate, and enthusiastic participation. Knop and Pope (1998) sum it up well:

> A complete Sport Education program should teach students how to compete, how to win and lose, how to understand the sport culture, how to prepare for participation, and how to analyze sport in a variety of settings. . . . For this to occur, all students need to have opportunities presented in a safe, controlled environment. The responsibility for selecting, planning, sequencing, and delivering this kind of [instruction] falls on the teachers' shoulders. At the same time, teachers must build student accountability into the plan and determine how to reward student involvement in their own learning. (p. 48)

Despite some of the criticisms directed at competitive sport on all levels, the educational potential of positive sport experience remains powerful. There are few human endeavors that can promote the variety of learning and developmental activities inherent in sport. The Sport Education model should be viewed as a means of recapturing the most positive attributes of our sport culture in order to teach them to the next generation of sport participants, our children and youth.

LEARNING ACTIVITIES

1. Make a list of five activity units (e.g., movement skills, fitness, softball, tennis, golf) that might be taught in a physical education program. Next, determine an appropriate grade level (P, K–2, 3–5, 6–8, 9–12) for teach-

ing each of those activity units. Now, write two major learning outcomes for those units. Then, go through the process of selecting an instructional model, shown in Chapter 2, to determine if Sport Education would be an appropriate model for teaching that activity to children at that grade level.

2. If Sport Education is appropriate for that activity, grade, and goals, mention three things that make it appropriate. If Sport Education is not appropriate for that activity, grade, and goals, mention three things that make it inappropriate.

3. Write an annotated lesson plan for a complete Sport Education season. Be sure to include all the decisions that must be made in all four parts of the season: organization and practice period, preseason, regular season, and a post-season or culminating event.

4. Write an assessment plan for all duty roles to be assigned in your Sport Education season.

TOPICS FOR REFLECTION & SMALL-GROUP DISCUSSION

1. I have suggested in this chapter how the Sport Education model is aligned to achieve one or more of the NASPE standards. Take a moment to review those alignments (refer back to Exhibit 11.1). After that, make some notes about whether you agree with those alignments, and then share them in your small group. When you have arrived at your final thoughts, please share them on the IMPE website Forum for others to review, and check back for replies.

2. Mention three ways Sport Education is similar to Direct Instruction and three ways it is different.

3. In general, which types of students are placed at an advantage in this model, and which students are at a disadvantage?

4. Why is it so important to allow students to make, and be responsible for, decisions in this model?

5. Why do you think many physical education teachers are attracted to the Sport Education model? What about it makes you willing to try it?

SUGGESTED READINGS FOR SPORT EDUCATION

Bulger, S. M., Mohr, D. J., Rairigh, R. M., & Townsend, J. S. (2007). *Sport education seasons.* Champaign, IL: Human Kinetics.

Siedentop, D. (1994). *Sport education: Quality PE through positive sport experiences.* Champaign, IL: Human Kinetics.

Siedentop, D., Hastie, P. A., & van der Mars, H. (2011). *The complete guide to sport education* (2nd ed.). Champaign, IL: Human Kinetics.

Tannehill, D. (Ed.) (1998). Sport education. Two-part feature presented in the *Journal of Physical Education, Recreation & Dance,* May (Vol. 69, No. 4) and June (Vol. 69, No. 5).

Townsend, S. J., Mohr, D. J., Rairigh, R. M., & Bulger, S. M. (2003). *Assessing student outcomes in sport education.* Reston, VA: National Association for Sport and Physical Education.

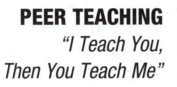

PEER TEACHING
*"I Teach You,
Then You Teach Me"*

T hink back to when you were a child, trying to learn all of the many things children learn outside the formal schooling process. Besides your parents, who were your most frequent teachers? Most likely your friends, playmates, and siblings first taught you many of the basic social, communication, cognitive, and psychomotor skills that you took into and through your early years in school. You probably learned how to play sports, ride a bicycle, jump rope, sing songs, and play games like hopscotch by being told how and shown by your siblings and friends. It is rare for adults to be around while children play during the day in their neighborhood, so young people rely on each other to teach them how to do the many things they learn as they grow up. Even in school, you probably still learned much from your fellow students, although most of your academic teaching was carried out by your teachers. We have known for a long time that children can teach other children and that in some ways those peer teachers can be as or more effective than adult teachers. Wagner (1990) presents a history of Peer Teaching that begins as early as the classical Greek period with Aristotle and extends uninterrupted into modern-day educational settings. Peer Teaching takes many forms and is conducted under a variety of labels, but its most fundamental feature is clear: to structure a learning environment in which some students assume and carry out many of the key operations of instruction, directly, assisting other students in the learning process.

The Peer Teaching model evolved from a number of teaching strategies that share the common feature of students helping other students learn. Many of these Peer Teaching strategies were developed as variations within Direct Instruction, so the basic operations of these models are often similar—differing mainly in who carries them out in class.

Three concepts related to the Peer Teaching model need to be clarified and kept in mind throughout this chapter. First, the Peer Teaching model obviously relies on strategies that use students to teach other students, but it becomes the Peer Teaching model *only* when a teacher plans for and follows a model-based approach—like the one presented in this chapter. Second, Peer Teaching is not the same as *partner learning,* in which students are paired together for one or more learning activities to learn "side by side." In order for instruction to be Peer Teaching, one student must be given the explicit responsibility to carry out several key instructional operations normally assumed by the teacher. There must be a clear tutor–learner role delineation, even though those roles can be reversed on a regular basis. Third, Peer Teaching is not to be misinterpreted as Cooperative Learning (Chapter 10) on a smaller scale. True, Cooperative Learning does feature students teaching other students, but that model uses a very different overall plan and places students into small "teams" that stay together for an entire content unit. Also, in Cooperative Learning, students most often learn together rather than actually teach each other.

The most recognizable version of Peer Teaching in physical education is Mosston and Ashworth's (2002) Reciprocal Style, in which one student is designated as the Observer (the tutor) and the other student is designated as the Doer (the learner). This style does maintain the most essential feature of Peer Teaching, but it is meant to be used as a temporary task structure and is not usually designed as the only instructional strategy in a content unit. Physical education teachers have been using the Reciprocal Style strategy for many years, but it differs somewhat from the Peer Teaching model presented in this chapter.

OVERVIEW

As mentioned earlier, the Peer Teaching model can be considered a variation of Direct Instruction. As you learned in Chapter 8, Direct Instruction places the teacher in charge of making and implementing nearly all content, managerial, task, and instructional decisions in a unit and lesson. In the Peer Teaching model, the teacher retains control over all of those same elements, except one: instructional interactions that occur during and after students' learning trials. That important responsibility is delegated to students called tutors, who have been trained to observe and analyze other students' practice attempts.

The reality for most physical education teachers is that because they have a large number of students in a class, it is practically impossible to directly observe every practice attempt made by every student as it occurs. Even when a teacher achieves a high feedback rate, each individual student is likely to receive only a few feedback comments in a lesson. To illustrate the point even more, let's assume that a teacher gives performance feedback in class at the rate of 2 per minute in a 30-minute lesson with 40 students. That means he makes a total of 60 feedback statements during the entire class. So, if those feedback comments are evenly distributed, each student would receive only 1.5 feedbacks *per class* from the teacher. If, say, each student averaged 30 skill attempts in class, only 5 percent of those attempts would have been observed by the teacher and given performance feedback. Even though there is some debate over the role of performance feedback in the learning process in physical education (Rink, 2003), it would be difficult to think that student learning would occur faster with so little feedback.

Terminology in the Peer Teaching model can sometimes be confusing. To reduce the potential for confusion, let's differentiate among four terms that will be used frequently in this chapter:

1. *Tutor:* A specific student temporarily assigned the role of teacher

2. *Learner:* A specific student who practices under the observation and supervision of a tutor

3. *Dyad:* A tutor–learner pair

4. *Student:* The general term used to describe students in class when they are not in the role of tutor or learner

The Peer Teaching model is based on an accepted trade-off intended to reduce the problem of too little teacher observation of practice attempts and very limited feedback received by students. Actual *opportunities to respond* (OTR) in class are essentially cut in half in the Peer Teaching model, since each student spends approximately one-half of the activity time as a tutor and approximately one-half practicing as a learner. However, when in the learner's role, each student in effect has a private tutor to observe and analyze each practice attempt—increasing the effectiveness of that learning time. And, when in that role, the tutor cognitively engages in a way that can increase her own comprehension of the task, thereby contributing to improved practice when it is her turn. Even though students typically get fewer OTR in Peer Teaching, the increased effectiveness of practice time will allow the teacher to cover considerably more, not less, content in a unit of instruction.

Proponents of Peer Teaching also point to the social learning that occurs within the model. Both members of the dyad become dependent on each other in ways that do not occur in other teaching models. The tutor must pay close attention to the task presentation and task structure given by the teacher, apply good concentration when observing skill attempts, have good verbal communication skills when giving cues and feedback, and be sensitive to the abilities and feelings of his temporary charge. The learner must be willing to accept the tutor's comments, to ask questions when the tutor is not clear, and to practice diligently under direct observation of each attempt. As students alternate between these two roles in class, they begin to develop a relationship based on a shared level of responsibility not given to them in most other teaching models.

The Peer Teaching model also has great potential to enhance students' cognitive development in physical education. In order to be a good tutor, a student must grasp key performance cues and understand the relationship between those cues and the outcome of each practice attempt. Using golf as an example, it is not helpful for the tutor to simply state the obvious: "Your shot went off to the right." The tutor must be able to identify the source of mistakes and provide good learning cues for the next attempt: "It went to the right because you lifted your head on the backswing, and that caused you to open the club face. Be sure to keep your head down throughout the whole swing next time." In essence, the tutor is developing problem-solving skills that can improve his own level of understanding and performance of movement skills.

One of the things that makes Peer Teaching an instructional model and not just partner learning is the degree to which the tutors are prepared and trained for their role as teacher-of-the-moment. In order for the model to be most effective, the teacher must help tutors understand and carry out the operations for which they will assume responsibility. It is not simply telling one student to "go teach" another student. A good training plan for the tutoring role should include:

1. Clarification of the learning objectives
2. Expectations of tutors (what they should and should not do)
3. Task presentation and check for understanding
4. Task structure and check for understanding
5. How to communicate errors to learners
6. How to provide praise appropriately
7. How to practice safely
8. How to assess mastery or task completion
9. Knowing when to ask questions of the teacher

Keep in mind that the Peer Teaching model calls for the tutors to lead only a small portion of the instructional process; the teacher retains much of the decision making and leadership—much like the Direct Instruction model. Research by Ellis and Rogoff (1986) suggests that many students are not capable of seeing the big picture in a content unit, nor are they able to orchestrate more than a small portion of the complex learning environment. Tutors can carry out some of the teacher's plans for instructional operations, but the tutors are rarely able to make those plans on their own. Ellis and Rogoff report that tutors could handle only two of the three key instructional components typically carried out by the teacher: task management, instructional information, and social management. Therefore, the tutor's role is probably best limited to receiving directions from the teacher and acting as the teacher's proxy in tasks with limited time and complexity. However, that limitation should in no way keep a teacher from selecting the Peer Teaching model in physical education. Due to the nature of many physical education learning activities, the tutor's ability to "be the teacher's eyes, ears, and voice" in directly observing the learner's practice attempts can serve a vital role in the learning process.

Greenwood, Carta, and Kamps (1990) compared the advantages of teacher-mediated and student-mediated instruction, and found that Peer Teaching fared quite favorably (see Exhibit 12.1). This analysis makes it clear that students can benefit greatly from engagement in the Peer Teaching model, despite some of the stated disadvantages. Actually, many of the disadvantages will be reduced or eliminated completely the more times a teacher uses this model and is able to anticipate some of the inherent problems.

In the end, the Peer Teaching model comes with the same stipulation as every other model in this book: when the model is selected to match a unit's learning goals, can meet the contextual demands for the unit, and is implemented according to the model's design, it will effectively increase student achievement of stated learning goals in physical education.

Comparing teacher-mediated and peer-mediated instruction.		EXHIBIT 12.1
TEACHER FACTOR	**TEACHER-MEDIATED**	**PEER-MEDIATED**
Advantages:		
Pupil/teacher ratio	High	Low
Engaged time	Variable	High
Opportunities to respond	Low	High
Opportunities for error correction	Low	High
Immediacy of error correction	Delayed	Immediate
Opportunities for help and encouragement	Few	Many
Opportunities for both competitive and cooperative learning experiences	Few	Many
Motivation	Teacher support	Peer plus teacher support
Disadvantages:		
Peer training requirements	Few	Many
Quality control requirements	Few	Many
Content coverage	Good	Variable
Peer selection	Not required	Required
Curriculum adaptations	Few	Many
Costs	High	Low
Ethical concerns	Few	Increased

From Greenwood, Carta, and Kamps (in Foot, Morgan, & Shute, 1990, p. 191)

ALIGNMENT WITH NASPE NATIONAL STANDARDS

E xhibit 12.2 shows the alignment of the Peer Teaching model with the NASPE standards. As you can see, Peer Teaching is consistently and strongly aligned with standards 1, 2, and 5. Its alignment with standards 3 and 4 will be strong in units that focus on fitness outcomes but not strong in units that focus on other learning outcomes. Its alignment with standard 6 depends on the match between the learning task of the moment and each of the components in this standard.

FOUNDATIONS

Theory and Rationale

To the degree that the Peer Teaching model is based on Direct Instruction, it shares much of the theory and rationale of Direct Instruction. That is, Peer Teaching is a mastery-based model that strives for high rates of student OTR,

EXHIBIT 12.2 Alignment of Peer Teaching with NASPE National Standards.

NASPE STANDARD	ALIGNMENT RATING	COMMENTS
1. Demonstrates competency in motor skills and movement patterns needed to perform a variety of physical activities	1	Achieved by better efficiency during practice time
2. Demonstrates understanding of movement concepts, principles, strategies, and tactics as they apply to the learning and performance of physical activities	1	Achieved when the tutor observes and analyzes the learner's practice attempts and provides feedback
3. Participates regularly in physical activity	1–3	Will vary according to the learning task of the moment
4. Achieves and maintains a health-enhancing level of physical fitness	2–3	Stronger alignment for fitness units when the tutor becomes a "personal trainer" for the learner
5. Exhibits responsible personal and social behavior that respects self and others in physical activity settings	1	Strong alignment due to the assignment of teaching responsibilities to the tutor
6. Values physical activity for health, enjoyment, challenge, self-expression, and/or social interaction	1–3	Strong alignment for enjoyment, challenge, self-expression, and social interaction; weak alignment for health, unless the content is fitness

Ratings categories:
1. Strong alignment
2. Moderate alignment
3. Weak alignment

high rates of augmented feedback (from tutors, not the teacher), and a brisk pacing through unit content. That way of structuring the teaching–learning process is founded on theories and principles of training developed by B. F. Skinner and other behavioral psychologists. However, the main feature of Peer Teaching, arranging for students to teach each other, originates from quite different theories of human learning, most notably those about social learning, cognitive development, and constructivism.

Social learning theory states that humans learn by interaction with their environment, especially interactions with other people. According to social learning theorists like Albert Bandura (1977), we learn from other people by imitating them, listening to them, talking to them, and observing the results of their own behavior. This theory is strongly based on behavioral psychology, with a particular emphasis on the role of other humans in the learning process. The formalization of tutor–learner interactions in the Peer Teaching model recognizes the important role other people play in our own learning.

The theories of noted cognitive developmentalist Jean Piaget also contribute to the rationale within the Peer Teaching model. Piaget theorized that humans progress through a series of stages in their development of intellectual abilities. We develop cognitive schemas that allow us to give meaning and structure to the world around us, and we progress through those stages in a rather predictable manner, based on physiological and environmental factors. According to cognitive learning theories, students who engage in shared learning develop problem-solving skills that foster intellectual development by requiring both tutor and learner to "figure out" more than they would in teacher-directed instruction. Just placing a student in the role of teacher/tutor presents an entirely new set of intellectual and social challenges that must be met in order to fulfill that role well.

Constructivist learning theory lends a third contribution to the theories that support the Peer Teaching model. Social constructivists place a strong emphasis on the process of learning, especially those processes that foster a democratic environment and allow students to use what they already know as the basis of interactions with peers. Therefore, social constructivists would support the one feature of the Peer Teaching model that separates it from Direct Instruction. However, the social constructivists would be much at odds with the rest of the Peer Teaching model, which places the teacher in a direct role at most times.

The fact that the Peer Teaching model draws from three different learning theories can be problematic for teachers who strongly believe in one view of learning over the others—unless they can come to recognize the commonalities among those theories and not allow the differences to deter them. The model's strength actually stems from those commonalities, as they merge for the benefit of student learning in all three domains: the psychomotor, the cognitive, and the affective.

The underlying rationale for the Peer Teaching model is rather simple. The teacher is able to use her content, managerial, and supervisory expertise to make the major planning decisions in a unit of instruction and in each lesson. Because one teacher is unable to observe and provide feedback for the large number of learners' practice attempts that can occur in physical education, students are trained and assigned to carry out those functions as tutors of other students (learners) who are engaged in practice attempts. The practicing learners get the benefit of increased instructional interactions that lead to improved learning. While carrying out the functions of teacher, the tutors engage intellectually and socially in ways that enhance development in the cognitive and affective domains. It is a win-win-win situation for all involved: the tutor, the learner, and the teacher.

Assumptions About Teaching and Learning

The Peer Teaching model assumes certain principles about teaching and about learning; these principles are listed separately below.

Assumptions about teaching

1. The teacher must retain control over many decisions related to unit content, class management, task presentation, and content progression in order to maximize the use of time and other resources.
2. The teacher can train tutors to carry out the key function of providing learners with instructional information.
3. The peer teaching dyad fosters development in all three domains.

Assumptions about learning

1. Learning in the psychomotor domain is facilitated by the increased monitoring and feedback provided by tutors.
2. Learning in the cognitive domain is facilitated for the tutors as they observe, analyze, and instruct practicing learners.
3. Affective/social learning is facilitated for both participants in the dyad as they assume differentiated roles in the teaching–learning process.
4. Tutors and learners develop problem-solving skills by having to work cooperatively to assist each other in completing assigned learning tasks.

The Major Theme of Peer Teaching: "I Teach You, Then You Teach Me"

As you already know, the basic task structure in the Peer Teaching model is for pairs of students, or dyads, to alternate in the roles of tutor and learner after the teacher has provided the task presentation. Essentially, one assumes the role of tutor and one assumes the role of learner for a short period of time; then they switch roles at the teacher's direction. Neither one is the tutor or learner on a permanent basis, so from their point of view, "I teach you, then you teach me" is an accurate theme for Peer Teaching.

Learning Domain Priorities and Domain Interactions

Domain priorities

Because students will assume two very different roles in the Peer Teaching model, it is necessary to discuss learning domain priorities and domain interactions from both perspectives. The model fosters learning in all three domains, but the type of learning that occurs will depend on which role a student is fulfilling at a particular moment. As learners, students will be engaged primarily in the psychomotor domain as they practice motor skill attempts in learning activities. It is possible for a teacher to use Peer Teaching for cognitive concepts, but that strategy would be somewhat inefficient since all students can learn the concepts at the same time, thus gaining nothing from peer instruction. So, for the learner in the Peer Teaching model, the domain priorities are typically:

First priority: Psychomotor learning

Second priority: Cognitive learning

Third priority: Affective/social learning

The second and third priorities for the learner are often reversed, as he interacts with the tutor to learn listening, trust, and other affective/social skills within the dyadic relationship.

As tutors, students will have different domain priorities in the Peer Teaching model. They will focus primarily on the cognitive components of the task: understanding the key performance cues given by the teacher, understanding the task structure demands, observing the learner's skill attempts for errors, and communicating the results of each skill attempt back to the learner in the form of feedback and cues for the next try. In trying to learn and carry out the momentary responsibilities of instruction, tutors strongly engage in the affective domain—learning about themselves and the needs of the learner. Though it is possible for the tutor to acquire some cognitive knowledge that can help her when it is her turn to practice, that link places the psychomotor domain third for the tutor in this model. So, the domain priorities for the tutor in the Peer Teaching model are typically:

First priority: Cognitive learning

Second priority: Affective/social learning

Third priority: Psychomotor learning

Domain interactions

The domain interaction for the learner in the Peer Teaching model works this way: He must accept and process verbal and modeled (cognitive) information from the tutor in order to master the current psychomotor task. Those processes have an "overlay" of affective/social interaction between the tutor and the learner that determines the atmosphere for those communications and impacts the learner's ability to master the task of the moment.

The domain interaction begins for tutors in the cognitive domain, as they acquire all of the task and content information needed for that role. It is when they provide instructional information to the learner that they must draw on affective/social and psychomotor knowledge to do that effectively. If the tutor is not sensitive to the learner's abilities and feelings, the learner is likely to ignore or reject the tutor's feedback. If the tutor cannot provide reasonably close models of the learner's mistakes and/or proper cues for the next trial, the learner will make slow or no progress. So, the tutor's cognitive knowledge will be the source of interactions with the learner, delivered through a combination of affective/social and psychomotor abilities.

Student Developmental Requirements

Student readiness for learning. As you just learned, many of the features of Peer Teaching must be discussed from two perspectives: that of the tutor and the learner. The same goes for student readiness to learn under this model. Tutors will need to be able to assume their specific responsibilities as teacher for short periods of time. They must be able to comprehend the task presentation and task structure and have the communication skills needed to pass those on to the learner. They must know the key performance cues of the task to be learned and how to recognize mistakes when they observe them. For that, they need good verbal and modeling skills to convey clear and correct information to the learner about completed tasks. As tutors, they also need to be understanding and patient with learners who are slow to master the task. In short, they need to be ready to be *teachers,* just like the adult teacher in the class.

As learners, students must be willing to take direction from peers—and sometimes peers who are not as highly skilled as they are. And, like the tutors, they must be understanding, patient, and cooperative with some tutors who are learning to teach for the first time. They must also be ready to receive both praise and criticism from their tutor, who is charged with correcting any mistakes they see in the learner's performance.

Student receptivity to the model. Because of the dual roles students assume in the Peer Teaching model, the profile for learning preferences will be different for the tutor and the learner. Based on the Reichmann and Grasha (1974) scheme, the tutor will most likely prefer the participative, collaborative, and independent attributes of the model. The learner will most likely prefer the attributes of participant, collaborative, and dependent, much like students in the Direct Instruction model. Teachers who use Peer Teaching should expect that some students will like being tutors but not learners, and vice versa.

Validation of the Model

Research validation

It is somewhat difficult to establish clear research validation for Peer Teaching because the feature of "students teaching students" occurs in several models of instruction. Some research reports on Peer Teaching will include any strategy that has this feature, even if it takes place within another model, such as Cooperative Learning (Ward & Lee, 2005). In a brief review of Peer Teaching (Foot, Morgan, & Shute, 1990), peer teaching (used in various models) has been shown effective in increasing achievement in several subject areas, such as mathematics, science, and language arts.

A limited amount of research has been completed on Peer Teaching in physical education. Ward and Lee (2005) reviewed 28 studies in physical education that used what they labeled *peer-assisted learning* (PAL), which is a different term for describing Peer Teaching. They report that most of these studies focused on the implementation of PAL, and not on measured learning outcomes. They concluded that peer-based instruction can be used with students as young as third graders, that tutors can provide high rates of feedback and other instructional information to learners, and that students can readily be taught to work collaboratively with each other. They also comment that most benefits from peer-based instruction come from adequate training of tutors for that role.

Craft knowledge validation

As noted by Wagner (1990), teachers have been using some form of Peer Teaching for over 3,000 years, starting with Aristotle and the ancient Greeks. The fact that this strategy has been practiced for such a long time and has been developed into a more formal instructional model in the past 30 years provides strong evidence that teachers in all subject areas find it feasible and effective for many learning outcomes. Again, this is not the same as just placing students in learning pairs, but it is rather the more formally operationalized plan and decisions that get one student to *teach another* for a period of time.

Teachers have found Peer Teaching highly effective in adaptive physical education settings, by having a higher-skilled student take on the role of individual tutor for a student with learning disabilities (Houston-Wilson, 1997; Webster, 1987). Although the higher-skilled student does learn important lessons about communication and others' needs, this student does not receive reciprocal instruction, often making this method a one-way street.

It is difficult to determine how much true Peer Teaching occurs in physical education today (Ward & Lee, 2005). It is likely that teachers use this as a temporary *strategy* in many kinds of learning tasks but do not sustain it across many learning tasks and entire content units. Most physical education teachers probably practice this under the name of the Reciprocal Style described by Mosston and Ashworth (2002).

Intuitive validation

A physical education teacher cannot provide all the direct observation and instructional information needed by every student practicing movement skills and concepts in class. There are usually just too many students for one teacher—even for one teacher plus a teacher's aide. We also know that students at nearly all grade levels can comprehend the necessary performance cues, observe them as other students execute them, and provide feedback for each practice attempt. Since many students can carry out a limited range of these key teaching operations in class, it makes good sense to use them as additional teaching resources for physical education, increasing learning levels for both students in the dyad. Turning this strategy into a formal model of instruction improves the design and implementation of this powerful way to teach in physical education, making a good case for intuitive validation.

TEACHING AND LEARNING FEATURES

Control

Exhibit 12.3 shows the control profile for the Peer Teaching model as it is used in physical education. Each element of the profile is explained in detail below.

1. Content selection. The teacher maintains complete control of the content and its sequencing in the Peer Teaching model. He decides what will be included in the unit, the order in which learning tasks will be sequenced, and the performance criteria used to determine mastery of each task. All students simply receive the content listing from the teacher and proceed through it.

2. Managerial control. The teacher determines the managerial plan, class policies, and specific procedures that students follow in the Peer Teaching model. The tutors are given a small degree of managerial responsibility within instructional tasks, such as arranging the practice area, orienting the learner to the task, and monitoring for safety.

3. Task presentations. These occur in two ways. The first is controlled by the teacher as she informs tutors of performance cues, task structure, and mastery criteria and then checks for understanding (A). After that, it is controlled by the individual tutor who relays that information to the learner to initiate practice on the assigned task (B).

4. Engagement patterns. The teacher decides and then assigns students to each role and determines the rotation plan within each task. Obviously, the predominant task structure is dyadic, but it is possible to use groups of three when the class consists of an uneven number of students. Students alternate between the roles of tutor and learner according to the teacher's plan.

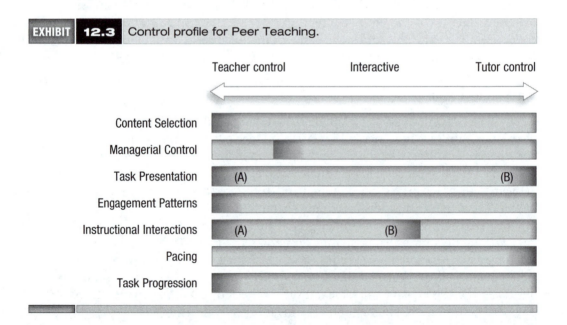

EXHIBIT 12.3 Control profile for Peer Teaching.

5. Instructional interactions. Two paths are used for instructional interactions in the Peer Teaching model. The first path (A) is between the teacher and the tutors of the moment. That initial communication is controlled by the teacher, who gives tutors the needed task presentation and task structure information, checks for understanding, and then lets them pursue their role. The teacher continues interacting only with the tutors, *not the learners,* except on rare occasions. The teacher's communications with the tutors should be highly interactive, using questions more often than direct statements to develop the tutors' observation, analysis, and communication skills (B). The idea is to promote problem-solving skills rather than simply using the tutor as a "conduit" to the learner. For example, if the teacher observes that a learner is not doing the correct step in a dance sequence, she should not make a comment to the learner. Instead, the teacher should ask the tutor to "watch carefully" to see if the learner is making any mistakes and then get the tutor to identify the incorrect movement pattern and communicate that to the learner.

The second path (B) is between the tutors and the learners. It should also be highly interactive, as they work cooperatively to structure and pursue assigned learning activities. The tutor is free (and expected) to make comments to the learner and to ask questions. The learner is expected to do the same. The tutor should provide the learner with all the information usually given by the teacher during learning activities: cues, guides, feedback, questions, and encouragement should all occur at very high rates before and after each practice attempt.

6. Pacing. After the teacher gives the task presentation and task structure information to the tutors and the tutors relay that to the learners, the learners can begin to practice at their own pace. Along with the tutor, the learner determines when each practice attempt will begin and how long it will last.

7. Task progression. The teacher decides the content listing for each unit and when learning activities will change within it. The teacher also decides when each dyad switches from tutor to learner, and vice versa. However, it is possible for the teacher to state a performance criterion for each task and allow student pairs to go to the next task on their own when they both have completed the current task. This can reduce management time significantly.

Inclusiveness

The Peer Teaching model can accommodate a wide range of student ability levels and previous experience with the content, making it highly inclusive. Students at low ability levels get many more monitored practice tasks and have the opportunity to learn in the role of tutor. Students of higher ability can refine their skills with the added monitoring and information given by the tutor, and they can develop increased analytic skills when they take over as tutor.

It must be emphasized that the Peer Teaching model is not to have more-skilled students always serve as tutors for less-skilled students. There must be reciprocity in the process: "I teach you, then you teach me."

Learning Tasks

The dyadic arrangement in the Peer Teaching model increases the efficiency of practice for the learner and gives the tutor an opportunity to develop movement skill analysis knowledge. It also provides both students in the dyad the opportunity to develop personal, social, and verbal communication skills. All of those benefits come with some limitations within the key operations of task presentation and task structure when the Peer Teaching model is used in physical education.

Task presentation

The process of providing the tutors with task presentation information is quite direct in this model: the teacher shows the tutors a model of the skill or task to be practiced, along with the key performance cues they must relay to the learners and watch for during each practice attempt. The presentation process is essentially the same as that in Direct Instruction. It is very important that the teacher regularly check for understanding to make sure the tutors know what instructional information to communicate to the learners, and how to do so. The teacher can use instructional media, such as videos, drawings, and photographs, to give the task presentation to the tutors.

The teacher has a few options when it is time for the tutors and learners to switch roles, since the tutor group will already be aware of the task and its key performance cues:

1. Before they switch, the teacher can ask the tutors to repeat all the performance cues to their learners.

2. The teacher can conduct a brief task presentation himself for the new learners, checking for understanding often.

3. The teacher can ask the new tutors to recall what they just learned, wanting to hear them cite the key performance cues for the task they will now be teaching.

Task structure

The dyad pattern of Peer Teaching limits the kinds of task structures to those that allow one learner to practice while one tutor observes. Drills, self-space tasks, stations, and brief in-class cognitive tasks are typically the kinds of task structures used in Peer Teaching.

The teacher can develop simple observational checklists for tutors to use as they watch each learner's practice attempts. The checklist would show all the key performance cues and allow the tutor to check off each time she sees the learner perform a cue correctly. This strategy is especially helpful for younger students who might forget one or more of the key cues from the task presentation.

Content progression

The teacher moves the class through the planned learning activities in the same way as in Direct Instruction. The unit is broken into a series of progressively more difficult or complicated learning tasks, and the students progress through them in the planned order. The teacher can plan for the second rotation on a task to be slightly briefer because the new learners will already have been tutors for that task and the new tutors will not have to make a new task presentation. The new learners can start to practice right away.

Engagement Patterns for Learning

As the name of the model implies, the predominant engagement pattern in Peer Teaching is the dyad, or pair. When the number of students dictates, it is possible to place them in groups of three, with each one taking a turn as the tutor. The teacher gives the task presentation and task structure information to the tutors, who in turn relay that information to the learners. When the learners have completed the task, or the teacher decides it is time, the tutors and learners switch roles.

Teacher and Student Roles and Responsibilities

Each instructional model will have certain operations that need to be completed to allow the model to function according to its design. Some of the operations are carried out by the teacher; others are carried out by one or more students. Exhibit 12.4 shows the major operations within the Peer Teaching model and indicates who is responsible for completing them during each lesson.

EXHIBIT 12.4	Teacher and student roles and responsibilities in Peer Teaching.
OPERATION OR RESPONSIBILITY	**PERSON/PEOPLE RESPONSIBLE IN PEER TEACHING**
Starting class	The **teacher** starts the lesson.
Bringing equipment to class	The **teacher** brings the needed equipment to class.
Dispersing and returning equipment	Each **partner group** gets the equipment needed for the activity and returns it when finished.
Roll call (if needed)	The **teacher** calls the roll.
Task presentation	The **teacher** shows and describes each movement skill or concept to the tutors. The **tutors** then show and describe each movement skill or concept to the learners.
Task structure	The **teacher** explains the task structure to the tutors. The **tutors** then explain the task structure to the learners.
Instructional interactions	**Path A:** The teacher uses questions to interact with the tutors. **Path B:** The tutors provide the learners with cues, guides, feedback, and encouragement.
Assessment	The **teacher** determines how each task will be assessed. The **tutor** assesses the learner (e.g., with a checklist).
Monitoring learning progress	The **teacher** determines when it is time to go on to new content.

Verification of Instructional Processes

Because students assume two different roles in the Peer Teaching model, it is necessary to identify a set of benchmarks for each role and for the teacher. These benchmarks, listed in Exhibits 12.5–12.7, verify that the Peer Teaching model has been implemented with an acceptable degree of faithfulness, increasing the likelihood that the stated learning outcomes will be achieved.

Assessment of Learning

Peer Teaching is most often recommended for use with discrete learning activities that can be pursued with individual student engagement patterns: one learner practices while her tutor observes. That feature suggests using Peer Teaching for relatively simple movement patterns and concepts that the tutor can view as the learner practices them. More dynamic engagement patterns, such as competitive games, do not allow many opportunities for the tutor to interact with the learner while the action occurs—although it is possible for them to interact once the game has paused or stopped. By design, the Peer

EXHIBIT 12.5 Peer Teaching teacher benchmarks.

BENCHMARK	HOW TO VERIFY
Unit content is broken into a series of small learning tasks, leading to larger learning goals.	Review the teacher's task analysis, content listing, and content progression prior to the start of the unit.
Teacher reviews previous day's content.	Review teacher's lesson plan to include a set induction that covers this.
Teacher presents a clear and effective task presentation to tutors.	1. The teacher checks often for understanding in the task presentation. 2. The teacher observes learners as they begin to practice. Are they doing the task correctly?
Teacher presents a clear task structure.	The teacher observes learners as they begin to practice. Are they engaged in the way described by the teacher?
Teacher uses a brisk pace through content progression.	1. Teacher plans a series of small learning tasks. 2. Teacher has quick transitions between planned class segments and role changes within learning activities.
Teacher primarily uses questions to interact with tutors during learning activities.	Record the frequency and types of questions directed by the teacher to tutors.
Learning tasks have a mastery criterion.	1. Check lesson plan. 2. Use written assessments to verify learners' mastery.
Regular content reviews are made.	1. Check the unit plan. 2. Record the timing and focus of each review.

Peer Teaching student learner benchmarks.	🖶 EXHIBIT 12.6
BENCHMARK	**HOW TO VERIFY**
Learners understand task presentation.	Count the number of learners who are doing the skill/movement/concept as it was initially described by the teacher.
Learners understand task structure.	Count the number of learners who: a. are engaged according to the teacher's directions to tutors. b. have modified the task. c. have withdrawn from the task.
Learners have high rates of OTR.	1. Count the number of practice attempts (if frequency is the best indicator of OTR). 2. Measure how much actual practice time learners get (if time is the best indicator of OTR).
Learners have high rates of ALT.	Monitor a sampling of learners with a valid ALT-PE recording instrument.
Learners get high rates of positive and corrective feedback.	Record and analyze the tutors' feedback to learners.
Learners have mastered content.	Learners complete and pass regular assessments monitored by tutors.

Peer Teaching student tutor benchmarks.	🖶 EXHIBIT 12.7
BENCHMARK	**HOW TO VERIFY**
Tutors comprehend task presentation.	1. Count the number of correct answers when the teacher checks for understanding. 2. Monitor each tutor's task presentation to the learner, noting correct and incorrect information.
Tutors comprehend task structure.	1. Count the number of correct answers when the teacher checks for understanding. 2. Allow pairs to set up the learning environment and the learners to begin practice. Scan and count the number of learners who: a. are engaged as directed by the teacher. b. have modified the task. c. are off-task.
Tutors provide high rates of positive and corrective feedback.	Monitor the type and rate of feedback from the tutor to the learner.
Tutors and learners work cooperatively.	Monitor interaction patterns within dyads.
Tutors can analyze movement skills/concepts correctly.	Teacher and tutor use an identical checklist while observing the same learner and compare records after each attempt.

Teaching model permits many opportunities for a tutor to observe a learner who is engaged in repetitive and relatively simple movement activities in a static situation, making the use of observational checklists most appropriate for assessment purposes.

Checklists are widely used as assessment devices in physical education because it is easy for the tutor to watch performance in the psychomotor domain and then to record which parts of the movement or skill were performed correctly. The teacher trains the tutor what to watch for and how to determine if a movement or outcome is correctly executed. The key is to match the number and complexity of checklist items with the tutor's ability to discern them in motion. Before the students switch roles, the tutor makes an assessment to determine how many of the performance cues the learner demonstrated.

Checklists can also be used to assess the tutor. Based on the information given in the task presentation, the teacher can make up a list of all performance cues that the tutor should tell the learner and monitor on each practice attempt. The teacher can observe a tutor interacting with his learner and use the checklist to note the types of interactions, their accuracy, and their "tone" (either negative or positive).

Checklist assessment techniques can help both the learner and the tutor. The learner benefits from having specific feedback for each component of the performance, while the items on the checklist remind the tutor of the key performance cues for the task when the roles switch.

IMPLEMENTATION NEEDS AND MODIFICATIONS

Teacher Expertise

Physical education teachers who use the Peer Teaching model will need to have particular strengths in the knowledge base presented in Chapter 3. Many of these areas are similar to those needed for Direct Instruction—but with a slightly different slant to address the needs of both tutor and learner.

Implementing developmentally appropriate instruction. Teachers must address developmental issues that pertain to the learner's need to be engaged safely in meaningful tasks, with high rates of OTR. It benefits neither the learner nor the tutor to have a lot of waiting time between practice attempts. The teacher must ensure that the learner can comprehend the task presentation and task structure information and that the level of task difficulty matches the learner's stage of development. The learner must also be willing and able to accept both praise and criticism (in the form of negative performance feedback) from a peer.

There are also questions about the developmental appropriateness that pertain to students in the role of tutor. The teacher must ask herself if tutors have the intellectual ability (to comprehend task information and monitor practice attempts), the level of responsibility (to assume some of the teacher's functions), the communication skills (to provide accurate feedback and cues), and the maturity (to work for the benefit of the learner) necessary to be "the teacher for the moment." If tutors are not ready for their role, the model's key feature will not work, greatly reducing its effectiveness.

Task analysis and content progression. The teacher must know the movement skills or concepts to be learned in the unit and also be able to break each one into its component parts so that a sequence of learning tasks can be formulated and presented to students. Students then progress through this sequence of tasks, alternating as tutor and learner throughout the unit.

Assessment. Tutors most often serve as the assessors in the Peer Teaching model. They observe learners' skill attempts and help to verify mastery of each learning task. The teacher's assessment expertise is needed to design and communicate assessment techniques to the tutors, such as the observational checklists just described. Depending on the tutor's observational and communication skills, the model permits other alternative assessment strategies, such as video analysis and rubrics.

Social/emotional climate. The Peer Teaching model relies heavily on the moment-to-moment interactions between the tutor and the learner. It will not work if both members of the dyad are not comfortable in those roles and do not care about each other's learning. It is up to the teacher to create an atmosphere that allows both members of the dyad to feel secure in this arrangement and to be willing to work as tutors for the benefit of others. The tutors must be sensitive to the learner's abilities and needs, especially when the learner is having difficulty and the needed feedback is not positive. The learners must be aware not only that the tutors can make mistakes and do not have the same level of expertise as their teacher but also that negative feedback is not meant personally. The teacher can promote a positive climate by having regular discussions with the class to reinforce examples of good tutor and learner role behavior and by reminding all students of the shared responsibility that occurs in the model.

Key Teaching Skills

The needed repertoire of effective teaching skills in the Peer Teaching model will be similar to that required by the Direct Instruction model, except for some interactions with the tutors as they work with learners.

Planning. The Peer Teaching model calls for the teacher to break unit content into discrete tasks that lead to identified learning objectives (see the unit plan for Peer Teaching on the IMPE website). The teacher will need to plan for all aspects of those tasks so that the tutors and learners can engage quickly once the teacher completes the task presentation.

Time and class management. The Peer Teaching model requires some extra attention to how time is allocated to lesson segments and how transitions are managed. Because students alternate between the roles of tutor and learner, there are more transitions during classes—with the potential for a loss of momentum. Teachers must establish routines and procedures for these transitions, to ensure that little practice time is lost when students change activities and roles. Particular attention must be given to providing students with approximately equal amounts of time in each role.

Task presentation and task structure. These are critical areas of effective teaching skills necessary for the Peer Teaching model. The teacher must make good task presentations to the tutors and check for understanding often so that the tutors know what to look for as they observe the learners and can provide helpful comments. Task structure is equally important, since the teacher will let each pair of students set up the learning environment and become engaged in the task as the teacher intends. If the teacher has provided tutors with good information about task presentation and task structure, the tutors will be more effective as they assume their temporary teaching responsibilities. The teacher must be careful to give necessary safety information to all students and must be sure that the tutors understand and follow these safety guidelines.

Communication. Verbal communication is used most often in Peer Teaching, as the teacher informs the tutors about the task presentation and task structure. The key point to remember here is that the teacher must communicate well enough so that the tutors can *teach* the content to the learners, so it is important to check for understanding frequently.

Instructional information and use of questions. While the dyads are engaged in the task, the teacher interacts only with the tutors—and in a very indirect mode. Because the teacher is trying to develop the tutor's analysis and communication skills, the primary mode of interaction involves questions that promote problem-solving abilities. The teacher should not say things like, "Billy is not using the correct grip on the bat. Go and show him how to do it correctly." Instead, the teacher might say, "I think Billy is having some problems with his swing. Watch his next try carefully, and see if you spot an error in his grip." Billy (the learner) takes another swing, after which Debbie (the tutor) says to the teacher, "He has a gap between his top hand and his bottom hand—I'll go tell him." The teacher says, "Not just yet. Why is that not a good way to hold the bat?" Debbie thinks for a moment and replies, "Because it causes him to lose control and miss the ball." The teacher acknowledges that correct answer and then says, "Good. Now go and tell him how to fix it, and keep watching to be sure he doesn't keep doing it."

Review and closure. The review segment of a lesson within the Peer Teaching model must address all the kinds of learning that occurred in class: what students learned as they practiced, what they learned when they taught, and what they learned while interacting with their partners. All of these outcomes are related, and the teacher must tie them together for students to see the "big picture" of what happens when they take turns teaching each other in physical education class.

Contextual Requirements

The main contextual need in Peer Teaching is having sufficient space and equipment for half of the class to be practicing at one time. That requirement cannot be compromised at all in this model. Beyond that, the Peer Teaching model can be used for a wide variety of movement content and in nearly every kind of activity area in schools. It works especially effectively with large classes, since it provides every practicing student with his own tutor for the moment and requires only enough equipment and space for half of the class for any learning activity.

Selecting and Modifying Peer Teaching

The Peer Teaching model can be used in a wide range of settings and content areas within physical education programs. The major factor to be considered when deciding whether to use Peer Teaching is the level of student learning the teacher wishes to achieve, more than the content itself. For example, Peer Teaching can be used effectively in all individual and team sports, but it should be limited to noncompetitive activities because the dynamics of game situations rarely allow for students to interact in the tutor–learner roles. Therefore, Peer Teaching would be an appropriate model for beginner and intermediate levels but not for advanced students who will be engaged in competitive games more often. Recognizing that feature of the Peer Teaching model, I would recommend it for the following types of physical education content units:

1. Movement skills and concepts
2. Individual sports (skill learning)
3. Team sports (skill learning)
4. Recreational activities
5. Dances with prescribed steps (e.g., line, square, folk)
6. Fitness performance
7. Personal fitness concepts
8. Personal fitness training programs
9. Aquatics (swimming and diving)

Grade-level adaptations

The Peer Teaching model will be more effective when student developmental levels can accommodate the full range of observational, communication, and problem-solving abilities needed for the role of tutor. However, it is possible to greatly reduce the number and complexity of role requirements for tutors, so you can use the Peer Teaching model with some lower grade levels. Exhibit 12.8 shows some grade-level adaptations for using Peer Teaching in physical education.

EXHIBIT 12.8	Grade-level adaptations for Peer Teaching in physical education.	
GRADE LEVELS	**SELECT PEER TEACHING?**	**POSSIBLE ADAPTATIONS**
Preschool	No	
K–2	No	
3–5	Yes	1. Give task presentation to all students at once, eliminating the need for tutors to do it. 2. Get the tutors to watch for one key element at a time. Add more as the tutors' observational skills increase.
Middle school/junior high	Yes	1. Limit the number of key elements the tutors will look for (no more than three or four). 2. Use simple checklists to remind tutors of what to watch for. 3. Train students how to be good, sensitive communicators.
High school	Yes	The full Peer Teaching model can be implemented without adaptation.
College/adult	Yes	The full Peer Teaching model can be implemented without adaptation.

Adaptations to accommodate diverse groups of learners

Peer Teaching can be a highly inclusive model for physical education if the teacher clearly gives the tutors enough training and direction to perform that role effectively and then monitors the tutors as they carry out those teaching functions. Exhibit 12.9 lists some strategies that address a variety of special learning needs found in many schools today.

PLANNING TIPS FOR PEER TEACHING

Detailed examples of a unit and lesson plan for Peer Teaching in physical education are shown on the IMPE website. Teachers who choose to use the Peer Teaching model can benefit by following a few additional planning tips:

1. Set clear expectations for tutors, telling them that they are your "eyes, ears, and voice" in that role.

2. Teach the tutors what it means to be an effective teacher. Show them what you do to help students learn. Allow time for that training in every lesson plan.

3. Be sure to assess the learners and the tutors. This reinforces the importance of the teaching role to the tutors.

Strategies adapting Peer Teaching for diverse groups of learners.   **EXHIBIT 12.9**

FOR STUDENTS WITH HEARING AND/OR SPEECH IMPAIRMENTS:

1. Give the tutors task sheets or checklists that show the key components of the skills they will teach.
2. Move these students closer when making the task presentations.

FOR STUDENTS WITH SIGHT IMPAIRMENTS:

1. Use a larger font for task cards and checklists.
2. Do not ask students to look for very small or fast-moving key components. Ask them to focus on more easily visible parts of skill performance with their learners.

FOR STUDENTS WITH PHYSICAL DISABILITIES:

1. Adapt the skill to be learned and/or equipment to promote higher levels of performance for all students.
2. Teach these students the tutoring role as you would all other students, but get them to verbalize instructions and movements that they cannot perform themselves.
3. Teach all tutors to recognize the abilities of these students and what to look for when identifying a skilled performance.

FOR STUDENTS WHO DO NOT SPEAK ENGLISH:

1. Use student translators, when available. Pair matching bilingual students with non-English speakers.
2. Provide task presentations in appropriate language, or use translated closed-caption media when possible.

FOR LOWER-SKILLED STUDENTS:

1. Encourage tutors to be patient and understanding with students who learn at a slower rate.
2. Provide extra encouragement and praise to the slower learners.
3. Encourage teams to think about ways to involve all members.

FOR STUDENTS WITH BEHAVIOR DISABILITIES:

1. Provide students with behavior disabilities with extra encouragement for their participation, especially as tutors.
2. Focus on the contribution to be made by students with behavior disabilities, not the potential for misbehavior.

4. It is acceptable to pair higher- and lower-skilled students in Peer Teaching. The lower-skilled student can be taught what to look for and how to provide effective feedback, without being a proficient performer.
5. When the tutors and learners switch roles during a learning activity (e.g., a drill or stations), the new tutors do not need a new task presentation. They already know the task structure and were taught the key components by the original tutors. If you need to verify that the new tutors know their role, do a quick check for understanding while the new learners practice the skill.
6. Peer Teaching will call for more transitions than other models, so be sure to plan these into the lesson, and make them as efficient as possible.

UNIT AND LESSON PLAN EXAMPLES FOR PEER TEACHING INSTRUCTION

Y ou will find several complete unit plans with lesson plans for Peer Teaching on the IMPE website. It is not recommended that you follow these examples exactly as they are presented. The context, specific learning objectives, and content of your own unit will require you to make changes in these examples to allow the Peer Teaching model to lead to the most effective instruction in your situation.

SUMMARY

One of the most underused resources in teaching today is students. Children teach other children every day during playtime around the house and neighborhood, yet most instructional strategies and models are designed for only one adult teacher, who cannot provide all students with regular observation and feedback during practice time. To the degree that students are mature and skilled enough to assume some of the necessary functions of instruction, they should be used as an in-class "teacher corps" to help their peers and themselves achieve more in physical education. The Peer Teaching model is designed to do precisely that, promoting learning outcomes in all three domains and across a variety of physical education content.

I end this chapter by repeating one of the early precautions about the Peer Teaching model. It is much more than simply placing students in pairs and arranging for them to learn alongside each other for a short period of time or even a few learning tasks. It becomes and remains the Peer Teaching model only when the teacher plans for, prepares, and monitors students who assume the role of tutor on nearly every learning task in the unit. Only then will the full range of student learning outcomes be achieved through this model.

LEARNING ACTIVITIES

1. Make a list of five activity units (e.g., movement skills, fitness, softball, tennis, golf) that might be taught in a physical education program. Next, determine an appropriate grade level (P, K–2, 3–5, 6–8, 9–12) for teaching each of those activity units. Now, write two major learning outcomes for those units. Then, go through the process of selecting an instructional model, shown in Chapter 2, to determine if Peer Teaching would be an appropriate model for teaching that activity to children at that grade level.

2. If Peer Teaching is appropriate for that activity, grade, and goals, mention three things that make it appropriate. If Peer Teaching is not appropriate for that activity, grade, and goals, mention three things that make it inappropriate.

3. For one activity unit at one grade level (e.g., middle school volleyball, high school tennis), write a complete list of content to be taught in that unit with Peer Teaching.

4. Pick one of the major goals identified in Learning Activity 1, and design an assessment strategy for monitoring student learning during this unit.

5. Write an annotated lesson plan for each of the first three lessons of this unit.

TOPICS FOR REFLECTION & SMALL-GROUP DISCUSSION

1. I have suggested in this chapter how the Peer Teaching model is aligned to achieve one or more of the NASPE standards. Take a moment to review those alignments (refer back to Exhibit 12.2). After that, make some notes about whether you agree with those alignments, and then share them in your small group. When you have arrived at your final thoughts, please share them on the IMPE website Forum for others to review, and check back for replies.

2. Mention three ways Peer Teaching is similar to Direct Instruction and three ways it is different.

3. In general, which types of students are placed at an advantage in this model, and which students are at a disadvantage?

4. Why is it so important to teach the tutors how to teach?

5. Few students have ever been placed in the teaching role in physical education class, so they might be a bit shy or hesitant to "be the teacher." What can you do to help them be more comfortable in this role?

SUGGESTED READINGS FOR PEER TEACHING

Foot, H. C., Morgan, M. J., & Shute, R. H. (Eds.) (1990). *Children helping children*. Chichester, England: John Wiley & Sons.

Mosston, M., & Ashworth, S. (2002). *Teaching physical education* (5th ed.). San Francisco: B. Cummings. (See esp. Chapter 5, The Reciprocal Style [Style C].)

INQUIRY TEACHING
Learner as Problem Solver

As you will recall from Chapter 1, teacher-directed instruction became the predominant approach to teaching physical education in the late 1800s. That method went unchallenged for over 60 years, even as physical education programs began to shift away from sport-centered content. The first and perhaps biggest challenge to teacher-directed instruction emerged in the 1960s from a fast-growing, vocal group of advocates for programs based on the development of intellectual ability, problem solving, and generic movement skills. Labeled *movement education,* such programs have since become the basis for a large number of physical education programs, most notably in the elementary grades. Some teachers retain the original "movement education" label while others use the broader term *movement-based physical education* to denote the philosophy, content, and teaching methods to which they adhere. By whatever label, programs with *movement* in their name share some common characteristics that are relevant to this book of instructional models.

As just mentioned, the "movement movement" (Locke, 1970, p. 208) was perhaps the first significant programmatic shift away from sport-centered curriculums in physical education. The major learning outcomes in sport-centered programs involve the development of skills, knowledge, and tactics needed for proficiency in a given game form (e.g., basketball, soccer, hockey). The content of any such program is the list of sports to be taught during the school year. Teachers instruct by showing and telling students how to be proficient performers and then giving students time to practice under the teacher's supervision. Of course, you know this as the Direct Instruction model from Chapter 8. But the content of movement-based programs is quite different, at times even directly opposed to sport-centered programming. Taken from a variety of sources, the major purposes of movement-based programs are:

1. The development of basic and generic movement skills that may or may not be precursors to those needed in more complex sport forms (In other words, it is OK if the learned movement does not have any direct application to a known sport—it is also OK if it does.)

2. The development of problem-solving and other intellectual abilities as they apply to human movement

3. The development of expressive and creative movement

It is clear to the advocates of movement-based programs that direct instruction will not work at all to help students achieve these goals. As you know, different objectives should lead to different kinds of instruction. The content of movement-based physical education has remained prominent in our field today, while the most important outcome from the "movement movement" has been the development of an array of inquiry-based strategies used to teach physical education. The method for movement-based teaching has been given several names: problem solving, exploration teaching, child-centered teaching, discovery teaching, and indirect teaching. Regardless of the name, all movement-based instruction shares one important characteristic: rather than the teacher showing and telling students how to move, she uses questions to prompt student engagement in both the cognitive and psychomotor domains. Essentially, the teacher asks a question that leads to some type of student thinking, which in turn leads to a "movement answer" displayed by students. The types of questions can vary, as can the types and level of student thinking and movement answers.

Because question-based learning is at the center of this kind of instruction, the term *Inquiry Teaching* will be used in this chapter to describe this array of strategies that can be defined as an instructional model. No formal Inquiry Teaching model has been developed for physical education, but the unique characteristics of question-based teaching, and the many recognizable strategies included within it, do formulate a coherent set of procedures that teachers can use to promote student thinking, problem solving, and exploration in physical education. And, although those strategies were originally developed for movement- based programming, they can be used effectively to teach a wide range of physical education content today.

The Inquiry Teaching model described in this chapter shares some similarities with other models in this book, most notably Cooperative Learning (Chapter 10) and Tactical Games (Chapter 14). Like the Inquiry Teaching model, those models use problem-solving teaching strategies. However, there are many differences that make the Inquiry Teaching model unique. Cooperative Learning is based on the team structure for learning activities. Inquiry Teaching uses many kinds of structures, but most often it relies on individual student thinking. Because of the scoring rubrics used by the teacher and communicated to students in the Cooperative Learning model and the situation-based activities in the Tactical Games model, those models typically lead to a narrower range of answers and movements. Inquiry Teaching can allow students to explore a wide range of answers (both cognitive and psychomotor), especially creative ones that are "not obvious."

All physical educators use questions in their teaching. Question-asking is a basic pedagogical skill. However, just using questions from time to time does not constitute teaching by the Inquiry Teaching model. It becomes Inquiry Teaching when entire units of instruction are based on questioning strategies and when question-asking is used nearly exclusively as the way to develop students' intellectual, physical, and emotional abilities in physical education. As with all other models in this book, using something "a bit" or "from time to time" does not qualify as model-based instruction. As you will see in this chapter, Inquiry Teaching is much more than asking students a question and "letting them go at it." When applied according to the model outlined here, Inquiry Teaching requires specific kinds of planning and pedagogical skills that are quite different from other models and that are just as engaging for the teacher as for students.

OVERVIEW

As stated in the introduction to this chapter, there is no formally designed Inquiry Teaching model for physical education. The model presented here is derived from a number of inquiry and problem-solving strategies that physical educators have been using for many years under many different names:

1. Student-centered teaching
2. Problem solving
3. Exploration teaching (Barrett, 1970)
4. Guided discovery (Mosston & Ashworth, 2002)

Because each of those terms describes one or more strategies that are used for short periods of class time, they do not comprise a teaching model in and of themselves. In order to form them into an actual model of teaching, their most common characteristic—using questions to guide learning—will be used as the foundation. The design of the Inquiry Teaching model owes a large debt to those strategies, but as you will see, the Inquiry Teaching model encompasses much more than any one of them.

Perhaps the most important feature of Inquiry Teaching is that student learning occurs in the cognitive domain first—and at times, exclusively. Students are asked questions that get them to think for themselves or, perhaps, along with one or more peers. Cognitive learning is sometimes the only type of learning sought by the teacher. More typically, however, the cognitive engagement is used as the prerequisite or stimulus for answers expressed in the psychomotor domain: students think first, then express their answer through some type of movement. The interaction between the cognitive and psychomotor domains will depend on the kind of student learning the teacher desires.

There are a number of ways to classify the development of student learning, and thus the kinds of questions used, in the Inquiry Teaching model. As discussed in Chapter 5, one of the most common schemes is the taxonomy devised by Bloom et al. (1956), which has six levels of cognitive knowledge. Based on the kind of knowledge sought with the learning activity, the teacher emphasizes questions at one level more than others, to make sure that students have the prerequisite knowledge for that task. Bloom's taxonomy can be used to differentiate between lower-order and higher-order knowledge, based on the position in the taxonomy. Lower-order learning includes *knowledge* (recognition and recall), *comprehension* (translation, interpretation, and extrapolation), and *application* (using previous knowledge to solve problems). Higher-order learning includes *analysis* (explanation of parts and function), *synthesis* (creativity used to make something new), and *evaluation* (judging the worth or merit of something). A teacher targets the level of knowledge intended in a given learning activity and uses questions that promote verbal and movement answers at that level. Higher-order questions are not necessarily better than lower-order ones; the appropriateness of a question depends on the degree to which it matches the targeted knowledge level and promotes that kind of student learning.

Some entire physical education curriculums are strongly based on Inquiry Teaching. Movement education, educational games, and skill themes (Graham, Holt/Hale, & Parker, 2009) all promote the development of intellectual abilities, which then work to help students be expressive, creative, and skillful in the psychomotor domain. These curriculums are used in many schools in the United States and abroad, most often at the elementary grades. The roles of teacher-as-question-asker and student-as-problem-solver are central in these programs, making Inquiry Teaching an effective model for them. But, as you will see in this chapter, the Inquiry Teaching model can also be effective with a wider range of content and in all grade levels.

ALIGNMENT WITH NASPE NATIONAL STANDARDS

 xhibit 13.1 shows the alignment of the Inquiry Teaching model with the NASPE standards. As you can see, Inquiry Teaching is consistently and strongly aligned with all standards except standard 4. Because the Inquiry

	EXHIBIT 13.1
Alignment of Inquiry Teaching with NASPE National Standards.	

NASPE STANDARD	ALIGNMENT RATING	COMMENTS
1. Demonstrates competency in motor skills and movement patterns needed to perform a variety of physical activities	1	Especially strong alignment for basic movement patterns
2. Demonstrates understanding of movement concepts, principles, strategies, and tactics as they apply to the learning and performance of physical activities	1	Strong alignment for all components
3. Participates regularly in physical activity	1–3	Will vary according to the learning task of the moment
4. Achieves and maintains a health-enhancing level of physical fitness	3	Weak alignment for fitness development tasks, due to primary focus on cognitive outcomes
5. Exhibits responsible personal and social behavior that respects self and others in physical activity settings	1	Strong alignment as students learn individually and in small groups
6. Values physical activity for health, enjoyment, challenge, self-expression, and/or social interaction	1–2	Strong alignment for all outcomes, except health

Ratings categories:

1. Strong alignment
2. Moderate alignment
3. Weak alignment

Teaching model has such a strong emphasis in the cognitive domain, it is not well suited for repetitive movements and exercises that promote increased fitness.

FOUNDATIONS

Theory and Rationale

The Inquiry Teaching model described in this chapter is based on a number of recognizable cognitive learning theories. Among some of the theories that contribute to the Inquiry Teaching model are Bruner's (1961) theory of discovery learning, Ausubel's (1968) meaningful reception learning, and very recently, constructivism—espoused by many contemporary educational theorists. Because of its current prominence, constructivism will be used here as the major theory that informs the Inquiry Teaching model. Actually, there are many constructivist viewpoints, but they all share some common ground, outlined in the next section about assumptions.

The basic rationale behind the Inquiry Teaching model is that learners need to process content cognitively before they can express that knowledge through movement. Therefore teachers should ask questions to get learners to think of possible answers and then give learners time to transfer those answers into movement. Part of that transfer occurs when learners are encouraged to explore and develop several movement patterns that answer the prompting question.

Assumptions About Teaching and Learning

The Inquiry Teaching model assumes certain principles about teaching and about learning; these principles are listed separately below.

Assumptions about teaching

1. The teacher's main pedagogical function is to stimulate student thinking, which then leads to development in the psychomotor domain.
2. Questions are the most prominent type of discourse from teacher to student.
3. The teacher facilitates student learning, prompting students with carefully thought-out questions that promote student exploration and creativity.
4. Teachers' questions should match students' intellectual abilities.
5. The teacher's role combines direct and indirect instruction. It is direct when the teacher plans for and leads students into a certain kind of engagement with the content. It is indirect once the teacher has prompted students into thinking about and exploring movement problems for solutions.

Assumptions about learning

1. Learning occurs best when the learning activity has personal meaning to the student.
2. Learners enter an activity with different sources of prior knowledge that they use to construct new knowledge and meanings.
3. Learning in the cognitive domain precedes learning in the psychomotor domain.
4. Learning is essentially a problem-solving process in which the learner uses prior knowledge and meaning to create solutions that can be expressed verbally and/or through physical movement.
5. Like all other kinds of learning, cognitive development occurs best when the complexity of the problem-solving task closely matches the learner's developmental abilities.

The Major Theme of Inquiry Teaching: Learner as Problem Solver

Although there are many recognized inquiry-based teaching strategies used in physical education today, they all share one common characteristic: they approach learning as a problem-solving process. The teacher frames the problem by asking a question, gives students some time to create and explore one or more plausible solutions, and then asks students to demonstrate their solutions as the evidence that learning has occurred. Typically, students must solve the problem in the cognitive domain before they can formulate the "movement answer" that shows they understand the key concept and have solved the problem posed by the teacher's question. Tillotson (1970) indicates that the problem-solving process has five steps (pp. 131–132):

1. *Identification of the problem.* The teacher knows the concepts that students need to learn, the skills to be mastered, and how to prompt students with questions that lead them through a well-planned sequence.

2. *Presentation of the problem.* The teacher asks one or more focused questions that frame the learning task and its embedded problem(s) for students.

3. *Guided exploration of the problem.* The teacher observes students as they attempt to solve the problem, providing cues, feedback, and facilitative questions.

4. *Identifying and refining the final solution.* The teacher uses those cues, feedback, and facilitative questions to refine the students' thinking and to lead them to one or more plausible solutions.

5. *Demonstration for analysis, evaluation, and discussion.* After they have completed the task by devising a solution to the problem, students (individually or in groups) demonstrate their solutions to the rest of the class. Those demonstrations serve as prompts for the teacher and other students to analyze—not to be critical, but to allow the rest of the class to benefit from their thinking and moving.

Tillotson's basic description obviously places problem solving as the organizing center of the teaching and learning process, nicely formulating the theme of "learner as problem solver" for the Inquiry Teaching model presented in this chapter.

Learning Domain Priorities and Domain Interactions

Domain priorities

The Inquiry Teaching model is strongly based in the cognitive domain, even for physical education instruction. Students are prompted into some level of thinking by the problem or question the teacher gives them. They then solve the problem or answer the question cognitively and fashion one or more movement answers from that. Typically, the domain priorities for the Inquiry Teaching model will be:

First priority:	Cognitive learning
Second priority:	Psychomotor learning
Third priority:	Affective learning

However, many teachers who use Inquiry Teaching will place affective learning ahead of psychomotor learning to promote students' self-awareness, exploration, creativity, and self-esteem. The cognitive domain maintains the highest priority, but the next priority is more to help students feel good about themselves in the movement environment than to develop skilled movement patterns. The rationale is to provide students with stimulating and positive movement experiences that will lead to increased enjoyment and additional participation.

Domain interactions

The domain interaction, then, will depend on which domain has second priority for each learning activity. For example, if the teacher is trying to get students to solve problems and then demonstrate skilled movement after some "thinking time," then learning in the cognitive domain should facilitate learning in the psychomotor domain. Affective learning then occurs when students feel good about their ability to "think better and move better." If the teacher wants to promote affective learning as the second priority, then student thinking can lead to any number of creative solutions that allow students to feel good about "thinking and moving," even if their motor answers are not highly skilled or proficient.

Student Developmental Requirements

Student readiness for learning. Student development in the cognitive and psychomotor domains, separately and together, determines their readiness for the Inquiry Teaching model. Students must be able first to understand the problem as the teacher frames it—to comprehend the problem-solving task or question—and must have a reasonable chance of working through an answer at the targeted cognitive level. The teacher must know her students' abilities in these areas and prepare learning tasks that match the student developmental stage at that point in time. But it is not enough that students arrive at answers only in the cognitive domain. They must have a level of psychomotor development that will allow them to move in ways that manifest their cognitive answers. They must "know" their answer(s) in both domains to achieve the primary goal of the Inquiry Teaching model—to "think and then move." When students have learned answers in a sort of linear fashion—first thinking, then moving—they are ready to learn interactively in those domains. That means they will be able to combine their thinking with their moving in ways that make moot the question "Are they thinking or moving right now?" At this point, they are doing both, and each domain facilitates the other to make a unique learning experience. Thinking and moving within complex games represents this kind of interaction. Therefore, the teacher must know the developmental requirements for each task/problem given to students and be sure that students are ready for that level of challenge.

Student receptivity to the model. Using the Reichmann and Grasha (1974) profile for student learning preferences, the Inquiry Teaching model will be most attractive to students who are classified as participant, collaborative, and independent. It must be emphasized that this profile applies more when students are engaged in the problem-solving process and somewhat less when the teacher is framing the problem to be solved. That framing will often take on many attributes of the Direct Instruction model, as the teacher controls the pacing of the lesson and interactions with students.

Validation of the Model

Research validation

As explained earlier, the Inquiry Teaching model presented in this chapter includes several strategies that rely on the teacher to frame and ask questions and rely on the students to "think, then move." Siedentop and Tannehill (2000) call this "teaching through questions." Mosston and Ashworth (2002) coined the most recognized label, "guided discovery," which means that the teacher uses carefully planned questions to guide students in the process of discovering new knowledge for themselves. Harrison, Blakemore, Buck, and Pellett (1996) call it "inquiry learning" but describe it more as a one-time strategy than as the complete model shown here. Even though inquiry-based teaching, in those forms and others, has been part of physical education instruction for many years, we have little research verification that it can promote the kinds of achievement its proponents claim. One of the very few studies was completed by Schempp (1982), in which students (grades 1–5) worked in shared decision–making groups for eight weeks. At the end of that time, those students showed significantly higher scores on originality, elaboration, and a total "creativity composite" than students who were instructed with teacher-centered decision making.

One version of Inquiry Teaching called "critical thinking" (McBride, 1992) has some research support behind its use in physical education. Ennis (1991) reported that elementary students were able to develop better cognitive-analytic skills within a unit taught with the critical thinking approach. McBride and Bonnette (1995) found that critical thinking skills could be increased in non–physical education settings such as sports camps.

Some of the lack of research support for the Inquiry Teaching model can be attributed to the variety of teaching strategies that use questions but do not fully follow the Inquiry Teaching model. In addition, large numbers of practitioners began to use Inquiry Teaching as part of movement-based programming and chose to validate it through the accumulation of craft knowledge, instead of waiting for support in research literature. Teaching as question-asking became "the way they taught," and they simply carried on with it.

Craft knowledge validation

Inquiry-based teaching has been prominent in physical education for about 50 years. Under several different names and procedures, teacher-as-question-asker has been the main pedagogical approach of a large number of teachers in the United States and abroad, particularly in Great Britain. Entire programs have been designed and implemented for physical education content that is most effectively taught exclusively, or in large part, with inquiry-based instruction, such as:

1. Movement education
2. Educational gymnastics
3. Skill themes (Graham, Holt/Hale, & Parker, 2009)
4. Group initiatives and New Games
5. Dance

The prominence of these and other types of physical education programs indicates that many teachers use some form of inquiry instruction, even if not the Inquiry Teaching model presented here. Many teachers use Mosston and Ashworth's (2002) guided discovery style in their lessons, expanding the number of teachers who are familiar with this approach. This widespread use of forms of Inquiry Teaching in physical education gives strong support for its effectiveness in promoting students' thinking, creative movement, and self-esteem—all three of which appear to be growing as goals for contemporary physical education instruction. Although we lack research validation in physical education, it is difficult to ignore the fact that so many teachers use inquiry and problem-solving approaches in their gyms.

Intuitive validation

Intuitive validation for the Inquiry Teaching model comes from a combination of motor learning principles and the commonsense use of Bloom's taxonomy. Motor learning experts agree that cognition plays a fundamental role in psychomotor learning. Learners must have basic cognitive abilities in order to comprehend and carry out the demands of nearly all movement tasks. In the strictest sense, we must think (consciously or unconsciously) before we move. Yet there is much disagreement on the manner in which those domains interact in a given situation for a learner, including the exact way that cognitive development contributes to motor development (Rink, 2003).

If you will recall, Bloom's taxonomy in the cognitive domain outlines a hierarchy of knowledge categories, starting with simple recall and advancing to evaluation. Each stage of cognitive development requires the learner to engage in increasingly more complex and difficult tasks, thus calling for different teaching strategies. So-called lower-order learning can be accomplished with mostly direct techniques: the teacher shows and/or tells students, who then attempt to recall or reproduce what they have just heard or observed. Following from that, so-called higher-order learning is typically pursued with mostly indirect techniques in which students attempt to synthesize previous knowledge, create new knowledge, or make value judgments. These higher-order outcomes cannot be effectively achieved with direct techniques; the teacher must find ways to *facilitate* student learning without providing actual answers. It stands to reason that Inquiry Teaching can serve these purposes, providing a sound rationale and validation for its use in many kinds of physical education instruction and content.

TEACHING AND LEARNING FEATURES

Control

Exhibit 13.2 shows the control profile for the Inquiry Teaching model as it is used in physical education; each element of the profile is explained below. As you can see, the teacher retains control over nearly all of the instruction but does let students control one key category—engagement patterns. Once the teacher frames the problem and students begin to think and move, the students determine how they will be engaged as they explore possible answers. Although this is only one characteristic in the total profile, it does allow the model to work as it is designed, providing students with the kind of engagement needed for cognitive development.

1. Content selection. In the Inquiry Teaching model, content constitutes the cognitive knowledge, concepts, and movement patterns that the teacher wants students to learn, contained within each of the problems to be solved. The teacher determines all the content in this model by deciding what will be taught (explored, solved, and so forth) in the unit and each lesson.

2. Managerial control. The teacher determines the managerial plan and specific class procedures in the Inquiry Teaching model. When managerial tasks overlap with learning tasks, such as setting up learning stations, selecting equipment, and making teams, the teacher allows students to make some decisions.

3. Task presentations. The teacher decides what task presentations will be used to frame the problem that students will be asked to solve in the learning task. Task presentations take the form of questions that the teacher communicates

Control profile for Inquiry Teaching.   **EXHIBIT 13.2**

to stimulate students' thoughts and then their movement. The teacher will plan a content progression for each class and use questions to move students through that progression. It is important to note that the task presentation should provide students only with enough information to clarify the task and its parameters; the teacher should stop short of giving students information that he wants students to learn for themselves. So, although the task presentation leads to student-controlled engagement, the teacher still retains control over this function in this model.

4. Engagement patterns. When the teacher has framed the problem, students are given much of the control in pursuing the solution(s), especially for higher-order cognitive tasks. Students can explore possible solutions, work with other students, try new things, change equipment, or change body positions as they attempt to "think through" the problem of the moment.

5. Instructional interactions. The Inquiry Teaching model becomes highly interactive once students engage in the problem solving, particularly when the problem is complex or has several steps in it. The nature of this interaction is interrogatory, not didactic. That is, the teacher uses questions, not direct statements, to stimulate student thinking and the exploration of movement patterns.

6. Pacing. The teacher controls the overall pacing in the unit and each lesson. She decides when new tasks or problems will begin and how much time will be allocated for each one (A). Students control the pacing within the time allocated for each task by deciding how long they need to think about solutions, how many times to practice possible solutions, and when they are finished with a task—that is, when they have the problem solved (B).

7. Task progression. The teacher determines the list and sequencing of learning tasks for the unit and each lesson. This progression should lead students toward increasingly more complex problems to solve, developing cognitive, psychomotor, and affective abilities. Students might be asked periodically, "What do you think should come next?" but the teacher retains control by guiding students to an answer he has already determined to be correct or appropriate.

Inclusiveness

Inquiry Teaching is highly inclusive. After the teacher frames the problem and communicates it to students, all students have an opportunity to work toward a solution and to fashion their own cognitive and movement answers. And, if the teacher is trying to foster divergent thinking, almost every answer that students can come up with is acceptable. There are few wrong answers that might exclude students who don't understand the concept or movement pattern to be mastered. Everyone gets a chance to think and then move, and nearly every answer contains something for which the student responding receives reinforcement from the teacher and classmates.

Learning Tasks

Task presentation

As defined in this book, Inquiry Teaching leads students through a series of planned learning tasks in which they attempt to solve one or more problems framed by the teacher in the form of a question. The problem is almost always given verbally by the teacher, although she might use some print and visual media, such as task cards, cue cards, and DVDs. After the problem has been framed, the teacher signals the students to begin "thinking and moving" within a stated task structure. Many of the problems within Inquiry Teaching are small ones that students can solve in little time. Because of this, there will often be many task presentations, or questions, used rapidly within a single task structure. (See the lesson plans for Inquiry Teaching on the IMPE website, for example.)

Task presentations in the Inquiry Teaching model look very different from those used for more direct models. In the Inquiry Teaching model, the teacher does not show and explain a concept or movement to the class and then ask students to reproduce it. Actual teacher demonstrations are used rarely, only when it is clear that students cannot solve the problem on their own after a lot of "thinking and moving." Essentially, the task presentation has two main components: framing the task and asking a question.

In framing the task, the teacher should provide students only with enough information to allow them to understand the task and the problem to be solved. When that is done, the teacher signals students to begin "thinking and moving." Framing the task means putting it into some context and giving students a point of reference. It can also include words that modify the task or increase the level of complexity. The last part of the framing process involves simply asking students a question to indicate the cognitive and/or movement problem they need to solve in the immediate task. Exhibit 13.3 presents an example of framing the task and asking the questions for a short series to develop second-graders' knowledge of balancing concepts and balancing skills. Notice that the teacher uses the first part of the task presentation to make sure students understand the basic concept of balancing. Without that knowledge, the students would not be ready for the series of balancing tasks that follows. The task structure (described more fully in the next section) is simple, allowing all students to "think and move" on their own once each question is asked. The teacher clearly has a content progression in mind, consisting of a series of small, increasingly more complex problems for the students to solve.

Task structure

Inquiry Teaching can use a wide variety of task structures within which students "think and move." The task structure will provide students with the parameters for their engagement, including one or more of the following:

1. Space to be used
2. Equipment to use or select from

EXHIBIT	13.3	Framing the task and asking the questions to develop knowledge of balancing concepts and balancing skills.

Teacher: What does it mean to "balance"?

Students: To be able to stay up without falling or losing your place.

Teacher: Good. When do you use balance?

Students: When we walk and run.

Teacher: Yes, but are those the only times? How about when you kick a ball, or throw a ball, or spin yourself around? What happens if you lose your balance while doing those things?

Students: We will fall down.

Teacher: Yes. What else can happen?

Students: If you lose your balance when kicking, the ball won't go where you aimed it.

Teacher: Good. Now, I want you to think for a moment about what you can do to keep your balance when you are standing in place. (Teacher allows five seconds of wait time.)

Students: Mary: "You can lift your arms."

                Megan: "You can keep both feet on the floor."

                Jose: "You can try to stand up straight."

Teacher: OK. In your *self-space,* can you show me one way to balance while standing just on one foot?

(Students "think and move" for about one minute.)

Teacher: Great! I see lots of you showing me good examples of one-foot balancing. Now, can you balance on two feet at a low level?

(Students "think and move" for about a minute.)

Teacher: I see a lot of creative balancers! Now, can you show me how to keep your balance while touching three different body parts to the floor?

(Students "think and move" for about two minutes.)

---

3. Grouping (individual, partner, small group, large group)
4. Safety information
5. Time limit for completing the problem

Extending the example of the second-grade balancing lesson, the teacher could begin to use some different task structures to increase the cognitive and psychomotor problems for the children. Students would "think, then move" after each question is asked. See Exhibit 13.4. The task presentations are very brief, and the task structure changes several times, building on the previous structure. In task 4, the teacher introduces students to the concept of counterbalancing, anticipating that they will not be able to fit everyone on the shape at one time with individual balancing. They will need to learn how to use each other in ways that allow them all to balance on the shape.

| Task structures for a balancing lesson. | EXHIBIT | 13.4 |

1. Partner up with the person closest to you. Can you and your partner show me two ways to balance while making contact with each other?

2. One of the persons from each of the partner pair should go to the box in the center of the gym and take one of the shape pieces in any size you wish. [The box contains a variety of flat pieces of geometric shapes, ranging from small to large.] Now, with your partner can you show me how to balance while standing on your shape, with each of you having only one foot on the shape? Which size shape is it harder to balance on? Why?

3. Now, you and your partner find another pair to join up with, so you have a group of four. Can you try balancing all four of you on one shape? Is this easier or harder than before? Why?

4. For this last task you are going to have to really think hard and experiment in your group. Combine with another group to make a group of eight. Each group should get one shape and place it on the floor so that it is not near another group's shape (for safety). I will give you four minutes to complete this task. Listen carefully. Try to balance all eight persons on the shape, so that no one has more than one foot touching it. You may choose any shape and size your group wishes. If you can do this with a large shape in less than four minutes, try it with a smaller shape. Go.

Task structures similar to those used in the Tactical Games model (Chapter 14) can also work in the Inquiry Teaching model. Students can be placed in lead-up or modified games for a short time, followed by questions from the teacher to teach tactics, strategy, game skills, and rules. Highly open task structures can allow students to explore and be creative as they learn, for example, expressive movement and some forms of dance. The teacher might play a musical piece and give students 10 minutes to devise a short dance that expresses the emotions they hear in the music. Each student must then do a short performance, followed by an explanation of their movement interpretation of the music. As you have recognized by now, the task structure in the Inquiry Teaching model need only be prompted by a question in order to let students "think and move" in response to that question.

Content progression

Moving students through content in the Inquiry Teaching model happens in two simultaneous dimensions. The first dimension relates to the concept or skill to be learned, such as dribbling, passing, playing defense, or fitness. Just like in other models, the teacher puts the learning activities into a developmentally appropriate order that moves students from simple to more complex learning outcomes. (For example, see the Inquiry Teaching lesson plan on the IMPE website.) The second dimension is based on the levels in Bloom's taxonomy (refer to Chapter 5) and applied within each of the content sections. More will be discussed on that taxonomy later in this chapter, but the key question for the teacher is, "At what cognitive *and* psychomotor levels do I want students to learn this content?" If lower-level outcomes are targeted, then the teacher uses questions that get students engaged in activities promoting only knowledge or comprehension (e.g., understanding health-related fitness concepts like resting heart rate and being able to take it accurately). If higher-order outcomes are targeted, then the teacher must ask questions that lead students through the lower-order outcomes and into levels such as synthesis or evaluation (e.g., designing their own fitness programs and becoming skilled at fitness-enhancing exercises).

Engagement Patterns for Learning

The Inquiry Teaching model can use many different engagement patterns as students pursue solutions to the problem framed by the teacher. Students can "think and move" individually, in pairs, in small groups, in temporary teams, in large groups, and even as an entire class. The most appropriate engagement pattern will be determined by the complexity of the problem and the degree to which the teacher wants students to interact with others in its solution.

Teacher and Student Roles and Responsibilities

Each instructional model will have certain operations that must be completed to allow the model to function according to its design. Some of the operations are carried out by the teacher; others are carried out by one or more of the students. Exhibit 13.5 shows the major operations within the Inquiry Teaching model and indicates who is responsible for completing them during each lesson.

EXHIBIT 13.5 Teacher and student roles and responsibilities in Inquiry Teaching.

OPERATION OR RESPONSIBILITY	PERSON/PEOPLE RESPONSIBLE IN INQUIRY TEACHING
Starting class	The **teacher** begins class with a set induction.
Bringing equipment to class	The **teacher** brings the equipment or delegates that task to students.
Content listing	The **teacher** determines the list of cognitive and movement problems to be presented in the unit.
Task presentation	The **teacher** makes task presentations by framing each learning task or problem for students.
Task structure	The **teacher** typically decides the task structure for each task/problem but can allow students to make their own groups when such a structure is used.
Content progression	The **teacher** decides when the class will move on to new learning tasks/problems.
Assessment	Two options: 1. The **teacher** provides students with comments and feedback on the quality of their cognitive and movement answers. 2. **Students** can view and critique other students' answers.

Verification of Instructional Processes

Teachers who use the Inquiry Teaching model can learn the benchmarks for their own and student behavior patterns. These benchmarks, outlined in Exhibits 13.6 and 13.7, verify that the Inquiry Teaching model has been designed and implemented with an acceptable degree of faithfulness, increasing the likelihood that the stated student learning outcomes will be achieved. Following these benchmarks closely also separates Inquiry Teaching from "just asking questions" in class from time to time within other models.

Assessment of Learning

Assessment in the Inquiry Teaching model takes several forms, due to the multiple levels of knowledge to be assessed and the need to assess both cognitive and psychomotor learning—sometimes separately and sometimes simultaneously. No single assessment technique will be adequate for all the possible kinds of learning that can happen in this model. Using a variety of informal, formal, traditional, and alternative approaches, teachers will need to develop their own assessment techniques that focus on each targeted learning outcome.

Inquiry Teaching teacher benchmarks.	EXHIBIT 13.6
BENCHMARK	**HOW TO VERIFY**
Unit content is based on a list of cognitive and movement knowledge areas to be learned by students.	Examine the teacher's unit plan.
The teacher frames each task/problem for students.	The teacher should write out each task/problem to be given to students on a lesson plan.
The teacher makes content progressions based on taxonomic levels.	The teacher should classify each task/problem according to Bloom's hierarchy and show a developmentally appropriate progression throughout the unit.
The teacher plans questions for each task/problem.	The teacher should write out a list of potential questions to be used in each task/problem.
The teacher monitors student engagement during tasks/problems.	Record the pattern of teacher movement during tasks/problems.
The teacher uses questions to facilitate student learning (rather than direct statements).	Record and monitor the teacher's verbal interactions with students.
The teacher provides students with adequate time to complete tasks/problems.	Observe and record the number of students who have completed a task/problem when the teacher moves to the next task/problem.
The teacher assesses student learning in the targeted domain(s) and level(s).	The teacher uses a checklist to indicate students' successful completion of tasks/problems given to them.

EXHIBIT 13.7 Inquiry Teaching student benchmarks.

BENCHMARK	HOW TO VERIFY
Students understand the problem as framed by the teacher.	Observe students right after the teacher indicates they should begin to "think and move." Students should quickly show evidence of thinking through the problem and should begin to explore movement answers soon after that.
Students understand the task structure as explained to them by the teacher.	Once engaged in the task/problem, students should show evidence of working toward answers that correspond to the structure as described by the teacher.
Students have the appropriate level of cognitive and movement knowledge demanded by the task/problem.	1. Student engagement is purposeful. 2. Students ask few clarification questions. 3. Students do not alter the task/problem as described by the teacher. 4. Students find the task/problem challenging but can complete it in a reasonable amount of time.
Students have learned to "think and move."	1. Use questions to check for student understanding. 2. Students can provide more than one answer to divergent questions. 3. Students can explain the processes they used to complete tasks and solve problems.
Students achieve higher-order learning (when that is targeted).	1. Students move creatively and purposefully. 2. Students' cognitive and movement answers match. 3. Students can critique others' answers. 4. Students need little direction to take on complex and longer tasks/problems.

Informal assessment

When the teacher has planned a series of short, fast-paced learning tasks or problems, it is likely that informal assessment will be the most practical way to go. Most of this assessment will be based on the teacher's observation of students as they think and move to develop answers to questions from the teacher. The teacher should begin the assessment process during lesson planning, when questions are framed and developed. For each question, the teacher should ask himself, "What will my students *say and/or do* to indicate that they have answered this question?" Convergent questions will lead to one or a few correct answers, while divergent questions will lead to several answers that the teacher will consider as indicators of student learning. By observing and counting the number of students who have formulated correct/acceptable answers to each question, the teacher can determine if student learning has occurred. It is helpful for the teacher to establish a "threshold" percentage (e.g., 80 percent) for each task/problem. When that percentage of the students has demonstrated correct/acceptable answers, the teacher moves to the next learning task.

A teacher can also *check for understanding* at the class level as an informal assessment strategy by asking the class to respond to the same question at one time and noting how many students provide a correct or acceptable answer. This is done frequently and quickly in class, with simple question stems like "Who knows . . . ?" or "Who can tell me . . . ?" or "How many of you were able to . . . ?" It is important to allow sufficient *wait time* so that each student can formulate his or her own answer, giving the teacher a better picture of student learning. Wait time is a period of five to eight seconds that elapses from the end of the question to the teacher taking answers from students.

Formal and traditional assessment

It is appropriate for a teacher to use traditional, formal assessment techniques to assess some lower-order learning outcomes in the Inquiry Teaching model. Short quizzes, computer-based tests, the completion of worksheets, and simple skills tests can provide the teacher with assessment information when learning is targeted at the levels of knowledge, comprehension, and application. These techniques have less validity and are often impractical in the assessment of higher-order outcomes.

Alternative assessment

Alternative assessment techniques can be used for all levels of learning in the Inquiry Teaching model, especially for the higher-order outcomes. When questions are framed creatively to reflect "real world" learning, the assessment will become highly authentic as well. The inquiry teacher can use several alternative ways to assess learning in this model:

1. Student-peer observation with a checklist
2. Student-peer critiques of other students' answers
3. Student self-assessment with a checklist
4. Student journals that explain how they arrived at answers
5. The Game Performance Analysis Instrument (GPAI) (Griffin, Mitchell, & Oslin, 1997) for game and other application-level outcomes (see Chapter 14)
6. Student-generated movement and media presentations
7. Check sheets based on the relevant levels of knowledge

Exhibit 13.8 shows an example of this last assessment technique, which the teacher could use in a single unit of instruction or keep over a longer time—even two or three years—to document student progression through knowledge levels in one area. The top of the check sheet indicates the area being assessed—balance. The columns are divided into the two major domains of learning to be assessed: cognitive (through students' verbalization of answers) and psychomotor (through students' ability to move). Each level of knowledge lists one indicator of student learning that must be observed (heard and seen) by the teacher. The teacher determines whether these indicators prove that the student has learned about balance at each level and in both domains.

EXHIBIT **13.8** Student check sheet for balance knowledge.

MOVEMENT CONCEPT: BALANCE   Name: _____

LEVEL ASSESSED	COGNITIVE INDICATOR(S)	MOVEMENT INDICATOR(S)
Knowledge	Can provide his/her own definition of "balance" when asked Achieved ☐	Can follow along with the teacher on several examples of static balancing Achieved ☐
Comprehension	Can identify when a person is "in balance" or "off balance" Achieved ☐	Can show the teacher two examples of being "in balance" and two examples of being "off balance" Achieved ☐
Application	Can identify three games or sports in which balance is important Achieved ☐	Can demonstrate the different kinds of balancing movements used in those three games or sports Achieved ☐
Analysis	Can correctly predict what will happen to a person's balance (increase or decrease) when changing from one position to another Achieved ☐	On the teacher's cue, can demonstrate how to increase or decrease his/her balance from a given starting position Achieved ☐
Synthesis	Can explain the importance of center of gravity in keeping one's balance Achieved ☐	Can show three ways to change his/her own center of gravity in a static balance position Achieved ☐
Evaluation	With a score sheet, can observe another student's gymnastics routine and correctly score that student's balance performance Achieved ☐	Can demonstrate the correct balancing movements for any part of the other student's performance that was scored low Achieved ☐

IMPLEMENTATION NEEDS AND MODIFICATIONS

Teacher Expertise

Teachers who use the Inquiry Teaching model will need to have particular expertise in several areas of the proposed knowledge base presented in Chapter 3.

Learners. Inquiry teachers will need to consider students' cognitive and psychomotor abilities to use the model effectively. Student ability will determine the degree to which students are able to comprehend questions used by the teacher and to engage in the problem-solving process. Teachers should have good knowledge of the stages of cognitive development and be able to place students at the correct stage.

Learning theories. There are many cognitive learning theories in education today. Inquiry teachers should be familiar with those that contribute to the foundation of the Inquiry Teaching model: constructivism, discovery learning (Bruner, 1961), and Jean Piaget's theories on child growth and development. The key here is for the teacher to recognize which part of each theory is applied in the Inquiry Teaching model. No single theory, nor the teaching strategies set forth in it, can fully encompass the scope of the Inquiry Teaching model.

Developmental appropriateness. The strong emphasis on cognitive learning that then leads to outcomes in the psychomotor domain makes the teacher's knowledge of learning levels critical in this model. The teacher must not only know the cognitive level at which each question is aimed, but also understand how that level will manifest itself through movement; both levels should match students' developmental stage. Determining developmental appropriateness is particularly complicated in this model, since the teacher must know if the students are intellectually ready to take on the problem and, most important, if they are able to execute a corresponding movement answer for it. It does not benefit students if they can think of an answer but do not have the ability to demonstrate that knowledge in the psychomotor domain.

Cognitive and psychomotor learning taxonomies. The Inquiry Teaching model is strongly based on Bloom's levels of cognitive learning. Therefore, teachers must know this classification system well and be able to recognize indicators of cognitive and psychomotor learning at each level. For example, if the teacher asks a simple knowledge question ("Can you show me where to make contact with the ball when you kick it?") but the student's movement answer remains only at the comprehension level (the student shows and explains the difference between a pass and a shot on goal), the teacher must be able to identify the mistake and redirect the question so that the student responds at the appropriate level the next time.

Task analysis and content progression. A task analysis for Inquiry Teaching involves a combination of cognitive concepts and psychomotor performance demands. Rather than list a sequence of skills to be mastered and performance criteria to be met, the teacher analyzes each part of the unit content for the kinds of cognitive knowledge students will need to acquire as they progress through the unit. This requires that the teacher be knowledgeable about those concepts, along with the motor performance cues included within them. Exhibit 13.9 shows an example of a typical task analysis for the tennis serve, including both the skills and concepts required by each task. The teacher would instruct students in each component of the task, working toward performance proficiency.

This kind of task analysis would lead the teacher to design a two-dimensional content progression: one based on the concepts needed for the skill and one based on the performance of the movement patterns it includes. The series of learning tasks would allow students first to learn each concept by responding to questions asked by the teacher and then to explore the movement pattern needed to execute each concept in the tennis serve.

EXHIBIT 13.9 Task analysis for a tennis serve.	
SKILLS	**CONCEPTS**
1. Stance	force, balance, weight transfer
2. Grip	force, friction, effect of grip on contact angle and ball spin
3. Toss	arm extension, accuracy, timing
4. Contact point	angle of contact
5. Follow-through	momentum, power, accuracy, preparation for return
6. Strategy	first service, second service, singles, doubles, anticipation of return, "no man's land"

Content progression is based on student advancement through the various levels of Bloom's taxonomy, until they have reached the level targeted by the teacher. Beginning students would be likely to progress through the lower-order types of learning, while more advanced students would focus on higher-order problems and tasks within each area included in the unit.

Movement content. By now you get the idea that the content taught within the Inquiry Teaching model is not just skill performance in sport, fitness, games, dance, and so on. It is skill performance in combination with knowledge of the concepts that are needed to understand each movement form and that contribute to proficient performance. When the learning goal is to promote student expression and meaning, those become the focal points of the moment. Therefore, to be an effective teacher in this model, the inquiry teacher must have a more comprehensive knowledge of physical education (movement) content than, for example, a teacher using only direct instruction. This knowledge will lead the teacher to observe student movement from a different perspective. When a mistake is observed, the inquiry teacher will not simply provide the student with corrective feedback. The teacher should determine what knowledge the student lacks and ask key questions to get the student to think through alternative response patterns that will be transformed into an appropriate movement answer the next time.

Assessment. Student learning in the Inquiry Teaching model can be assessed with traditional and alternative techniques. It is possible to assess lower-order learning with written tests and regular checks for understanding during lessons. Checklists can also verify that students have demonstrated verbal and movement answers to major concepts in a unit. Higher-order learning is more difficult to assess, because it often requires a teacher's subjective judgment and interpretation of student answers. The key to all types of assessment in the Inquiry Teaching model is the teacher's own knowledge of which cognitive and movement answers given by students are appropriate or inappropriate and, specifically, how those answers represent students' learning of the embedded concepts. In many ways, it is a matching process: the teacher asks a question that leads to student responses. The teacher must then determine which answers fall within a range of acceptable answers, which would indicate the desired kind of student learning targeted by the teacher.

Curriculums. It is possible to use the Inquiry Teaching model to teach any movement content at any grade level. However, the origins of the model are strongly rooted in several curriculum programs that rely heavily on this approach to teaching:

1. Movement education
2. Educational gymnastics
3. Skill themes
4. Educational dance
5. Group initiatives and New Games

The teacher will need to become familiar with the principles and specific content taught in these curriculums, in order to adopt the Inquiry Teaching model for each one.

Key Teaching Skills

Teachers who use the Inquiry Teaching model must apply effective teaching skills in unique ways to allow the model to facilitate the learning objectives planned in content units. Some of these skills are described in detail below, and some are exemplified in the Inquiry Teaching lesson plan on the IMPE website.

Planning. The teacher's list of knowledge areas to be learned by students provides the starting point for unit planning with the Inquiry Teaching model. The teacher decides the progressions and levels of knowledge to be covered in the unit and then plans a sequence of questions, problems to be solved, and specific learning activities for student engagement. This will look like the planning process for Direct Instruction in many ways, except that the content will be a strong combination of cognitive and performance outcomes.

Lesson planning in the Inquiry Teaching model is less structured than for other models, since it is often difficult to anticipate how long it will take students to complete each problem-solving task and how long question-based interactions need to be to help students grasp the knowledge of the moment. Because students' ability to take on new problems given by the teacher depends so much on their previous knowledge, the teacher must ensure that students have grasped the prerequisite knowledge. "Covering" concepts should not take precedence over having students learn the targeted concepts in each lesson.

It is strongly advised that the inquiry teacher not "wing it" through the problem-solving progression in a lesson. The lesson plan should include how each problem will be framed, the specific problems to be solved, a list of questions to ask students before they become engaged, student movement patterns to be monitored, and follow-up questions to ask when students are engaged in learning activities. This kind of planning can prepare the inquiry teacher for many possible student answers and movement patterns, giving her time to plan some of the interactions before the class begins. Most inquiry lessons cannot be completely scripted before class begins, but the most effective ones are those in which the teacher has correctly anticipated a good number of the students' verbal and movement answers and is ready to use those answers as "teaching moments." For example, when trying to teach middle school students the concept of correct offensive spacing in soccer, the teacher can anticipate that the students will initially "bunch up" around the ball and have no open passing lanes. From that expectation, the teacher can prepare to ask questions like, "Why is your team not making any passes?" or "Is that the best way to move the ball toward the goal?" or "How do you help the defense when you do that?" or, after stopping play, "Can you show me where you should be when the ball is at midfield?"

Time and class management. In inquiry lessons, the teacher has control of the flow and pacing of planned learning activities. Time and class management may look somewhat informal, but in reality the teacher maintains close control of how the lesson proceeds and is well aware of the time each activity takes to complete. The teacher will monitor students to make sure they are properly engaged during learning activities and are following all class rules. It is important that the teacher have a firm but flexible management plan that allows students time to develop their problem-solving abilities and also maintains a steady pace for the class.

Task presentation and task structure. Inquiry teachers must have three key pedagogical skills: the ability to frame problems for students, excellent questioning skills, and the ability to design learning tasks that simultaneously challenge students intellectually and physically.

Framing the learning problem. The inquiry teacher must be able to "set the stage" for the upcoming learning problem, regardless of the problem's size and complexity. Set induction can be used effectively to alert students to the importance of the knowledge they will learn and the context in which they will apply it. This will also increase student interest in the upcoming task. When teaching younger students, it is often helpful to create a story line that goes with the lesson's sequence of learning tasks, allowing the children to place themselves in the story and act out the part of a certain character. This also helps them relate class activities to familiar stories, people, characters, and places.

Questioning students. Good questioning skills include a number of different elements, such as question level, question type, wait time, and use of probes.

1. *Levels of questions.* The teacher must apply his skill in using questions at three times: at the end of the problem framing when the initial question directs students to be engaged, during engagement in the problem-solving process, and during the lesson review. At all three times the teacher's most critical skill is matching the level of questions with the intended level of stu-

dent learning. Questions for each level share some common *stems* that can be used to prompt student engagement regardless of the particular content. Exhibit 13.10 shows some examples of question stems that can be used in physical education.

2. *Types of questions.* Questions at the levels of knowledge, comprehension, and application typically lead to one or a few correct answers. These are referred to as *convergent questions,* because they require the learner to sort out and identify one or a limited number of potentially correct answers. Questions at the levels of analysis, synthesis, and evaluation typically lead to any number of plausible answers that solve the problem posed by the teacher. Because they stimulate learners to "branch out" in their thinking, they are labeled *divergent questions.* The skilled inquiry teacher must be aware of the types of questions to ask students, so that answers can be assessed appropriately. You can refer to Exhibit 13.10 for examples of questions at each level.

3. *Wait time.* The major purpose of the Inquiry Teaching model is to get students to use their intellectual abilities to solve problems silently or verbally and then follow with a "movement answer." It is therefore essential that students have time to formulate answers on their own, before other students are allowed to tell or show their answers. Research has shown that waiting at least five to eight seconds before allowing any student to answer convergent questions increases all students' academic performance. A wait time of 15 or more seconds should be used for divergent questions (Tobin, 1987).

4. *Probes.* Borich (1992) recommends that inquiry teachers regularly use probes, or redirects. A probe is a question that follows a student's answer in order to:

   a. *Elicit clarification.* Get the student to rephrase, reword, or refine the original answer (e.g., "I didn't understand that answer. Can you say it in another way for me?").

   b. *Solicit new information.* When the student has given a partially correct or nearly acceptable answer, the teacher asks for more details (e.g., "That was close. Can you give me some more information?").

   c. *Redirect the flow.* The teacher gently, positively rephrases the question when the student has not made a correct answer. Without using harsh or abrupt language, the teacher cues the student to "think again" (e.g., "That wasn't the answer I was looking for. Can you give it some more thought and try again?").

Designing challenging tasks. The questions used in Inquiry Teaching determine the task structure to a large degree. Some questions require students to work alone, while other questions direct students to work in pairs, small groups, or large groups. Some questions demand very short periods of engagement time (particularly convergent ones), while other questions (higher-order, divergent) will need more time—perhaps as long as three to five minutes. The

EXHIBIT 13.10	Some common question stems for Inquiry Teaching.	
LEVEL	**SOME COMMON STEMS**	**EXAMPLES**
Knowledge	"Who can show me . . . ?"	"Who can show me the correct way to do the first part of the 'electric slide'?"
	"Who can tell me . . . ?"	"Who can tell me where you stand when your partner is serving in tennis doubles?"
Comprehension	"Can you explain . . . ?"	"Can you explain why your partner's shots keeping going off-line?"
	"Why would you . . . ?"	"Why would you want to play a zone defense in basketball?"
	"How do you get [something] to happen?"	"How do you get your badminton opponent in position to make an overhead smash shot at her?"
Application	"Can you combine . . . ?"	"Can you combine a slide and a gallop? If so, please show me how to do that."
	"Knowing what you know now, can you tell me . . . ?"	"We just discussed the offensive strategy for passing in flag football. Knowing that, and if you are on defense, how would you try to prevent the offense from succeeding?"
	"How is [something] similar to . . . ?"	"Can you show me three ways that playing defense in floor hockey is similar to playing defense in team handball?"
Analysis	"How is [this] different from . . . ?"	"How does the badminton low, short serve set up your opponent differently than the high, deep serve? When would you use each one?"
	"Why would you not . . . ?"	"Why would you not stretch cold muscles?"
	"Analyze . . . "	"I am making a shape with my body. Can you analyze it for the class? How stable is it? Is my balance good or bad? Why?"
Synthesis	"What will happen if . . . ?"	"What do you think will happen if you use a longer implement to strike the lighter ball?"
	"Can you make a new . . . ?"	"Can you and your partner make a new dance from this music?"
	"If [something] changes, how will you compensate?"	"If you change your center of gravity, what will you need to do to increase stability?"
Evaluation	"What should [someone] have done . . . ?"	"When Molly had the basketball on the right wing on the fast break, what should she have done to move her defender more?"
	"Is it better to . . . or . . . ?"	"Is it better to hit this putt fast or slow? Why?"
	"Why do you . . . ?"	"I see you running regularly. Why do you do that so often?"
	"Is that the right way to . . . ?"	"I see you use the two-handed grip for your forehand shots. Is that the right technique?"

teacher will need to use her expertise to fashion questions, determine the best task structure to answer each one, and allocate the appropriate amount of problem-solving time to students.

Communication. As you might expect, communication skills in the Inquiry Teaching model center on the abilities to frame the problem or task and to use questions as the primary pedagogical strategy to promote intended learning outcomes. Teachers need to be clear and concise in both areas, giving students only what they need to know to define the problem and the parameters for their engagement. Students cannot be expected to be properly engaged if they do not understand the problem to be solved at any given moment.

As you know by now, the inquiry teacher uses very few direct communications to students. The major idea is to "ask, not tell," so when the teacher wishes for students to learn, he must find ways to ask questions that will prompt students into "thinking first, then moving" to explore, solve problems, and develop several plausible answers. For a few times, the teacher might need to give students clues, or even direct answers, to help them get "unstuck" on their way to more complex answers. Such clues should be limited, however.

The teacher communicates other types of instructional information in the form of comments to students while they are engaged and feedback when students give or show answers. Comments during engagement should support students' efforts, giving small hints that students are "on the right track," or direct them toward the process of problem solving. Feedback should be directed toward process and outcomes demonstrated through students' answers. It is also possible for the teacher to use other students to provide feedback, helping those students develop analytic and evaluative knowledge.

Review and closure. The lesson review should be consistent with the level of questions asked by the teacher during class. If the teacher has targeted the level(s) of intended student learning, the review questions can serve as an informal assessment strategy as well as a way to "tie it all together" and alert students to the next lesson's content. The teacher must be careful not to overextend the level of questions in the review, making them too difficult given the students' ability to answer them. It is important to focus on what students have *learned*, not what they don't yet know in the unit. The closure should follow the overall design of the Inquiry Teaching model, with the teacher asking students what needs to be done to finish the lesson (e.g., where equipment should go, how much time they have until their next class, and what students need to remember for next time).

Contextual Requirements

The Inquiry Teaching model has few contextual demands, so it can be used in almost any physical education setting. The three main factors to consider are activity space, equipment, and time. The task structure will determine the need for activity space. It can range from needing only enough room for every student to move safely in her personal space to needing large spaces for group explorations and problem solving. It is important that all students (or groups of students) have enough equipment to prevent having to wait to take turns. The discovery process will be ineffective if one student has to wait and watch another student solve the problem. For the waiting student, the learning process will then be imitation, not creative problem solving. Finally, all students should have an adequate amount of time to engage in the problem-solving process. Some students will take longer than others, but all students should be given ample time to "think and then move" for themselves. Again, if the class progresses at a pace that is too fast for some students, those students will learn simply by imitating their peers' answers, or they may not learn at all.

Selecting and Modifying Inquiry Teaching

As you learned in the beginning of this chapter, the Inquiry Teaching model as presented here merges strategies used in several physical education curriculum models, such as movement education and skill theme learning—curriculums used mainly in elementary school programs. "Teaching by questioning" is used regularly in those curriculums, but it can also be applied in many other physical education content areas and grade levels. I would recommend Inquiry Teaching as an effective model for the following physical education content areas:

1. Movement education/movement concepts
2. Educational gymnastics
3. Educational games
4. Dance
5. Group initiatives and New Games
6. Personal fitness concepts
7. Sport and activity concepts
8. Skill themes

The key thing to remember is that the model emphasizes the process of "thinking, then moving," so it can work with nearly any form of content—not just those listed. If the teacher wishes to develop students' cognitive knowledge in a way that leads to enhanced movement performance, then the Inquiry Teaching model is an appropriate choice.

Grade-level adaptations

The Inquiry Teaching model can be effective at all grades if the levels of cognitive and psychomotor problems given to students match their developmental readiness. Exhibit 13.11 shows some possible ways to match tasks to various grade levels.

GRADE LEVELS	SELECT INQUIRY TEACHING?	POSSIBLE ADAPTATIONS
Preschool	Yes	1. Limit to knowledge level. 2. Focus on student attention and listening skills.
Elementary	Yes	1. Frame the task/problem clearly. 2. Check for understanding before and during. 3. Use shorter tasks/problems.
Middle school/ junior high	Yes	No adaptations needed. The full Inquiry Teaching model can be implemented.
High school	Yes	1. Focus on higher-order learning. 2. Use fewer, longer tasks/problems. 3. Promote answers that require media and technology.
College/adult	Yes	1. Focus on higher-order learning. 2. Use fewer, longer tasks/problems. 3. Promote cognitive answers that require media and technology.

Grade-level adaptations for Inquiry Teaching in physical education. **EXHIBIT 13.11**

Adaptations to accommodate diverse groups of learners

Inquiry Teaching can be a highly inclusive model for physical education if the teacher asks questions that students can understand and if students have the cognitive and physical abilities to develop answers to those questions. Exhibit 13.12 lists some strategies that address a variety of special learning needs found in many schools today.

PLANNING TIPS FOR INQUIRY TEACHING

eachers who choose to use this model can benefit by following a few additional planning tips:

1. Always remember that the content progression should move students to higher levels of cognitive and physical proficiency.
2. "Ask, don't tell" as much as you can and as often as you can. Do not get into the habit of giving students the solutions to learning tasks/problems. In this model, students should try to come up with those answers themselves.
3. There can be a tendency to "shoot from the hip" with questions in this model. But until you have a lot of experience and truly understand how to progress through the content with questions, it is best to prepare your questions ahead of time and write them into your lesson plans.

EXHIBIT | **13.12** | Strategies adapting Inquiry Teaching for diverse groups of learners.

FOR STUDENTS WITH HEARING AND/OR SPEECH IMPAIRMENTS:

1. Move these students closer when asking questions or giving directions.
2. Write the questions/tasks on cards that students can read.
3. Allow time for students with speech impairments to give their verbal answers completely. Use *redirects* when you cannot fully understand verbal answers (e.g., "Can you tell me a little more about . . . ?" "Did you really mean to say . . . ?" "Can you tell me that in your own words?")

FOR STUDENTS WITH SIGHT IMPAIRMENTS:

1. Use a larger font for task cards.
2. Do not ask students to perform very small or fast movements that require keen visual abilities. Get them to focus more on larger body movements.

FOR STUDENTS WITH PHYSICAL DISABILITIES:

1. Ask questions that promote higher levels of developmentally appropriate performance for all students.
2. Accept movement answers that are within their abilities.
3. Give them more time to devise movement answers.

FOR STUDENTS WHO DO NOT SPEAK ENGLISH:

1. Use student translators, when available. Pair matching bilingual students with non-English speakers.
2. Provide task presentations in appropriate language, or use translated closed-caption media when possible.
3. When using examples as part of the question/task description, give examples that include other cultures.

FOR LOWER-SKILLED STUDENTS:

1. Give students more time to "think, then move."
2. Provide extra encouragement and praise to the slower learners.
3. Use *divergent* questions that allow for a wide range of acceptable answers.

FOR STUDENTS WITH BEHAVIOR DISABILITIES:

1. Provide students with behavior disabilities with extra encouragement for their participation and creativity in devising answers.
2. Use task structures that allow for individual engagement if students cannot work cooperatively.
3. Focus on the contribution to be made by students with behavior disabilities, not the potential for misbehavior.

4. Be very clear with your questions; students will devise answers based on *their* understanding of the question—not yours.
5. Allow ample time in your lesson for students to think about answers and to experiment with several possible ones.
6. Monitor your patterns for calling on students to give answers. Be sure that all students get approximately equal chances to give verbal and/or movement answers.

UNIT AND LESSON PLAN EXAMPLES
FOR INQUIRY TEACHING INSTRUCTION

Y ou will find several complete unit plans with lesson plans for Inquiry Teaching on the IMPE website. It is not recommended that you follow these examples exactly as they are presented. The context, specific learning objectives, and content of your own unit will require you to make changes in these examples to allow the Inquiry Teaching model to lead to the most effective instruction in your situation.

SUMMARY

The Inquiry Teaching model as presented in this chapter is designed from instructional strategies used in several physical education curriculum models, such as movement education and skill theme development. Those and many other approaches use questioning as the primary instructional interaction pattern that prompts learners to "think, then move." There is enough commonality in those approaches to merge them into the Inquiry Teaching model, which can help teachers formally design and implement question-based instruction for many content areas and grades in physical education.

All physical education teachers use questions in their instruction, and good questioning skills are necessary in nearly every model presented in this book. However, the difference in the Inquiry Teaching model is that the use of questions is not unplanned or sporadic. Asking questions and framing learning tasks in the form of problems are the most essential pedagogical operations in this model. There are some new conceptualizations of teaching that are likely to make inquiry-based teaching even more prominent in physical education. Constructivist teaching strategies are becoming more and more commonplace in all subjects, and they share many of the same attributes as Inquiry Teaching, particularly getting students to formulate new knowledge from existing knowledge, prompting students to learn by exploring, and placing the teacher in the role of facilitator of student learning.

Used in physical education for over four decades, question-based teaching has emerged as the primary strategy for movement education and movement-based programs in elementary programs. With the recent development of other student-centered strategies and instructional models, along with the promotion of cognitive learning outcomes in physical education (NASPE, 2004), a formal Inquiry Teaching model like the one presented here offers an effective way to teach a wide variety of program content at all grade levels in physical education.

LEARNING ACTIVITIES

1. Make a list of five activity units (e.g., movement skills, fitness, softball, tennis, golf) that might be taught in a physical education program. Next, determine an appropriate grade level (P, K–2, 3–5, 6–8, 9–12) for teaching each of those activity units. Now, write two major learning outcomes

for those units. Then, go through the process of selecting an instructional model, shown in Chapter 2, to determine if Inquiry Teaching would be an appropriate model for teaching that activity to children at that grade level.

2. If Inquiry Teaching is appropriate for that activity, grade, and goals, mention three things that make it appropriate. If Inquiry Teaching is not appropriate for that activity, grade, and goals, mention three things that make it inappropriate.

3. For one activity unit at one grade level (e.g., third-grade skill themes, middle school volleyball, high school tennis), write a complete list of content to be taught in that unit with Inquiry Teaching. Remember that the content should be based mostly on cognitive learning outcomes.

4. Pick one of the learning outcomes identified in Activity 1, and design an assessment strategy for monitoring student learning.

5. Write an annotated lesson plan for each of the first three lessons of this unit. Be sure to show the level for each question/problem you give to students.

TOPICS FOR REFLECTION & SMALL-GROUP DISCUSSION

1. I have suggested in this chapter how the Inquiry Teaching model is aligned to achieve one or more of the NASPE standards. Take a moment to review those alignments (refer back to Exhibit 13.1). After that, make some notes about whether you agree with those alignments, and then share them in your small group. When you have arrived at your final thoughts, please share them on the IMPE website Forum for others to review, and check back for replies.

2. Mention three ways Inquiry Teaching is similar to Direct Instruction and three ways it is different.

3. In general, which types of students are placed at an advantage in this model, and which students are at a disadvantage?

4. Why is it so important for teachers using this model to "ask, don't tell"?

5. Inquiry Teaching is rarely used in high school physical education, but it is used extensively in lower grades. Discuss some reasons for this.

SUGGESTED READINGS FOR INQUIRY TEACHING

Dillon, J. T. (1988). *Questioning and teaching: A manual of practice.* New York: Teachers College Press.

Graham, G., Holt/Hale, S., & Parker, M. (2009). *Children moving: A reflexive approach to teaching physical education* (8th ed.). Boston: McGraw-Hill. (Note: Inquiry Teaching model for skill theme teaching)

Mosston, M., & Ashworth, S. (2002). *Teaching physical education* (5th ed.). San Francisco: B. Cummings. (Note: Chapter on guided discovery style)

Stanley, S. (1977). *Physical education: A movement orientation* (2nd ed.). New York: McGraw-Hill.

chapter

14

TACTICAL GAMES
*Teaching Games
for Understanding*

The largest single content area in most physical education programs is the teaching and learning of sport-related games. Other movement forms are constantly being introduced into physical education, but it is safe to say that traditional games content still remains the biggest part of most schools' curriculum—particularly in middle grades through college. Except for a few innovative curriculum and instruction models like Sport Education (Chapter 11), little has changed in the way teachers plan and implement games units: students get a brief time to practice isolated skills, followed by an introduction to game rules, with an extended time to play the game for the rest of the unit. Students who do not enter the unit with existing game skills and knowledge are not likely to improve as the unit progresses. This approach favors students who come to the unit with previous experience and abilities in the game being taught. Moreover, this approach is likely to focus mainly on skill development and, to a lesser extent, on the strategies needed to play the game well.

But the teacher is not entirely at fault in this scenario. Students like to play games much more than they like to practice game skills in repetitive drills, and they'll often show great resistance when directed to work on discrete skills that they perceive as having little to do with game performance. Once a teacher tells a class that they are starting a games unit (e.g., soccer), there is one predictable question that students will ask: "When do we get to play?" That question will be asked early and often in the unit, until the games segment actually begins. Experienced teachers also know that one of the "faux pas" of physical education is to start the games segment of a unit and then later direct students back into drills. Student resistance can become almost a rebellion at that point!

The most difficult part of this scenario is that physical education students are rarely ready for the complexities of game play when that segment of a unit begins. Many of them do not possess the skills or tactical knowledge needed to carry on even a semblance of the game, so the game becomes an exercise in futility and frustration, defined by poor play. The irony is that many students think the best way to learn a game is to play the full version of it, so they would rather keep the overall game structure than revert to skill development through drills, lead-up games, or modified games.

The Tactical Games model cleverly uses student interest in the game structure to promote the skill development and tactical knowledge needed for competent game performance. In traditionally taught game units, the teacher plans a progression from basic drills to more complex skills, followed by explanations of rules and the playing of the game's full version. In the Tactical Games model, the teacher plans a sequence of learning tasks that have a gamelike structure to develop students' skills and tactics, leading to modified or full versions of the game. These gamelike tasks and modified games are called *game forms.* The model emphasizes the development of tactical knowledge that facilitates skill applications in smaller versions of the game so that students can apply that learning in the full version when the time comes. In a sense, students are always "playing the game" as they work on essential skills and tactics in a developmentally appropriate sequence.

As the name indicates, the organizing center of the Tactical Games model is *tactics,* the combination of strategy and skill needed to perform in game and gamelike situations. For instance, in a softball unit the goal would not be for students to "learn how to field ground balls." Rather, students would strive to learn situational applications of fielding ground balls—positioning, decision making, and understanding that lead to the correct execution of fielding skills according to the demands of the game form situation. Tactics and skills develop in the sequence of game forms, each of which contains a stated *tactical problem* that defines the learning objective for the current task (Griffin, Mitchell, & Oslin, 1997). It is essential that students solve the tactical problem by knowing the correct position, options, and plays in the given situation. Performance follows from that understanding. For example, in a traditionally taught softball unit, the teacher would divide the content into familiar skills such as catching, fielding, batting, and base stealing. In a Tactical Games softball unit, the content would be defined by tactical problems such as advancing runners, situational hitting, and defensive positioning. When students understand the importance of each concept, they then acquire the tactical knowledge and skills needed to execute those in a game form, modified game, or full game.

OVERVIEW

The Tactical Games instructional model evolved from a British conceptualization of games teaching called *teaching for understanding* (Bunker & Thorpe, 1982). Dissatisfied with the ways that games content was typically taught (such as some of the ways just mentioned), Bunker and Thorpe argued that physical education programs should attempt to teach the underlying principles of games so that students really understand each game's structure and tactics, along with the necessary performance skills. This approach also emphasized the use of developmentally appropriate versions of games at all grade levels, making it rare for students to play full, adult versions of games. Bunker and Thorpe promoted the notion of *games classification* to help students understand the underlying structure of each game by identifying common attributes among similarly classified games. Almond (1986) suggested that nearly all games taught in a physical education program can be classified into one of four types: invasion, net/wall, fielding/run scoring, and target. Examples of each type are shown in Exhibit 14.1.

Games classifications and examples.		EXHIBIT 14.1
GAME TYPE	**EXAMPLES**	
Invasion	Basketball	Hockey (ice, field, floor)
	Football	Lacrosse
	Net ball	Soccer
	Ultimate games	
Net/wall	*Net:*	*Wall:*
	Badminton	Handball
	Pickleball	Racquetball
	Table tennis	Squash
	Volleyball	
Fielding/run scoring	Baseball	Cricket
	Kickball	Softball
Target	Croquet	Billiards
	Bowling	Golf

Adapted from Almond, L., 1986, pp. 71–72.

Games with the same classification share many common features that students can be taught to recognize and carry over to other games in that category. Basic concepts like positioning, off-the-ball movements, with-ball skills, playing offense, playing defense, and tactics become the building blocks within each category, with direct attempts made to teach students how to generalize those concepts and apply them to similar games. For instance, the concept of defensive positioning is quite similar for soccer, basketball, and hockey. Students would be taught the concept of defensive positioning in ways that will allow them to apply it to those three games, building on their tactical awareness and skills from one game to the next.

Bunker and Thorpe (1982) based their *Teaching Games for Understanding* (TGFU) model on six components, using a particular game as the organizing center in the instructional unit (see Exhibit 14.2).

- Step 1 introduces the game, including its classification and an overview of how it is played.
- Step 2 serves to promote student interest in the game by teaching students its history and traditions.
- Step 3 develops students' tactical awareness by presenting the major tactical problems within the game.

EXHIBIT 14.2 The Teaching Games for Understanding model.

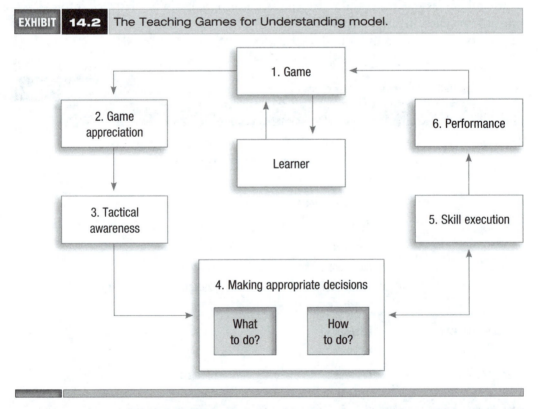

From Thorpe, R., Bunker, D., & Almond, L. (1986). *Rethinking Games Teaching.* (Used with permission by R. Thorpe, Sr. Editor).

- Step 4 uses gamelike learning activities (game forms) that teach students to recognize when and how to apply tactical knowledge.

- Step 5 begins to combine tactical knowledge with skill execution, again in gamelike activities.

- In Step 6, students develop proficient performance ability, based on this combination of tactical and skill knowledge, and they apply that knowledge in game forms or full versions of games.

As you can see, the learning of motor skills does not come until Step 5, which is the *first* step in many traditional approaches to teaching games in physical education.

In the last 15 years, several U.S. physical educators have collaborated with the British developers of the TGFU model. Although still very much based on the work of Rod Thorpe, David Bunker, and Len Almond, the American version has evolved into a more formal instructional model called Tactical Games (Griffin, Mitchell, & Oslin, 1997). The Tactical Games approach is now being used by more and more physical education teachers at all grade levels, offering an interesting and effective way to teach traditional games content in an untraditional way. The model established by Griffin, Mitchell, and Oslin will be the one presented in this chapter; however, it must be noted that their model owes a huge debt to the work of Thorpe, Bunker, and Almond.

The Tactical Games model is based on a sequence of developmentally appropriate game and gamelike learning activities (game forms) that focus on tactical problems for students to solve—first cognitively and then through the execution of skilled motor performance. The teacher begins by determining the most essential tactics needed to play the game. This becomes the content listing for each unit of instruction. For example, in basketball for middle school students, the most essential tactics might involve:

1. Moving the ball on offense

2. Shot selection

3. Off-the-ball movements

4. Defensive guarding (zone and player-to-player)

5. Positioning for rebounding

6. Fast breaks

7. Out-of-bounds plays and defense

The teacher would then design a series of learning activities within each tactical area. The first learning activity in each area would be a game form, starting with simple game forms and progressing to more complex ones. During each game form, the teacher analyzes students' tactical knowledge and abilities, identifying gaps in their understanding and skills that need to be practiced. The teacher can then decide whether to have students remain in the game form or practice skills in drill structures. To use the model as it is designed, teachers should incorporate the game form structure as much as possible, to keep the focus on tactical applications of skills. Repetitive, static drills should be used only to develop the most basic skills needed to participate in the simulation activities.

According to Griffin, Mitchell, and Oslin (1997), the game forms should be *representative* of the full game and use *exaggerated* situations to focus on tactical skill development. To be *representative* means that the game form contains realistic situations that students will face in the full game. To be *exaggerated* means that the game form is set up in a way that forces students to focus only on the tactical problem of the moment. For example, if teaching students the offensive and defensive tactics of the "rundown" play in baseball, the teacher should stage the learning activity so that it looks like a real rundown; the distances between bases are regulation, all players start in the correct fielding positions, and base running rules are in effect. That makes the game form representative. By isolating the rundown play and practicing it many times, students remain focused on that tactical problem for an extended period, rather than just the few times it might occur in the flow of a game. Within those repetitions, each student would have the opportunity to participate in all the positions involved in the rundown—something not likely to happen in a real game. In combination, the repetition and the varied participation provide the exaggeration feature of the game form.

Doolittle and Girard (1991) discuss the role of the tactical problem in the model and how the teacher can prompt students to solve it with targeted questions. The tactical problem is the key concept that students must understand in order to execute the situated skill proficiently from each involved position. Think back to the previous example of the rundown play in baseball or softball. If you are the runner, what might be the most important tactical problem to solve, once you are in that situation? How would you improve your chances of getting to a base safely? The teacher would ask students to consider some tactics for that scenario before the game form begins as well as during it. After students tell the teacher a viable solution, they then try to execute that solution in the game form. But it all starts with solving the tactical problem cognitively.

ALIGNMENT WITH NASPE NATIONAL STANDARDS

Exhibit 14.3 shows the alignment of the Tactical Games model with the NASPE standards. As you can see, the Tactical Games model is strongly and consistently aligned with standards 1 and 2. Its alignment with standard 3 will depend on the specific game being learned; high-activity games (e.g., badminton, Ultimate, tennis) have a stronger alignment than low-activity games (e.g., softball). Alignment with standard 4 is typically weak because learning tasks in this model focus on skill and tactics—not on tasks that promote physical fitness.

NASPE STANDARD	ALIGNMENT RATING	COMMENTS
Alignment of Tactical Games with NASPE National Standards.		EXHIBIT 14.3
1. Demonstrates competency in motor skills and movement patterns needed to perform a variety of physical activities	1	Strong alignment for skills needed for game play
2. Demonstrates understanding of movement concepts, principles, strategies, and tactics as they apply to the learning and performance of physical activities	1	Strong alignment for all components
3. Participates regularly in physical activity	1–3	Will vary according to the game being learned
4. Achieves and maintains a health-enhancing level of physical fitness	3	Weak alignment for fitness development, due to primary focus on skills and tactics in games
5. Exhibits responsible personal and social behavior that respects self and others in physical activity settings	2	Moderate alignment as students periodically interact to solve tactical problem
6. Values physical activity for health, enjoyment, challenge, self-expression, and/or social interaction	1–3	Strong alignment for enjoyment, challenge and self expression; moderate alignment for social interaction; weak alignment for health

Ratings categories:

1. Strong alignment
2. Moderate alignment
3. Weak alignment

FOUNDATIONS

Theory and Rationale

The Teaching Games for Understanding model and the Tactical Games model presented in this chapter both recognize the central role of games in nearly all physical education programs. But, in an attempt to improve student interest and learning in this large program content area, both models were developed in direct contrast to ways we typically teach games. It is the developers' way of not "throwing the baby out with the bathwater." Game content still constitutes the largest content area in physical education, so it is essential that we explore alternative and effective ways to teach it.

The basic theory for the Tactical Games model is not explicitly stated, but it is possible to suggest a theory by analyzing the key features in the model's design. It contains many of the attributes of constructivism, a cognitive learning theory that allows learners to make new learning from previous knowledge, in an attempt to foster understanding—not just to recall memorized facts or execute static skills. The use of the tactical problem in situated game forms and the emphasis on cognitive learning that precedes motor performance are strongly based on constructivist learning theories.

Griffin, Mitchell, and Oslin (1997) provide three major rationales behind the Tactical Games model. First, students' *interest and excitement* in games and game forms become positive motivators within the predominant task structure in the model. In some sense, students are always playing the game or some version of it, keeping interest and excitement high. Because students are almost always applying tactics and skills in gamelike situations, they are likely to see more clearly and immediately the need for knowledge development, further increasing their interest in learning activities. Second, *knowledge is empowering.* Students' increased understanding of the game allows them to be better players and less reliant on the teacher for their participation and decision making. Third, students can *transfer their understanding and performance* from game to game when applicable. Since games with the same classification contain many similar tactical problems, it is possible to teach game concepts that students can transfer to other like games, reducing the time they need to become proficient in new games.

Assumptions About Teaching and Learning

The Tactical Games model assumes certain principles about teaching and about learning; these principles are listed separately below.

Assumptions about teaching

1. The teacher is able to identify the major tactical problems in a game and organize each learning task to focus on the development of solutions to the inherent problem.

2. The teacher uses games and modified game forms to design learning tasks that develop the tactical awareness and motor skills needed to perform in the game.

3. The teacher is the primary source of games expertise but provides the students with indirect learning opportunities to engage with tactical problems.

4. All games and game forms must be developmentally appropriate versions for students at the grade level being taught. There is no expectation that students need to learn full-scale, adult versions of games.

Assumptions about learning

1. Most students find game participation to be more interesting, motivating, and authentic than skill development drills that have little application to game play.

2. Students can develop tactical awareness and decision-making abilities when those become the primary objectives of instruction.

3. Tactical awareness is prerequisite to performance skill, but students must eventually have both types of knowledge to perform well in games.

4. Tactical awareness and decision making should be taught from a constructivist approach, using a planned progression of learning activities based on tactical problems.

5. Tactical awareness and other types of student learning will transfer from game to game within similar classification categories.

The Major Theme of Tactical Games: Teaching Games for Understanding

As you can see, the major theme for the Tactical Games model is the label used for its predecessor, developed by Bunker and Thorpe (1982), "teaching games for understanding." This theme summarizes the single most important learning outcome in the Tactical Games model: to facilitate a deep level of understanding that can be applied in game and gamelike situations and can be transferred to other similar games. This theme also denotes the primary emphasis on students' tactical awareness and decision-making abilities.

Learning Domain Priorities and Domain Interactions

Domain priorities

The model's most basic assumption is that motor skill performance will be more proficient if it follows cognitive learning. It is important that students know *what* to do and *how* to do it in game settings, but in the Tactical Games model the *what* comes first (Griffin, Mitchell, & Oslin, 1997). This provides a clear statement of the domain priorities in the Tactical Games model:

First priority: Cognitive learning
Second priority: Psychomotor learning
Third priority: Affective learning

Domain interactions

The domain interaction in the Tactical Games model is also quite clear. Students solve a given tactical problem first in the cognitive domain, which in turn facilitates game-situation performance in the psychomotor domain. At some point, it is necessary for students to execute tactical decisions to demonstrate how well they have solved the situated problem, but again, the skill development components follow from the cognitive problem-solving activities.

The affective domain comes into play when students learn to combine their tactical awareness with motor performance to produce authentic learning outcomes, improving their appreciation of the game and their own self-esteem. As in many other models, learning in the affective domain occurs mostly through indirect interactions with learning in the other domains.

Student Developmental Requirements

Student readiness for learning. The Tactical Games model relies on students' ability to comprehend game and gamelike learning tasks and their embedded tactical problems. Therefore, students will need to have sufficient listening and intellectual abilities in order to benefit from the Tactical Games approach. Of course, the instruction and all learning tasks can be adjusted to meet students' levels, but if students do not have the capacity to make tactical decisions at any level, the model should not be used.

Student receptivity to the model. The Tactical Games model uses mostly directed teaching. Interactive questioning strategies encourage students to solve tactical problems; but by and large the teacher controls much of the learning environment, so the student learning preference profile will closely resemble that of Direct Instruction and appeal to students whom Reichmann and Grasha (1974) would classify as avoidant, competitive, and dependent. As mentioned in Chapter 2, those labels should not be given a negative interpretation. They simply describe how some students prefer the instructional environment to be designed and determine which students would be most receptive to learning under the Tactical Games model.

Validation of the Model

Research validation

Tactical Games is very new to physical education instruction. To date, little research has been completed on the model, so it is difficult to know if and when it can be used most effectively. Griffin, Oslin, and Mitchell (1995) compared the Tactical Games approach with skill-based techniques (Direct Instruction) in middle school net games classes. They reported that students had more interest and motivation in the Tactical Games classes but did not differ on the amount of skill knowledge acquired with either technique. Using the Game Performance Analysis Instrument as an authentic measure of student learning in game settings, the researchers found that students who received Tactical Games instruction had better performance in two important areas: court position and decision making. The GPAI is discussed more fully in the assessment section of this chapter.

Some early studies of the tactical model showed mixed results in its effectiveness. Turner and Martinek (1992, 1995) used the tactical model and a skill-based model in two middle school field hockey units of different lengths. There were few significant differences in the shorter six-week unit: the tactical students showed more improvement in two of the game performance variables. In the longer nine-class unit, the tactical students showed more improvement in procedural knowledge and game decision making. McPherson and French (1991) studied college tennis classes to test for differences between a tactical approach and a skill-based approach. The tactical groups were not given skill instruction initially, which resulted in significantly lower skill scores for that group. However, when given skills instruction as part of the model, their scores quickly improved. No differences were reported for knowledge gains or games performance.

Using TGFU, Turner (1996) compared the tactical model with a skills-technique approach in a seventh-grade field hockey unit. His results indicated that the TGFU students improved significantly more in skill development, declarative knowledge, and game performance. By using student interviews, he also reported that the TGFU students enjoyed the gamelike structure, giving those students more satisfaction than their counterparts undergoing technique-based instruction.

A 1996 monograph of the *Journal of Teaching in Physical Education* featured two research reports of studies conducted on the Tactical Games model compared with other approaches for teaching skills and tactics to ninth-grade students. In their summary of those studies, Rink, French, and Graham (1996) surmised that the tactical approach was no more effective than a skill-based approach in promoting student achievement, decision making, or positive affect. They cautioned that the tactical model might tend to develop tactics too far ahead of skill, so that students understand *what* to do but are no more able to execute the needed skill in game play than students who learn skill first and then tactics.

Oslin and Mitchell (1998) studied the degree to which a small sample of ninth-grade students were able to transfer tactical knowledge across two net games units. Although studies like this are supportive of the Tactical Games model, overall results are still very preliminary and cannot provide research-based validation for the Tactical Games model at this time, as noted by Chandler (1996) and Rink, French, and Graham (1996). Oslin and Mitchell (2006) conducted a major review of the numerous studies, including those cited above, completed on the TGFU model and other models that share very similar designs but are known by different labels. They called these "game-centered approaches" (GCA) (p. 627). Their summary findings indicate that: (1) GCA promoted improvement in skill performance in nearly all of the studies; (2) students who were taught with GCA consistently showed significant improvement in game knowledge and tactical decision making during game play; and (3) students' active involvement in games increased when instructed with GCA.

That does not mean the Tactical Games model is ineffective, since many of the findings show that tactically taught students improved at least as much as skill-taught students in skills, knowledge, decision making, and game performance. The completed research would suggest that the tactical model is one of several viable ways to teach games to students, even if it is not demonstrably superior in some respects.

Craft knowledge validation

One teacher's experience with the Tactical Games model has now become typical of how TGFU is viewed in our field. Rebecca Berkowitz (1996), writing in the *Journal of Physical Education, Recreation & Dance*, outlined her own philosophical shift from "teaching skill" to "teaching tactics":

> Changing the way I teach games has been an enlightening and challenging endeavor. For me and my students, the tactical approach appears to have been beneficial. It has made me rethink my philosophical view of teaching

for skill proficiency. Even though skill proficiency was my major focus, it was never an outcome in my classroom. Now [with the tactical approach] improvement can be seen in my students' game play performance and their understanding of the game. I think I am accomplishing more now, and I see my students truly succeeding and enjoying physical education. (p. 45)

In recent years, a growing number of teachers, including those in the United States and several other countries, have used the Tactical Games model on a regular basis. Some physical education programs now base their entire curriculum on this instructional model. This model has a strong following among teachers and teacher educators in physical education, many of whom are active members in a new special interest group with its own website (www.tgfu.org/) and who regularly participate in an international conference devoted entirely to this model.

It seems apparent that the use of the Tactical Games model will continue to grow, for two reasons: First, many teachers can learn this model with only a little training because it contains many features of how coaches instruct athletes in sports. Second, the inherent student interest in this approach provides strong motivation and enjoyment for them to be actively engaged and to learn in physical education classes.

Intuitive validation

Some would argue that the Tactical Games model goes against many of the traditional strategies we use for teaching games to students. Chandler (1996) suggests that the lead-up games used in the model do not adequately represent full-game situations and can give students a false sense of accomplishment because the game forms do not have the immediacy and reality of the game situations they simulate. By citing their research and that of others, Rink, French, and Graham (1996) suggest that the inherent practice of teaching tactics before skill is not the correct sequence for learning. They argue that students need to have mastered at least the rudiments of skill before they are introduced to situated tactics.

Despite the power of these arguments, there is still much about the use of the Tactical Games model that makes good sense in physical education. First, we know that students of all ages like to play games, so using games and game simulations as the major task structure is appealing and will hold students' interest. Second, most physical education teachers know games content well, providing a strong base of expertise. Admittedly, the Tactical Games approach requires a shift from "teaching skill" to "teaching tactics" (Berkowitz, 1996), but many teachers' personal histories in sport will make that a relatively simple transition. Third, the games structures provide ongoing authentic learning tasks for students. They need to learn in "real time" so that they can use their tactical and skill knowledge immediately—not at some unknown time in the future. Finally, the Tactical Games approach takes a developmental perspective by not placing students in full-scale adult versions of games right away and then throughout a unit. It recognizes that students need to learn tactical awareness, decision making, and performance skills through progressively more complex tactical problems and structures. All of this adds up to an innovative and defensible way to teach the most popular curricular content area in nearly all physical education programs.

TEACHING AND LEARNING FEATURES

Control

Exhibit 14.4 shows the control profile for the Tactical Games model. Each element of the profile is explained in detail below.

1. Content selection. Content in the Tactical Games model comprises the sequence of tactical problems that students solve throughout the unit. After selecting the game to be learned in the unit, the teacher makes a list of tactical problems and plans the game and gamelike situations that students will use to develop tactical awareness and decision making. This function is controlled entirely by the teacher.

2. Managerial control. The teacher controls decisions about the managerial plan, class policies, and specific procedures in the Tactical Games model. Letting the teacher maintain managerial control improves efficiency as students progress through the series of game forms and drills. This model can require increased amounts of managerial time to set up each learning activity and to get students engaged for practice, so it is often best that the teacher take direct control of those procedures.

3. Task presentations. The teacher is viewed as the main resource for games knowledge, so he will be the one who plans and implements learning tasks that

Control profile for the Tactical Games model.   EXHIBIT 14.4

develop tactical awareness and decision making. The teacher poses the tactical problem by using deductive questions to get students to solve the problem before engaging in the simulation to combine tactics and skills. Therefore, the task presentation part of the profile is strongly teacher-controlled, with some interaction with students as they respond to questions.

4. Engagement patterns. The teacher determines all of the learning tasks and their structure, gets students to solve the tactical problem, and then directs students to practice the game form or drill. To that point, the engagement patterns are very much teacher-controlled. After that, students can practice on their own and are allowed to make several decisions that determine their engagement patterns.

5. Instructional interactions. The teacher initiates most of the instructional interactions, first by using deductive questions to help students solve the tactical problem and then by providing students with cues and feedback during the game forms and drills. The profile indicates that the model is somewhat interactive in this dimension because, even after the tactical problem is solved, the teacher should continue to use deductive questions to further develop students' understanding.

6. Pacing. While engaged in game forms, students make their own decisions about when to begin and end practice trials, giving the model a strongly student-controlled approach in this element of the profile.

7. Task progression. The teacher determines when each learning activity is over and when students will move to the next tactical problem and its learning task(s). Therefore, the model is strongly teacher-controlled in this dimension.

Inclusiveness

The Tactical Games model can become inclusive for all students if the teacher considers differing levels of cognitive and skill performance abilities. The model is not inherently inclusive when all students are expected to progress through the tactical problems and learning tasks at the same rate. More experienced and more highly skilled students can come to understand things faster and better, leaving other students still figuring out current tactical solutions while the class moves to new problems. Because learning in the model is built on previous understandings and performance skills, students' needs are not served if the class progresses before everyone is ready. Instead, the teacher should identify groups of students with about the same level of understanding and ability and allow those students to move together in groups through the series of tactical problems—rather than all students in class at once. Groups that move through the sequence faster can advance to modified and full games when their tactical awareness and skills predict proficient performance. Groups that go more slowly will spend extra time on simple game forms and modified games, providing them with the appropriate level of complexity to develop their awareness and skills. In this way, the model can be inclusive because all students are working at their own level, even if not progressing at the same rate. The model is also inclusive in that all students engage in the game forms, modified games, or full games. There should be little waiting time in this model, because every student works on some aspect of game skills and tactics in every learning task.

Learning Tasks

Four primary kinds of learning tasks are used in the Tactical Games model: game forms, situated skill–development drills, modified games, and full games. Each type of task will have its own task presentation and task structure, but all of them will center on student solutions of tactical problems. The sequence of four tasks just listed does not represent the task progression used in the model. According to Griffin, Mitchell, & Oslin (1997), the teacher presents a tactical problem that will carry through a full sequence of tasks. That sequence begins with a *game form,* a modified version of the full game that is used to assess students' tactical and skill knowledge in a targeted area of that game. Exhibit 14.5 provides some examples of initial game forms and elements of tactical awareness that can be assessed in them.

Examples of initial game forms and elements of tactical awareness that can be assessed in them.		**EXHIBIT 14.5**
GAME	**GAME FORM**	**USED TO ASSESS**
Basketball	Three-on-three half court	1. Defensive positioning 2. Off-the-ball movement 3. Rebounding positioning 4. Freeing up the shooter 5. Defensive communication
Volleyball	Two vs. two	1. Defensive positioning against attacks 2. Offensive passing 3. Team communication 4. Serving tactics
Golf	Putt-Putt (mini golf, putting only)	1. Stance and aiming line 2. Judgment of ball speed 3. Judgment of "break"
Lacrosse	Half-field scrimmage (one team stays on offense, one team stays on defense)	1. Establishing defensive position 2. Marking 3. Off-the-ball movement 4. Finding gaps in the defense 5. Team communication

After the game form has been played, the teacher identifies student needs related to tactics and skills and then designs one or more *situated skill drills* that target those areas. Following the drills, students can return to the initial game form or progress to *modified games*. A modified game uses many aspects of the full game—but with some planned changes in rules, scoring, field/court size, and length of the game. These modifications should reflect students' developmental readiness and should allow certain aspects of the game to come into play more often to give students more in-game skill practice and repetition of key tactics. Exhibit 14.6 shows some examples of game modifications and what each change is designed to do.

The final type of learning task is the *full game*. The full version does not have to be the adult form of the game; it can be any developmentally appropriate version that includes all or nearly all aspects of the game in ways that allow students to practice tactics and skills with maximum participation. At times it will be difficult to tell the difference between modified games and developmentally appropriate full versions, but that is OK. The important thing is that students participate in the fullest version of the game *for them*. It is also not necessary to include the formalities that accompany many full-game versions, as the Sport Education model would do. The idea is to get students in the game quickly and to give them many opportunities to learn tactics and skills in game situations.

Task presentation

The task presentation to be used in the Tactical Games model will depend on the type of learning task it introduces. Since each type of task has distinct purposes and leads to a different kind of task structure, task presentations will vary in this model.

EXHIBIT 14.6	Examples of game modifications and their purposes.	
GAME	**MODIFICATION**	**TO FOCUS ON**
Floor hockey	Teams cannot shoot on goal until all players have touched the puck.	1. Getting open 2. Teamwork 3. Communication
Soccer (elementary grades)	Reduce the width and length of the field by half and reduce the size of the goal.	1. Increased opportunity to touch the ball and to play defense 2. Off-the-ball movement 3. Shooting accuracy
Ultimate Frisbee	Increase the allowed possession time after catches.	1. Off-the-disk movement 2. Passing decisions 3. Communication
Badminton	No overhead smashes are allowed.	1. Offensive accuracy and touch shots 2. Longer rallies

Task presentation for game forms. The teacher should explain how the game form relates to the full version of the game and why it is important from a tactical perspective. The teacher gives students only the information needed to visualize and understand the game form or the situation (applicable rules, how the situation occurs, which players are involved). Then the teacher uses deductive questions to help students arrive at one or more feasible solutions (for example, see the lesson plans for Tactical Games on the IMPE website). Once they are there, the teacher explains the task structure and gets students actively engaged in decision making and skill practice in the learning task, observing students to assess their level of awareness and proficiency in that situation (refer to Exhibit 14.5). This task ends with the teacher and students identifying areas of tactical awareness and skills that must be developed in more isolated and repetitive learning tasks—most often drills.

Task presentation for situated skill drills. When students' needs for tactical awareness and skill development have been identified, the teacher ends the game form task and plans a progression of skill learning tasks (see the lesson plans on the IMPE website). By starting with the game form, the teacher can identify more authentic learning needs for students and get students to understand how important those needs are for playing the game well. In much the same way as in Direct Instruction, the teacher presents skill drills to students by explaining and modeling the movement patterns to be learned and providing verbal cues to students. An extra dimension is included to make students aware of the tactical importance of the skill and how the skill is used to solve the tactical problem of the preceding game form task. Therefore, it is important that the teacher explain not only how to perform the skill but also why and how it should be used when students return to the game form or go on to modified games or full games.

Task presentation for modified games. Modified games are designed to reduce the tactical and performance complexity of full games, allowing students to focus on certain aspects with multiple attempts. The task presentation for modified games should include an explanation of how the modified game relates to the full game (differences and similarities), why and how rules have been changed, and the tactical objectives of the modified version. By stating the tactical objectives, the teacher can lead into one or more tactical problems presented in the modified game. As mentioned before, the teacher should explain the modified game but allow students to deduce the answers to the tactical problems.

Task presentation for full games. This task presentation looks much like the one for modified games. The teacher sets the stage for the game, explains the tactical objectives, and poses the tactical problems that students must solve before the game begins. When the teacher is confident that students have good tactical awareness and the prerequisite skills, the full game becomes an appropriate learning environment.

Task structure

The task structure depends on the type of task the teacher plans at each stage of the model: game form, situated skill drill, modified game, and full game. Because all tasks are game-like, much of the structure will be revealed to students during the task presentation and the solving of the tactical problem. Students cannot deduce the answer to the tactical problem without knowing a lot about the way each task will be set up. After the tactical problem is solved and the basic task structure is explained, the teacher needs only to give students information about allocated time, safety, and the exact place for each learning station.

Task structure for game forms. In a sense, game forms are simulations of common situations that can occur in modified and full-game contexts: a rundown in softball, a goal line defense in flag football, a breakaway in hockey, or an opponent coming to the net in tennis. The teacher constructs a learning task that gives students a reasonable representation of that situation in order for students to practice and assess tactical awareness, decision making, and the needed skills. The teacher must know the situation well enough to identify which players are involved; how the situation occurs in the flow of the game; and how to provide students with a challenging, authentic game form. Remember, by this time the students will already have solved the tactical problem in the cognitive domain, so the objective of task structure is to give them repeated opportunities to make and execute the needed tactical decisions.

Task structure for situated skill drills. Many different drills can be designed to help students develop the necessary skills for executing tactical decisions. And many different task structures can be used: individual practice, paired practice, small groups, and large groups. The instruction for skill drills will closely resemble that of the Direct Instruction model with one important difference: the teacher poses the tactical problem to students before the drill begins. In Direct Instruction, the teacher will show and tell students how to perform the movement proficiently and then ask students to imitate that example. In the Tactical Games model, the teacher encourages students to understand what the skill is and how it needs to be carried out to meet the tactical demands of the drill being practiced. The teacher also goes to great lengths to help students understand the need for the skill in game applications. Once students reach that level of understanding (that is, they solve the tactical problem), the teacher should engage students in a drill designed to promote both tactical and skill knowledge at the same time. Therefore, the task structure should allow students many opportunities to make and carry out tactical decisions, rather than simply perform a number of automatic repetitions.

Task structure for modified games. The task structure for modified games must be both representative and exaggerated (Griffin, Mitchell, & Oslin, 1997). To be representative means that the modified game closely resembles one or more aspects of the full version of the game so that students are practicing in a realistic environment and making authentic tactical decisions. When modifying game rules, boundaries, the size of the goal, and so forth, the teacher must be careful to retain the most essential features of the game in its modified version. At the same time, the task structure exaggerates certain aspects of the game, giving students more opportunities to practice isolated tactical decisions and skills. Exaggeration helps students to focus on those certain aspects by eliminating or reducing the possibility of other aspects occurring in the typically unpredictable flow of a game. For instance, if a teacher engages students in a half-court game of basketball, both teams will have many opportunities to practice and execute tactical decisions about offensive patterns, set defense, and rebounding. By eliminating fast breaks, this half-court structure reduces the complexities of the full-court game and provides many more "teaching moments" for the tactical and skill knowledge being learned.

Keeping the tactical problem as the focal point of the learning activity, the teacher will first explain the modified game and then present the tactical problem to students before the game begins. If preparing for a half-court basketball game, the teacher might ask a number of key tactical questions:

1. The teacher asks the offense, "What is your main goal for each possession?" The offense replies, "To score a basket." The teacher then asks, "How do you increase your chances of doing that?"

2. "Who has the advantage in a half-court situation, the offense or the defense?"

3. The teacher asks the defense, "What is the main difference between a zone defense and a player-to-player defense? When should you use each type?"

The modified games task structure is crucial in the Tactical Games model because it provides a direct bridge between skill tasks and full games. It allows students to develop game-based decision-making abilities and to apply skills in highly authentic situations that will occur often when they play the full game later. Teachers should bear in mind that the modified game structure will be the culminating structure for many units, particularly when students are at the novice stage of tactical and skill development.

Task structure for full games. Only when students have demonstrated sustained competence in modified games should they play full versions of a game. In modified games, the teacher can make informal and formal assessments of students' knowledge, which then helps the teacher decide if the class should progress to full versions of the game. Again, the full version is not automatically played in every unit; students must be ready for that task structure.

The task structure for full games will tend to resemble a practice scrimmage used by coaches in many sports. The teacher should watch for "teaching moments" that occur in the game and interject when appropriate to get students to focus on tactical awareness, tactical decisions, and game skills. However, when play is stopped momentarily, each teaching moment should pose a tactical problem to students.

Metzler (1990) suggested some useful ways teachers can structure game tasks and interject in them:

1. *Instant replay.* The teacher stops the game and resets the last play so that players can have the chance to review and change their tactical decisions. Only the results of the original play count in the scoring.

2. *Player–coach.* The teacher enters the game for a strategic purpose: to manipulate certain situations to promote students' tactical and skill practice. For instance, the teacher is the pitcher for both teams in a softball game and deliberately pitches in ways that force certain situations to occur (hitting ground balls, hitting to the opposite field); or the teacher enters a basketball game as the point guard on one team and uses that position to control the pace of the game.

3. *Situations.* During the course of the game, the teacher stops play to ask a question to check tactical awareness and decision making before a particular situation happens in the game. For instance, in a doubles tennis match, the teacher would ask one partner, "What will you do if your partner has to come to the net when that's your territory?" With runners on first and second and one out in a softball game, the teacher would ask the right fielder, "What do you do if you catch a deep fly ball?"

4. *TV analyst.* After the teacher notices a pattern emerging during a game, she stops the game to ask, "What's going on, and how do you change it?" For instance, if one team in a soccer match has had several breakaway shots on goal, the teacher would ask the defensive team, "Why is that happening?" and "What does your team need to do to stop that?"

The important feature of the full-game structure in the Tactical Games model is that the focus remains on tactical awareness, tactical decisions, and skill execution, so the teacher must use a lot of interactive teaching that gets students to think about and solve the large number of tactical problems that occur in most games. Only then can the full-game structure differ from simply "playing games" in class.

Content progression

The organizing center for content in the Tactical Games model is the *tactical problem,* a situation that typically arises in a game or game form that requires the simultaneous application of skill and tactical knowledge. The key thing to understand in this model is that the content is not skill-based (e.g., stealing a base, kicking a ball, or striking an object). The content is based on the learning of tactical awareness and proper execution that meets the demands of a specific situation. The content will therefore be defined differently—from a conceptual perspective (e.g., maintaining defensive positioning, attacking the goal, moving to the open spot, or using the game clock advantageously). Griffin, Mitchell, and Oslin (1997) state that tactical problems can be defined at four levels of increasing complexity. If the game form is soccer, and the tactical problem is "attacking the goal for a shot," the tactical problem *for the passer* could be ordered this way:

Level I	Understanding my position relative to the goal, the defenders, and my teammates

Level II   Understanding when (and how) to advance the ball myself and when (and how) to pass it

Level III   Understanding how the defense will move if I attack and how to react to that; anticipating when a teammate is moving into an open spot and recognizing the most effective timing and way to get the ball to her for a shot

Level IV   If I shoot the ball, knowing when to shoot, where to aim it, and how to execute the shot. If I pass the ball, knowing when to pass it (and to whom), what kind of pass to make, and how to execute it most effectively

Players at other positions would learn the tactical problems from their perspective: defender, goalkeeper, or offensive teammate. To progress on the content, the teacher would plan one or more game forms and situated learning tasks at each level to allow students to become aware of the tactical problem and to practice its recognition and execution at each level.

Engagement Patterns for Learning

The four major task structures in the Tactical Games model—game forms, situated skill drills, modified games, and full games—lead to three different engagement patterns for students. In skill drills, students are likely to practice the same task individually. Each student would have her own practice space and needed equipment. The engagement pattern in gamelike simulations and modified games will be small groups, with each group having enough students to make the simulation or modified game focus on the tactical problem at hand. The teacher may or may not use the last type of engagement pattern, depending on student readiness for regulation game play. Of course, this third engagement pattern will be determined by the game being played: individual, dual, small team (e.g., basketball), or large team (e.g., football).

Teacher and Student Roles and Responsibilities

Each instructional model will have certain operations that must be completed to allow the model to function according to its design. Some of the operations are carried out by the teacher; others are carried out by one or more students. Exhibit 14.7 shows the major operations within the Tactical Games model and indicates who is responsible for completing them during each lesson.

Verification of Instructional Processes

Teachers who use the Tactical Games model can learn the benchmarks for their own and student behavior patterns. These benchmarks, outlined in Exhibits 14.8 and 14.9, verify that the model has been designed and implemented with an acceptable degree of faithfulness, increasing the likelihood that the stated student learning outcomes will be achieved.

EXHIBIT 14.7 Teacher and student roles and responsibilities in Tactical Games.

OPERATION OR RESPONSIBILITY	PERSON/PEOPLE RESPONSIBLE IN TACTICAL GAMES
Starting class	The **teacher** usually begins class as a whole for the first game form and tactical problem.
Task presentation	The **teacher** will make the task presentation. It is also possible to use instructional media to show students a tactical situation.
Stating the tactical problem	The **teacher** sets the stage for each situated learning task and then gives the tactical problem to students.
Solving the tactical problem	**Students** can think on their own or work in small groups to solve the tactical problem.
Dispersing and returning equipment	Most learning tasks will use a small-group structure, so each **group of students** can get and return its needed equipment.
Task structure	**Students** set up each task (learning station) as directed by the teacher.
Assessment	The **teacher** should design the assessment technique for each task. Once designed, it can be used either by students or by the teacher.

EXHIBIT 14.8 Tactical Games teacher benchmarks.

BENCHMARK	HOW TO VERIFY
Teacher uses a tactical problem as the organizing center for learning tasks.	Check content listing, with tactical problems written out.
Teacher begins each unit segment with a game form to assess student knowledge.	Check unit plan.
Teacher identifies needed tactical and skill areas from game form.	Teacher can make a list of tactical areas in each unit segment and make a written assessment of students' knowledge in each area after observing each game form.
Teacher uses deductive questions to get students to solve the tactical problem.	1. Check teacher's lesson plan. 2. Make a list of all questions asked and student responses.
Teacher uses clear communications for situated learning tasks.	Observe students as they organize each task. Students should quickly set up and engage in the task according to the teacher's directions.
Teacher uses high rates of guides and feedback during situated learning tasks.	Record the content and frequency of the teacher's instructional interactions.
Teacher provides a review that includes the tactical problems of the lesson.	1. Check the teacher's lesson plan. 2. Record the number of times the teacher checks for understanding at the end of each lesson.
Assessment.	1. Check the teacher's unit and lesson plans. 2. Review the teacher's checklists for tactical decision making and skill execution (e.g., use the GPAI).

BENCHMARK	HOW TO VERIFY
Tactical Games student benchmarks.	EXHIBIT 14.9
Students are given time to think about deductive questions regarding the tactical problem.	1. Observe the teacher's use of wait time. 2. Make a record of how many times each student is called on to answer.
Students understand how to set up situated learning tasks.	Observe students as they organize each task. Students should quickly set up and engage in the task according to the teacher's directions.
Students are making situated tactical decisions.	1. Record correct and incorrect answers students give to teacher's questions during learning tasks. 2. Observe students' tactical decision making and skills during learning tasks.
Game modifications are developmentally appropriate.	Observe students as they are engaged. Does the modification make the game too simple or too complex for them?
Students are able to progress on tactical knowledge as they move along in the task progression.	Monitor game forms, modified games, and full games with the GPAI. Note which game performance components are not demonstrated as the complexity of learning tasks increases. Some drop-off will occur each time the complexity increases, but the drop should be only temporary.
Students have learned tactical awareness, decision making, and situated skills.	Monitor students with the GPAI or another authentic assessment technique.

Assessment of Learning

The major learning objective in the Tactical Games model is to get students to make and carry out tactical decisions in games and gamelike learning activities. Student achievement represents a combination of knowing what to do and how to execute it correctly in game contexts. That well-defined objective helps teachers devise valid and authentic assessment techniques when using this model, because the "assessment question" is clear and direct: "To what degree can students make correct tactical decisions and carry them out in the flow of game play?"

Assessment in the tactical model should focus on students' abilities to make and execute tactical decisions while playing a game. The game can be a full game, a modified game, or a game form that represents a specific aspect of the game. In addition, assessment should be authentic—based on observations made during game play. With that in mind, there are two primary forms of assessments in the Tactical Games model: objective game statistics and evaluations of students' decision-making and performance abilities.

Assessment with game statistics

If you were coaching a team (for instance, floor hockey), how would you answer someone who asked you, "How did your team play in its last game?" Most likely you would use the game score as the major indicator of performance. Winning or losing can tell you if the primary goal was accomplished, but it does not always indicate how well the team played. In order to better assess your team's play, you would probably look to the statistical summary for that game. Such a summary might show things like the number of shots on goal each team took, where those shots were taken from, which players took the shots, time of possession, turnovers, other errors, and total penalty time for both teams. With a complete set of game statistics, you would be able to assess many aspects of each player's performance, based on his or her position. For classes in the Tactical Games model, each student could be given a summary report that would include the statistics relevant to that student's position, with a written assessment of performance.

Assessment of tactical decision making and skill execution

Assessing student performance with game statistics can be useful, but that information will not tell the teacher how well students made and carried out tactical decisions during the game. For instance, the summary statistics for goal keeping in floor hockey will show how many shots were taken on goal and the percentage of saves, but they will not show how often the goalkeeper made situationally correct decisions and actions—one very good measure of tactical knowledge. Griffin, Mitchell, and Oslin (1997) have devised a valid authentic system for assessing tactical knowledge in a wide variety of games typically taught in physical education. The GPAI is a generic template that can be adapted to many types of games in order to assess students' tactical knowledge. The GPAI includes seven common components of game performance, shown in Exhibit 14.10.

EXHIBIT 14.10	GPAI components of game performance.
COMPONENT	**CRITERION FOR ASSESSING PERFORMANCE**
Base	Appropriate return of the performer to a home or recovery position between skill attempts
Adjust	Movement of performer, either offensively or defensively, as required by the flow of the game
Decision making	Making appropriate choices about what to do with the ball (or projectile) during a game
Skill execution	Efficient performance of selected skills
Support	Off-the-ball movement to a position to receive a pass when player's team has possession
Cover	Providing defensive help for player making a play on the ball or moving to the ball (or projectile)
Guard or mark	Defending against an opponent who may or may not have the ball (or projectile)

Reprinted, by permission, from L. L. Griffin, S. A. Mitchell, and J. L. Oslin, 1997, *Teaching Sport Concepts and Skills: A Tactical Games Approach* (Champaign, IL: Human Kinetics), 221–222.

When using the GPAI for a specific game or game form, the teacher would identify which of the seven components apply to that situation and determine one or more criteria on each component that indicate good tactical decisions and performance. The GPAI focuses on three aspects of performance for each component: decisions made (appropriate or inappropriate), skill execution (efficient or inefficient), and support (appropriate or inappropriate). The teacher would then observe each student in the course of the game and record appropriate/inappropriate and efficient/inefficient instances of tactical knowledge and performance for each selected component.

Using a soccer example from Griffin, Mitchell, and Oslin (1997), Exhibit 14.11 shows how the GPAI can be used to assess students' tactical knowledge in three game performance components.

Exhibit 14.12 shows the GPAI record of the teacher's observations during a 10-minute three-vs.-three modified soccer match. The field was shortened to an area about 40 yards square, with goals at two ends. Each x indicates an instance in which a student was viewed making a tactical performance.

From the teacher's record, it is possible to calculate several measures of tactical game performance for each student. Exhibit 14.13 shows how the various GPAI scores are calculated, with Matthew's record being used to determine his scores in the abbreviated match.

As Griffin, Mitchell, and Oslin (1997) are quick to point out, a student's game performance score is a ratio, not a percentage or an absolute score. That means it reflects a balance between appropriate/inappropriate and efficient/inefficient instances such that students with more positive occurrences in a game will not necessarily score higher than students with fewer positive instances. What counts is making fewer tactical mistakes for each positive tactical opportunity. The highest GPAI scores occur when students have more positive instances relative to the number of negative instances. This scoring method encourages students to make good tactical decisions and fewer nega-

Sample GPAI assessment of a soccer player deciding when to pass to a teammate or shoot on goal.	EXHIBIT 14.11
GPAI COMPONENT	**CRITERIA**
Decision making	1. Player attempts to pass to an open teammate.
	2. Player attempts to shoot when appropriate.
Skill execution	Reception—Control of pass and setup of the ball.
	Passing—Ball reaches target.
	Shooting—Ball stays below head height and is on target.
Support	The player appeared to support the ball carrier by being in or moving to an appropriate position to receive the pass.

Reprinted, by permission, from L. L. Griffin, S. A. Mitchell, and J. L. Oslin, 1997, *Teaching Sport Concepts and Skills: A Tactical Games Approach* (Champaign, IL: Human Kinetics), 221–222.

EXHIBIT 14.12	Completed GPAI for 10-minute three-vs.-three soccer game.					
	DECISION MADE		**SKILL EXECUTION**		**SUPPORT**	
NAME	**A**	**IA**	**E**	**IE**	**A**	**IA**
Matthew	xxxxxx	x	xxxxxx	x	xxxxxxx	xxxx
Laura					xxx	xxx
Sudha	xxxxx	x	xxxxx	x	xxxx	x
Kelly	xx	x	xxx	x	xxxxx	xx
Peter	xxx	xx	xx	xxx	xx	x
Alison	x	xx	x	xx	xxxxxxx	x
KEY	A = appropriate		IA = inappropriate	E = efficient	IE = inefficient	

Reprinted, by permission, from L. L. Griffin, S. A. Mitchell, and J. L. Oslin, 1997, *Teaching Sport Concepts and Skills: A Tactical Games Approach* (Champaign, IL: Human Kinetics), 221–222.

EXHIBIT 14.13	Matthew's GPAI scores for the 10-minute match.
INDEX	**HOW TO CALCULATE**
Game involvement	number of appropriate decisions + number of inappropriate decisions + number of efficient skill executions + number of inefficient skill executions + number of appropriate supporting movements
Decision-making index (DMI)	number of appropriate decisions made ÷ number of inappropriate decisions made
Skill execution index (SEI)	number of efficient skill executions ÷ number of inefficient skill executions
Support index (SI)	number of appropriate supporting movements ÷ number of inappropriate supporting movements
Game performance	[DMI + SEI + SI] / 3

Matthew's GPAI assessment:

    Game involvement = 6 + 1 + 6 + 1 + 7 = 21

    Decision making + 6 ÷ 1 = 6

    Skill execution = 6 ÷ 1 = 6

    Support = 7 ÷ 4 = 1.75

Matthew's game performance index = (6 + 6 + 1.75) / 3 = 4.58

Reprinted, by permission, from L. L. Griffin, S. A. Mitchell, and J. L. Oslin, 1997, *Teaching Sport Concepts and Skills: A Tactical Games Approach* (Champaign, IL: Human Kinetics), 221–222.

tive ones. An analysis of Matthew's performance would indicate that he had some kind of involvement about every 30 seconds (21 chances in 10 minutes); in this modified game structure, that is not a high level of involvement, so the teacher would find ways to get him more in the flow of the action. However, his game performance index showed that he made only one inappropriate decision or action for every 4.58 appropriate ones. That indicates he was very effective in instances when he did have direct involvement in the game.

IMPLEMENTATION NEEDS AND MODIFICATIONS

Teacher Expertise

Teachers who use the Tactical Games model will need to have particular expertise in several areas of the knowledge base presented in Chapter 3.

Developmentally appropriate instruction. Games—even modified games and game forms—can become complex instructional settings that require a relatively high level of cognitive and psychomotor readiness on the part of students. It is very important that the complexity of the current tactical problem and the skill needed to execute tactical decisions match students' ability level. Teachers must be able to analyze the concepts and skills in each tactical situation and then design an appropriate game form, drill, or modified game to help students acquire that knowledge. Perhaps a teacher's two most important instructional decisions occur when students go from modified games to a full-game version—or as they go back to modified games when the full game appears to be too complex or demanding for them.

Learning domains and objectives. The Tactical Games model is based on an interaction between the cognitive and psychomotor domains; the teacher gets students to solve a tactical problem through a series of deductive questions and then directs students to execute tactical decisions within the various kinds of task structures. Teachers will need to keep that domain interaction in balance so that students can actually execute the skills called for by the tactical solution. It is not desirable to have students come up with very complex tactical solutions that are well beyond their physical abilities to perform.

Teachers who use the Tactical Games model will need to know how to identify and state tactical problems to students. The solutions to those problems become some of the main instructional objectives within this model, and they form the basis of tactical learning progressions (Doolittle & Girard, 1991). Therefore, teachers must translate tactical problems into learning tasks that facilitate those objectives.

Task analysis and content progression. Task analysis in the Tactical Games model is different from that in other models in this book. Remember that Tactical Games content is not determined by a list of skills to be learned in a given order. Rather, content is based on the tactical knowledge and skills needed to play a game proficiently. Therefore, the teacher begins the task analysis process by analyzing the tactical requirements of each game and considering students' developmental stage. The resulting list of tactical areas becomes the content listing for the unit, presented to students as tactical problems. From there, the teacher plans the unit's series of learning tasks that will help students solve and execute the tactical problems.

It is essential in the Tactical Games model that the teacher be able to correctly assess student readiness for each of the four main task structures: game forms, situated skill drills, modified games, and full games. Those structures form the plan, or stages, for task progression to occur within the model. Remember that a Tactical Games lesson will begin with a game form that is used to assess students' tactical awareness, decision making, and skills. While students are in the game form, the teacher must assess which tactical knowledge and skills students need most and then plan a sequence to promote that knowledge. All of that must be considered along with students' developmental readiness, and adjustments must be made for the complexity and physical demands of each learning task.

Games content. It almost goes without saying that teachers must have strong expertise in games taught with the tactical model. Teachers must know each game well enough to be able to identify the tactical demands, to formulate tactical problems, and to design developmentally appropriate game forms and other task structures. This familiarity goes well beyond game rules and basic strategies. The teacher must know all playing positions and the most typical tactical situations that can occur in the flow of a game so that she can design authentic game forms and modified games.

Assessment. Students demonstrate tactical knowledge in two learning domains in this model: the cognitive (knowing what to do) and the psychomotor (knowing how to do it proficiently). Furthermore, they must demonstrate that knowledge in games and gamelike situations. Therefore, assessment in the tactical model should rely mainly on authentic techniques, implemented while students are actively engaged. Teachers can make some assessment of students' declarative knowledge by asking them to think about and verbally solve tactical problems, but the major focus should be assessing tactical knowledge in action.

Griffin, Mitchell, and Oslin (1997) developed the GPAI specifically for use with the Tactical Games model. Described earlier in this chapter, the GPAI is essentially a performance scoring system that a teacher can use to observe and assess various components of game performance to determine if students are making and executing tactical decisions during game play. Teachers who plan to use the Tactical Games model should become proficient with the GPAI or be able to design their own games assessment checklists. (Refer to Exhibits 14.10–14.13.)

Key Teaching Skills

Many of the teaching skills that prove effective for the Tactical Games model are similar to those used in Direct Instruction. In addition, teachers will use some deductive questioning skills to help students solve the tactical problem within each learning task.

Planning. The Tactical Games model requires some planning prior to the start of the unit, but most of the planning will occur once the teacher has assessed the students' initial tactical knowledge and skills. The teacher can plan ahead for the first game form, which is used to determine students' tactical knowledge and skill. What the teacher observes in that game form will decide what comes next—either a modified game (if students are ready) or a series of skill drills. From there, the teacher should grasp what students need and which learning tasks can help them learn best. The tactical problem serves as the starting point for every learning task after the initial game form. The teacher will need to formulate the tactical problem ahead of time and prepare a series of deductive questions and learning tasks that will lead students toward its solution.

Time and class management. Learning tasks should be designed to simulate game situations, and the teacher will need to pay particular attention to details in planning each skill drill, game form, and modified game. Good planning will facilitate higher rates of engagement and more opportunities for students to practice their situated game skills. Learning tasks should be organized so that all students are actively engaged and transitions between tasks are efficient. This will reduce the likelihood that transitions will cause a loss of momentum in a lesson.

Task presentation and structure. Task presentations in the tactical model closely resemble many of those used in Direct Instruction, with the added element of deductive questions to help students solve the tactical problem before each task begins. Task presentations should include an explanation of the tactical importance of the skill or situation to be practiced and the key tactical decisions to be made. The teacher should stop short of telling students the one or more correct tactical decisions to make, allowing students to solve the tactical problem themselves. Teachers should review the guidelines for effective questioning techniques presented in Chapter 5. It will be especially important to use the *wait time* technique with deductive questions to make sure all students get the opportunity to formulate their own solutions before one is presented publicly.

Communication. Communication skills are important in the Tactical Games model because of the many situated learning tasks given to students. Those tasks require the teacher to give a full and clear explanation of the situation to be practiced and the major tactical decisions that need to be made. If students don't understand the situation or the tactical problem, they are less likely to devise an acceptable solution.

Instructional information. Most of the instructional information comes from the teacher in the form of task presentations and verbal interactions while students practice. The key skill for teachers is to recognize when to "ask, not tell" students about solutions to the tactical problem. The model expects students to work out solutions on their own, a process that increases their understanding and learning.

As students practice the situated learning tasks, the teacher should give high rates of verbal guides and feedback. Guides are statements given to students while they are actively engaged. During the game forms, modified games, and full games, the teacher should observe the flow of action and alert students to upcoming situations, cueing them to make tactical decisions (without giving students the answers, it should be emphasized) in the course of game events. For example, in a volleyball three-vs.-three modified game, the teacher would observe the ball coming over the net to a team, note their positioning, and cue them to make the right adjustments before the ball arrives. Augmented feedback from the teacher is important because many practice situations will be quite complex; students may realize when a mistake has been made, but in order to prevent it from happening the next time, they will need feedback on why it occurred.

Review and closure. The tactical problem(s) presented to students in a lesson should form the focal point of the lesson review. The teacher can restate the problem(s) and let students respond with the correct solution as one last check for understanding. The review can also be used to preview tactical problems and learning tasks planned for the next lesson. The teacher could even choose to give students the next tactical problem and ask them to think about solutions before the upcoming lesson, providing a nice way to start the following class. The closure should also allow enough time for equipment to be returned to its proper place, and it should end with an orderly dismissal.

Contextual Requirements

The Tactical Games model can be used in nearly all physical education contexts. The major requirements are to have sufficient equipment and teaching space to allow all students to engage without waiting turns. When there is not enough equipment or space for all students to participate in the same situated learning task, I recommend that the teacher plan other tasks that have different equipment and space requirements. The Tactical Games model can support a high degree of flexibility, giving it very few contextual limitations in physical education units.

It is possible to use the Tactical Games model with very young learners, even first and second graders. If the games they will play are developmentally appropriate, they will have simple tactical problems to become aware of and learn to solve. For example, many elementary physical education teachers use tag games in their programs. Those games look simple but contain a number of tactical problems, such as recognizing and moving to a "safe" space; anticipating others' (e.g., the tagger's) movements in a dynamic environment; and choosing and executing evading actions like dodging, faking direction, and changing speed.

Selecting and Modifying Tactical Games

The Tactical Games model is obviously designed to teach students how to make and execute tactical decisions in the context of games. Those games can be the more formal versions of sport or any game that requires a degree of tactical knowledge to play it well. I would advise using this model with the following types of physical education content:

1. Low organizational games (tag games, group games)
2. New Games and other creative games
3. Individual and dual sports
4. Team sports

Grade-level adaptations

The Tactical Games model can instruct students across a wide range of developmental stages if the teacher carefully matches student ability with the tactical complexity and skill requirements needed to play the game proficiently. Exhibit 14.14 shows some possible adaptations for different grade levels.

Adaptations to accommodate diverse groups of learners

The Tactical Games model can be highly inclusive for physical education if the teacher devises game forms that simulate full versions of the game and that allow all students to learn the skills and tactics in them. Exhibit 14.15 lists some strategies that address a variety of special learning needs found in many schools today.

Grade-level adaptations for Tactical Games in physical education.		EXHIBIT 14.14
GRADE LEVELS	**SELECT TACTICAL GAMES?**	**POSSIBLE ADAPTATIONS**
Preschool	No	
Lower elementary	Yes	1. Choose tactically simple games. 2. Focus on decision making, not performance. 3. Do not emphasize competition.
Upper elementary	Yes	1. Choose tactically simple games. 2. Focus on skill development first. 3. Use more game forms as learning tasks. 4. Do not use full versions of team sport games.
Middle school/ junior high	Yes	1. Use mostly modified games. 2. Use full games rarely and cautiously. 3. Focus on skill development along with tactics.
High school	Yes	1. Use a high proportion of modified games over full games. 2. Use full games only when students have demonstrated they are ready.
College/adult	Yes	None needed. Use the full model when students have demonstrated their readiness for increasing tactical complexity and skill applications.

| EXHIBIT | **14.15** | Strategies adapting Tactical Games for diverse groups of learners. |

FOR STUDENTS WITH HEARING AND/OR SPEECH IMPAIRMENTS:

1. Move these students closer when asking questions or giving directions.
2. Use diagrams and other visual aids, such as a large "white board," to let students see the tactical patterns being taught.

FOR STUDENTS WITH SIGHT IMPAIRMENTS:

1. Use "on the court or field" examples that show a play or pattern in "real life" size.
2. Modify game space and equipment to provide better tracking.

FOR STUDENTS WITH PHYSICAL DISABILITIES:

1. Design tactical problems that promote higher levels of developmentally appropriate performance for all students.
2. Explore ability-appropriate solutions to tactical problems (e.g., showing how a "pick" is set in wheelchair basketball).

FOR STUDENTS WHO DO NOT SPEAK ENGLISH:

1. Use student translators when available. Pair matching bilingual students with non-English speakers.
2. Provide task presentations in appropriate language, or use translated closed-caption media when possible.
3. Use games and game forms that interest students from other cultures.

FOR LOWER-SKILLED STUDENTS:

1. Focus on simpler tactical problems.
2. Provide additional examples to make points about tactical problems.
3. Provide extra encouragement and praise to the slower learners.
4. Use divergent questions that allow for a wide range of acceptable solutions to tactical problems.

FOR STUDENTS WITH BEHAVIOR DISABILITIES:

1. Provide students with behavior disabilities with extra encouragement for their participation and creativity in solving tactical problems.
2. Use task structures that allow for individual engagement if students cannot work cooperatively.
3. Focus on the contribution to be made by students with behavior disabilities, not the potential for misbehavior.

PLANNING TIPS FOR TACTICAL GAMES

 eachers who choose to use this model can benefit by following a few additional planning tips:

1. Always remember that content is based on tactical problems, not skill. For example, the focus of a basketball lesson might be "moving to get open for a shot," not "shooting."

2. Make the game form as simple as possible, but also ensure that it is highly authentic. That is, it should contain elements that are similar to the full version of the game.

3. Do not keep the class in the game form too long. Once one or more tactical problems are identified, transition out of the game form. For example, do not play a three-vs.-three volleyball game form to 15 points. It takes too long, and the tactical problem(s) can almost always be identified after a few points are played.

4. When using game forms that are new to students, you can probably anticipate what the tactical problems will be and plan situated learning tasks ahead of time.

5. As much as possible, get students to identify the tactical problem for themselves. If they can figure out problems on their own and see a need to improve in an aspect of the game, they will be more likely to apply themselves in the situated learning tasks.

6. Make sure that the situated learning tasks contain some degree of authenticity regarding the game and focus on the tactical problem at hand. For example, do not let students simply play "catch" back and forth with a softball. Rather, put some element in the task that makes it somewhat gamelike (e.g., catching on the run, throwing to a moving target, mixing up ground balls and fly balls).

7. Give ample time in the lesson for students to experiment with several possible solutions to a tactical problem. There is rarely only one way to make a play in games.

8. Assess students in authentic situations (e.g., game forms and full-game versions). Do not use skills tests to assess in this model.

UNIT AND LESSON PLAN EXAMPLES FOR TACTICAL GAMES INSTRUCTION

You will find several complete unit plans with lesson plans for the Tactical Games model on the IMPE website. It is not recommended that you follow these examples exactly as they are presented. The context, specific learning objectives, and content of your own unit will require you to make changes in these examples to allow the Tactical Games model to lead to the most effective instruction in your situation.

SUMMARY

As mentioned in the beginning of this chapter, the Tactical Games model is very new to physical education instruction, even though its predecessor, the Teaching Games for Understanding model, was developed nearly 20 years ago. Physical education teachers have used games instruction for more than 100 years in U. S. schools, and the Tactical Games model offers a fresh and innovative way to approach that key part of school curriculums. Teachers who choose to use this model should be aware that they will not just be teaching games content with a slightly new twist. The Tactical Games model begins the process of teaching games content to students from a very different perspective, with very different objectives and teaching strategies. This model can be a refreshing and creative way for veteran teachers to instruct content they have taught many times. For new teachers, the Tactical Games model could become "their way" to teach games content to students of all ages.

LEARNING ACTIVITIES

1. Make a list of five activity units (e.g., tag games, softball, track and field, New Games) that might be taught in a physical education program. Next, determine an appropriate grade level (P, K–2, 3–5, 6–8, 9–12) for teaching each of those activity units. Now, write two major learning outcomes for those units. Then, go through the process of selecting an instructional model, shown in Chapter 2, to determine if Tactical Games would be an appropriate model for teaching that activity to children at that grade level.

2. If Tactical Games is appropriate for that activity, grade, and goals, mention three things that make it appropriate. If Tactical Games is not appropriate for that activity, grade, and goals, mention three things that make it inappropriate.

3. For one activity unit at one grade level (e.g., third-grade tag games, middle school New Games, high school tennis), write a complete list of content to be taught in that unit with Tactical Games. Remember that the content should be based on the identification and solution of tactical problems.

4. Pick one of the major goals identified in Learning Activity 1, and design an assessment strategy for monitoring student *tactical* learning.

5. Write an annotated lesson plan for each of the first three lessons of this unit. Be sure to show the game forms and tactical problems in each lesson.

TOPICS FOR REFLECTION & SMALL-GROUP DISCUSSION

1. I have suggested in this chapter how the Tactical Games model is aligned to achieve one or more of the NASPE standards. Take a moment to review those alignments (see Exhibit 14.3). After that, make some notes about whether you agree with those alignments, and then share them in your small group. When you have arrived at your final thoughts, please share them on the IMPE website Forum for others to review, and check back for replies.

2. Mention three ways that Tactical Games is similar to Direct Instruction and three ways it is different.

3. In general, which types of students are placed at an advantage in this model, and which students are at a disadvantage?

4. Why is it so important in this model always to base the content on tactics, not skills?

5. Many physical education teachers are attracted to this model when they first learn about it. What about Tactical Games makes it attractive to teachers?

SUGGESTED READINGS FOR TACTICAL GAMES

Griffin, L. L., & Butler, J. I. (2005). *Teaching games for understanding: Theory, research and practice.* Champaign, IL: Human Kinetics.

Griffin, L., Mitchell, S., & Oslin, J. (1997). *Teaching sport concepts and skills: A tactical games approach.* Champaign, IL: Human Kinetics.

Mitchell, S. A., & Oslin, J. L. (1999). *Assessment in games teaching.* Reston, VA: National Association for Sport and Physical Education.

Mitchell, S. A., & Oslin, J. L. (2003). *Sport foundations for elementary physical education: A tactical games approach.* Champaign, IL: Human Kinetics.

Mitchell, S. A., Oslin, J. L., & Griffin, L. L. (2003). *Sport foundations for elementary physical education.* Champaign, IL: Human Kinetics. (Note: Excellent resource for using Tactical Games in lower grades)

Thorpe, R., Bunker, D., & Almond, L. (1986). *Rethinking games teaching.* Loughborough, England: Authors.

15

TEACHING PERSONAL AND SOCIAL RESPONSIBILITY
Integration, Transfer, Empowerment, and Teacher–Student Relationships

Almost since physical education programs have been in schools, we have sought to teach more than the skills and knowledge of sport, fitness, dance, and games. As a profession, we have tried to teach children and youth personal values and pro-social behaviors that contribute to the education of the whole person. These outcomes have been directly or indirectly expressed in every major set of curriculum standards in our field, beginning as early as 1910, when Clark Hetherington included character education—the development of moral, social, and personal characteristics—as one of the four main goals of his "New Physical Education" (Van Dalen & Bennett, 1971). Within the Seven Cardinal Principles of Education adopted by Congress in 1917, physical educators took on the goal of promoting ethical character development in school programs. In some form or other, the development of moral, ethical, and social outcomes has been part of our profession's stated goals since that time.

But, even though physical educators have expressed those kinds of outcomes for nearly a century, learning outcomes derived from skill and cognitive performance have clearly dominated the content, structure, and instruction of school programs. The failure to adequately address moral, personal, and social outcomes in physical education may be attributed to four factors. First, historically schools were hesitant to promote these outcomes, because they were often thought to be best taught at home by parents and other family members. Essentially, it was "not the school's business" to provide values education. Second, even if schools did try to teach moral and social values, there was the question of "Whose values should students learn in public schools in a diverse culture?" Third, the curriculum in most U. S. schools is designed to promote a limited set of learning outcomes, increasingly defined as what students need to know to perform well on standardized tests of learning. Because outcomes derived from moral and social values either *cannot* be tested (like math skills) or *should not* be tested (this would imply a judgment of one's character), they have been marginalized in U.S. school curriculums. "If it can't be tested and measured, it can't be in the curriculum," or so it goes. Fourth, until relatively recently we had no instructional model that could effectively focus on and promote the development of personal, moral, and social outcomes in schools and in physical education. Even if we wanted to do that, we really didn't know how!

In the past three decades, two important changes have occurred to kindle a keen interest in teaching to achieve the outcomes expressed in the NASPE standards. The first change has been our society's realization that schools have the obligation to promote these outcomes. Many citizens and professionals will admit that our so-called social fabric has seemed to deteriorate, and many of those critics point to the erosion of the family unit—our most traditional institution for passing along our society's values to future generations. If that kind of learning is not taking place in the home, then it becomes the school's obligation to provide it. The second change involves the approach to values education itself. The key question of "Whose values get taught in schools?" is a central issue in our diverse culture. To teach the values of one or a few groups in the culture simply goes against our notions of democracy and free speech. However, although we should not even attempt to agree on the question of whose values to teach, few people will argue that children and youth should not learn to be responsible for themselves and others around them. That perspective shifts the focus from teaching values to teaching children and youth to think, decide, and act in ways that contribute to positive personal and social outcomes in settings involving physical activity—in physical education class and beyond the school building.

OVERVIEW

he model for teaching personal and social responsibility has evolved since the publication of *Beyond Balls and Bats: Alienated (and Other) Youth in the Gym* by Don Hellison in 1978. Dr. Hellison first developed the model as a way to teach physical education to inner-city youths who were known to be at risk in several places: in school, at home, as gang members, and as participants (and victims) in violent crimes. Many of them attended school just because their only other option was incarceration; one more failure would have a heavy cost. Hellison quickly realized that the needs of these students went far beyond what a traditional approach to physical education could provide, thus the title, *Beyond Balls and Bats,* of his first book. By his own admission, Hellison's initial goal was to promote character development in physical education, hoping to make his students "better people" who could withstand some of the social inequities in their world. But that approach did not seem sufficient; the problems were too severe, and his direct impact was too limited. He needed to find a different perspective:

> I needed a much clearer purpose and set of goals as well as some intervention strategies, and quickly! I came to realize that helping my students to take more responsibility for their own development and well-being and for contributing to the well-being of others was perhaps the best contribution I could make, especially given the personal and social problems my students faced. (Hellison, 2003, p. 5)

The venue for his new vision would be physical education class; the medium would be the activity content taught in his physical education program. The approach would become the Teaching Personal and Social Responsibility (TPSR) model.

The main idea behind TPSR is that much of the content taught in physical education programs allows students opportunities to practice and learn how to take responsibility for themselves and others. But the key is that responsibility and physical activity (skill and knowledge) are not *separate* learning outcomes; they must be pursued and achieved at the same time in TPSR. We all know that achievement in all forms of physical activity, particularly sports, relies on the demonstration of both personal and social initiative. Individuals know that much of their personal success depends on recognizing their teammates' abilities and accepting their own responsibility to work with their teammates toward common goals. Learning to recognize, accept, and act on those personal responsibilities in physical activity settings is the single most important outcome in the TPSR model. But, as you will learn in this chapter, this objective is a lot easier for a teacher to state than to accomplish.

The TPSR model works within the regular content of the physical education program and can be embedded in the planned learning activities of any physical education lesson (Hellison, 2011, p. 24). The strategies and learning activities of TPSR are used when personal and social development are the main learning goals. For example, a teacher could be using Peer Teaching in a middle school fitness unit and incorporate several TPSR strategies to help students make better decisions for themselves and for others while they are in the role of tutor.

It needs to be noted that TPSR is not a "deficiency" model, to be used only when students show patterns of improper behavior and poor decision making. TPSR strategies can provide all students a safe environment in which to practice, learn positive behaviors, and develop productive decision-making habits.

ALIGNMENT WITH NASPE NATIONAL STANDARDS

Exhibit 15.1 shows the alignment of the TPSR model with the NASPE standards. As you can see, this model is strongly and consistently aligned with standards 5 and 6—perhaps stronger than any other model. Its alignment with standards 1, 2 and 4 is either moderate or weak because of the high priority on the development of personal and social decision making. TPSR's alignment with standard 3 is also weak for that same reason.

FOUNDATIONS

Theory and Rationale

The TPSR model is not based on explicit theories of teaching and learning. However, it does draw strong support from a social-problems perspective (Hellison, 2011) that reveals a clear need to help underserved and disenfranchised youth cope with the many risks they face in today's society, such as

EXHIBIT 15.1	Alignment of Teaching Personal and Social Responsibility with NASPE National Standards.	
NASPE STANDARD	**ALIGNMENT RATING**	**COMMENTS**
1. Demonstrates competency in motor skills and movement patterns needed to perform a variety of physical activities	3	Weak alignment unless combined with another model
2. Demonstrates understanding of movement concepts, principles, strategies, and tactics as they apply to the learning and performance of physical activities	2	Weak alignment unless combined with another model
3. Participates regularly in physical activity	1–3	Will vary according to the unit content taught with TPSR
4. Achieves and maintains a health-enhancing level of physical fitness	3	Weak alignment for fitness development, due to primary focus on personal and social development
5. Exhibits responsible personal and social behavior that respects self and others in physical activity settings	1	One of the best models for achieving this standard
6. Values physical activity for health, enjoyment, challenge, self-expression, and/or social interaction	1, 3	Strong alignment for enjoyment, challenge, self-expression, and social interaction; weak alignment for health

Ratings categories:

1. Strong alignment

2. Moderate alignment

3. Weak alignment

violence, gang affiliation, drug and alcohol addictions, alienation, attending underachieving schools, and poor health. Of course, these problems are not limited to minority youth who live in areas of urban poverty; the problems now cut across all social, ethnic, and economic groups in our country, occurring in every town, city, and region. The TPSR model was first developed to help at-risk inner-city youth, but one of the reasons it has shown increased popularity in recent years is that the problems just named are no longer found only in core urban areas. Teachers at nearly all schools in the U. S. have large numbers of students who can be served by this approach to instruction.

Although TPSR does lack an explicit theoretical foundation, it is backed by a sound rationale for its need and its use in physical education programs. That rationale is based on the recognition that the content of physical education programs (sport, fitness, dance) provides opportunities for students to learn how to take responsibility for themselves and others and to make positive personal and social choices in a "safe" setting, under the guidance of a qualified educational professional. A "safe" setting allows students to learn and practice choices that can help themselves and others, without the serious consequences associated with life outside of school. As you will see later, as students make those positive choices in school physical education settings, teachers can make direct attempts to show students how to make the same positive choices in settings outside of school.

Part of the rationale supporting TPSR comes from the inherent nature of most activities taught in school programs, particularly those associated with individual and team sports. Success or failure in sport is almost always due to a combination of effort, preparation, support, and sharing. Team sports offer obvious examples, as members of the team must do their individual jobs *and* work together to reach the team's goals. But even individual sport athletes (golfers, tennis players) rely on many other people (coaches, trainers, and loved ones who give support); the athlete is just the most visible member of this team. All members of the team must recognize their special role and take responsibility for doing what is needed for the team's success. Physical education programs provide regular and meaningful opportunities for students to learn decision-making skills that affect their welfare and that of those around them. TPSR provides an instructional plan designed to optimize such learning opportunities.

Assumptions About Teaching and Learning

The TPSR model has developed from a distinctly organic method, largely stemming from Hellison's own trial-and-error approach in finding out "what works" to help students learn personal and social responsibility in physical activity settings. Rather than assuming to know what his students needed and how to teach them, Hellison developed TPSR from his daily interactions with students and their teachers in schools, on playgrounds, and in other community settings. The current assumptions about teaching and learning in TPSR came out of those interactions and have been validated by numerous teachers in many physical education programs.

Assumptions about teaching

1. Responsibility for self and others can be taught with a high level of intent. That is, a teacher can promote those outcomes through recognized strategies and progressions, similar in many ways to teaching motor skills, knowledge, fitness, and dance. A teacher can start "where the students are" and go from there in a reasonably well-planned sequence.

2. Teachers should not separate content learning in physical education programs from the learning of responsibility and decision making. That is, it is not acceptable to promote one set of outcomes over the other or to pursue them individually.

3. Teaching is best done by empowering students to make positive personal and social decisions in physical activity settings and then assisting students in carrying out those decisions.

Assumptions about learning

1. Learning must be student-centered. The activity content must have some meaning to students and provide ample opportunity for them to practice positive decision making.

2. Some level of structure can be planned to teach responsibility, but learners must be expected, and allowed, to progress in uneven patterns. Success *and* failure provide opportunities for learners, if properly managed by the TPSR teacher.

The Major Theme of TPSR: Integration, Transfer, Empowerment, and Teacher–Student Relationships

Hellison (2003) outlines four main themes that define the TPSR model of instruction: "Integration, Transfer, Empowerment, and the Teacher–Student Relationship."

1. *Integration* means that the teacher does not separate the learning of physical activity content from the learning of personal and social responsibility. The TPSR teacher maintains the connection between these outcomes by engaging students in content that provides the opportunity for learning responsibility at the same time.

2. *Transfer* means that the TPSR teacher makes every attempt to move students from being responsible in the relatively controlled setting of the gym to making positive decisions in less predictable settings in school, after school, and in the community.

3. *Empowerment* means that students learn to recognize and act on the large degree of self-determination they have over many of life's outcomes. The idea is to let students know they are not victims of life; they are *in charge* of much of what happens in their lives.

4. The *teacher–student relationship* is the most essential component of TPSR, and the most difficult for teachers to learn and apply. Most of the interactions

in TPSR are based on personal relationships built on experience, honesty, trust, and communication. They take time to foster and make both the teacher and the student vulnerable to emotional harm. But, when established, the teacher–student relationship opens a two-way path for them to move *together as equal partners* through TPSR's interactive learning process.

Learning Domain Priorities and Domain Interactions

Domain priorities

TPSR offers a holistic approach to teaching. It tries to promote outcomes in all three major learning domains by constantly integrating affective learning with motor performance and cognitive knowledge. Contrary to many people's beliefs, the model does not prioritize affective outcomes over the others. Many teachers who hear the message of TPSR hear only the social/affective part of that message; they do not note the part that says teachers should still strive to help students be competent, knowledgeable, and fit.

Domain priority is determined by the focus of the current learning activity, which will certainly change many times in a lesson and unit. As Hellison indicates, the initial domain priority is determined by the teacher's stated learning objective in the cognitive or psychomotor domain; at that point, TPSR looks no different from all the other models in this book. However, when student engagement in planned learning tasks presents an opportunity to develop personal and social skills, those skills take precedence—but are addressed within the same learning activity as before. That is, students might still be participating in the same initial drill, but goals related to other issues, such as being safe around others, behaving well, and helping others learn, receive increased emphasis.

Domain interactions

In TPSR, all three domains interact in dynamic and often unpredictable ways. Domain priority can shift at any time, causing domain interactions to shift. The TPSR teacher must constantly ask herself, "What is the primary goal here/now, and how does working on that goal affect the other learning domains?"

Levels of Personal and Social Responsibility

TPSR teachers must always keep in mind that the content in this model is not defined by outcomes in the cognitive and psychomotor domains. It is defined by student learning that demonstrates increased levels of personal and social responsibility in physical activity settings. "Getting better" in this model means making better positive decisions and taking more positive actions that affect individual students and those around them. Students' current development of those attributes and their improvement over time are based on a five-level scheme in the TPSR model. Hellison (2011) explains the current description of each level, shown in Exhibit 15.2. To understand the levels best, you should read Exhibit 15.2 from the bottom to the top. Also, you should know that the teacher always targets student progression one level above the general level

EXHIBIT 15.2	Levels of responsibility indicating student readiness for TPSR.	
LEVEL	**DESCRIPTOR**	**COMPONENTS (MAJOR LEARNING GOALS)**
5	Outside the gym	■ Trying these ideas in other areas of life ■ Being a positive role model for others, especially younger kids
4	Helping others and leadership	■ Care and compassion ■ Sensitivity and responsiveness ■ Inner strength
3	Self-direction	■ On-task independence ■ Goal-setting progression ■ Courage to resist peer pressure
2	Participation and effort	■ Self-motivation ■ Exploration of effort and new tasks ■ Courage to persist when the going gets tough
1	Respecting the rights and feelings of others	■ Self-control ■ The right to peaceful conflict resolution ■ The right to be included and to have cooperative peers

Reprinted by permission from D. Hellison (2011), *Teaching Responsibility Through Physical Activity*, 3rd ed. (Champaign, IL: Human Kinetics).

they currently display: students who are working on the components of level 3 have already consistently demonstrated appropriate decisions and actions at level 2.

Student Developmental Requirements

In most instructional models, student readiness to learn and receptivity to engaging in ways designed in the model are viewed as mostly constant phenomena. If students do not have the prerequisite skills, knowledge, and dispositions needed for a given model to work, the teacher is advised to select a different model. In TPSR, student readiness and receptivity are not viewed as fixed sets of attributes; in fact, as part of its fundamental design, the model actually tries to intentionally change students' readiness and receptivity to learning.

Student readiness for learning. In TPSR, two kinds of readiness must be considered. The first kind is the student's physical and cognitive readiness to learn the content of the unit, the same readiness that applies to every other teaching model in this book. A second kind of readiness is needed in TPSR to indicate whether the student is prepared to learn personal and social responsibility in addition to the physical activity content.

The teacher will determine readiness and receptivity based on the categories that describe each student's current level of responsibility (see Exhibit 15.2). After the teacher understands each student's present level, or the predominant level among all students in a class, he then selects lesson content and strategies for developing personal and social responsibility to match that level. Readiness is therefore used as a starting point for the TPSR teacher, and all instructional decisions proceed from that point.

Student receptivity to the model. Student receptivity is also dynamic in the TPSR model. The teacher will determine the degree to which each student is avoidant/participatory, competitive/collaborative, and dependent/independent and use that as a starting point to decide content and specific strategies for moving students closer to the participatory, collaborative, and independent ends of those categories. Receptivity to learn within the model is determined by the same scheme used to categorize student readiness, which is shown in Exhibit 15.2.

The TPSR model is the only model in this book that tries to change student readiness and receptivity, and in many ways, that is the major purpose of the model: to help students change their degree of readiness to learn content and responsibility and to increase their willingness to enter into the process of making that happen within the model.

Validation of the Model

Research validation

Research on TPSR has not been extensive, but it does show some evidence that the model effectively promotes the learning outcomes stated for it. In a review of literature on TPSR, Hellison and Walsh (2002) cite 26 studies done on the model. It should be noted that many of these studies did not take place in school physical education settings. Rather, they were conducted in after-school and other community-based programs.

Hellison and Walsh (2002) summarize strong evidence that within programs, TPSR leads to participant improvement in key learning areas like self-control, effort, helping others, self-worth, self-direction, teamwork, and communication skills. There is also solid evidence that attributes such as self-control, effort, and self-esteem learned in TPSR are transferable to other settings (level 5). TPSR participants show a greatly reduced dropout rate and an increased willingness to be a positive force in the community.

Hellison and Walsh (2002) cite evidence that cross-age teaching opportunities (a TPSR strategy, and a form of Peer Teaching) can promote improved problem-solving skills, more concern for others, better self-confidence, and a better acceptance of constructive criticism. More recently, Li et al. (2008) reported that students who demonstrated higher levels of personal and social responsibility enjoyed physical education more than students who exhibited low levels. A researcher in New Zealand (Gordon, 2010) found that students were able to develop a stronger understanding of personal and social responsibility in physical education but showed no evidence of transferring those behaviors to other settings (i.e., out of school). Wright and Burton (2008) studied a full unit of TPSR at a high school and reported that the TPSR model could be used to effectively promote "life skills" for students, thus verifying the major outcomes described for this model.

Although there has not been extensive research on the TPSR model to date, the available results support the model as an effective way to teach personal and social skills and responsibility. These outcomes occur in the original setting (physical education or other programs) and can be transferred to settings in the larger community. It should be noted that many physical education teachers have completed action research studies on TPSR that have not been published in scholarly journals. This leads to the belief that much more is known about this model than can be found in journals.

Craft knowledge validation

The TPSR model has been developed from the experiences of Don Hellison, his graduate students, and colleagues and teachers across the United States and several countries around the world. In many ways the model developed according to "what worked" when Hellison and others tried to teach personal and social responsibility in physical education programs. The sharing of effective strategies in the TPSR model has occurred in many ways: in books, in professional journals, at conferences, in the many workshops led by Hellison and other leading proponents of the model, and through a large informal network that now extends across the United States and into many other countries. That networking has led to the formation of the TPSR Alliance to promote the use of this model in physical education and other programs with a physical activity component. The TPSR Alliance website, found at www.tpsr-alliance.org, is a valuable resource and "community center" for teachers who use this model.

Even with that network, craft knowledge validation of the TPSR model is challenged for two reasons. The first reason is that few teachers actually use the complete model; many of them will use the familiar scheme for categorizing student levels of responsibility (Exhibit 15.2) but incorporate few if any of the interactive strategies to be discussed later in this chapter. The second reason is that success with the model is highly idiosyncratic: it depends on the teacher's ability to make and implement decisions that might work only in that specific context. So, when another teacher tries that same thing, she might experience failure rather than success. Because the model relies so much on minute-to-minute interactions between the teacher and students, and between students themselves, there are many different situations in which it is difficult to determine patterns for those interactions that will always work.

That is not to say that TPSR has not been successful for a large number of teachers. It has, and teachers provide many testimonials to its success in a wide variety of contexts. The problem arises when we try to find commonalities among those successes that can guide others to use the model effectively in their own situations.

Intuitive validation

The foundation of TPSR can be used as the basis for validating it intuitively. That is, if physical education teachers wish to help students develop positive patterns of personal and social responsibility, then those outcomes must be given direct attention and taught like any other essential content in a program. As you will recall, learning in the affective domain in most other models happens indirectly, as a byproduct of learning in the cognitive and psychomotor domains. In the TPSR model, learning in the affective domain is intentionally planned and developed, like any other content in the program, by a series of sequential learning experiences and teacher–student interactions. So, if a teacher really wants students to learn positive personal and social responsibility, then it makes sense to approach that learning with a model that promotes those outcomes intentionally and directly, leading to higher levels of success.

TEACHING AND LEARNING FEATURES

Control

The control profile for TPSR is described in two parallel tracks. The first track is determined by how the teacher has planned for students to learn the content in the cognitive and psychomotor domains—that is, how they will learn the knowledge and skills that lead to improved performance in physical activity. The profile for this track will reflect the way the teacher plans task presentation and task structure. For example, if Peer Teaching is the model being used in conjunction with TPSR, the profile for task presentation and task structure will be the same as Peer Teaching. The second track is determined by how the teacher interacts with students to promote the development of personal and social responsibility *within* the stated physical activity content. Two kinds of learning can be pursued: cognitive/psychomotor and affective/social. If students have demonstrated the ability to make positive personal and social decisions, the TPSR strategies can be used to reinforce present behavior patterns. If students cannot make positive decisions in those areas, then the teacher incorporates one or more TPSR strategies in the unit to develop positive patterns. Exhibit 15.3 shows the control profile for the second track of TPSR as it relates to decisions and operations developed specifically for that model—when personal and social learning is directly addressed. Each element of the profile is described below.

1. Determination of levels. The teacher determines the level for each lesson focus after identifying students' present levels (Exhibit 15.2) and then plans appropriate learning activities. Remember, these levels are based on personal and social responsibility, not the typical cognitive and psychomotor content found in other instructional models.

2. Managerial control. When students are at the lower levels of responsibility, the teacher maintains direct control over managerial decisions and actions (A).

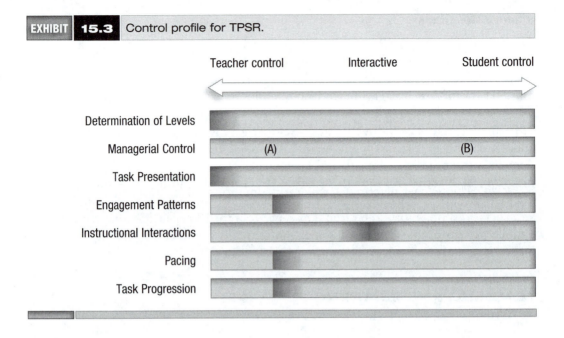

EXHIBIT **15.3** Control profile for TPSR.

As students demonstrate higher levels of responsibility, the teacher can give them more input and control over class management operations (B).

3. Task presentations. In TPSR, task presentations that address personal and social responsibility typically start with the teacher's observations and assessment of students' present levels. For instance, the teacher might observe that too many students are arguing with the official in a volleyball match and stop the match to bring that to the attention of the class. The teacher then states that such behavior is indicative of level 2 (effort and cooperation) and tells students that he thinks by now they should be at the next level (self-direction). So, to work on that, the teacher decides to use a Goal-Setting Plan in the next 15 minutes of the match, explaining that plan to students as a task presentation.

4. Engagement patterns. The TPSR model uses a variety of engagement types, but the teacher decides how students will engage at any given time. Since the teacher knows students' current level, as well as the appropriate strategies for working to improve personal and social responsibility, the teacher makes the engagement pattern decision and communicates it to students. As Exhibit 15.3 indicates, the teacher can give some of this control to students, once they have shown the ability to make and carry out decisions at a higher level of responsibility.

5. Instructional interactions. One of the hallmarks of the TPSR model is the way in which teachers interact with students on a minute-to-minute basis. Remember that one of the key themes in the model is teacher–student relationships. These relationships build from a regular pattern of verbal and nonverbal interactions between the teacher and students. Only in cases when student safety is immediately threatened should the TPSR teacher directly order students to do or stop some kind of behavior. In all other situations, the teacher interacts with students in a manner that allows them to see their behavior for what it is, understand its consequences, and negotiate new behavior patterns. In many ways the teacher's role is similar to that of a counselor, who helps someone see what he is doing and how it affects his life and those around him and encourages him to initiate new patterns of behavior.

6. Pacing. The teacher determines when it is time for students to move to the next level. When students have shown a consistent pattern of decisions and actions at their current level, the teacher starts to use strategies at the next level to move students a little further along in personal and social development.

7. Task progression. In TPSR, learning tasks are planned by the teacher within each of the levels. All tasks within one level contain about the same degree of complexity and individual responsibility for personal and social development. The TPSR teacher plans a number of these tasks within each level, looking for improvement in affective development along the way. The decision to move from one task to the next depends on how well students respond to each task and when the teacher thinks that the current task has accomplished what it was supposed to.

Inclusiveness

The TPSR model is highly inclusive because all students can be placed within one of the levels and instructed according to their current personal and social development. All students therefore have a "starting point" that the teacher can use when designing developmentally appropriate tasks that move students to a higher level of responsibility. Inclusion in TPSR is further promoted when students are able to make decisions about which level they ultimately aspire to and when they assume a large degree of self-responsibility for reaching it. People who have a high degree of self-determination in their lives find goals to be more meaningful to them, and they generally succeed more than people who are *told by others* what their goals are and how to reach them.

Learning Tasks

Because the content in TPSR is different from that in models that do not directly promote the development of personal and social responsibility, the learning tasks used in TPSR are unique. In fact, rather than call them learning tasks, Hellison (2003) labels them *strategies*—ways that a teacher gives students opportunities to learn decision making and behaviors within each of the five levels. Exhibit 15.4 shows some examples of these strategies, their purpose, and how they would be presented to students in this model.

EXHIBIT	15.4	Sample strategies for each of the five levels of student development (Hellison, 2003).

LEVEL 1 STRATEGIES

STRATEGY	PURPOSE	TASK PRESENTATION TO STUDENTS
Inclusion	To get students to understand that everyone has the right to participate and not be subject to humiliation in the process	Setting guidelines for picking teams: 1. Teams must be fair and agreed on by all. 2. As team members are chosen, they all get to decide about the next choice (no "captain's only" choices). 3. Teams must alternate choices between boys and girls. 4. Students may not ridicule a team's choices. 5. Everyone must play every position during the game.
The Accordian Principle	To get students to understand that they can play a favorite activity as long as they follow the guidelines. When they fail to do that, the activity ends; so the activity could last five minutes or the whole class period.	1. Explain that the activity will last until: a. Three major violations occur. b. Six minor violations occur. c. Student safety is jeopardized.
Sit-Out Progression	This is done with individual students, to get them to make their own choices about participating or not. The rules are set up ahead of time so they know what the consequences will be. If they **choose** to misbehave, the consequences will be enforced by the teacher.	1st violation: Some signal from the teacher (warning). 2nd violation: "Get under control or sit out now." 3rd violation: The student sits out and returns only after a designated time. 4th violation: The student sits out until the teacher and student can negotiate a remediation plan. 5th violation: Referral to school administration or home.
Grandma's Law	To get students to participate in the current low-interest activity so they can do a high-interest activity later	Teacher: "I know you don't like aerobics, but if you do that for the next 15 minutes without a lot of griping, you can play basketball the rest of the period."
Five Clean Days	To promote consistency within the level 1 decisions and actions. Used to prevent "backsliding" from the current level to level 0.	A student is given a list of positive decisions and actions at level 1. This is her personal plan. If she follows that plan for five consecutive days with no violations, she can progress to level 2.

LEVEL 2 STRATEGIES

STRATEGY	PURPOSE	TASK PRESENTATION TO STUDENTS
Modifying Tasks	To get students to understand different levels of difficulty on skill or fitness tasks	Start with a "baseline" task, one with a moderate level of difficulty (e.g., stationary passing of a football from 10 yards apart). After students have practiced that for 10 minutes, make the task easier or harder and have them practice another 10 minutes. Note their reactions and level of participation after the baseline task changes each time.

Continued.	EXHIBIT 15.4

LEVEL 2 STRATEGIES, *continued.*

STRATEGY	PURPOSE	TASK PRESENTATION TO STUDENTS
Self-Paced Challenges	To get students to understand their abilities within a given skill or fitness task	Give the students a series of learning tasks (e.g., volleyball serving, bumping, setting) and have them try each task 10 times, keeping track of successful attempts. From that, they can start to see which position in volleyball they might be best suited for.
Intensity Scale	To get students to make their own rating of effort and participation	Give students a learning task and ask them to practice for 10 minutes. At the end of the 10 minutes, ask them to rate their own level of participation: 1 is nonparticipant/no effort, 10 is the highest level of participation/effort. For the next activity, group students according to their level on the previous activity.
Teaching by Invitation	To empower students with self-choice	Set up five stations for passing skills, each with a different level of difficulty. Allow students to determine the level that gives them a balance of challenge with success. Afterward, ask them to discuss how they chose their own level.

LEVEL 3 STRATEGIES

STRATEGY	PURPOSE	TASK PRESENTATION TO STUDENTS
On-Task Independence	To promote individual decision making and action by working without direct supervision by the teacher	1. Students read and follow a set of task cards for learning tennis serves. 2. Students complete a pre-class stretching routine without the teacher's lead. 3. Each student makes up his own cardio workout to be in his target heart rate zone for 15 minutes.
Goal-Setting Plan	Going beyond independence to meet personal goals	1. Students design and implement their own plans to lose a designated amount of weight. The amount they want to lose is up to them. 2. Students make and reach a goal for a number of consecutive "clean days." That number is up to them.
Counseling Time	To get students to understand the relationship between their decisions, actions, and goals	1. The teacher recognizes that a student has set unreasonable goals and talks with the student to clarify the process of setting and reaching realistic goals. 2. Sometimes a student wrongfully blames others for her failure to meet goals. When the teacher recognizes this, he talks with the student to clarify her own decisions and actions that contributed to that failure and helps her take more self-control in the future.

(continued)

| EXHIBIT | 15.4 | Continued. |

LEVEL 4 STRATEGIES

STRATEGY	PURPOSE	TASK PRESENTATION TO STUDENTS
Peer Teaching	To provide students with opportunities to develop sensitivity to others and accept responsibility	1. Teacher puts students in pairs or small groups. One student in each pair/group is designated as the leader. 2. The teacher explains the upcoming task to the leaders, who will be expected to teach that to their groups. 3. The teacher discusses with the leaders the qualities of being a good leader. 4. The teacher directs the leaders to work with their groups. 5. The teacher walks around to find good examples of leadership and highlights those to the class at the end of the lesson.
Group Goal Setting	Going beyond independence to meet goals set by the group	1. The teacher puts students in groups of four to six, making the groups as heterogeneous as possible. 2. The teacher explains to the groups that they must determine a goal related to the current fitness unit. They will have two weeks to reach that goal. 3. Each group meets to discuss and set an appropriate goal. 4. The teacher consults with each group to help them set a challenging but realistic goal.

LEVEL 5 STRATEGIES

STRATEGY	PURPOSE	TASK PRESENTATION TO STUDENTS
Community Volunteer	To provide opportunities to develop in settings with no direct supervision from the teacher	1. The teacher identifies several community organizations that are looking for part-time volunteer coaches. 2. The students are asked to pick one organization and to volunteer for two hours after school one day a week. 3. The teacher gives physical education credit for those hours.
Class Leader	To allow students to help others reach their next level of development	The teacher asks a level 5 student to conduct an "awareness talk" for a group of level 2 students.

Reprinted by permission from D. Hellison, *Teaching Responsibility Through Physical Activity,* 2nd ed. (Champaign, IL: Human Kinetics), 29–34, 36.

In TPSR, not only are the learning tasks unique but the model also uses a unique format for physical education lessons. Each lesson should include five components (Hellison, 2011, p. 27):

Relational time	Brief personal interactions between the teacher and individual students. These can occur either before or after class, and they serve to let students know that the teacher is aware of them on a personal level. These interactions could include things like acknowledging a student's birthday or making compliments about appearance (clothing, new hairstyle, and so forth).
Awareness talk	This formally begins the lesson. The teacher brings the students together as a group and reminds them of the importance of making good decisions for themselves and their classmates. It should also include a mention of what level(s) will be focused on in the lesson, with reminders of what those levels mean.
Physical activity	This is the largest part of the lesson and includes all the drills, games, and other physical activity content to be learned in the lesson. Student behavior during this part of the lesson provides the opportunity for students to learn and practice at each TPSR level and for the teacher to look for "teaching moments" that will prompt personal and group interactions in class.
Group meeting	This occurs near the end of the lesson. Its purpose is to provide time for the teacher to review the lesson as it relates to the major learning outcomes and levels of TPSR. For example, the teacher could compliment the class because all of them were working well at level 2 during the earlier floor hockey game. This time can also be used to preview the next class for students.
Self-reflection time	After the group meeting, the teacher provides students with the opportunity to conduct some brief self-evaluation of their decisions and actions in the lesson, focusing on how those decisions and actions relate to one or more of the TPSR levels. This can also be used to allow students the opportunity to set new goals for themselves.

Engagement Patterns for Learning

It is important to remember that all the learning strategies in TPSR have roots in some type of physical activity content and are used on an "as needed" basis. So the teacher will plan a lesson that involves skill development, games, exercise, and so on, and then use one of the TPSR strategies as the situation demands. Therefore, the engagement patterns in TPSR will be very specific to each situation. For example, sometimes the teacher will give an awareness talk to one student; at other times the teacher will need to present the awareness talk to the entire class. (A sample lesson format for TPSR can be found on the IMPE website.)

The common characteristic of all TPSR engagement is dialogue, between the teacher and one or more students or between two or more students. This dialogue allows all participants an opportunity to be heard, ask questions, and share in the decision-making process.

Teacher and Student Roles and Responsibilities

Each instructional model will have certain operations that must be completed to allow the model to function according to its design. Some of the operations are carried out by the teacher; others are carried out by one or more students. Exhibit 15.5 shows the major operations within the TPSR model and indicates who is responsible for completing them during each lesson.

EXHIBIT 15.5 Teacher and student roles and responsibilities in TPSR.

OPERATION OR RESPONSIBILITY	PERSON/PEOPLE RESPONSIBLE IN TPSR
Starting class	The **teacher** usually starts class by acknowledging at which level(s) students are working and by providing some overview of the lesson.
Task presentation	The **teacher** will make the task presentation of the activity content for the lesson.
Identifying problems related to personal and social development	The **teacher** observes students in the activity content and identifies behaviors that need attention with a TPSR strategy.
Selecting the TPSR learning activity	The **teacher** decides which TPSR learning activity is appropriate for the situation, based on the identified problem. The **teacher** informs the involved student(s) about why the TPSR activity is needed right now.
Setting the parameters of the TPSR activity	The **teacher and the involved students** discuss the upcoming TPSR activity to decide how long it might last, what its purpose is, and what outcomes (resolutions) are expected.
Problem resolution	**Students** are responsible for engaging in the TPSR activity with good effort, an open dialogue, and respect for others.
Assessing the outcomes	The **teacher** should state clearly to the students what is expected of them in resolving the problem and assess their effort in working toward that resolution.

Verification of Instructional Processes

Teachers who use the TPSR model can learn the benchmarks for their own and student behavior patterns. These benchmarks, listed in Exhibits 15.6 and 15.7, verify that the model has been designed and implemented with an acceptable degree of faithfulness, increasing the likelihood that the stated student learning outcomes will be achieved.

TPSR teacher benchmarks.   🖶 **EXHIBIT** **15.6**

BENCHMARK	HOW TO VERIFY
Teacher plans a regular lesson of physical activity content.	Check the lesson plan.
Teacher is aware of each student's level of responsibility.	Teacher has a record of each student's progression through the levels, including current level.
Teacher identifies needed TPSR learning activity.	The teacher observes students in the physical activity content and notes behavior that indicates a need to use one of the TPSR learning activities.
Teacher explains the need for the TPSR activity.	Observe the teacher's explanation.
Teacher sets clear expectations for the upcoming TPSR activity.	Teacher checks for understanding often.
Teacher allows students to participate in the decision-making and goal-setting processes.	1. Observe the teacher's interactions with students. 2. Ask students if they feel that they were allowed to participate.
Teacher does a review and closure to discuss student progress regarding personal and social responsibility.	1. Check the teacher's lesson plan. 2. Observe and record the teacher's interactions with students in the review and closure segment.

TPSR student benchmarks.   🖶 **EXHIBIT** **15.7**

BENCHMARK	HOW TO VERIFY
Students know their own level.	1. Ask students to tell their level. 2. Ask students to give examples of behaviors and decisions at their level.
Students understand why the TPSR learning activity was needed.	Observe students as the teacher explains, to determine if they agree with what the teacher saw.
Students make an honest effort in the TPSR activity.	Observe students while they engage in the TPSR activity, and note events that indicate their effort.
Students do not "backslide" (go back to a lower level too often).	Monitor student behavior according to the levels, and note behavior that is indicative of a lower level than their present one. (Occasional backsliding is to be expected, but frequent backsliding is not.)

Assessment of Learning

Assessment in the TPSR model is based on the five levels of responsibility. Students should know what behaviors are indicative of each level (especially their current level) and show that they can demonstrate the behaviors of their level consistently. When they have shown consistency at their current level, they can gradually be given opportunities to demonstrate decisions and behaviors at the next level.

However, student knowledge of the levels is not good enough in this model; students should *demonstrate* their progression through the levels with the appropriate decisions and behaviors. Therefore, much of the assessment in TPSR should be authentic, conducted within the learning activities themselves.

Assessing knowledge of the levels

Because the levels form the basis of progression through the TPSR model, students will need to know what each level means and what decisions and behaviors are included at each level. The teacher can give simple written tests that ask students to match each level's label with the level's decisions and behaviors. The teacher can also assess knowledge interactively by checking for understanding with students (e.g., asking them to categorize an example of a decision or behavior within a particular level).

Assessing student decisions and behaviors

The five levels of responsibility can be used to design rubrics for assessing students' decisions and behavior in the TPSR model. Refer back to Exhibit 15.2 for the descriptors used within each level. Students can be assessed on their ability to demonstrate the appropriate decisions and behaviors that define their present level by noting what they do in class and looking for instances of agreement or disagreement with that level's characteristics. Those assessments can be performed by the teacher, by peers in class, or with self-assessment. For example, if a student is at level 3, self-direction, she should demonstrate the following decisions and behaviors in a tennis lesson:

1. Completing tasks without teacher supervision
2. Being able to do self-assessments
3. Being able to set self-goals
4. Being able to resist negative external influences

She could take a few moments near the end of class to *reflect and recall* specific instances when she followed the guidelines for that level:

1. I finished my stretching routine without asking the teacher for help.
2. After my stretching, I went right into my practice task on my own.
3. I decided that I would get five good serves in a row before the end of the lesson.
4. Jerry tried to get me to stop practicing and play a joke on Hector, but I told him no and kept practicing.

A similar way to assess is to use a *checklist* to note if the student made level-appropriate decisions or behaviors in class. For example, a student at level 1 in a soccer lesson could ask a peer to observe him during class and record if the behaviors listed were observed (see Exhibit 15.8).

Another effective strategy is the *behavioral contract*. Negotiated by the teacher and student, the contract states very clearly what is expected of the student (within her level) and what the consequences will be for successful and unsuccessful completion of the contract. It is signed by the teacher and the student, making it a true contract, not just a verbal agreement. Exhibit 15.9 shows an example of a contract used to get a student to have five "clean days" in a row. A "clean day" is any day that the student does not backslide from her current level by making decisions and behaving in ways that indicate a lower level.

Checklist for assessing whether a student made level-appropriate decisions and behaviors in class.	🖶 EXHIBIT	15.8

Name:	Level:		Date:	
I participated without interfering with others.		YES		NO
I participated safely around others.		YES		NO
I used self-control during the game when things went wrong.		YES		NO
I used peaceful conflict resolution when I disagreed with others.		YES		NO

Observed by: _____

A behavioral contract for level 2.	🖶 EXHIBIT	15.9

Date: _____

I _____ agree that I will complete five clean days in a row at level 2,
      (Student name)

starting on _____ and ending on _____ . If I complete five
      (Date)   *(Date)*

clean days in a row on those days, _____ will allow
                                      (Teacher name)

me to have a self-choice activity day during the following week. Clean days will be assessed by

_____ , according to the guidelines of level 2.
      (Teacher name)

Signed: _____
               Student

_____
               Teacher

It is a good idea for teachers to negotiate with students when assessing in TPSR. By taking part in the process, students get opportunities to make decisions that will have a direct effect on them in physical education. They can also learn how to make realistic decisions for which they will be held accountable—which is really the essence of the TPSR model.

IMPLEMENTATION NEEDS AND MODIFICATIONS

Teacher Expertise

Teachers who use the Teaching Personal and Social Responsibility model will need to have particular expertise in several areas of the knowledge base presented in Chapter 3.

Physical activity content. TPSR teachers must know physical activity content in a different way than in most other models. They need to know how each potential content area fits within the five levels of responsibility. That is, what is it about the content can be used to provide level-appropriate opportunities for student development? For example, when getting students to progress to level 1, the teacher should choose content that will be highly interesting to students. If they are not interested, they are not likely to participate. And, for instance, if a majority of the students are not yet at level 1, the teacher should not choose activities that offer opportunities for students to harm each other with equipment, including activities such as softball (bats and balls), tennis (racquets), or hockey (sticks).

Student development. The effective TPSR teacher will have good knowledge of child and adolescent development, especially emotional maturity and social skills. If students simply do not have the maturity to handle the decisions and behaviors at a certain level, the teacher should not try to force them to get there.

Environmental factors. Many of the behaviors and attitudes that students exhibit relative to personal and social responsibility are not learned in school. They are learned at home or in the community and then transferred to the school setting. In order for the TPSR teacher to use a holistic approach to address those problems, he should possess a solid understanding of the factors that can influence student behaviors.

Communication. At the heart of TPSR "in action" is a dialogue between the teacher and students. The teacher must be able to express herself clearly, directly, honestly, and consistently to avoid sending mixed signals to students or making agreements that can't be kept later.

Empowering students. One of the key learning outcomes in TPSR is empowerment for students to make and carry out their own decisions in a physical activity setting. This means that the teacher should help students make those choices and should allow them to experience the consequences, both positive and negative. Students can learn through success *and* failure, if they understand their contribution to the outcome. So, the TPSR teacher will not only give students the latitude to make many of their own decisions but will also be prepared to provide students with opportunities to reflect on those choices after providing an outcome.

Key Teaching Skills

Teachers will need two sets of teaching skills in this model. The first set depends on the physical activity content of the moment—the skills and knowledge teachers are getting students to learn in physical education class. The second set of skills comprises those skills needed to help students develop personal and social responsibility within the TPSR model. These skills will be used on an "as needed" basis when there are opportunities to promote the development of responsibility in lessons.

Counseling. In many ways, the TPSR teacher is a counselor—someone who can see differences between observed student behavior and socially appropriate behavior, make the student aware of problems in that area, and then help the student improve decision making. This process can have several steps:

1. Making the student aware of her behavior and its potentially negative consequences
2. Getting the student to acknowledge that a problem exists
3. Placing the behavior at one of the TPSR levels
4. Setting goals for improvement
5. Negotiating a plan for improvement
6. Providing support for the student's efforts to improve
7. Promoting regular reflection and interaction to prevent backsliding

Even though the steps are sequential, the student's progression might not follow that sequence. The TPSR teacher will need to know when to "go ahead," when to "take a few steps back," and when to allow students more time in any one stage.

Listening and questioning. A key part of the counseling process is listening—giving students a chance to explain their decisions and actions and hearing it from their point of view. In order to fully understand a student's point of view, the TPSR teacher must be skilled at asking questions that help clarify what the student said. Not all students can express themselves clearly, especially about their feelings; thus, the TPSR teacher should be able to ask questions that allow students an "entry point" for saying things that are sometimes difficult.

Showing honesty. Honesty is not a skill—it is a personal characteristic. A teacher either has it in his interactions with students or does not. However, the TPSR teacher can learn to *show* honesty in interactions with students in ways that gain students' trust. Some of that honesty comes from the teacher "being himself" and not trying to dress, act, and talk like his students. Other aspects of honesty come from being firm when needed, fair at all times, and willing to explain decisions as a teacher to students—even when those decisions are not popular with them.

Another way to show honesty with students and to truly gain their trust is to "walk the walk, not just talk the talk." That means the TPSR teacher should ask nothing of her students that she cannot do herself and that the teacher should model the very highest levels of personal and social responsibility at all times. Now, that does not mean the TPSR teacher can't "backslide" herself at times, but it does mean that when backsliding happens, the teacher can use the situation as a teaching moment for students and can make the same commitment to change for the future that she would ask of her students.

Using playfulness and a sense of humor. These personal characteristics need to be applied skillfully in the TPSR model. The teacher and students take on a high level of risk in many of the TPSR strategies; they put much of themselves "on the line" as they express their feelings and make decisions in sometimes very public ways. The TPSR teacher will know how to make that process less threatening to students and how to use TPSR strategies in the spirit of play— sometimes by being lighthearted and sometimes even humorous.

Reflecting. TPSR teachers constantly ask students to reflect on their decisions and behaviors. Because the TPSR model requires so many unanticipated decisions and actions on the teacher's part, teachers must develop good self-reflection habits and skills as well. TPSR teachers do not always have the luxury of extensive prior thinking; events happen quickly, and decisions must be made on the spot. Sometimes only well after an incident can teachers determine the quality and consequences of their decisions, but they must reflect in this way in order to be a little better prepared the next time they face similar circumstances and decisions.

Contextual Requirements

The TPSR model can be used in any setting and combined with any physical activity content. However, when deciding to use TPSR, a teacher does not consider the usual contextual factors, such as facilities, equipment, time, and content. Rather, he decides to use TPSR by assessing students' present level of personal and social responsibility to determine if there is a need for further development in those areas. If students are showing age/stage-appropriate levels of personal and social development, then there is no need to use TPSR. But if students have not developed to an appropriate level, the teacher can use TPSR to move them to higher levels.

Because Hellison established the TPSR model with inner-city, seriously at-risk students for many years, many physical educators mistakenly believed that only those kinds of students needed TPSR and that the only appropriate context for TPSR was the inner city. However, it is clear today that youth in every kind of community and in every kind of school show signs of underdeveloped personal and social responsibility. Thus student decision making and behaviors, not local context, will determine the need for TPSR.

Selecting and Modifying TPSR

As you just read, TPSR is used on an as-needed basis—when a teacher wishes to focus on students' personal and social development. So, the first rule for selecting TPSR is to identify a need for it. This can be done by reviewing the levels of responsibility and observing students to determine their current level. (Teachers can expect to see some variation in level among students in a class.) If this observation reveals that students have not developed to a level appropriate for their age, the teacher can then begin to use TPSR strategies and learning activities.

Unlike other instructional models, there are no guidelines for modifying TPSR for different grade levels. Teachers can use the whole model at any grade level they choose. What does get modified is the way in which a teacher applies each TPSR strategy and learning activity. Teachers should use simpler versions of each strategy and activity for students in lower grades and at lower levels of responsibility. When students are at higher levels of responsibility and maturity, the strategies and activities can be more complex and demanding.

Adaptations to accommodate diverse groups of learners

The TPSR model can be highly inclusive for physical education if the teacher accurately assesses students' present responsibility levels, knows how to apply the specific strategies to all students, and designs a safe environment for developing positive decision making and social interactions. Exhibit 15.10 lists some strategies that address a variety of special learning needs found in many schools today. Note that these examples are for the TPSR model, not the model being used to promote cognitive and/or psychomotor outcomes.

PLANNING TIPS FOR TPSR

eachers who choose to use the TPSR model can benefit by following a few additional planning tips:

1. Always know each student's current level, and plan the majority of lesson activities at the predominant level in the class.
2. Provide ample time for the TPSR strategy to work. In this model, process leads to progress, so give the strategy enough time to work.
3. Expect and plan for "backsliding"—when students behave and make decisions at lower levels. This is to be expected.
4. Use written contracts as much as possible. This removes all doubts about what you and the student agreed to do and prevents potentially negative interactions.

EXHIBIT 15.10 Strategies adapting TPSR for diverse groups of learners.

FOR STUDENTS WITH HEARING AND/OR SPEECH IMPAIRMENTS:

1. Move these students closer when asking questions or giving directions.
2. Provide written examples whenever possible.
3. Modify game space and equipment to provide increased participation.
4. Use hand and body gestures that convey specific messages to students (e.g., "thumbs up," "OK" signal, hugs).

FOR STUDENTS WITH SIGHT IMPAIRMENTS:

1. Use large body movements and verbal communication to express specific messages (e.g., waving arms, raised voice).
2. Modify game space and equipment to provide increased participation.

FOR STUDENTS WITH PHYSICAL DISABILITIES:

1. As much as possible, learn the nature of the disability and how it can affect the student's willingness and ability to participate in physical activity.
2. Modify game space and equipment to provide increased participation.
3. Explore ability-appropriate patterns and decision making (e.g., listening to the student's honest assessment of her ability to complete a task, asking, "How will I know you are doing it correctly?" or "What can I do to help you?").

FOR STUDENTS WHO DO NOT SPEAK ENGLISH:

1. Use student translators when available.
2. Pair matching bilingual students with non-English speakers.
3. Learn and use some key phrases that allow a basic level of communication.
4. Understand the culture of all students and how that can affect their interest, participation, and behavior in physical activity settings.

FOR LOWER-SKILLED STUDENTS:

1. Do not put them in potentially embarrassing situations.
2. Understand and act on the relationship between a student's skill ability and his behavior in physical activity settings.
3. Provide additional examples to make points.
4. Provide extra encouragement and praise to the slower learners.

FOR STUDENTS WITH BEHAVIOR DISABILITIES:

1. Provide students with behavior disabilities with extra encouragement for their participation and creativity in solving tactical problems.
2. Frequently relate their behavior to the level it demonstrates, and provide extra praise whenever they "kick it up a level."

5. Personal and social learning take priority over other outcomes in this model. Do not be afraid to take time away from things like skill development when students' patterns indicate the need to focus on decision making.

6. Develop personal and social learning in the same way as other domains: start at the student's current level, and build from there. Do not expect too much too soon.

UNIT AND LESSON PLAN EXAMPLES FOR TPSR INSTRUCTION

You will find several complete unit plans with lesson plans for the TPSR model on the IMPE website. It is not recommended that you follow these examples exactly as they are presented. The context, specific learning objectives, content of your own unit, and the predominant levels of responsibility of your students will require you to make changes in these examples to allow the TPSR model to lead to the most effective instruction in your situation.

SUMMARY

Teaching Personal and Social Responsibility is not a stand-alone model like the others in this book. It should be used within any content unit in a physical education program and can be interwoven with any other instructional model on an as-needed basis. In every instructional model, students are given some level of responsibility for themselves—and often, for classmates. As the teacher observes the students' level of responsibility, she must decide if that level is appropriate for that point in their development. If students have developed appropriately, then the strategies and activities of TPSR can be used to reinforce positive patterns. If students have not developed appropriately, then the teacher can select and use TPSR to help them reach higher levels of personal and social responsibility in physical education settings and beyond.

The TPSR model is not easy for teachers to learn, because it involves many decisions and actions that cannot be planned and that must be carried out in the flow of busy classes. TPSR teachers must be good at making decisions "on their feet," and many of those decisions involve judgments about students and themselves. But once a teacher has command of the TPSR model, it can promote some of the most important learning outcomes in the physical education program, outcomes that can affect the lives of students well beyond the gym walls.

LEARNING ACTIVITIES

1. Make a list of five patterns of student behavior and/or decision making that that might occur at different grade levels (P, K–2, 3–5, 6–8, 9–12). Explain how you would determine the level for each pattern on the scale shown in Exhibit 15.2 in this chapter.

2. For each of those patterns, identify one or more appropriate TPSR strategies that you could implement to take students to the next level.

3. Write an annotated plan to show how you would implement each strategy with a group of students in a physical education class.

4. Tell how you will assess the effectiveness of each TPSR strategy used. That is, how will you know the students have improved or moved to a higher level?

TOPICS FOR REFLECTION & SMALL-GROUP DISCUSSION

1. Discuss the potential of the TPSR model in promoting the NASPE standards for K–12 physical education in our schools today. Which standards can this model promote, and which ones might it fall short on?

2. Discuss why a teacher who uses TPSR might want to have some expertise in counseling and conflict resolution.

3. Explain why TPSR should not be viewed as a "deficiency" model.

4. Why has the need for TPSR gone far beyond applications for at-risk children in inner-city settings?

SUGGESTED READINGS FOR TPSR

Hellison, D. (1983). Teaching self-responsibility (and more). *Journal of Physical Education, Recreation & Dance, 54*(n), 23–28.

Hellison, D. (1985). *Goals and strategies for teaching physical education.* Champaign, IL: Human Kinetics.

Hellison, D. (2003). *Teaching responsibility through physical activity* (2nd ed.). Champaign, IL: Human Kinetics.

Hellison, D. (2011). *Teaching responsibility through physical activity* (3rd ed.). Champaign, IL: Human Kinetics.

O'Sullivan, M. O., & Henninger, M. (2000). *Assessing student responsibility and teamwork.* Reston, VA: National Association for Sport and Physical Education.

references

Alberto, P. A., & Troutman, A. C. (2008). *Applied behavior analysis for teachers: Influencing student performance* (8th ed.). Columbus, OH: Merrill.

Alexander, K., Taggart, A., & Luckman, J. (1998). Pilgrims progress: The sport education crusade down under. *Journal of Physical Education, Recreation & Dance, 69*(5), 21–23.

Alexander, K., Taggart, A., & Thorpe, S. (1995, November). Teacher renewal through curriculum innovation: Australian teachers tell their stories. Paper presented at the Australian Association for Research in Education.

Almond, L. (1986). Reflecting on themes: A games classification system. In R. Thorpe, D. Bunker, & L. Almond, eds. *Rethinking games teaching* (pp. 71–72). Loughborough, England: Authors.

American Alliance for Health, Physical Education, Recreation and Dance. (1989). *AAHPERD tennis skills test manual.* Reston, VA: AAHPERD.

Anderson, W. (1980). *Analysis of teaching physical education.* St. Louis: C.V. Mosby.

Annarino, A. (1976). Individualized instructional materials. In *Personalized learning in physical education* (pp. 64–76). Washington, DC: AAHPERD.

Ausubel, D. P. (1968). *Educational psychology: A cognitive view.* New York: Holt, Rinehart & Winston.

Bandura, A. (1977). *Social learning theory.* Englewood Cliffs, NJ: Prentice Hall.

Barrett, K. R. (1970). Exploration—A method for teaching movement: Discussion and summary. In R. T. Sweeney, ed. *Selected readings in movement education* (pp. 141–146). Reading, MA: Addison-Wesley.

Baumann, J. F. (1988). Direct Instruction reconsidered. *Journal of Reading Behavior, 31*, 714.

Bennett, R. G., & Hastie, P. A. (1997). The implementation of the sport education curriculum model into a collegiate physical activity course. *Journal of Physical Education, Recreation & Dance, 68*(3), 62–73.

Berkowitz, R. J. (1996). A practitioner's journey from skill to tactics. *Journal of Physical Education, Recreation & Dance, 67*(4), 44–45.

Blitzer, L. (1995). "It's a gym class . . . What's there to think about?" *Journal of Physical Education, Recreation & Dance, 66*(6), 44–48.

Bloom, B., Englehart, M., Furst, E., Hill, W., & Krathwohl, D. (1956). *Taxonomy of educational objectives: The classification of education goals. Handbook I. Cognitive domain.* New York: McKay.

Borich, G. D. (1992). *Effective teaching methods* (2nd ed.). New York: Merrill.

Bredekamp, S. (Ed.) (1987). *Developmentally appropriate practice in early childhood programs serving children from birth through age 8.* Washington, DC: National Association for the Education of Young Children.

Bredekamp, S., & Copple, C. (Eds.) (1996–97). *Developmentally appropriate practice in early childhood programs* (rev. ed.). Washington, DC: National Association for the Education of Young Children.

Brophy, J. E. (1987). Synthesis of research on strategies for motivating students to learn. *Educational Leadership, 45*(2), 40–48.

Bruner, J. S. (1961). The act of discovery. *Harvard Educational Review, 31*, 21–32.

Bulger, S. M., Mohr, D. J., Rairigh, R. M., & Townsend, J. S. (2007). *Sport education seasons.* Champaign, IL: Human Kinetics.

Bunker, D., & Thorpe, R. (1982). A model for teaching games in secondary schools. *Bulletin of Physical Education, 18*, 5–8.

Canter, L., & Canter, M. (2001). *Assertive discipline* (3rd ed.). Santa Monica, CA: Canter and Associates.

Carlson, T. B., & Hastie, P. A. (1997). The student social system within sport education. *Journal of Teaching in Physical Education, 16*, 176–195.

Chandler, T. (1996). Teaching games for understanding: Reflections and further questions. *Journal of Physical Education, Recreation & Dance, 67*(4), 49–51.

Cheffers, J., Mancini, V., & Martinek, T. (Eds.) (1980). *Interaction analysis: An application to nonverbal activity* (2nd ed.). Association for Productive Teaching.

Clark, C. (1983). Research on teacher planning: An inventory of the knowledge base. In D. C. Smith, ed. *Essential knowledge for beginning educators* (pp. 5–15). Washington, DC: American Association of Colleges for Teacher Education.

Cleland, F., & Pearse, C. (1995). Critical thinking in elementary physical education: Reflections on a yearlong study. *Journal of Physical Education, Recreation & Dance, 66*(6), 30–38.

Coker, C. (1996). Accommodating students' learning styles in physical education. *Journal of Physical Education, Recreation & Dance, 67*(9), 66–68.

Coker, C. (1998). Observation strategies for skill analysis. *Strategies, 11*(4), 17–19.

Cooper Institute for Aerobic Fitness. (1994). *FITNESSGRAM.* Dallas: Author.

Cregger, R. (1994). *Effects of three presentation formats in a PSI college level bowling course.* Unpublished doctoral dissertation, Virginia Polytechnic Institute and State University, Blacksburg.

Cregger, R., & Metzler, M. (1992). PSI for a college physical education basic instruction program. *Educational Technology, 38*(8), 51–56.

Cuseo, J. (1992). Cooperative learning vs. small-group discussions and group projects: The critical differences. *Cooperative Learning and College Teaching, 2*(3), 5–10.

Deutsch, M. (1949). A theory of cooperation and competition. *Human Relations, 2*, 129–152.

Dillon, J. T. (1988). *Questioning and teaching: A manual of practice.* New York: Teachers College Press.

Doolittle, S., & Girard, K. (1991). A dynamic approach to teaching games in elementary PE. *Journal of Physical Education, Recreation & Dance, 62*(4), 57–62.

Dugas, D. (1994). Sport education in the secondary curriculum. In D. Siedentop, ed. *Sport Education: Quality PE through positive sport experiences* (pp. 105–112). Champaign, IL: Human Kinetics.

Dunn, R. (1996). *How to implement and supervise a learning styles program.* Alexandria, VA: Association for Supervision and Curriculum Development.

Dunn, R., & Dunn, K. (1993). *Teaching secondary students through their individual learning styles.* Boston: Allyn and Bacon.

Dunn, R., Dunn, K., & Price, G. (1989). *Learning styles inventory.* Lawrence, KS: Price Systems.

Dyson, B. (2005). Integrating cooperative learning and tactical games models: Focusing on social interactions and decision making. In J. Butler and L. Griffin, eds. *Introduction to teaching games for understanding* (pp. 149–168). Champaign, IL: Human Kinetics.

Dyson, B. P., Linehan, N. R., & Hastie, P. A. (2010). The ecology of cooperative learning in physical education. *Journal of Teaching in Physical Education, 29*, 113–130.

Ellis, S., & Rogoff, B. (1986). Problem solving in children's management of instruction. In E. C. Mueller and G. R. Cooper, eds. *Process and outcome in peer relationships* (pp. 60–69). New York: Academic Press.

Ennis, C. (1991). Discrete thinking skills in two teachers' physical education classes. *Elementary School Journal, 91*, 473–487.

Foot, H. C., Morgan, M. J., & Shute, R. H. (Eds.) (1990). *Children helping children.* Chichester, England: John Wiley & Sons.

Frieberg, H. J., & Driscoll, A. (1996). *Universal teaching strategies* (2nd ed.). Boston: Allyn and Bacon.

Gallahue, D. L. (1982). *Developmental movement experiences for children.* New York: Wiley.

Gallahue, D. L., & Cleland, F. (2003). *Developmental physical education for today's children* (4th ed.). Madison, WI: Brown & Benchmark.

Good, T. L., & Brophy, J. E. (1990). *Educational psychology: A realistic approach* (4th ed.). New York: Longman.

Goodrich, H. (1996–97). Understanding rubrics. *Educational Leadership, 54*(4), 14–17.

Gordon, B. (2010). An examination of the responsibility model in a New Zealand secondary school physical education program. *Journal of Teaching in Physical Education, 29*, 21–30.

Graham, G. (2001). *Teaching children physical education: Becoming a master teacher* (2nd ed.). Champaign, IL: Human Kinetics.

Graham, G., Holt/Hale, S., & Parker, M. (2009). *Children moving: A reflexive approach to teaching physical education* (8th ed.). Boston: McGraw-Hill.

Graham, G., Hopple, C., Manross, M., & Sitzman, T. (1993). Novice and experienced children's physical education teachers: Insights into their situational decision making. *Journal of Teaching in Physical Education, 12*, 197–214.

Graham, K. (1988). A qualitative analysis of an effective teacher's movement task presentations during a unit of instruction. *The Physical Educator, 11*, 187–195.

Grant, B. (1992). Integrating sport into the physical education curriculum in New Zealand secondary schools. *Quest, 44*, 304–316.

Grant, B. (1994). High school touch rugby and tennis. In D. Siedentop, ed. *Sport Education: Quality PE through positive sport experiences* (pp. 83–92). Champaign, IL: Human Kinetics.

Greenockle, K., & Purvis, G. (1995). Redesigning a secondary school wellness unit using the critical thinking model. *Journal of Physical Education, Recreation & Dance, 66*(6), 49–52.

Greenwood, C. R., Carta, J. J., & Kamps, D. (1990). Teacher-mediated versus peer-mediated instruction: A review of educational advantages and disadvantages. In H. C. Foot, M. J. Morgan, & R. H. Shute, eds. *Children helping children* (pp. 177–206). Chichester, England: John Wiley & Sons.

Gregorc, A. F. (1982). *Gregorc style delineator.* Maynard, MA: Gabriel Systems, Inc.

Griffin, L., Dodds, P., & Rovegno, I. (1996). Pedagogical content knowledge for teachers: Integrate everything you know to help students learn. *Journal of Physical Education, Recreation & Dance, 67*(9), 58–60.

Griffin, L., Mitchell, S., & Oslin, J. (1997). *Teaching sport concepts and skills: A tactical games approach.* Champaign, IL: Human Kinetics.

Griffin, L., Oslin, J., & Mitchell, S. (1995). An analysis of two instructional approaches to teaching net games. *Research Quarterly for Exercise and Sport, 66* (Suppl), A–64.

Griffin, L. L. & Butler, J. I. (2005). *Teaching games for understanding: Theory, research and practice.* Champaign, IL: Human Kinetics.

Grineski, S. (1996). *Cooperative learning in physical education.* Champaign, IL: Human Kinetics.

Gurvitch, R., Metzler, M., & Lund, J. (Eds.) (2008). Model-based instructional in physical education: The adoption of innovation. *Journal of Teaching in Physical Education, 27*, 447–589.

Gusthart, J. L., Kelly, I. M., & Rink, J. E. (1997). The validity of the Qualitative Measures of Teaching Performance Scale as a measure of teacher effectiveness. *Journal of Teaching in Physical Education, 16*, 196–210.

Hannon, J. C., & Ratliffe, T. (2004). Cooperative learning in physical education. *Strategies, 17*(5), 29–32.

Harlow, A. (1972). *Taxonomy of the psychomotor domain.* New York: McKay.

Harrison, J., Blakemore, C., Buck, M., & Pellett, T. (1996). *Instructional strategies for secondary school physical education* (4th ed.). Dubuque, IA: Brown & Benchmark.

Hastie, P. A. (1998). Applied benefits of the sport education model. *Journal of Physical Education, Recreation & Dance, 69*(4), 24–26.

Hastie, P. A. (in review). A Review of Research on Sport Education: 2004 to the Present.

Hellison, D. (1983). Teaching self-responsibility (and more). *Journal of Physical Education, Recreation & Dance, 54*(n), 23–28.

Hellison, D. (1985). *Goals and strategies for teaching physical education.* Champaign, IL: Human Kinetics.

Hellison, D. (2003). *Teaching responsibility through physical activity* (2nd ed.). Champaign, IL: Human Kinetics.

Hellison, D. (2011). *Teaching responsibility through physical activity* (3rd ed.). Champaign, IL: Human Kinetics.

Hellison, D., & Walsh, D. (2002). Responsibility-based youth programs evaluation: Investigating the investigations. *Quest, 54,* 292–307.

Hensley, J. E., East, W. B., & Stillwell, J. L. (1979). A racquetball skills test. *Research Quarterly, 50,* 114–118.

Hensley, L. (1997). Alternative assessment for physical education. *Journal of Physical Education, Recreation & Dance, 68*(7), 19–24.

Hetherington, C. (1910). Fundamental education. *The Physical Education Review, 15,* 629–635.

Hicks, D. (1998). *A fourth grade Ultimate Frisbee Sport Education season.* Unpublished masters' collaborative action research project, Georgia State University, Atlanta.

Hilke, E. V. (1990). *Cooperative Learning.* Bloomington, IN: Phi Delta Kappa Educational Foundation.

Hopple, C. (1995). *Teaching for outcomes in elementary physical education: A guide for curriculum and assessment.* Champaign, IL: Human Kinetics.

Housner, L., & Griffey, D. (1985). Teacher cognition: Differences in planning and interactive decision making between experienced and inexperienced teachers. *Research Quarterly for Exercise and Sport, 56,* 45–53.

Houston-Wilson, C. (1997). Peer tutoring: A plan for instructing students of all abilities. *Journal of Physical Education, Recreation & Dance, 68*(6), 39–44.

Johnson, D. W., Johnson, R. T., & Holubec, E. J. (1994). *The new circles of learning: Cooperation in the classroom and school.* Alexandria, VA: Association for Supervision and Curriculum Development.

Jonassen, D. H., & Grabowski, B. L. (1993). *Handbook of individual differences, learning, and instruction.* Hillsdale, NJ: Lawrence Erlbaum.

Jones, D. (1992). Analysis of task systems in elementary physical education classes. *Journal of Teaching in Physical Education, 11,* 411–425.

Jones, D., & Ward, P. (1998). Changing the face of secondary physical education through sport education. *Journal of Physical Education, Recreation & Dance, 69*(5), 40–45.

Joyce, B., & Weil, M. (1972). *Models of teaching.* Englewood Cliffs, NJ: Prentice Hall.

Joyce, B., & Weil, M. (1980). *Models of teaching* (2nd ed.). Englewood Cliffs, NJ: Prentice Hall.

Joyce, B., & Weil, M. (1996). *Models of teaching* (5th ed.). Englewood Cliffs, NJ: Prentice Hall.

Kauchak, D. P., & Eggen, P. D. (1998). *Learning and teaching: Research-based methods.* Boston: Allyn and Bacon.

Keller, F. (1968). Goodbye, teacher! *Journal of Applied Behavior Analysis, 1,* 79–88.

Keller, F. S., & Sherman, J. G. (Eds.) (1974). *The Keller Plan handbook.* Menlo Park, CA: W. A. Benjamin.

Keller, F. S., & Sherman, J. G. (1982). *The PSI handbook: Essays on Personalized Instruction.* Lawrence, KS: TRI Publications.

Keller, J. (1983). Motivational design of instruction. In C. Reigeluth, ed. *Instructional-design theories and models: An overview of their current status* (pp. 383–434). Hillsdale, NJ: Erlbaum.

Kinchin, G. D. (2006). Sport education: A review of the research. In D. Kirk, D. Macdonald, & M. O'Sullivan, eds. *The handbook of physical education* (pp. 596–611). London: Sage.

King, A. (1992). From sage on the stage to guide on the side. *College Teaching, 41*(1), 30–35.

Knop, N., & Pope, C. (1998). Design, redesign, and dissemination of sport education. *Journal of Physical Education, Recreation & Dance, 69*(5), 46–48.

Kolb, D. A. (1981). Learning styles and disciplinary differences. In A. W. Chickering, ed. *The modern college* (pp. 232–255). San Francisco: Jossey-Bass.

Kounin, J. (1970). *Discipline and group management in classrooms.* New York: Holt, Rinehart and Winston.

Krathwohl, D., Bloom, B., & Masia, B. (1964). *Taxonomy of educational objectives: The classification of education goals. Handbook II. Affective domain.* New York: McKay.

Lambert, L. T. (1999). *Standards-based assessment of student learning: A comprehensive approach.* Reston, VA: National Association for Sport and Physical Education.

Lambert, L. T. (2007). *Standards-based assessment of student learning* (2nd ed.). Reston, VA:

National Association for Sport and Physical Education.

Lavay, B. W., French, R., & Henderson, H. L. (2001). *Positive behavior management for physical education* (2nd ed.). Champaign, IL: Human Kinetics.

Li, W., Wright, P. M., Rukavina, P. B., & Pickering, M. (2008). Measuring students' perception of personal and social responsibility and the relationship to intrinsic motivation in urban physical education. *Journal of Teaching in Physical Education, 27,* 167–178.

Locke, L. F. (1970). The movement movement. In R. T. Sweeney, ed. *Selected readings in movement education* (pp. 208–212). Reading, MA: Addison-Wesley.

Lowry, W. H., & Thornburg, M. S. (1988). A working bibliography on the Keller Plan (PSI). Unpublished bibliography.

Lund, J. (2000). *Creating rubrics for physical education.* Reston, VA: National Association for Sport and Physical Education.

Lund, J., & Tannehill, D. (2010). *Standards-based physical education curriculum development* (2nd ed.). Boston: Jones and Bartlett.

Lund, J. L., & Kirk, M. K. (2010). *Performance-based assessment for middle and high school physical education* (2nd ed.). Champaign, IL: Human Kinetics.

Mager, R. F. (1984). *Preparing instructional objectives* (rev. ed.). Belmont, CA: Fearon.

Manross, D., & Templeton, C. (1997). Expertise in teaching physical education. *Journal of Physical Education, Recreation & Dance, 68*(3), 29–35.

Maslow, A. H. (1970). *Motivation and personality* (2nd ed.). New York: Harper and Row.

McBride, R. (1992). Critical thinking: An overview with implications for physical education. *Journal of Teaching in Physical Education, 11,* 112–125.

McBride, R., & Bonnette, R. (1995). Teacher and at-risk students' cognitions during open-ended activities: Structuring the learning environment for critical thinking. *Teaching & Teacher Education, 11,* 373–388.

McCaslin, M. M., & Good, T. L. (1996). *Listening in classrooms.* New York: HarperCollins College Publications.

McPherson, S., & French, K. (1991). Changes in cognitive strategy and motor skill in tennis.

Journal of Sport & Exercise Psychology, 13, 26–41.

Metzler, M. (1979). *The measurement of Academic Learning Time in physical education.* Doctoral dissertation, The Ohio State University, Ann Arbor, MI: University Microfilms, No. 8009314.

Metzler, M. (1984). Analysis of a Mastery Learning/Personalized System of Instruction for teaching tennis. In M. Pieron & G. Graham, eds. *The 1984 Olympic scientific congress proceedings, Volume 6: Sport pedagogy* (pp. 63–70). Champaign, IL: Human Kinetics.

Metzler, M. (1986, April). *Teaching tennis by the Keller Method: A comparison between "traditional" and PSI-based instruction.* Paper presented at the Annual Meeting of the American Educational Research Association, San Francisco.

Metzler, M. (1989). A review of research on time in sport pedagogy. *Journal of Teaching in Physical Education, 8,* 87–103.

Metzler, M. (1990). Teaching during competitive games: Not just playin' around. *Journal of Physical Education, Recreation & Dance, 61*(8), 57–61.

Metzler, M. (2000). *Instructor's manual for the Personalized Sport Instruction Series.* Boston: Allyn & Bacon.

Metzler, M., & McCullick, B. (2008). Introducing innovation to those who matter most—The P–12 pupils' perceptions of model-based instruction. In R. Gurvitch, M. Metzler, & J. Lund, eds. Model-based instructional in physical education: The adoption of innovation (pp. 512–528). *Journal of Teaching in Physical Education, 27,* 447–589.

Mitchell, S. A., & Oslin, J. L. (1999). *Assessment in games teaching.* Reston, VA: National Association for Sport and Physical Education.

Mitchell, S. A., & Oslin, J. L. (2003). *Sport foundations for elementary physical education: A tactical games approach.* Champaign, IL: Human Kinetics.

Mitchell, S. A., Oslin, J. L., & Griffin, L. L. (2003). *Sport foundations for elementary physical education.* Champaign, IL: Human Kinetics.

Morine-Dershimer, G. (1985). *Talking, listening, and learning in the elementary classroom.* New York: Longman.

Mosston, M. (1966). *Teaching physical education*. Columbus, OH: Merrill.

Mosston, M., & Ashworth, S. (2002). *Teaching physical education* (5th ed.). San Francisco: B. Cummings.

Napper-Owen, G. (1994). . . . And justice for all: Equity in the elementary gymnasium. *Strategies, 8*(3), 23–26.

National Association for Sport and Physical Education. (1992). *Outcomes of quality physical education programs*. Reston, VA: Author.

National Association for Sport and Physical Education. (2004). *Moving into the future: National standards for physical education* (2nd ed.). Reston, VA: Author.

National Association for Sport and Physical Education. (1995). *Looking at physical education from a developmental perspective: A guide to teaching*. Reston, VA: NASPE Motor Development Task Force.

Oberteuffer, D., & Ulrich, C. (1962). *Physical education: A textbook of principles for professional students* (3rd ed.). New York: Harper & Row.

Orlick, T. (1982). *The second cooperative sports and games book*. New York: Pantheon.

Oslin, J., & Mitchell, S. (1998). *An investigation of tactical transfer in new games*. Paper presented at the AAHPERD National Convention, Reno, NV.

Oslin, J., Mitchell, S., & Griffin, L. (1998). The game performance assessment instrument (GPAI): Development and preliminary validation. *Journal of Teaching in Physical Education, 17*, 231–243.

Oslin, J. L., & Mitchell, S. A. (2006). Game-centered approaches to teaching physical education: A review of the research. In D. Kirk, D. Macdonald, & M. O'Sullivan, eds. *The handbook of physical education* (pp. 627–651). London: Sage.

O'Sullivan, M. O., & Henniger, M. (2000). *Assessing student responsibility and teamwork*. Reston, VA: National Association for Sport and Physical Education.

Phillips, D. C., & Soltis, J. F. (1991). *Perspectives on learning* (2nd ed.). New York: Teachers College.

Poole, J., Sebolt, D., & Metzler, M. (1996). *PSIS student workbook for volleyball*. Dubuque, IA: Kendall-Hunt.

President's Council on Physical Fitness and Sports. (1985). *The Presidential Physical Fitness Award Program*. Washington, DC: Author.

Rauschenbach, J., & Vanoer, S. (1998). Instant activities: Active learning tasks that start a lesson out right. *Journal of Physical Education, Recreation & Dance, 69*(2), 7–8.

Reichmann, S. W., & Grasha, A. F. (1974). A rational approach to developing and assessing the validity of a student learning styles instrument. *Journal of Psychology, 87*, 213–223.

Rink, J. (Ed.) (1996). Tactical and skill approaches to teaching sport and games. *Journal of Teaching in Physical Education, 15*(4).

Rink, J. (1997). Teacher education programs: The role of context in learning how to teach. *Journal of Physical Education, Recreation & Dance, 68*(1), 17–24.

Rink, J. (2009). *Teaching physical education for learning* (6th ed.). Boston: McGraw-Hill.

Rink, J. (2003). Effective instruction in physical education. In S. Silverman & C. Ennis, eds. *Student learning in physical education: Applying research to enhance instruction* (2nd ed.) (pp. 165–186). Champaign, IL: Human Kinetics.

Rink, J., French, K., & Graham, K. (1996). Implications for practice and research. In J. Rink, ed. Tactical and skill approaches to teaching sport and games (pp. 490–502). Monograph, *Journal of Teaching in Physical Education, 15*(4).

Rink, J., & Werner, P. (1989). Qualitative measures of teaching performance scale (QMTPS). In P. Darst, D. Zakrajsek, & V. Mancini, eds. *Analyzing physical education and sport instruction* (2nd ed.) (pp. 269–276). Champaign, IL: Human Kinetics.

Rosenshine, B. (1979). Content, time, and direct instruction. In H. J. Walberg & P. L. Peterson, eds. *Research on teaching: Concepts, findings, and implications* (pp. 28–56). Berkeley, CA: McCutchan.

Rosenshine, B. (1983). Teaching functions in instructional programs. *Elementary School Journal, 83*, 335–350.

Rowe, M. (1986). Wait time: Slowing down may be a way of speeding up! *Journal of Teacher Education, 37*, 43–50.

Safrit, M. J. (1995). *Complete guide to youth fitness testing*. Champaign, IL: Human Kinetics.

Schempp, P. (1982). Enhancing creativity through children making decisions. In M. Pieron & J. Cheffers, eds. *Studying the teaching in physical education* (pp. 161–166). Leige, Belgium: International Association for Physical Education in Higher Education.

Schempp, P. (1997). Developing expertise in teaching and coaching. *Journal of Physical Education, Recreation & Dance, 68*(2), 29.

Schiemer, S. (2000). *Assessment strategies for elementary physical education.* Champaign, IL: Human Kinetics.

Schunk, D. H. (1996). *Learning theories: An educational perspective* (3rd ed.). Englewood Cliffs, NJ: Merrill.

Sherman, J. G. (1974a). PSI: Some notable failures. In J. G. Sherman, ed. *Personalized system of instruction: 41 germinal papers* (pp. 120–124). Menlo Park, CA: W. A. Benjamin.

Sherman, J. G. (Ed.) (1974b). *Personalized system of instruction: 41 germinal papers.* Menlo Park, CA: W. A. Benjamin.

Shuell, T. J. (1986). Cognitive conceptions of learning. *Review of Educational Research, 56,* 411–436.

Shulman, L. (1987). Knowledge and teaching: Foundations of the new reform. *Harvard Educational Review, 15*(2), 4–14.

Siedentop, D. (1973). How to use personalized systems of instruction in college teaching. *NCPEAM Proceedings,* 11th annual meeting. Kansas City, 116–125.

Siedentop, D. (Ed.) (1994). *Sport education: Quality PE through positive sport experiences.* Champaign, IL: Human Kinetics.

Siedentop, D. (1998). What is sport education and how does it work? *Journal of Physical Education, Recreation & Dance, 69*(4), 18–20.

Siedentop, D. (2004). *Introduction to physical education, fitness, and sport* (5th ed.). Boston: McGraw-Hill.

Siedentop, D., Hastie, P. A., & van der Mars, H. (2011). *The complete guide to sport education* (2nd ed.). Champaign, IL: Human Kinetics.

Siedentop, D., Mand, C., & Taggart, A. (1986). *Physical education: Teaching and curriculum strategies for grades 5–12.* Palo Alto, CA: Mayfield.

Siedentop, D., & Tannehill, D. (2000). *Developing teaching skills in physical education* (4th ed.). Mountain View, CA: Mayfield.

Silverman, S., & Ennis, C. (Eds.) (2003). *Student learning in physical education: Applying research to enhance instruction* (2nd ed.). Champaign, IL: Human Kinetics.

Silverman, S., Tyson, L., & Krampitz, J. (1993). Teacher feedback and achievement: Mediating effects of initial skill and sex. *Journal of Human Movement Studies, 24,* 97–118.

Slavin, R. E. (1977). Classroom reward structure: An analytic and practical review. *Review of Educational Research, 47,* 633–650.

Slavin, R. E. (1980). Cooperative learning. *Review of Educational Research, 50,* 315–342.

Slavin, R. E. (1983). *Cooperative learning.* New York: Longman.

Slavin, R. E. (1988). *Student team learning: An overview and practical guide* (2nd ed.). Washington, DC: National Education Association.

Slavin, R. E. (1990). *Cooperative learning: Theory, research, and practice.* Boston: Allyn and Bacon.

Slavin, R. E. (1995). *Cooperative learning: Theory, research, and practice* (2nd ed.). Boston: Allyn and Bacon.

Snow, R., Corno, L., & Jackson III, D. (1996). Individual differences in affective and conative functions. In D. C. Berliner and R. C. Calfee, eds. *Handbook of educational psychology* (pp. 243–310). New York: Macmillan.

Stanley, S. (1977). *Physical education: A movement orientation* (2nd ed.). New York: McGraw-Hill.

Stevens, R. J., & Slavin, R. E. (1995). The cooperative elementary school: Effects on students' achievement, attitudes, and social relations. *American Educational Research Journal, 32,* 321–351.

Strand, B. N., & Wilson, R. (1993). *Assessing sport skills.* Champaign, IL: Human Kinetics.

Stroot, S., & Morton, P. (1989). Blueprints for learning. *Journal of Teaching in Physical Education, 8,* 213–222.

Tannehill, D. (Ed.) (1998). Sport education. Two-part feature presented in the *Journal of Physical Education, Recreation & Dance,* May (Vol. 69, No. 4) and June (Vol. 69, No. 5).

Thorpe, R., & Bunker, D. (1986). The curriculum model. In R. Thorpe, D. Bunker, & L. Almond, eds. *Rethinking games teaching* (pp. 7–10). Loughborough, England: Authors.

Thorpe, R., Bunker, D., & Almond, L. (1986). *Rethinking games teaching*. Loughborough, England: Authors.

Tillotson, J. (1970). Problem-solving. In R. T. Sweeney, ed. *Selected readings in movement education* (pp. 130–135). Reading, MA: Addison-Wesley.

Tishman, S., & Perkins, D. (1995). Critical thinking and physical education. *Journal of Physical Education, Recreation & Dance, 66*(6), 24–30.

Tobin, K. (1987). The role of wait time in higher cognitive level learning. *Review of Educational Research, 57,* 69–95.

Townsend, S. J., Mohr, D. J., Rairigh, R. M., & Bulger, S. M. (2003). *Assessing student outcomes in sport education*. Reston, VA: National Association for Sport and Physical Education.

Turner, A. (1996). Teaching games for understanding: Myth or reality? *Journal of Physical Education, Recreation & Dance, 67*(4), 46–48, 55.

Turner, A., & Martinek, T. (1992). A comparative analysis of two models for teaching games. *International Journal of Physical Education, 24*(4), 15–31.

Turner, A., & Martinek, T. (1995). Teaching for understanding: A model for improving decision making during game play. *Quest, 47,* 44–63.

Van Dalen, D., & Bennett, B. (1971). *A world history of physical education: Cultural, philosophical, comparative* (2nd ed.). Englewood Cliffs, NJ: Prentice Hall.

Wagner, S. (1990). Social and historical perspectives on peer teaching in education. In H. C. Foot, M. J. Morgan, & R. H. Shute, eds. *Children helping children* (pp. 21–42). Chichester, England: John Wiley & Sons.

Wallhead, T., & O'Sullivan, M. (2005). Sport education: Physical education for the new millennium? *Physical Education and Sport Pedagogy, 10,* 181–210.

Ward, P., & Lee, M-A. (2005). Peer-assisted learning in physical education: A review of theory and research. *Journal of Teaching in Physical Education, 24,* 205–225.

Watts, R. (1998). *A middle school pickleball sport education unit*. Unpublished masters' collaborative action research project, Georgia State University, Atlanta.

Webster, G. E. (1987). Influence of peer tutors upon Academic Learning Time—Physical education of mentally handicapped students. *Journal of Teaching in Physical Education, 6,* 393–403.

Wood, T. M. (1996). Evaluation and testing: The road less traveled. In S. J. Silverman & C. D. Ennis, eds. *Student learning in physical education: Applying research to enhance instruction* (pp. 199–219). Champaign, IL: Human Kinetics.

Wood, T. M. (2003). Assessment in physical education: The future is now! In S. J. Silverman & C. D. Ennis, eds. *Student learning in physical education: Applying research to enhance instruction* (pp. 187–203). Champaign, IL: Human Kinetics.

Woods, A., & Book, C. (1995). Critical thinking in middle school physical education. *Journal of Physical Education, Recreation & Dance, 66*(6), 39–43.

Wright, P. M., & Burton, S. (2008). Implementation and outcomes of a responsibility-based physical activity program integrated into an intact high school physical education class. *Journal of Teaching in Physical Education, 27,* 138–154.

Yoder, L. (1993). Cooperative learning and dance education. *Journal of Physical Education, Recreation & Dance, 64*(5), 47–51, 56.

subject index